Betty M. Chambers 1

Wednesday's Child

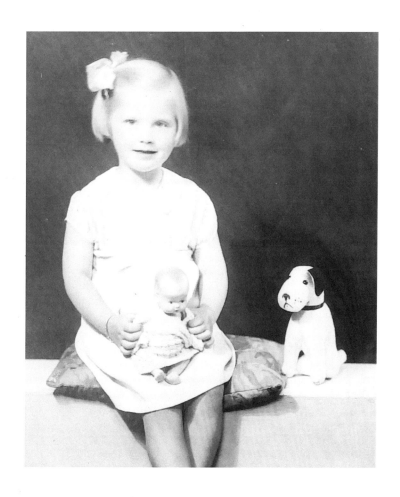

Monday's child is fair of face

Tuesday's child is full of grace

Wednesday's child is full of woe

Thursday's child has far to go

Friday's child is loving and giving

Saturday's child works hard for a living

But the child that is born on the Sabbath Day

Is bonny and blithe and good and gay

First published December 2023

The right of Professor Jonathon Chambers FREng to be identified as the Author of this work has been asserted by him in accordance with the Copyright, Designs and Patent Act 1988

ISBN 978-1-3999-6753-2

Printed by Peterborough Printing Services, Peterborough

DEDICATION

This book is dedicated to the memory of the loving family of Bill, Con, Betty and Leslie Boyden, my exceptional maternal grandparents, mother, and uncle (and godfather).

Con, Betty, Leslie and Bill Boyden in the 1940s

Contents

Appendices

Notes

All photographs in the book are from the family's own collection.

The name Jonathon was often shortened to Jono by Betty, and Alison is known as Connie to many.

Every effort has been made not to edit unnecessarily the material written by Betty. The style of her later content may be indicative of the progression into dementia.

Both forms of the spelling of the fenland town Whittlesey and more historic form Whittlesea were adopted by Betty, and these have not been changed.

Quotes in the text are generally from local newspapers but the full sources were not recorded.

Foreword

Betty undertook this research for the benefit of her family but it has a much wider value. She began by looking at the distinctive character of Norfolk, a county with wide open horizons and beautiful sunsets. Her Boyden family have been traced to 1630 when her ancestor Robert was christened in North Elmham. The family story has been careful slotted in the larger picture of what was happening in the country as a whole. Betty studied under a respected professor at London University so her research has been meticulous.

There is a great deal of information about Betty's Boyden family and her mother's Garfield family. She obviously had a great deal of affection for them. Her father, Bill, was a soldier in the First World War and she was curious to know about his service. This took her to the Army Museum in Chelsea where she discovered that he drove army vehicles transporting troops and supplies between the trenches. I was privileged to be with her for that visit, one of many we did together.

Coming to Betty's life, we find the same detailed and well-researched information. Of particular interest is the way of life during the Second World War. She recalled the Movietone and Pathe Gazette news reports in the days when films ran on and on and you could stay in the cinema all day. There were childhood games and memories of living during a war. No-one likes a war but they were interesting times.

Education was always an interest. After the Grammar School, she went to a Teacher Training College. This was a very different route from that taken these days in order to qualify as a teacher. Betty had an interesting and varied teaching career and the *History of Education* was the subject she chose to study at London University

Betty married Arthur Chambers who was in the Royal Navy. She has been equally careful with her research into his family as well. There are some excellent descriptions of the journey taken on HMT Empire Clyde to the Far East, a section in her book which she has entitled *A Slow Boat to China*. The description of sailing through the Suez Canal is particularly atmospheric. Then there was Aden, Columbo, Singapore and eventually Hong Kong.

Family was important to her and she writes about her three children, David, Jonathon and Alison. After her retirement she was able to join Professor Jonathon on many of his academic lecture tours, visiting many other far-flung places and describing them so well. Jono has completed Betty's book which she was unable to finish because of ill health. He also has very high standards and he has kept me informed of its progress. It is a privilege to be able to contribute to Betty's book and I remember our times together with affection.

Dr. Anne Allsopp
25th September 2023

Preface

In concert with many people researching the history of their family, I regret not asking questions of my parents and grandparents. During my mother's later years, she gave me some valuable facts about her family while, over time, my father dropped snippets of information about his life. Unfortunately, I took little notice and now need to mine my memory to retrieve these gems and use them, with official sources and other family memories, to create a reasonably accurate history. My grandparents could also have responded to the most probing enquiries but without questions how could they have given answers? Despite these difficulties, I have attempted to put together a document for my children, grandchildren and later generations so that they will know from where they came from, and which serves as a piece of social history. Initially, an attempt is made to set the family within the wider society when the poor were deemed insignificant and not worthy of being individually recorded. This is followed by the story of the family and the memories of my life.

Dr. Betty M. Chambers MBE

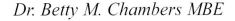

Betty didn't have opportunity to complete this work as in her twilight years she succumbed to dementia. Therefore, as her son Jonathon who became her primary carer, I have completed the document and recorded Betty's final years.

Acknowledgements

Mum retired from her teaching career in 1994 at the age of 60 and then enjoyed many years of research. We often sparred for access to the desktop computer in the home office.

During her retirement a major desire was to complete her life story and much of the material in this book was written by her. I committed to complete it for her.

I wish to acknowledge my brother David and sister Alison, together with Mary Crowson and Dr. Anne Allsopp, who have helped considerably to complete this project.

Emeritus Professor Jonathon Chambers FREng FIEEE DSc(Imperial)

Introduction

I was born on Wednesday 21st February 1934 at Charnwood Nursing Home in London Road, Peterborough. According to the old nursery rhyme, my life was destined to be 'full of woe', but the prediction was wrong. My early years were full of love and, during my adult years, distress and sadness have been outweighed by happiness and success. My story is, therefore, not one of triumph over cruelty and adversity but one of comfortable family life with kind and gentle parents, affectionate relatives, and true friends. Had I been born in some of the big towns and cities of the British Isles my experiences might have been different. There, living conditions for the working classes were frequently crowded, food was often short and illness a real concern. Hours of work, if work was available, were long with wages low and leisure limited. Peterborough, however, did not experience the worst effects of unemployment during the 1930s and family life was becoming more comfortable. Areas of considerable poverty existed in the city, but generally housing was of a better standard, food adequate and more nutritious; and children, with parents like mine, were protected from any harshness. My birth in a nursing home at a time when home births were the norm resulted from the fact that my parents were living 'in rooms' in Queen's Walk. After their marriage, they had been unable to find a house at a rent they could afford, but, despite his limited means, my father considered professional care to ensure the safety of his wife and child worth the cost. He was William Boyden, and was responsible not only for my family name, but also for my Christian name! My mother, named Constance Irene by her parents, Albert and Florence Garfield, but always known as Con, spent much time during her pregnancy reading novels with Irish themes and decided that I must have an Irish name. She chose Shelagh Maureen, but Bill disagreed, and insisted that Con's sister, Betty, 'had been good to Con' and I should be named after her. He won and when he registered my birth the name on the certificate was, indeed, Betty. I kept the Maureen, however, and was christened Betty Maureen at St. Augustine's Church Woodston on Easter Sunday 1st April 1934 with Auntie Betty as my godmother.

Dr. Betty M. Chambers MBE

The Boyden Family in Early Days

On the world scene or in national events my Boyden ancestors have made no significant mark. They have consistently been of the lower class, very poor and close to the land, but always labouring not owning. They were resilient people who weathered the storms of life, both literally and physically, and although they had few home comforts frequently lived to a ripe old age. Their roots are in East Anglia, an area which has been inhabited since Neolithic times; archaeological evidence of Bronze and Iron Age settlement and activity is widespread. The indigenous people were the 'Iceni', a tribe, which, led by its queen, Boudicca, resisted the Roman occupation, but was finally defeated. The victors then, as they did in all corners of the empire, built roads and towns, and imposed their way of life. Britain remained a settled and orderly Roman province for more than 400 years, but eventually, the legions were withdrawn and tribes from Northern Europe took advantage of the situation and began to raid the east coast. The raids foreshadowed eventual settlement, and by the seventh century Roman Britain was a thing of the past, and East Anglia had become an Anglo-Saxon kingdom. This movement from Europe poses the intriguing question; did the Boydens arrive at this time? The name may have been derived from the Germanic word for bold or brave but there is no definite evidence to link the family to Norfolk until the 16th century. Records then indicate that life events forced the Boydens to move steadily westward and for the last two hundred years they have lived in The Fens, where visitors often find the flatness uninteresting and comment that it cannot be compared to the grandeur of mountains or the power of the sea. The real fen person, however, is most at ease where there is a vast expanse of the land, immense overarching skies and sunsets not easily equalled anywhere in the world.

Anglo-Saxon society was divided into distinctive classes, with a settlement being headed by a chief. Two groups of freemen, thanes and coerls (churls), defined by their land ownership, formed the next rank of society while the lowest level consisted of villeins and serfs, the latter being peasants, who were tied to the land. The Boydens, if Anglo-Saxon, belonged to this last group and were entirely subject to the chief. They lived in small dwellings, built with wattle and daub walls and thatched roofs, and relied on subsistence farming and fishing for their existence. The women had responsibility for preparing and cooking food, spinning fleece from sheep, weaving cloth and making clothes. Conversion to Christianity marked the Anglo-Saxon period and religious communities were widely established with repositories of learning. The ecclesiastical centre of North Norfolk was the village of North Elmham with a cathedral built in 673 of wood and roofed with thatch, and important in the Boyden history. Religious establishments faced, from the middle of the eighth century, an onslaught from the Vikings who raided, pillaged and burned buildings. These raiders later evolved into colonizers and the people of North Norfolk found themselves living in the Danelaw and, by 1016, being part of an Anglo-Scandinavian kingdom ruled by the Danish king, Cnut. It is unlikely that the Boydens arrived as marauding Vikings but that they adapted to living with the erstwhile invaders as they evolved into peaceful settlers. After Cnut's death, various claimants took the throne until Edward, known as the Confessor, was proposed as king by the Saxon Earl Godwine. Harold, Earl Godwine's son, became Earl of East Anglia, and then, in early 1066, king on Edward's death. In October, however, William, Duke of Normandy, defeated Harold at the Battle of Hastings and on Christmas day William the Conqueror was crowned king in Westminster Abbey.

William built on the administrative system of the Anglo-Saxons and created a feudal system with rigid class definitions, each group having specific duties. William presumed that all land belonged to the crown and maintained great areas for his personal use. The rest he leased to his barons, who in turn distributed the land surplus to their requirements to their knights. Barons and knights held their land under strict conditions: one of which was to prevent rebellion against Norman rule and another to provide soldiers whenever the king demanded. The barons built castles in order to deter hostility, while the knights established themselves in fortified manors in settlements where the peasants were on the bottom rung of society. They could not move without the Lord of the Manor's permission and were required to work for him on a specified number of days without payment. This fact prompts the question that, if the Boydens did not arrive with the Anglo-Saxons were they of Norman origin? It is possible that the name originated from the French 'Baudouin' (bold/brave friend), which was in common usage in Mediaeval France for both the highest and lowest members of society and, without doubt, soldiers of the conquering army. Boyden or Boydon, both spellings continue to the present century, may have been one corruption of Baudouin which over time developed into a surname.

The lives of peasants were continually hard with no freedom. Their homes continued to be one-roomed buildings with wattle and daub walls and thatched roofs. Wooden shutters closed over unglazed windows against inclement weather while the hard earth floors were covered with straw, if it was available, to give some warmth. Furniture was limited to simple wooden tables, stools or benches and chests for clothes. Life depended, as it had in Anglo-Saxon times, on subsistence farming and the hamlets had three large open fields which were cultivated commonly. The manor court decided the rotation of crops - barley, wheat, rye, oats, pulses - and the time of sowing. The fields were divided into strips and the villagers received the number of strips based on their status and every year one of the fields was left fallow to keep the soil fertile. After harvest the fields became pasturage for the animals. In north Norfolk, the land was sandy and stony which supported flocks of sheep which produced long coarse wool for weaving into cloth. Sheep fairs flourished and weaving worsted cloth, which took its name from the village of Worstead, became an important industry throughout the county. Flemish weavers brought their skills to Norfolk and a Weavers Guild was established. A percentage of the wool was exported to Flanders, through Cley next the Sea, a port that was as busy as it had been in Saxon times. The church continued as an important aspect of life in Norman times with the continuation of the building of monasteries while, in Norfolk, the frenzied construction of churches led to the county having more churches than any other area. Until 1072 North Elmham retained its ecclesiastical importance but, in that year, Bishop de Losinga moved to Thetford and North Elmham began a decline into a backwater. Despite its loss of status, the bishop continued to visit the village, built the parish church, and used the site of the Anglo-Saxon cathedral to construct a private chapel. In approximately 1370, Bishop Despenser of Norwich obtained the Lordship of the Manor to take advantage of the hunting and, in 1388, the villagers watched or were employed to transform the cathedral into a castle. Eighty years before, Edward I had introduced standard measures, and it is possible that those employed on the project measured in 'feet and inches' for the first time.

In contrast, King John made a definite impact on the common people, although they were unlikely to have been aware of the rebellion of the barons or the signing of the Magna Carta. It added nothing to their rights. They were also probably ignorant of the dispute between king and church, but when, in 1207, the Pope put an interdict on England, everyone was affected. The interdict virtually shut down the church. Family life was in limbo; there were no marriages, no funerals and no Sunday services until 1213, when the interdict was lifted. Three years later, John was in East Anglia pillaging the lands of the barons to finance his on-going war against the French. In October 1216, John travelled from Newark, in Lincolnshire, to King's Lynn to which he had recently granted a royal charter and where he was consequently very popular. He stayed only briefly before determining to return to Newark and decided to travel by way of Wisbech while his wagon train crossed the Wash via the Wellstream, a causeway, accessible at low tide by those who were familiar with the area. It is possible that the wagon train attempted to make the crossing without guides and disaster struck. The column of baggage carts, soldiers and servants became disorientated and were trapped when the tide rose. John's household effects, his wardrobe and perhaps his royal regalia and treasury were lost. The local fen people may have tried to find the treasure, which was no longer of use to John when he died a week later, but there is no accurate information about a search or if any artefacts were discovered.

Within two weeks of John's death, his son, at the age of nine, was crowned King Henry III and his reign lasted for 56 years. He was described as 'petulant and pious'. His petulance encouraged him to disregard the Magna Carta with the result that Simon de Montfort led a rebellion against him, while his piety was expressed by his rebuilding of Westminster Abbey and his support for the arts and learning. These interests did not touch the lives of people in North Norfolk, but had they been Londoners they would have been amongst the crowds that watched the arrival of the first elephant in England; a gift to Henry from the French King. Edward I followed his father Henry, but was not crowned until he returned from the crusades. The coronation was spectacular with a feast which included oxen, chickens, sheep, salmon, boars and game fowl; a meal in sharp contrast to the diet enjoyed by the peasants whose life, at this time, was becoming steadily more difficult. Harvests were poor and those with enough land began to enclose it in order to farm more efficiently to produce extra food for a growing population. Unfortunately, the poor were left with insufficient resources to feed their families, and many had no option but to become manual labourers for those who had more money. Then, in 1315-16, a serious famine struck; everyone went hungry, and the long-time rules of village life began to break down.

A scandal of tabloid proportions provided, as the news spread throughout the country, an on-going opportunity for salacious gossip and some relief from the constant hardship. The sexuality of Edward II was the cause. The titillating facts were that Edward I had banished Piers Gaveston on suspicion that the friendship between his son and Gaveston was of an inappropriate nature. Edward II, however, once he became king had Gaveston return, lavished titles and riches on him. Then, in 1308, to the dismay of the court, Edward made Gaveston regent while he crossed the Channel to marry Isabella of France. Despite the marriage, Edward's affection for his friend grew and Gaveston flaunted his power so openly that, in 1312, the barons captured and killed him. Edward was plunged into depression but, in November of the same year, Isabella gave birth to a son, an event which improved the king and queen's relationship and, by the early 1320s, the queen had given birth to three more children. Unfortunately, also by this time, Edward had established a relationship with a new friend, Hugh Despenser, and problems were mounting to an extent where Edward was forced to banish Despenser. The banishment was short-lived to the fury of Isabella who had tolerated Gaveston but was not prepared to be humiliated by a second affair. She left England for France where she lived openly with Roger Mortimer, who had already rebelled against Edward, and the pair began to plot to bring about his downfall. During October 1326, Isabella landed near the estuary of the river Orwell in Suffolk with an army of mercenaries, the royal fleet mutinied, and Londoners rioted in her support. Edward and Despenser fled to Wales. By November Isabella and Mortimer had the Great Seal of England and Edward was their prisoner. Isabella determined to wreak vengeance on Despenser. At a celebratory banquet she organised a mock trial and found Despenser guilty of 'unnatural practices'. He was put to a gruesome death while Edward II was forced to abdicate and, later, brutally murdered. Edward III, the new king was young, and Isabella and Mortimer controlled the court but within three years, Edward III had wrested back control and captured the couple. Mortimer was executed while Isabella was imprisoned at Castle Rising. The final episode of a more than 20-year saga ended in North Norfolk

If the royal 'goings on' had taken minds off the poor harvests, there was an event on the horizon that brought every thought back to survival. In 1348, Norfolk was devastated as was the whole country. Plague arrived in the southwest onboard ships. Rats lived amongst the cargo and harboured the fleas which carried the Black Death, and the disease spread like wildfire. East Anglia with its Fenland was one of the worst hit areas and the population was dramatically reduced with villages being abandoned or shrinking to a tiny huddle of dwellings. Burials were a daily occurrence as parents buried their children or the children became orphans when parents died. Animals were left untended and land untilled. The church taught that the plague was a judgement from God on human decadence. The poor largely accepted the teaching but as an insurance against the disease they wore sweet smelling herbs. The huge death toll resulted in there being too few peasants to do the work of the manor and they began to demand payment for their labour. Some labourers took advantage of the situation and climbed the social ladder, but the Boydens did not. They continued to work in the fields, and looked after the animals and enjoyed their very limited pleasures on holy days and when special events demanded celebration. Villagers enjoyed dancing, wrestling, and playing games of football or 'pitch' while in towns; bear baiting and cockfighting were also popular. News of the exploits of the Black Prince at the Battles of Crecy and Poitiers was greeted with enthusiasm and in villages there was great satisfaction that the foot soldiers, ordinary men with their longbows, had been instrumental in the success.

The Black Prince, son of Edward III, was not only a great soldier but also a great spender on extravagant clothes and jewels. The courtiers followed the fashion and were not enamoured when they saw the lower classes copying their way of dressing. They commented that the common people were 'getting above their station' and complained that, since the plague, the peasants were enjoying a higher standard of living and receiving pay for tasks that should have been done as feudal duty. The lords and knights became increasingly resentful and saw the clothes issue as a way of reasserting the class hierarchy. A law, detailing the dress of each level of society, was enacted. Royalty and nobles were permitted to wear ermine and pearls, peers and knights with an income of 400 marks a year had permission to wear cloth of gold and silver while the cloth used to make the garments of lesser knights could cost no more that six marks per yard. Tradesmen and others of the same social level were not permitted to spend more that 40 shillings on their outfits which were to have no embellishments. Despite the stories of their higher standard of living, peasants did not feature in the law! The untimely death of the Black Prince, in 1376, and that of Edward III a year later, led to Richard II becoming king at ten years of age. Perhaps because of his youth and inevitable lack of experience, Richard quickly made himself unpopular with the poor. In 1381, when he was 14 years old, he imposed a poll tax, a flat-rate tax levied on every household, to finance a war. The poor reacted against its unfairness and resisted the tax collectors. The resistance began in Essex but later spread across neighbouring counties. In Norfolk the rebels took over Norwich castle and plundered the area around the city. If the Boydens were not active in the uprising, they must have been supportive of demands for fairer treatment, the abolition of serfdom and the right to rent land at four pence an acre. Wat Tyler led the Kent rebels on a march to London where they confronted the king. Richard promised to grant the demands, but his promise was later rescinded, and Wat Tyler killed. The power of the lord of the manor remained intact but a shortage of labourers ensured that some feudal duties were not carried out without payment.

In 1399, if memories went back to 1327 people would make comparisons between the abdication of Edward II and current events. News which reached the peasantry reported problems between Richard II and the powerful barons. Richard had sent Henry Bolingbroke into exile for life and seized his inheritance. There was serious speculation on the possible outcome of this banishment. The actual outcome was that Bolingbroke returned from exile with a small band of supporters which swelled to a large army. Richard was forced to abdicate, and Bolingbroke was acclaimed as Henry IV. Henry did not make a significant mark on Eastern England; he spent almost all his 14 years as king in subduing rebels and fighting the Welsh in order to secure the country for his family. Memories of Edward II, however, were again stirred early in 1400 when news of the death of Richard II came with rumours that he also had been cruelly murdered. In 1413, Henry V, who was to become one of the most well-regarded and successful of English kings, succeeded. Henry's one aim was to gain the French throne and his campaigns in France were successful with his victory at Agincourt being legendary with the long bowmen deserving much credit. Before the battle, Henry roused his small fighting force which had been stricken by dysentery and hunger and impeded by rain and mud to a classic victory. London welcomed him joyously and the euphoria spread to all parts of the nation. Nine years later Henry was dead, and it was his baby son who was crowned King of England and France.

The two coronations did not presage a peaceful united Anglo-French nation. Instead, it foreshadowed 60 years of instability. Henry was just eight years old when Joan of Arc began her crusade to drive the English out of France. The villagers of North Norfolk were dismayed that the hopes they had had for Henry V's reign were dashed. In 1450, an uprising in Kent and Suffolk was of interest to the poor locally. Jack Cade, who was virtually unknown, led the rebellion and marched to London with his followers. One of the grievances was that feudal labour was continuing. This stance should have had the support of poor people, but Londoners turned against Cade and his supporters because of their violent behaviour. The uprising failed and the poor continued with their feudal duties. Five years later the country was ensnared in the Wars of the Roses, a civil war between the Lancastrians, whose emblem was the red rose and the Yorkists, who wore the white rose as their emblem. The Houses of Lancaster and York were descended from Edward III and were rivals for the crown, but the reasons for rivalry and the progress of the war was probably incomprehensible to country peasants although they may have discussed who was affiliated to which rose! The conflict lasted for more than 30 years and involved six changes of monarch. Many people were unable to remember a time without battles and were frequently unsure which king was ruling at a particular time. In Norfolk, the Paston family who had improved their status because of the 'Black Death' and lived in Castle Rising on the Norfolk coast did not escape the 'fall out' from the wars. Margaret Paston was forced to surrender the castle to the Duke of Norfolk and the Paston family was not permitted to return for seven years. Interestingly, although the lordly factions were fighting for supremacy, they were united in ensuring that those at the bottom of society did not develop delusions of grandeur. In 1463, a law restated that of a century before and defined what each class might wear after the lords had complained that it was difficult to tell a peasant from a squire or a squire from a knight. Lords were assigned gold, purple or sable, knights' satin, velvet and silk, squires nothing finer than damask while commoners were forbidden to wear scarlet or foreign cloth. Commoners, like the Boydens, could only afford wool!

Once the Wars of the Roses had ended at Bosworth with Henry Tudor becoming king, life for the peasants continued its hardworking way and a local incident would have been of greater interest to the people of North Elmham than royal deeds. In 1507, a huge fire destroyed more than half of Norwich! The blaze may have been visible to the villagers and, without doubt, proved an important talking point. Henry VII, however, proved himself a capable and astute ruler, a patron of the arts and a supporter of the church. England was a Catholic country and Henry founded new religious houses and encouraged pilgrimage. Pilgrimage to holy shrines was a duty that all levels of society believed important, and the foremost two shrines were Thomas Beckett's at Canterbury and Our Lady's at Walsingham, about 20 miles from North Elmham. The great and the good as well as the poor and humble made their way to Walsingham, including Henry VIII whose pilgrimage was meant to prove his Catholic credentials. The people of North Elmham attended mass and revered the host in a church that was full of colour. They listened to the priest and accepted his teaching but about 1529, they began to hear gossip that Henry was obsessed with his desire to produce an heir, was infatuated with Anne Boleyn, and wanted to divorce Queen Katharine. Then unbelievable news came! Henry had renounced his allegiance to the Pope, been proclaimed the head of the church, divorced Katharine, and married Anne Boleyn. The ordinary people had not been privy to the politics that had led to the establishment of the Church of England. They were in no position to foresee the mediaeval Cultural Revolution which was to hit them with Thomas Cromwell, the chancellor, leading the 'red guards'! Cromwell launched a propaganda campaign to 'persuade' the people that the country was sovereign and must not be subject to a 'foreign power', in other words the Pope's dominion must be ended. The use of the word 'Papa' as a way of referring to the Pope was banned; he was to be known only as the Bishop of Rome. The ordinary people found this restriction difficult to remember as they had grown up with 'Papa' on their lips. An insult to the new queen, or a reference to the king as a heretic, was to be treated as treason. The closing of the monasteries and abbeys, the treasures being plundered, the wealth being seized, the monks and nuns being assaulted, terrorized, and driven out into the countryside were watched stoically in North Elmham.

The sympathy of the people was with Katharine and the fact that Anne received no acclaim at her coronation indicated her unpopularity while her execution brought a real sense of relief and hope was that the execution would presage a return to life as it had been in the days of Queen Katharine. In 1536, a few months after Henry had married his third queen, Jane Seymour, a new pilgrimage swung into action. Ten thousand men primarily from the north but with a good representation from the east marched in the Pilgrimage of Grace to Doncaster to demand a return to the 'old ways'. The king initially agreed to the demands and the people were confident that the clock would be turned back, but Henry reneged on the promises and leaders of the pilgrimage were executed as an example that opposition to the 'new ways' would not be tolerated. More restrictions followed; pilgrimages, saints' days and the display of relics were banned while precious and venerated objects were smashed or burned. In 1538, the statue of the Virgin was taken from the Abbey at Walsingham to Chelsea and burned and, despite the Abbott's willingness to adopt the new ideas, the building was destroyed, and the treasure seized. The churchwardens of North Elmham decided that they could not stop the changes and should take advantage of them. They purchased stone from Walsingham, sold much of the North Elmham silver plate and destroyed the cross that held the 'relyques'. Yet, a number of the old ways were retained; the priest remained celibate and belief that Christ was present in the mass persisted. In North Elmham it was noted that the ceremonies had not changed, and the guild lights were still burning. Bibles in English were available, but Henry forbade women and the lower classes from reading them, the reason given was to prevent them being led astray. The poor felt that they had already been led astray! One constant, however, was the continuing wars with France. They had been a fact of life for longer than living memory, and, in 1545, the possibility of an attack on the East Coast sharply re-focused minds on the danger to Norfolk. King Francis aimed to control the Channel and as the English fleet sailed out to engage the French, the flag ship, the 'Mary Rose', capsized and sank. Seven hundred men were on board and only 40 were rescued, a tragedy that overshadowed the defeat of the French. Six months later the news which was on everyone's tongue was that of the death of King Henry and that the new king was a serious solitary boy of ten years.

Edward VI's coronation was one of great pageant and procession which he enjoyed as much as the citizens of London. The Boydens and their contemporaries celebrated from their perspective of rural Norfolk but could not imagine the crowds and spectacle. If there was an expectation that the new king would end the changes in the church, disappointment awaited. Edward, influenced by Cranmer, the Archbishop of Canterbury, and Edward Seymour, the Lord Protector, was eager to drive the Reformation more radically than ever. In 1549, the Catholic mass was made illegal, and the Book of Common Prayer made compulsory. In North Elmham, the churchwardens sold the silver monstrance, the censers and paxes, and removed 'the clothes yt hengo before yr roode loft' and 'ye ymages'. They also purchased Erasmus' 'Paraphrases' and in 1550, disposed of the 'common light', the altar cloths and the medieval service books, pulled down the high altar and moved it to a new place in the chancel. Older villagers found the sweeping away of all they had held precious unsettling and were sympathetic to the protests in Oxfordshire and Buckinghamshire against the new prayer book. In Norfolk, however, high prices and the enclosure of common land by landowners for sheep and cattle caused more resentment than the new prayer book and a serious uprising developed. Robert Kett, the leader, stood under an oak tree on Mousehold Heath, where the 10,000 who followed him camped in turf huts, roofed with boughs, to voice the demands of the poor. The primary demand was for the restoration of common land, and to demonstrate the serious nature of the demands. Norwich Castle was captured. The camp had been in place for seven weeks when troops were sent to disperse it and end the rebellion. According to reports, the troops acted brutally when a cheeky young lad made rude gestures and comments. They slaughtered 3,000 and hanged Kett from the keep of Norwich Castle. There was much anger! Four years after this incident, Edward VI was dead at the age of 18 years, but not before he had prohibited priests from wearing vestments, banned prayers for the dead and ordered punishment for anyone who attended a different form of worship. In just over 20 years, the church, which was the centre of villages like North Elmham had changed out of all recognition, and only those over 40 years of age could remember the old ways.

It is unlikely that the peasants of North Elmham heard about Lady Jane Grey's nine day 'reign' before it was over, but they would have known about the growing support for the Lady Mary, Queen Catharine's daughter, and perhaps were part of it. Mary left her house at Hunsdon, in Hertfordshire, as soon as she heard of Edward's death, travelled through Cambridgeshire, and raised her standard at Framlingham Castle in Suffolk. East Anglia was where she had her power base and, on the journey, she gathered thousands to her cause. Sailors mutinied against Queen Jane in favour of Mary and soldiers flocked to her banner. The reasons for supporting her were varied, some hoped for a return to the old religion, more remembered the unfair treatment of her mother and most believed it important that the will of Henry VIII should be honoured in the succession. In September 1553, news reached Norfolk that Mary had entered London in triumph where the streets were deep in flowers. Once Mary felt secure on the throne, she began her mission to return England to Rome. On 30th November 1554 she officially announced that the mission had been achieved. St Andrew's Day was proclaimed as an annual celebration of the event. The churchwardens in North Elmham had obeyed all the directions towards Protestantism and it is difficult to know the way they reacted to Mary's directives, but as news of Mary's fanaticism to cleanse the realm of heresy by burning reached the village, there was general alarm and then horror. North Elmham was fortunate, and no one was martyred, although there must have been many moments of fear as they heard about people going to the most terrible of deaths for the sin of reading the English Bible or having it read to them. A year before the first burnings, Mary's popularity had been dented by her marriage to Philip of Spain. Mary was desperate for a husband and an heir, but her desperation was translated as loving Spain more than England. Gradually, her unpopularity increased with news of her two phantom pregnancies, the loss of Calais to the French and the increase in prices and unemployment. In 1558, relief was palpable throughout the country on her death.

Sir Thomas Smith and People's Class

It is difficult to know the way in which the ordinary people in north Norfolk viewed the accession of Elizabeth. After the experience of the reign of Mary, there were many misgivings about another female monarch. The coronation of Elizabeth, however, marked the beginning of a reign of more than 40 eventful years; even as she processed to Westminster Abbey there were signs that questions of her suitability were fading. The citizens of London greeted her with affection, and, wearing her robes of cloth of gold, she responded by stopping to acknowledge their cheers. The people over whom Elizabeth reigned were, according to Sir Thomas Smith, in 1583, divided into four classes: gentlemen, citizens, yeomen and manual workers. The gentlemen included the nobility, landowners and knights of the shires, the citizens were merchants, and the yeomen farmers while no account was to be taken of the workers who were 'only to be ruled'. As they always had been the Boydens were in the latter category, but they and their neighbours in North Elmham had opinions and there were plenty of events in Elizabethan England about which they could comment. John Boyden who probably married Agnes Alison in Asmanhaugh in 1574/1576 in North Norfolk could have been connected with these Boydens (the exact dates and locations remain unclear). The marriage of Thomas Boyden and Emma Borne, in October 1575, in Dry Drayton, was recorded in the Cambridgeshire Registers of Marriage 1539-1812. Matters which raised their interest and concern were the marriage of the queen and religion. The question whether or whom the queen would marry was a constant discussion point almost to the end of her reign. Religion had a continuous high profile and in 1559, the Act of Supremacy and Uniformity re-established Protestantism in England. It restored the Book of Common Prayer but permitted priests to wear vestments and to continue some practices from the 'old ways'. Catholics were unable to accept this compromise and refuting the 'English Church' brought them danger. In 1577, Elizabeth made a glittering 'summer progress' through East Anglia and used this occasion to stress her determination that opposition to her religious decrees would not be tolerated. She imprisoned 22 prominent gentlemen Catholics but knighted several prominent Protestants and one or two Catholics who had agreed to conform. The common people understood the message, but, in North Elmham, there was little need to reinforce any religious message; the changes made by Henry VIII and Edward VI had been accepted without opposition and the village had avoided the excesses of Mary's re-imposition of the Catholic faith. Thus, the churchwardens reacted positively to the Act of Uniformity and installed a table of the Ten Commandments in the east end of the church, placed a poor box prominently and obtained a coffer with two locks for the parish register. Morning and evening services were conducted on Sundays as well as one service on each Wednesday and Friday. The morning service on Sundays included communion and sermon and frequently lasted almost four hours. Catechism lessons for the young were arranged for Sunday evenings but the young were not excited by them!

Elizabeth's reign was the time of exploration and a growing pride in being English. The news of the successful expeditions of Drake and Raleigh caused excitement but whether there was any understanding in North Elmham of the extent of the voyages, particularly Drake's circumnavigation of the world, is open to debate. Spain was the enemy, and much pleasure was expressed at the news of the capture of Spanish treasure, but, in early 1588, there was no pleasure and much fear. The news came that a Spanish Armada was sailing towards England with the intention of deposing Elizabeth in favour of Philip of Spain. Relief came in July when the Armada was finally defeated and driven by storms northwards. Anyone who was able to reach the coast from North Elmham would have been able to see the Spanish ships with the English in pursuit, many of which came from the North Norfolk ports and manned by Norfolk mariners. A year before there had been the news of the execution of Mary Queen of Scots; she had been a prisoner in England for almost 20 years. The stories and rumours of plots to make her queen in place of Elizabeth would have been the source of speculation over the years and it is likely that the common people believed that their queen was in danger and were happy at the news of Mary's execution. The event that most affected the poor of Elizabethan England came in 1601 with a harsh Poor Law, which was seen as necessary to deal with the increased number of poor peasants who were deemed a menace to society. The law stated that 'sturdy beggars' and out-of-work poor be returned to their native parish, and every parish be required to provide a poor house and to feed the destitute. To pay for these requirements a poor rate was levied. The Boydens would have been 'menaces to society' and subject to these regulations in the future! Elizabeth died in 1603, the majority of the population had known no other monarch and people mourned her and wondered what the future would bring.

James I was the future and was welcomed into England by the citizens of Berwick. He arrived in London in September 1603 and was crowned in Westminster Abbey. The people of North Elmham, with all their fellow countrymen, faced a time of change. England and Scotland were no longer separate, and James was to be known as King of Great Britain and the ordinary people found they lived in Great Britain of which England was just part. A new flag was designed - a combination of the flags of St. George and St. Andrew – to which everyone had to adapt. Two years into the reign, in 1605, the names of Guy Fawkes and Robert Catesby were on every tongue. As soon as news arrived in North Elmham that there had been a plot to blow up the king and Parliament there was gossip about the man Guy Fawkes, the gunpowder and the way it was secreted into the palace of Westminster with, probably, the wickedness of the Catholic Catesby and his fellow plotters. They may have approved of the horrible torture and death of the gunpowder traitors. James's determined Protestantism resulted in his desire that the Bible should be understood by the people, and he commissioned a new translation. This was published in 1611 and from then on anyone who could read had access to the Bible. It is highly unlikely that the Boydens could read but no doubt they admired the Bible when it arrived in the church. James had a special attachment to East Anglia because it provided him with the expanses of land where he could pursue his favourite hobbies of hunting and hawking and, in 1605, he had established a base in Newmarket and built a palace where he and his son, Charles, could relax and indulge in their passions of hunting, gambling, cockfighting, theatregoing, entertaining and horse-racing. Newmarket is about 80 miles from

North Elmham and the villagers had no opportunity to see the king, but news of his exploits and those of the prince would have been common knowledge. James's love of gaming and hunting brought the disapproval of a developing Puritan wing of Protestantism which advocated sombre dress and industry rather than leisure pursuits. In 1620, a group of Puritans, including 32 from Norwich, left Boston, a port in Lincolnshire across the Wash from North Norfolk, to find a new life in America where they could practise their religion as they wished. After a voyage of two-and-a-half months on board the ship the Mayflower, the pilgrim puritans arrived and the news of the successful passage was viewed as a feat of courage. Boydens did cross the Atlantic but not those from North Elmham, they showed no enthusiasm for emigration.

Five years later, in 1625, King James died and his second son, born in Scotland and named Charles was proclaimed sovereign.

North Elmham Boydens

Robert Boyden, my seven times great grandfather, was born in North Elmham. He was baptized in St. Mary's Church in 1630 and lived in the village throughout his life. Improvements in living conditions had been achieved since feudal times, but in small villages life remained hard for the poor, and Robert was born into a poor family. His parents afforded meat and fish very rarely and Robert's basic diet was bread and cheese and when harvests failed, which they did all too frequently, Robert went hungry. He did not experience the harvest failure of 1623, which was severe enough to cause famine, but lived through a time of great turmoil for the country. King Charles believed that he was king by divine right while the Parliament held that kingship implied a contract between the monarch and his subjects. Friction was inevitable and was exacerbated by the clash of religious allegiance: the suspected Catholicism of Charles thanks to the influence of his wife Henrietta Maria of France against the mainly Puritanism of Parliament. Neither king nor Parliament was willing to compromise, and civil war became inevitable. The nobility, landowners and Anglicans largely supported Charles, but the lower classes sympathised with the parliamentary side. East Anglia was a solid parliamentary stronghold, being the home of Oliver Cromwell. Robert worked in the fields from an early age and listened to the talk of war, although he did not fully understand the reasons for a probable conflict. He was about 12 years old when the civil war began, and he felt a certain excitement at the sight of local men being conscripted into the opposing armies but learned to be wary of soldiers as he watched them plunder the land to find food. No arrangements were made for feeding and quartering armies and soldiers were forced to fend for themselves by stealing food and finding shelter wherever they could.

In October 1642, the reports of the Battle of Edgehill, on the road to London, with its 3,000 dead and countless wounded brought home the enormity of the conflict to North Elmham, and the news that reached the village during the winter, and for much of 1643, was unsettling. The Royalists seemed the most effective militarily, and the outlook for parliamentary supporters was gloomy. In September 1643, the fighting came within 30 miles of North Elmham. The Earl of Manchester, who commanded the Eastern Association Army, in which Oliver Cromwell was a cavalry commander, occupied King's Lynn, as part of the strategy to prevent the king gaining support in East Anglia. After this skirmish, fighting was largely in the west of England, and North Elmham did not feel so involved until news came that the City of York was under siege by parliamentary and Scottish troops, that the area around the city was being destroyed and food stolen leaving the villagers to starve both with cold and hunger. There was great sympathy for the dispossessed people, but great satisfaction in July 1644, when North Elmham heard that the parliamentary soldiers under Sir Thomas Fairfax had routed the Royalist cavaliers at the Battle of Marston Moor, close to the City of York. That Cromwell had played a major part in the successful outcome was particularly welcome news in the village while the fact that the battle was as bloody as that at Edge Hill with 6,000 men dying in three hours must have been difficult to comprehend and was little discussed. Cromwell was once again the village hero when, in 1645, news of the Battle of Naseby, near Market Harborough and the New Model Army's decisive victory arrived. After the battle Charles took refuge with the Scots but, in 1646, he was handed over to the parliamentarians. Charles was held in Holdenby House in Northamptonshire and later transferred to Newmarket. On the way to Suffolk, Charles stayed in Hinchingbrooke House at Huntingdon and in Childerly Hall at Dry Drayton. Robert would not have been able to travel to see the convoy. Charles was popular in Newmarket and was entertained 'magnificently and dutifully by Edward Montague's wife Jemima'.

Charles' enjoyed his interlude in Newmarket as he was able to ride horses, but riding ended when he was taken to Caversham on the borders of Berkshire and Oxfordshire from where he was transferred to Hampton Court and thence to Windsor Castle. He escaped from the Castle and fled to the Isle of Wight but was recaptured and imprisoned in Carisbrooke Castle. Charles hoped that the Scots would come to his aid but, in 1648, their army was defeated at Preston. The Civil War was at an end and Charles was taken to London, tried for treason in Westminster Hall and beheaded in Whitehall. The news of the king's execution was greeted in North Elmham with relief and with expectations of a more peaceful life, but none of more comfort. Living conditions with poor hygiene meant that disease remained rife with the only possibility of cure being herbal remedies, and hunger and thirst after a long day at work continued to be assuaged by bread, cheese, and beer. Robert would have been interested to hear that Cromwell had returned victorious from Ireland, had become Lord General, and was ruling the country with a Council of State. Robert may also have heard that Cromwell had commissioned the Council of State to prepare a constitution to reflect gospel values and encourage the people to turn away from the things of the flesh towards things of the spirit. The Council failed but urged Cromwell to become the constitutional monarch. Cromwell refused but agreed to become the Lord Protector. In January 1653, Robert's marriage to Anne at North Elmham coincided with the start of the 'Protectorate'. The couple's expectations of this Godly Commonwealth were high. After all Cromwell, whom they admired, was in charge. Unfortunately, major generals controlled the country and worked to coerce the population into righteousness. Sunday was the only day that Robert and Anne had some limited leisure, but they found that all enjoyable activities were deemed profane. Taking part in or watching games or dancing was not permitted and the appearance of a maypole resulted in sanctions for the person who erected it. Alehouses were licensed and inspected, and fiddlers and gamblers purged. Robert and Ann were required to attend church and listen to fiery sermons delivered by ministers dressed in black. The bells no longer rang out over the village and there were no more church ceremonies and Christmas was not celebrated. Robert, in concert with other men of the village, was forced to guard his tongue; any swearing was punished by a fine while children, heard using bad language, were whipped. These harsh regulations alienated Robert and the majority of the population and were frequently ignored and often went unpunished. Cromwell gradually found it more and more difficult to achieve his desire; a peaceful tolerant God-fearing country and, in 1659, he died, and the Protectorate was soon at an end. Robert had mixed feelings about the death of someone who had been his hero but was too occupied with family matters to contemplate the changes Cromwell's death might bring.

In the year of Cromwell's death, Robert became a father when Anne gave birth to a daughter, Prudence, who was baptised on 1st of May 1659, and died almost immediately. Robert's second daughter, Ann, was baptized on 18th of October 1660, married to James Bolker on 29th June 1682 and a daughter was born in 1683. On 5th October 1682 Joseph Fuller married Mary Boyden who was a daughter of Robert and Anne and born in 1661/2. Katharine, daughter of Robert Boyden and his wife Anne, was baptised on 4th of February 1666. Alice was daughter of Robert Boyden and Anne and baptized on 19th January 1668. Robert son of Robert and his wife Anne was baptised on 4th March in 1670, while Lucy, daughter of Robert and Anne was baptized on 1st March 1672. John was baptized on 29th May 1677 while three of the remaining children were born in very significant years for the country. Ann arrived in the year that the monarchy was restored. The son of the beheaded Charles was invited to return, and, in May 1660, he landed in Dover and was crowned Charles II. It was an extravagant coronation which presaged the end of a Puritan ethos in the country. Robert and his village contemporaries welcomed the end of the austere society and found the stories of their 'merrie monarch' and his life of debauchery, something about which to snigger. Initially, Robert, the father, found the reports of the execution of those who signed the death warrant of Charles I and the exhumation and hanging of Oliver Cromwell at Tyburn unsettling but there were more serious concerns in North Elmham. The war with Holland was worrying in that the Dutch coast was very near Norfolk and a sea battle had taken place off Lowestoft. In the summer of 1664, however, the village was full of gossip about an approaching disaster! A comet was visible and was being interpreted as a harbinger of doom. Robert and Anne scanned the sky to see it and knew in 1665 that their fears and those of their neighbours were correct when news reached them that plague had struck London. Plague did not reach North Elmham, but fear of it did. One sixth of London's population died in 1665; the rich were able to run away from the city, but no-one was immune, and the disease reached far and wide. Katharine, Robert, and Anne's third daughter shared her birthday with the Great Fire of London. In September 1666, a small fire in Pudding Lane engulfed much of the old City of London. It burned for a week before the rain arrived to extinguish it. When Robert heard the news of the fire, he found it impossible to imagine the devastation. He had not visited London and could not comprehend the size of the capital. He was only able to be sorry for those who had nowhere to live, but was relieved that the fire meant an end to the plague. Robert died in March 1680 with Ann dying during 1689. Both were buried in the churchyard at North Elmham.

John Boyden, my six times great grandfather, was three years old in 1680, when his father died. John's birthday in 1677 was the day of the marriage of Mary, the niece of Charles, to William of Orange, an alliance that would become important to the future of the country. John was baptised on 29th May 1677 at North Elmham and during his early life, England was preoccupied by the religious problems of the succession to the throne. The cause of the preoccupation was the fear that Charles' heir, his brother James, who had converted to Catholicism, would return the country to the Roman Church. Catholic plots, mostly imagined but sincerely believed, caused panic. The king was determined that James should succeed him and, each time a political move was made to exclude him, Charles reacted by proroguing Parliament. The struggle continued until 1685, when Charles died having been received into the Catholic Church on his death bed, and James became king. John Boyden was eight years old and probably too young to have an opinion about this turn of events. James did, indeed, make every attempt to turn England back to the Catholic Church and, by mid 1688, when John was 11, Protestant concern was great. James had arrested bishops and promoted his Catholic supporters to positions of influence. William of Orange was called to intervene, and he reacted to the invitation and before the end of the year the Glorious Revolution was over. James had fled to France, and William with his wife Mary had arrived from Holland and they had become jointly king and queen. William's battles in Ireland and Scotland were to prevent James regaining the throne. In Ireland, William defeated James at the Battle of the Boyne, 1690, and during the campaign in Scotland the infamous massacre at Glencoe, 1692, occurred.

John would have heard the news of the various campaigns, but it did not change his life, neither did the successful measures by Parliament to limit the power of the king. In about 1706, John married Susannah. A daughter, Prudence, was born soon after the marriage but died and was buried on 27th July 1708. Their second child John also died in infancy and was buried on 20th September 1710. Their third child John was baptized on 26th October 1712, Hannah was baptized on 17th June 1716, Robert was baptized in 1718 and Samuel in 1720. The family lived in a small and poor dwelling with plain and simple furniture and their life continued at subsistence level with monotonous food, consisting largely of bread, butter, and potatoes, although John may have supplemented the diet with other vegetables if he had land available. Pottage was a daily meal, but meat was a rare luxury, usually enjoyed in the autumn when animals were slaughtered; they were too costly to feed during the winter. Beer had, over the generations, been the drink of the poor and it continued to be available, but gin became popular and, by 1695, was the cheapest beverage. King William had banned the import of French brandy and levied duty on spirits from Germany to encourage the import of gin from Holland. In 1695, British beer was taxed, and gin consumption escalated. Whether John migrated from beer to gin is unknown, but, in 1720, 'Gin Madness' was a major problem in London and gin's consumption must have increased throughout the country. John worked in the fields from dawn to dusk and the children joined him as soon as they were able. They did not have the opportunity to go to school. Susannah was also expected to help in the fields at busy times, but she had no relief from her responsibility for all the domestic tasks and making clothes for the family. In 1698, Celia Fiennes recorded her journeys around England and noted 'ordinary people both in Suffolk and Norfolk knit much and spin, some with a rock (distaff) and fusoe (spindle) as the French do, others at their wheels out in the streets and lanes'. Susannah would have used a distaff; she was too poor to own a spinning wheel. Leisure time was extremely limited, but the villagers made their own entertainment. They enjoyed dancing and singing, playing games, and watching puppet shows if the travelling puppeteers came by. Gambling with dice was popular with men and a growing number of them smoked clay pipes.

A Move to Holme Hale

When John's son Robert was born on 24th April 1718 and baptised on the same day at North Elham, George I was king. Queen Mary had died in 1694, King William had followed in 1702 and Queen Anne had reigned until 1714. Anne was the second daughter of James II, and the highlights of her reign were the defeat, in 1702, of the French by the Duke of Marlborough at Blenheim. The duke ensured this victory was noted by having a palace built and naming it Blenheim Palace. The Act of Union of 1707, formally united England and Scotland. Anne died without heirs; none of her twelve children survived her and she was succeeded by the Elector of Hanover, her second cousin, who became George I. The son of James II challenged George's right to the throne and landed in Scotland but was routed and fled back to France. Despite being the king, George did not speak English fluently, disliked the country and spent most of his time in Hanover. In 1727, when Robert was nine, George died, and his son became king. George II was equally unhappy to be in England and was no more popular, but these changes of monarch did not alter the lives of the poor. Hardship was the lot of Robert and his contemporaries while landowners expected them to work steadily, spend no money on alcohol, avoid bad company, keep no dogs, be quiet and content and never steal or swear. Robert left North Elmham in the 1730s; he was either searching for employment or had met Sarah who lived in Holme Hale. Whatever the reason, in 1743, he married her in Holme Hale and a daughter, Mary, was born in 1743 and a son, John, in 1750. It is unlikely that Robert visited Norwich on his journey to Holme Hale but if he had he would have been impressed by the city. Norwich, at this time was surrounded by a blackish wall, built of shiny flints, had 12 gates and many towers. Inside the walls were 36 churches and broad well-made roads wide enough for coaches and carts to pass. Country butchers rented stalls in one street and sold meat to the townspeople. A fish market was well away from the heart of the city and fruit and corn markets were held around the market cross. The Town Hall, built of timber and plaster in a squared pattern, was beside the Sealeing Hall in which a fair was held each Saturday, and a County Hall, a Sessions House and a Gaol were being built on the site of the castle.

The baptism of John Boyden, my four times great grandfather, was registered in Swaffham on 28th January 1750 but he was born in Holme Hale. This was approximately two years after 1st January had been adopted as New Year's Day. Before 1748, 25th March had been the official start of the year in England for at least five centuries. John's birth was also 10 years before George III came to the throne in 1760. In the middle of the 18th century, Britain had not become an easier place for the poor and uneducated like John. A succession of wheat harvest failures caused prices to soar dramatically with the result that there were food shortages and widespread riots. Power continued largely in the hands of the king, the aristocracy, and the church, and they used it for their benefit. John could not vote and had no part in decisions that regulated his daily life. The law remained harsh, and 160 offences carried the death penalty! In about 1777 a Norfolk vicar described a man being whipped through the streets and then hanged for stealing potatoes. Death was a daily occurrence and diseases killed young and old indiscriminately. During the last years of the century there were extremely cold winters with severe outbreaks of cholera and smallpox and consequent high numbers of deaths. Although it was at this time that Edward Jenner was experimenting with cowpox as a vaccine, live smallpox was being used as an inoculation against the disease by those who could afford it. Cuts were made in the arm, the smallpox inserted into the wounds and the recipient put on a special diet for a week. This procedure was dangerous and unhygienic and regularly life-threatening. The cost for this primitive procedure was about 5s, a sum unaffordable for the poor. Country herbal remedies were relied on for ill health while dealing with accidents and extraction of bad teeth was a task for a willing member of the family or a friend. A 'tooth drawer' was available at a cost but expertise was not guaranteed. A diary noted, 'Sent for…a man who draws teeth…he…drew my tooth but shockingly bad…he broke away a great piece of gum and … gave me exquisite pain all day…and my face swelled prodigiously. Gave the old man…2s 6d. He is too old I think to draw teeth, can't see very well'.

John was 23 years old when the Boston Tea Party occurred and two years later the American War of Independence began. At the same time France was in turmoil and as Britain had long regarded France as an enemy, tension was heightened. In 1780, the future seemed bleak and a fast was observed throughout 'the kingdom to beg Almighty God his assistance in our present troubles being at open rupture with America, France and Spain and a Blessing on our Fleets and Armies'. Preparations for conflict were obvious in Norfolk, and, in 1777, the Dragoons were exercising on Mousehold Heath, a large expanse of heath land outside Norwich and the following year the 'common soldiers' of the Western Battalion of the Norfolk Militia caused uproar when, with the support of the 'mob', they rioted against their officers because of a dispute over pay. The Militia was made up of men from the country villages and John was eligible to become a militia man. The terms of the Militia Act of 1757 required parishes to provide men for the militia and those between the ages of 18 and 50 were listed on muster rolls by the parish constables. Men were then elected to serve from the lists and their length of service was initially three years but after 1786 was increased to five. Militia men did not serve abroad and, during peace time, lived at home but were required to attend camp for training, and received an allowance from the parishes if they were on permanent duty. A John Boyden from Methwold served in the militia and, in 1784, a year after America achieved independence, was in difficulties and claiming poor relief from Feltwell which issued a 'return order' on him. The order required him to return to his own parish, which was listed as Methwold where other Boyden families lived. Holme Hale was the home parish of my four times great grandfather, and he does not seem to have served in the Militia.

Moving to The Fens

The harvest failures and shortage of food caused John Boyden to move west into The Fens and establish the fen line of Boydens. In 1785, he married Mary in Stow Bardolph, more information could possibly be found in either Stow Bardolph's or Wimbotsham's parish registers for where she was born, and in May 1786, their first child, Sarah, was born, the couple were in nearby Wimbotsham. Sarah's life was a brief eight weeks, and she was buried in the village in June 1786. The second child Noah, my thrice great grandfather, was born in the same village in 1787, two years before the French Revolution, and baptised 16th December 1792. Noah was followed in 1789 by a brother, Lazarus, and three further brothers, Robert in 1791, James in 1796 and William in 1800.

John and Mary spent their lives in Wimbotsham but news of revolution in France reached them and no doubt they became fearful that similar terrifying events would spread to Britain when they knew that the royal coach had been stoned by an angry crowd which chanted, 'Down with George!' John's major concern remained the support of his family although work was not always easily available and when John was successful in his search, the work was as an agricultural labourer, but farming methods were changing as a result of agricultural innovations. Viscount 'Turnip' Townsend and Thomas Coke of Holkham introduced new crops and a four-year rotation of planting while Jethro Tull's invention of a seed drill had already speeded sowing. Unfortunately, new ideas and new machinery reduced the number of men, like John, who were needed, although the work remained physically very hard with long days and poor pay. At harvest time, the wheat was cut by hand with sickles which had an edge like a saw and horses and carts were used to get it into barns as quickly as possible to keep it dry. This work had one advantage; the farmers usually fed the men well, gave them as much 'liquor' as they could drink, and paid a bonus to each worker when the harvest was finished.

Noah's childhood was dominated by the French Revolutionary and Napoleonic Wars and his adult years by poverty. The war against France began in 1792 when Noah was five and already working. The land battles went badly for Britain and her allies, and Noah would know that the adults around him were concerned about the successes of Napoleon. In 1798, Admiral Nelson, a Norfolk man, won a great sea victory at the Battle of the Nile and the war ended with the Treaty of Amiens, in 1802. By 1804 Napoleon was Emperor and making aggressive moves and the naval war resumed. In 1805, Nelson, although mortally wounded, defeated the combined French and Spanish fleets at Trafalgar. Noah was 18 years old and celebrated the victory and felt pride in Nelson but also sadness at the great man's death. On 2nd November 1813, Noah married Maria Reader, a Wimbotsham girl, in the village church. Neither had had the chance to learn to write and they each signed the marriage certificate with a cross. Noah was 26 and Maria was 22 and their hopes were high. Unfortunately, the continuing war caused rising inflation, and Norfolk was losing its premier position as the county of farming; and although enclosures were promoted as a way of ensuring the economic use of the land, they resulted in the poor losing their access to common land and being evicted from their homes. Wimbotsham was enclosed in 1801 and after their marriage Noah and Maria left for Denver. They were looking for a place to live and work. Denver was a village on the Great Ouse and its name came from the Anglo-Saxon word Dena-faer, the ford of the Danes. The move was unsuccessful and, in 1814, Noah and Maria were paupers living in Denver Poor House where their first child, a daughter, named Sarah, was born in November 1814 but survived only to December of the same year. The Battle of Waterloo at which Wellington finally defeated Napoleon was celebrated in 1815, but Noah and Maria, although relieved that the war was finally at an end, had little to celebrate. In 1816, a second child, a daughter, named Martha, was born and Noah had found work, but it was the year that Krakatoa, a volcano in Indonesia, erupted violently and caused a year in Britain, so cold that it was known as 'the year without a summer'. Conditions for Noah, Maria and the very young child were particularly harsh and keeping warm was almost impossible. Two sons followed Martha; Benjamin in 1818 and William in 1819 but the outlook for the family was grim. By the beginning of the 1820s employment prospects were again precarious; an economic depression was developing, and landowners began to cut wages and to sack labourers, while men discharged from the army after the Napoleonic wars were joining the labour market. Noah and Maria did not produce children for the next nine years but in 1828 a daughter Sarah was born. She died three years later as did her sister Sarah who was born in 1833 and died in 1838. The final child, John was born in 1835. Noah and Maria unfortunately and other families in their position also had the drainage of The Fens to face.

St. Mary's Church, Denver

Drainage of the Fenland had been undertaken since Roman times, but in the 17th Century systematic work began. Noted for his involvement is the fourth Duke of Bedford who led a group of speculators, known as the adventurers, who commissioned the Dutch engineer Cornelius Vermuyden to undertake work which included the construction of the Old and New Bedford Rivers. Work continued during the 19th century until the drainage of The Fens in East Anglia was completed and thousands of acres of black fertile land had become available for growing crops. The acres of black land, however, replaced a marshy environment which had provided self-sufficiency for numerous fen families and once their way of life was destroyed, they had no other option but to join the growing number of impoverished agricultural labourers and add to the number of the unemployed. The changes brought about by the Drainage Act of 1798 and that of 1802 for 'draining and preserving certain lands and fen grounds' in Denver and other nearby 'parishes' seems to have been the catalyst for Noah and his family leaving the village and travelling west into Cambridgeshire. The well-off travelled by horseback or post-chaise along roads which were no more than tracks and often controlled by turnpikes, but the poor could not afford this luxury and their journeys were primarily on foot, although a lift on a cart was a possibility. The family went to March, a distance of about 20 miles, where Noah's brother, William, was living. Noah, Maria and the children were in March in 1828, the year when the weather was the best since 1814 and the harvest good. In August, a second Sarah was born, and Noah and Maria must have thought their situation was improving, although there was no security; employment was by the day and poor relief subject to a scheme that reduced the amount paid. In 1829, all hopes were dashed, snow fell in October and the harvest was the worst for many years and Noah and his family, like his fellow labourers, were cold and hungry. Discontent and despair grew as pauperism increased. Noah could have been one of the labourers who turned to poaching and theft of food to feed their children, because Norfolk and Cambridgeshire, where new farming technology, maximum enclosure and fen drainage had occurred, were among the counties most affected by the conditions.

Further uncertainty was added when George IV died, and an election was triggered by the accession of William IV. The Whigs were returned, and rumours abounded about their intentions. The harvest of 1830 was again disappointing, and riots broke out. Machines were damaged and arson was rife. Meetings of the labourers demanded better pay – 13s 6d per week in winter and 15s in summer and more security of employment. The riots were not long lasting but over 500 people were transported as punishment for their part in them and over 600 imprisoned but it seems unlikely that Noah was charged with any offence. He had been earning about 8s 4d per week, but the rent of cottages was increasing and once he was out of work he returned to Denver with Maria and family in 1831. Martha, aged 15, died in March of that year and Sarah in the October, aged three years, probably of influenza as there were two major epidemics of this disease between 1831 and 1833, although there was a severe Cholera epidemic in 1831/1832 which could have been the killer. Noah found enough work to keep the family out of Denver Union, or Downham Workhouse as it was built in 1836, until 1838, but life was extremely precarious. Two more children were born during this time, a daughter, in 1833, who became the third Sarah, and, in 1835, John the third son and final child. In 1837, Queen

Victoria came to the throne, but the event did nothing to improve the life of Maria and Noah. Indeed, the Queen had little understanding of the conditions her subjects suffered in East Anglia and when she visited the region, she described them as sub-human specimens whereas Thomas Carlye who also came to The Fens and went to the poor house at St Ives was angry at the inhumanity he witnessed there. Noah and Maria, in concert with all poor people, had a terror of pauperism but by the time Sarah was five, they had no other option but to accept the inevitable and enter the union. They were subjected to the new regulations of the Poor Law Amendment Act, which brought in the New Poor Law and made conditions harsh; the philosophy being that bleak surrounding would deter the poor from entering the union. Men and women were separated and subjected to an unbending regime, where Sarah died in 1838. Maria and the baby did not survive long and, by 1841, both were dead. Perhaps all three were subject to one of the epidemics of influenza, typhoid, typhus, or cholera that occurred between 1836 and 1842. Noah left the union and went to live in Denver in the home of a farmer who employed him as a gardener. By 1851, Noah had moved to Hilgay and was lodging with a grocer and his family and at age 62 was once more working as an agricultural labourer. Ten years later Noah was in Downham Market Union and was listed as a pauper, but he was again a gardener. Whether he was obliged to do this or was a volunteer can only be guessed. His hard life came to an end in 1863 in Downham Union, but where he was buried is not known.

Noah and Maria's first son Benjamin was my great, great grandfather. Born in 1818 and baptised in Denver his childhood followed the tradition of the family, and he was an impoverished agricultural labourer from an early age. He cannot have been more than about nine when the family set out for March and whatever work was available, he would have had to do his share to keep food on the table. He returned to Denver where he and William, his brother, must have watched the windmill at Denver being built and perhaps was one of the first farm workers to help take wheat for milling to it. Although William remained at Denver and became a well-regarded member of the community, Benjamin decided that Denver had nothing to offer him when his parents were forced into the Denver Union. He was already 20 and independent and he left. He is not recorded on the census of 1841, so he was probably wandering the countryside picking up work wherever it was available and 'sleeping rough'. In about 1842, Benjamin reached Chatteris, a town which was founded, in 980, by a community of Benedictine nuns from Chartreuse in France, and in November 1843 married Mary Ann Watson. The banns noted that both Benjamin and Mary Ann were parishioners of Chatteris, although Mary Ann was born in Warboys, the daughter of Elias and Mary Watson. Elias was dead by 1841 and Mary was designated a work woman, and two younger siblings were listed, John, aged 15 and Elizabeth 13. Mary was 50 years old and ten years later she was in March and had become the housekeeper for a man named Thomas Darby, a widower aged 69 years. It is probable that Benjamin had obtained work in Chatteris while Mary Ann Watson was most likely a domestic servant. Their first child was born in Chatteris in 1844 and named William Watson. The successive children also had Watson, Mary Ann's maiden name, included in their name. William's brother and three sisters were Mary Ann Watson (1846), John Watson (1849), Elizabeth Watson (1852) and Harriett Watson (1860). In Chatteris,

Benjamin found work as a brick maker but about the time of the Great Exhibition in 1851 the family left Chatteris and went to Bardney in Lincolnshire where Elizabeth was born in July 1852 and baptised in September 1852. The reason for making the long journey to Lincolnshire can only be surmised. Perhaps Benjamin was no longer able to find work and decided to try his luck in Lincolnshire where he may have had contacts or relatives as there were Watsons in Bardney. Certainly, the newspaper of 13th April 1872 reported that 'agricultural labourers were in Whittlesea marketplace waiting for a meeting', but the speaker did not arrive, and the lack of work was not discussed.

The length of the time spent in Bardney cannot be easily judged but the family was in Whittlesey by 1860, the year of Harriett's birth. Elizabeth married Henry Redhead in 1881. Benjamin was working as an agricultural labourer, but later he became a brush maker which may have been a less arduous occupation. Initially, Benjamin and Mary Ann found a house in Arnold's Lane but moved to Scaldgate where they remained for more than 10 years. They spent their old age in Parkinson's Lane with relatively more comfort than Noah and Maria had had in their later lives. Mary Ann died in 1892 and Benjamin followed her in 1894, both are buried in Whittlesey cemetery.

Grave of William Watson Boyden the lighter man and Elizabeth in Whittlesea Cemetery

William Watson, my great grandfather, was 17 when the family arrived back in Whittlesea. William returned to working on the land but within a short time his life changed. The Boydens' neighbours in Arnold's Lane were members of the Harris family and William was attracted to Elizabeth Harris. He determined to marry her and achieved his ambition in 1863. Elizabeth's father was John Harris, her mother Alice and she had seven brothers and four sisters. At the time of William and Elizabeth's marriage John Watson Boyden, William's brother was an agricultural labourer, but he had been a waterman, and the year Elizabeth was born the family was living in East Delph, where many other watermen had their homes. It would seem that John Watson was the influence which persuaded William to leave the land and turn to the waterways. Better pay may have been a consideration for this decision. Another important persuasive aspect for William was that a child was soon expected, and he anticipated that employment would be more secure on the lighters. The drainage of The Fens had created water channels, usually referred to as drains, which, with the rivers, formed an extensive network of water ways, navigable from the seaports of the Wash as far as Northamptonshire and Bedfordshire. Before the building of Denver Sluice sea-going coasters sailed inland and in the late 17th century Daniel Defoe made an extensive journey through England and Wales and noted that King's Lynn was 'a well positioned port' and merchants used inland navigation to supply six counties, particularly with wine and coal. Once the sluice was completed, cargoes needed to be transferred to smaller vessels and lighters, based on traditional fen river craft, were the answer and they became the freight transport of the fen water ways. Lighters were double headed, stoutly constructed craft, generally in oak, about 13 metres in length and approximately three metres in beam. A smaller version of the lighter, which carried about two tonnes of freight, known as a 'fen butt,' was also constructed for use on the minor waterways. These two types of vessel did not require a great depth of water because they were flat bottomed and, individual craft could be linked together to form what was known as a 'gang'. A 'gang' could be managed by two men, one steering and one handling the horse on shore, making lighters an economic means of transport. Square canvas sails, similar to those used by the Vikings, propelled the vessels efficiently in wind while horses were necessary in calm conditions. When the sail was being used the horses were put in a lighter especially adapted for the animals (known colloquially as the 'oss boat) at the rear of the line of craft, and along the route certain establishments were required to provide stabling and food for the horses. One such place was the White Cock Inn on the Cock Bank, near Whittlesea, where the landlord, Jesse Dolby had to agree to this condition before taking on the public house.

William Watson appears to have been the last Boyden to travel the length of the water way system as a lighter/waterman in that his working life coincided with the last years when the waterways remained important freight carriers. The growth of the railways made it obvious that the days of the lighter men were rapidly coming to an end. William had been described as a 'scholar' in his childhood, but his time in school was limited and, without access to books and the need for him to work from his early years, he lost his ability to read or write and signed his marriage certificate with a cross. William Watson was not without practical skills, however, and demonstrated his abilities while working as part of a two-man crew with the responsibility of making up the 'gang' of the required number of lighters. A pole projected from the stern of each lighter which was joined to the preceding stern by a rope called a quarter bit while a 'seizing chain' joined the 'fore-lighter' to the second vessel which was equipped with a long 'steering pole'. 'Fest ropes' were attached to the 'steering pole' so that the helmsman on the 'fore-lighter' could direct the course of the gang. The 'fore-lighter' had a substantial mast supported by heavy stays so that it could be lowered for passing under bridges, and when lowered fitted into a building situated amidships called a tabernacle. Expertise to manage the complications of forming a gang and to navigate the waterways with long lines of lighters was not easily gained but was essential, while the work of loading the lighters and hoisting the sails needed strength and muscle. Each vessel was able to transport about 20 tonnes of cargo either agricultural produce to the Wash ports or imports such as coal and timber inland. The sails were hoisted manually by controlling lines when there was a following wind and again if the sails became wet. It was essential to ensure they were thoroughly dry before they were stowed to prevent the canvas from rotting. Strength was also essential if conditions made it necessary to propel the lighters by a 'quant' which was a long pole capable of reaching the bottom of the river or drain. The lighter man held the pole and ran the length of the lighter with the current which moved the craft forward. Normally, the lighters were towed by heavy horses; their strength was needed for the loaded vessels, and although the Shire is the horse of the fen country other breeds were used and any animal with prowess was highly prized. Unlike the canals of other parts of the country, the tow paths, known as haling ways, were rough and ready. Before the Haling Act of 1789 no regulation or organisation existed for maintenance or the use of the waterside paths, and even after the legislation, which aimed to reconcile the grievances of the landowners with the rights of the lighter men, disputes arose. The detail of the Act required that the towing ropes were attached to the masts of the lighters, which became, whether intended or not, an advantage to the lighter men if a disgruntled landowner obstructed the towpath. The horses were trained to loosen the long towing ropes and jump or negotiate an obstruction, and to leap to and from the horse boat and canal bank if the situation required it.

Lighter men were recognizable by their distinctive clothing. There were two types; one consisted of long blue waistcoats with hats made of otter fur, the second moleskin waistcoats with stocking caps, ending with tassels. Whether they indicated the particular job of the lighter man, or the particular owners of the vessels cannot immediately be noted. What is certain is that lighter men had a bad image, probably with some truth. Their language is reported to have been appalling, they were frequently accused of poaching and pilfering, and they were hell-raisers at isolated taverns when off duty. However, they were often welcomed by landlords for their generosity. There are reports that these landlords fired shot guns to alert the local men that the lighter men had arrived and there would be free beer for everyone. The lighter men were also regarded as being pugnacious and known for settling disputes with their fists, but when the very limited regulation was disregarded, there was no other way to settle complaints about obstruction of the haling ways by the lighter men or accusations of trespass on the part of the farmers. The families of the lighter men did not live on the lighters, their wives and families remained at home, with the wife shouldering the responsibility of looking after the children, so there was no domestic environment to soften the lighter men's reaction to problems. Although there were no families on board, house lighters provided accommodation which was needed for long runs, and some journeys were very long. Reports noted that, under certain conditions, particularly of the depth of water, the journey from Wisbech to Peterborough could take a month! The minimal facilities of the house lighters would not have proved adequate for a family; they were cramped and too low to permit standing while the floor space was largely taken up by bunks or lockers. It is likely that the lockers were the boxes which contained all the worldly goods of the lighter men. A small coal burning stove with its chimney projecting through the deck provided some warmth and was welcome on a bitter night. A 'cock boat' was carried on a 'gang' and was used to row to the bank if the lighters were anchored mid-stream.

After their marriage, William and Elizabeth lived in Fosters Lane and later moved to a small four roomed house in Cheap Lane, not far from St. Andrew's Church and within walking distance of The Fens. They produced seven children and Watson was included in their names with Thomas Watson arriving in 1864, William Watson in 1866, and John Watson in 1868/9. The first daughter, Mary Ann Watson, was born in 1870 with a second daughter, Emma Jane Watson, following in 1873. A fourth son, Elias Watson, was born in 1878, and the baby of the family, Alice Watson, came in 1881. Elizabeth ran the home and coped with a growing family, which she ruled with a rod of iron or rather a leather belt. William was on board various vessels during his career. In 1871 he was the 'foreman' on board 'The Brothers', moored in Wisbech, and in charge while the Master was on shore all night. Elizabeth was at home with three growing boys and a new baby! Ten years later just at the time Alice was born, William was the mate of the Black Vessel at Wadenhoe. John recalled that he sailed to Denver with his father when he was a child and, no doubt, lighters and lightermen were an important part of life to John and his siblings. John also spoke about the Floating Church, known as the Fenland Ark, although William Watson would not have used it. He was already dead when the Rev. George Broke became the incumbent of Holme Hale, where Boydens had lived, in 1895 and developed the floating church to serve those who could not get to a place of worship because of impassable roads and/or working on the waterways. The Ark remained in use until 1904 when Rev George retired to Holme Hale, where his wife had inherited the manor house.

The Boyden family was extremely poor, and Elizabeth needed the children to work as soon as they were able. In 1881, Thomas, William and John were already agricultural labourers and they had probably worked seven days a week from a very young age. They were all members of child agricultural gangs and daily made the long walk to the fields, beyond Black Bush and into Farcet Fen. The landowner directed what they did but their tasks probably included 'picking stones off the land, gathering twitch or weeds...driving horses at plough (or) cutting turnips for sheep'. John thought that he earned sixpence a week, but it is more likely that his wage was sixpence a day as contemporary reports indicate that at the age of eight this amount was the average with an increase of up to a shilling a day at the age of 11 or 12 years. John always insisted that he did not keep any of his earnings because his mother needed the money and that he did not go to school because of this financial need. He thought that he might have attended very briefly and had begun to learn to read and write but quickly forgot the skill when his mother obtained permission to remove him from school. This belief is unlikely to have been true because there was no compulsory attendance until the 1880 Education Act when children between five and ten years of age were required to attend and after that date John's four younger siblings went to school. John was already 11 years old in 1880 and not obliged to attend school, but perhaps he heard from his younger friends that they had obtained permission to stay out of school and he believed that his mother had indeed gained permission for him to work. In his old age, it worried me that he could not read the destinations of buses and surprised me that he signed his pension book with an X while Con wrote 'J. Boyden, his mark' beside it. Sometimes she drew the cross herself! Despite his inability to write he had no problems with managing his money and could estimate the size of a field down to the last rod, pole, or perch!

John Watson Boyden in The Fens

In the 19th century it was usual for agricultural employees to live at their workplace and John Watson Boyden was living and working on a farm at King's Delph in 1891. It seems, however, that he found, in the same year, an employer who would pay more money than his previous one and he had also found somewhere to lodge. He joined three other lodgers, Eliza Lewis, Martha Titman and William Corney in Farcet Fen. Eliza went to school, was able to read and write and became a domestic servant. Her father was a railway engine driver and Mary Ann, her mother. Eliza was born in Ramsey St. Mary's in 1871. and had three brothers and two sisters. John and Eliza became very friendly and four years later, in October 1895, they were married. He was 27 years old, and she was 24. The curate of St. Mary's Church Whittlesea officiated at the wedding which took place at St. Thomas' Church, Ponders Bridge where both were living. Eliza signed her name on the marriage certificate with confidence, John was unable to sign his name. John always referred to her as Liza and they continued to live in Farcet Fen and John remained an agricultural labourer. Liza died in March 1932, aged 61 years, two years before I was born, and I remember nothing about her. She appears in no photographs and John spoke about her very rarely. His one particular memory concerns the copper kettle which came from the Farcet Fen home. It was, according to John, made in Whittlesea and that Liza walked to the town to purchase it. Certainly, there are records of a number of tinsmiths operating at the time. It is unlikely that it was the only time she, John or the family walked to Whittlesea as there were John's parents and other relatives to visit. If the kettle or any other metal pot needed repair, Liza would have employed a tinker to do the work. Tinkers were itinerant handy men, usually referred to as didicoys. Packmen carried household linens from door to door so that items could be purchased. Agricultural wages were, however, at the bread line so Liza would only have been able to buy absolute necessities. It was not possible to buy books for reading and only schoolbooks would have been kept in cupboards.

In 1901, the Census included:

Parish of Pondersbridge; Church of St. Thomas

Head of family: John W. Boyden, age 32, birth about 1869

Wife: Eliza Boyden, age 30 born at Whittlesey

Children: Willie 4 years, Emma 2 years, Mary Elsie 3/12

Mother of Eliza, Mary Ann Lewis 67 years

Brother of Eliza, Fred Lewis 23 years

Living with family, Herbert Bull 19 years

In 1911 two families were sharing a home. The list of those in the house appears with the Lants who remained friends with the Boydens for many years.

Household Members:

John Lant 51   Caroline Lant 38 Ada Mary Lant 16 Majorie Stella Lant 1

John Boyden 42   Eliza Boyden 40 Willie Boyden 14 Emma Jane 12 Mary Elsie 10

                      Fred 7 Albert Ernest 5 Jesse Boyden 1

In 1911, the Census also detailed:

John Boyden	42	Farm Labourer	Mary Elsie	10	School
Eliza Boyden	40		Fred	6	School
Willie	14	Farm Labourer	Albert Ernest	5	School
Emma Jane	12	School	Jesse	1	

It was as an old man that I remember John, when he was slightly stooped but still quite tall. He had retained a good head of steely grey hair and had a bushy moustache that matched his hair exactly. In one ear he wore a gold earring which fascinated me. I wasn't accustomed to men having earrings. John explained that his mother had pierced his ear, using a burnt cork and needle, to aid his sight. John dressed as all good fen men did, in corduroy trousers with belt and braces, a flannel shirt, waist coat and cardigan, fastened by the top button only, and a flat cap. Strangely, he always referred to his cardigan as a 'ganzy', which is a corruption of Guernsey, the name of a Channel Island and that of a fisherman's jersey made in the island. John was hardy and did not appear to feel the cold; he had not had the experience of warm houses and hot water for washing.

At the beginning of the Second World War, John, with Emma and Albert were forced to leave their home, it was needed for working land workers, retired workers were not considered! Emma and Albert came to live in Farcet and John went to live in Wistow, where he died in 1951, aged 83 years. His funeral was held at St. Andrew's Church in Whittlesea, which is near his boyhood home. St. Andrew's is always referred to as the 'low church' because it is without a steeple unlike its partner church St. Mary's which is known as the 'high church'. Its designations have no association with their respective liturgies.

Bill

Bill was born in 1897 in a cottage surrounded by the flat farmland of Farcet Fen in the rural county of Huntingdon. The cottage was built with mud walls and a thatched roof like the homes of most poor fen people since earliest times. It was situated in Milk and Water, a name that conjures up a peaceful pastoral scene but in reality, such an impression was false. Bill was the eldest child of John and Eliza, and they gave him the name Willie which he disliked intensely. He tolerated William for official forms, but much preferred the simple tag 'Bill'! There were five other children, two sisters Emma Jane, born in 1899, and Mary Elsie in 1901 and three brothers, Fred, born in 1903, Albert Ernest in 1906 and Jesse in 1909. John and Eliza did not include Watson in their names, but like the preceding generations their life was hard as John was a poorly paid agricultural labourer. Even when John may have become a horse keeper, work that carried significant responsibility, increased rewards were negligible, even though horses were used in every aspect of farming and a horse keeper needed knowledge and ability. 'The man who knows minutely the habits and manner of treatment of…horses…(is a) first rate farm labourer (and) is truly as skilled as the first-rate mechanic or artisan.' John always aimed to do his work to the best of his ability. He was proud of the fact that he could plough a straight furrow and once said, on seeing a very badly ploughed field, that if he had produced such uneven rows, he would have got up in the night to do it again.

Bill Boyden (left), my Dad, with his family

Bill and his siblings attended Pondersbridge Church of England School about three miles distant and they walked to and fro everyday whatever the weather and, with no school meals provided, they carried a meagre mid-day meal with them. The children entertained themselves on the walk with various activities; one that they particularly enjoyed was walking on the parapet of the bridge above the river. Despite the danger they all survived. Bill was an able scholar and deserved the opportunity of secondary education but was denied it by the local vicar. The Rev. Mr. Hampton, who served the parish for 24 years, was the controlling school manager, and acted with the class consciousness that pervaded society at the time and he did not include Bill in possible candidates for the secondary school at Ramsey. He saw Bill as the son of a poor farm labourer and not worthy of or able to take full benefit from any education beyond an elementary school and chose a boy from a 'better home'. Bill never expressed his anger at this injustice but studied all his life, through correspondence courses, and became skilled in motor and mechanical engineering. He could turn his hand to any practical task and his mind to any problem that required a solution. Perhaps his treatment spurred him on to be more than an agricultural labourer although, when he left school, there was no other place to obtain work but on a farm. Bill frequently helped his father with the care of the horses even though he had not grown to his adult height of more than six feet and had difficulty reaching the heads of the animals. He also assisted on long cattle drives of as much as 30 miles taking the 'beasts' to market. The farmer was a man who understood that methods of farming would change, and he had obtained a tractor. This primitive machine, given the name 'Overtime', had been developed in America and quickly attracted an intense interest from Bill. He determined to teach himself to drive it, achieved his ambition and immediately possessed an expertise not shared by many of his peers. It was to have a very important benefit.

The First World War gave Bill his opportunity to 'escape' The Fens, although service on the Western Front was hardly a desirable destination. He was 17 years old in 1914 and, like the majority of his generation, felt it his duty to join the army. These young men were encouraged in various ways. There were Parliamentary recruiting meetings in Farcet but enlistment by agricultural workers was probably delayed until the end of August when the harvest was finished, and their presence was not so vital. By December 1914, the number of Farcet men who had 'answered the call' reached 55 and the village could no longer be criticised as 'not having done well' and 'was...well represented according to its size and population' but 'there were still many young men whose services would be welcome in H.M. Forces.' In the following years, 204 men from the village 'answered the call', one of which was Bill, although there is a mistake, and he was recorded as John Boyden. The 'roll of honour' lists those who were killed in the war. Bill was assigned to the Queen's Royal (West Surrey) Regiment as Huntingdon had been associated with this regiment for many years. Bill was at Ypres when General French wrote in his dispatches that 'a counterattack was made by the Northamptonshire Regiment in combination with the Queen's' and it may have been at this time that Bill met Joseph Peacock from Newark, a small village to the north of Peterborough who was serving in the Northamptonshire Regiment. Bill was also on the Somme and survived that battle and the war without injury and it was probably his tractor-driving ability which proved to be the major factor in his survival. He was detailed to drive vehicles which carried supplies to the front line, an essential task, and one that kept him from actual combat but did not shield him from witnessing the carnage.

Some of the major battles of the First World War began:

1st	Ypres	19th October 1914
2nd	Ypres	21st April 1915
3rd	Loos	25th September 1915
4th	Verdun	21st February 1916
5th	Somme	1st July 1916
6th	Vimy Ridge	9th April 1917 also termed Arras
7th	Ypres	31st July 1917 also termed Passchendaele

A story survives that, on one occasion, Bill overstayed his leave, but it cannot be true as he received his Victory medal. Certainly, in 1915, the farmers in several counties, including Huntingdonshire, needed labourers to help with the harvest and soldiers were given special dispensation of four weeks leave to do the necessary work. Bill must have been one of those men and the story was based on a misunderstanding. It could, however, be associated with demobilisation, which began in December 1918, one month after the end of the conflict. The local newspaper reported that several Farcet soldiers who were at home for Christmas had been told not to return and Bill could have been one of that number. It also attempted to raise spirits and, in February 1916 just five months before the beginning of the Battle of the Somme, noted that the Christmas season had been celebrated in order to 'keep the home fires burning for the sake of the boys across the water'. Every week the Peterborough Advertiser reported extensively on the war. It counted the weeks of hostilities and published news from individual servicemen and photographs of the wounded and killed, with the somewhat inappropriate heading 'The Lucky and the Unlucky'. On 16th November 1916, an 'unlucky' one was Joseph Peacock who died during the Somme offensive. Joseph was born in Newark, a small village to the north of Peterborough and served in the Northamptonshire Regiment but appears on the Farcet War Memorial with the list of men who joined the army from the village. Private J.G. Marriott took the news of Joseph's death in action to his parents. He told them that Joseph and a comrade were killed by a shell, and Joseph was buried within British lines and his name is on the Thiepval Memorial. The likelihood is that, when the opportunity arose, Bill visited the Peacock family to extend his condolences and met Minnie Louisa, Joseph's sister.

Bill and Minnie's acquaintance grew into friendship, then love and they married in 1922, when he was 25 years old, and she was 24. Bill had returned to farm work and the two went to live in Daintree Drove in Farcet Fen. Their happiness was short-lived when Minnie became seriously ill with stomach cancer and pneumonia, and died after seven weeks in February 1927 at her parent's home. A story, without verification is that the cancer resulted from an incident when Minnie is said to have attempted to stop a runaway horse and that the animal injured her stomach. She was buried in Eastfield Cemetery in Peterborough. The grief which Bill experienced is demonstrated by the inscription on her grave:

Minnie Louisa

The Dearly Beloved Wife of

Willie Boyden

Who fell asleep February 16th 1927

Aged 29 years

Sleep on beloved, sleep and take thy rest

Lay down thy head upon thy Saviour's breast

We loved thee well but

Jesus loves thee best

Minnie's death left Bill lonely in Farcet Fen. He pushed his war experiences and his short-lived marriage to the back of his mind and rarely mentioned them and certainly did not describe them in detail. I knew Minnie's sister and brother-in-law and visited them regularly with Con but was never told who they were. Minnie's sister worked with Con, and this might have been the reason that Con and Bill got together. Bill must have continued to stay in the house that he and Minnie lived in because in the Peterborough Advertiser on 21st June 1929 it was reported that William Boyden of Daintree Drove had applied artificial respiration, which Bill said he could do, with no result to a Mr. Jesse Papworth, also of Daintree Drove who had drowned in a dyke called the dipping place.

The Garfield Family

My maternal Garfield ancestors mirror very closely those of the Boydens. The meaning of 'gar' in the Anglo-Saxon poem Beowolf is spear but the word may also have described objects that were shaped like spears i.e., were triangular. Thus, Garfield became the distinguishing name of a man whose allocated piece of land was spear shaped. If this derivative is accurate then the Garfields were Saxon serfs, then Norman peasants with no freedom and despite some improvement in lifestyle during the following centuries were poor agricultural labourers from the time of the enclosures. In the 19th century they moved away from the land into the nearby city and became railway workers. My three times maternal great grandfather was Robert Garfield, and was born and baptised on 3rd June 1794 in Polebrook, Huntingdonshire. This county, until the second half of the twentieth century was sparsely populated and completely rural, where the poor were, almost without exception, agricultural workers. Like the Boydens they lived in small dwellings with wattle and daub walls, and wooden shutters to close the opening which let in light (there were no glass windows for the peasantry) in small villages or settlements and spent their lives ploughing, sowing and harvesting. The law was on the side of the rich and powerful and the Church of England wielded much control over their lives and this power was a grievance expressed in the highly charged meetings at the time of the 1830 riots. There was little time for leisure or education. Attendance at church on Sundays was perceived as mandatory and Holy Days were the only times of pleasurable activities. Robert married Mary who was also born in Polebrook. There was no work and/or housing for them because in 1818 when their first child, William, was born they had moved to Sibson about six miles distant from Polebrook. Sibson and its neighbouring settlement Stibbington are closely linked together, with few people being able to distinguish where one begins and the other ends. Sibson-cum-Stibbington, being on the A1 Road is a village that is more passed by than visited. William was followed by five brothers but only one sister, John in 1825, Ruth in 1830, Joseph in 1832, Edward in 1835, James in 1837 and Robert in 1840.

William was my great, great grandfather and seems to have spent all his life in Sibson, but he married Ann who was born in Oxford Street in London. It appears that she arrived on a coach from London and William fell in love with her. Down the years a story was that Ann was a lady but, in reality, she was a lady's maid. Her father was John Palmer, a tailor and she was, at 15 years of age, living with a number of young people and was designated as a F.S. (family servant). Ann did not return to London and remained in Sibson until her death in 1892 while William lived two more years. Their marriage took place, but the date is not easy to pinpoint. The registration index records the day as in early 1845, but the church marriage certificate is dated 13th August 1848, two years after the birth of their first child. William and Ann produced nine children, four daughters and five sons. Mary Ann arrived in 1846, John in 1849, Sarah in 1850, James in 1854, Thomas in 1856, Joseph in 1858, Sophy in 1859, Henry in 1861 and Ruth in 1864. John followed in his father's footsteps and became an agricultural labourer. There was no other option when he began his working life, but an opportunity arose that he grasped with both hands as did many of his contemporaries. The railways were developing rapidly, and Peterborough was becoming an important junction with five railway companies operating within the city. Many agricultural workers left the land for life in urban areas to take advantage of the better wages that the railways offered. Railway companies employed prospective engine drivers as engine cleaners and after they had proved their ability and had worked conscientiously, they were moved to employment as firemen. John was employed by the Midland Railway and when he married Sarah Rycraft, who was born in Nassington in 1848, the couple went to live in Bread Street Peterborough and, in 1871, he was recorded as a railway fireman. After the promotion, another period of probation followed before driver status was reached! He walked from Palmerston Road to his place of employment at the Midland Railway Engine Shed at Spital Bridge, a distance of about three miles. Sarah's younger brother James was an engine cleaner when he first moved to Peterborough and lived with her and John. Three children were born in Bread Street, John William in 1873, Albert Henry in 1875 and Emma Gertrude in 1877. The family then moved to 10 Lime Tree Terrace in Palmerston Road where the rest of the family arrived, Ethel in 1880, Ruth Elizabeth in 1883, Nellie in 1885 and Herbert in 1888. Finally, John and Sarah lived at 186 Palmerston Road with John William, who remained unmarried, until his death. John and Sarah were my maternal great grandparents and were part of a movement of nonconformists in Peterborough, which diluted the predominance of the Church of England. John was a staunch member of the Salvation Army and reportedly never used bad language; his favourite swear word was 'juggering'. It seems he also attended Fletton Baptist Church for over 35 years with Sarah where they were much appreciated. The party for the celebration of their Silver Wedding was particularly for John Garfield and his service of 50 years on the Eastern and Midland Railway celebration. They also celebrated their Golden Wedding. Mrs Garfield's party to celebrate her 90th birthday was held two years before her death, which was 1940.

The Garfield family around the 1930s with Albert and Florence together with their children including Constance, my mother, rear rightmost

School Days and Work Days

Con was the daughter of Albert Henry Garfield and his second wife Florence, who cared for Albert's four children when their mother died. She (Albert's first wife) was Eliza (Betty) Hart who was born in 1874 in the area known as Willington Quay in South Shields. Albert Henry followed his father and was employed by the Great Eastern Railway for 49 years. He began his work at Stratford in July 1890 as a fireman and later became an engine driver for 11 years. Working on the railway meant an irregular work pattern. A 'knocker-up' woke Albert when his shift began very early, and he was booked to go to Newcastle. Train crews did not take a train to the north and back to the south in a day; they stayed overnight, an arrangement known as 'lodging'. Albert made long-standing friendships with those people in whose homes he regularly stayed. In one he found a wife! Betty Hart came to Peterborough, lodged in 30 Cromwell Road and worked as a servant. Albert and Betty married in 1898 at St. Mark's Church; they shared the day with Albert's sister Gertrude and Herbert Neaverson with whom they had a double wedding. Albert and Betty went to live in Hankey Street and produced four children. They were Elsie, born 1900, Winifred Nellie who arrived in 1903, Herbert John Richard came in 1904 and the youngest Molly Sarah was born in 1907. Betty died in March 1910; she fell down the stairs. Florence Maud Allcock was working as the cook at the vicarage of St. John's Church in Priestgate at the time. She was born in Ipswich in 1887 and, in 1901, was a 'visitor' at the Crown Inn in Newmarket and living on her 'own means', which seems to indicate that she was travelling to Peterborough to take up employment at St. John's Vicarage. When exactly Florence met Albert is difficult to ascertain but the vicarage was very near the railway, and she agreed to leave her position and move to Woodston almost immediately after Betty's death. Florence visited Ipswich in April 1911 probably to explain to her parents that she felt obliged to care for the children who no longer had a mother, she was however already pregnant. Con was born in August 1911, only 17 months after Betty died and Albert and Florence were unmarried. Con was followed by a second infant which was also almost out of 'wedlock', being born in April 1913 when Albert and Florence had been married only in January of that year, at the registration office with two supporters present, Arthur P. Barnes and Eva J. Cracknell.

Con's birth was in Palmerston Road, but the family moved to 96 New Road just before her sister Florence was born. Albert renamed this new baby daughter! He took a first look at her, and remarked that she resembled Kaiser Bill, the German Emperor of First World War notoriety, and the name stuck. Two years later, in 1915, a son was born and named Kenneth Albert, but lived only a few months. Con recounted that she inspected the tiny coffin, and it was made from an orange box. A second son, Leslie Albert Charles was welcomed in 1916, Betty followed in 1918 and Margaret came a year later, the 'baby' of the family was born in 1922 and named Kathleen Ethel. The house in New Road was small for the large family with sleeping accommodation limited. Sharing beds was absolutely necessary. Although Albert's employment as an engine driver was well paid for the time, the family was not rich and clothes were 'handed down' by the older girls to their younger sisters.

The two boys were more fortunate, they were not included in the 'handing down' system. Albert was a good gardener and supplied the family with fresh vegetables and his wife Florence was a skilful cook, so the family was fed properly. Food was not permitted to be wasted however, and anything not eaten at one meal was presented at the next and cold. Con learned to eat parsnips under this regime, she disliked them cold more than she did when they were hot. In later life, Albert kept chickens; the eggs were stored with his whiskey in a large, locked box in his shed and, when his wife Florence needed eggs, she had to buy them from him! He also kept pigs, which were specially remembered on Christmas Day and given a taste of 'plum pudding'. This special treatment did not save them from slaughter, and they were killed on site and the joints cured in a large lead lined tray which rested on a table in the kitchen. Despite his fiery temperament and his intolerance of disobedience in his children, Albert was not cruel and worked hard to keep his family, but he was irascible, had a partiality to alcohol and demonstrated that he was not the easiest of men by calling his wife Florence Maud either Florrie or Maud depending on his mood. One of the routes he drove on the railway was between Wolferton (the nearest station to Sandringham on the line to Hunstanton) and Peterborough. On a number of occasions he drove a royal train in which King George V and Queen Mary were travelling over this route. When he left for retirement, he was praised for his work and wished a happy retirement and better health. Albert was presented with a chiming clock and Florence a handbag.

Con was educated at Woodston C. of E. School in Wharf Road from three years of age to 14 years when she left to begin work. Con was a spirited child and revolted against the indignity of wearing a pinafore in school to protect her clothes. She removed the dreaded item and hung it under her coat before going into class. Despite the pinafore she enjoyed school and generally behaved well although on one occasion she was sent to the head teacher because she was talking. He, however, merely expressed his disappointment in her behaviour and Con was so surprised she cried bitterly. On her return to the classroom, the teacher thought the copious tears indicated she had been caned and gave her sixpence to cheer her up! Con also managed to fall off a pavement on the way to school and, as a result, broke her arm and was taken to the Infirmary (now Peterborough Museum) by a young neighbour. The means of transport was a wooden pushchair with a seat made of carpet material and the painful jolting remained a vivid memory for many years. Con was certain that a 'Chinaman' with a pigtail x-rayed her arm in a darkened room and she was very frightened. The arm was put in a sling but later the doctors wanted to reset the bone. Albert refused, he said the arm was causing no problems and it never did although it remained slightly bent. At home, Con was 'the big sister' and on occasion looked after the younger members of the family when Albert and Florence went out. Con was permitted to have a friend with her and the two regularly pushed the clock forward so that they could put the children to bed as soon as possible in order to enjoy themselves! The activity that they frequently chose was cooking.

Once she left school, Con had a variety of employers. She became a 'day girl' for a city alderman and his daughter in a three-storey house in the cathedral precincts, and then worked in a small shop opposite St. John's Church for the Misses Hook who owned the business. The shop sold books and 'bits and bobs' and Con spent much time cleaning and dusting with an occasional trip to the home, in Broadway, of the Misses Hook where she scrubbed the front path and steps. She was also required to deliver advertising leaflets along Thorpe Road, and at that age she did not imagine that she would one day live in Longthorpe. Her enthusiasm for leaflet delivery was completely non-existent and she posted many of the papers down the drains rather than in letter boxes. After the retail experience, Con returned to her role as a 'day girl' at a fish shop in Midgate where there had been a serious fire and where the smell remained. Con was far from happy; she imagined the fire would re-occur and that she would be trapped and not rescued. The fear became a problem, and she obtained work at the Celta Mills where artificial silk was produced but this employment lasted just one week! The local corset factory then attracted her where her first task was cutting ribbon into lengths for straps. Con said that she found the work really exciting! Later she was promoted and became a sewing machinist. She put gores into corsets and, although she was not a great sewing expert, she stayed at the factory for almost two years.

Domestic service then became Con's metier. She became a kitchen maid at Laundimer House, a boarding house, at Oundle School. She lived at the house and bicycled home to Woodston on her days off. Her uniform was a blue dress, white apron and a frilled cap and she was subject to the Scottish cook. It was at Laundimer where Con made her two good friends, Dora and Ethel, and saw her first 'Baby Austin' which was owned by a master. Con was then persuaded by her sister Mollie, who was a parlour maid in Peterborough, to join her at Paston Hall, the home of Mr. F. Ihlee, Chairman of Baker Perkins. The move for Con was successful. Mr. Ihlee, always referred to as the 'boss', was a good employer and her time at Paston was very happy. The Hall was a grand building, surrounded by a beautiful garden in which stood a large green house where Con frequently *tried* a tomato. She was not on the lowest rung of domestic service at Paston and was a housemaid; her morning uniform was a dark dress with a plain white apron and in the afternoon the cap and apron were frilled. Mr. Ihlee was a keen model ship restorer and a full-sized prow hung over the main staircase. The restoration work was done in a large shed by his nephew and a factory worker and Con had the responsibility of keeping the two supplied with regular cups of tea and snacks. Mr. Ihlee showed his concern for Con when he noticed that she was having problems with her sight and sent her to the local doctor. Spectacles were prescribed, for which he paid, and Con wore glasses for the rest of her life. Ethel, Con's friend celebrated her 21st birthday while at Paston and naturally invited Con to the party, which was to be held at the home of Ethel's brother Bill and his wife, Annie. Annie was the sister of Minnie Louisa and had persuaded her sad brother-in-law to attend. Bill and Con met 'across a crowded room' and were attracted to one another. A period of 'courting' began with Bill travelling regularly to Paston on his motor bicycle, an Aerial Square-Four with a registration number of FL 8087. Eventually, he decided that he was not going to travel any more in bad weather and suggested they marry. Con agreed but before they did Mr. Ihlee rendered Con an important service. He ensured that the name of her registration of birth document was changed from Allcock to Garfield, the name she had always used. Canon Lethbridge, vicar of Paston is said to have signed the necessary forms and her birth certificate is dated 1932, the year of her marriage, and is noted as being officially sanctioned by the Registrar general. In the index of births, however, she can only be found under the name of Allcock.

Marriage and a Daughter

In October 1932, Bill and Con were married at St. Augustine's Church, Woodston. The Rev. Mr. Atkinson officiated, and the newspaper described it as a pretty wedding. Con was just 21 years old with Bill almost 15 years her senior. Con's wedding dress was turquoise georgette and lace, with a belt and diamante buckle, and a hat of the same colour. She carried white carnations and was given away by her brother Bert. Albert (her father) was in hospital in London. The best man was Bill's brother, Albert, and the bridesmaids were Con's sister Florence and Bill's cousin, Laura, from Ramsey Heights both of whom wore pink dresses. The wedding reception was held at the family home and the honeymoon was spent in London. The stay in the capital, although short, was a very happy time for Con and she particularly enjoyed her visit to Petticoat Lane.

On their return, Bill and Con lived at 78 Queen's Walk for 16 months and Bill, who had finally left his agricultural days, followed the tradition of the area and was working at the brickyards. In February 1934, just before my birth, Bill and Con were able to rent a house and moved to 111 Palmerston Road.

I was born in Charnwood Nursing Home and was taken to my first home which was within easy walking distance of 96 New Road and Con regularly took me to visit Florence and the family. I was Florence's first 'real' grandchild and always had a special place in her heart and was the centre of attention of my aunts and each was photographed with me while Margaret who lived next door loved to play with me. I was also taken on visits to Farcet Fen to the home of my grandfather, and Bill's sister and brother.

Florence (Grey Granny) and me

I was cocooned in the sidecar of Bill's motor bike for the journey and while I was a baby, I was put to sleep in it during the visit. Not many babies had the honour of sleeping in such a prestigious sidecar in that it was called a Swallow and the firm which built it was the forerunner of the Jaguar car manufacturer.

Bill and Con's meeting had much to do with chance but led to a long and happy marriage. It was Bill's second marriage and he had been devastated when he became a widower. Bill and Con decided to move to Farcet in 1935 when I was about a year old. They rented a house in Peterborough Road, to make Bill's journey to his work at the brickyards at King's Dyke, near Whittlesea, much easier. Unfortunately, the move did not result in settled security but worry and insecurity. Grovedale was the name of the rented house but very soon after Bill and Con with me had taken up residence the owners decided they required it for their daughter who was to be married. Bill and Con were given notice to quit and they had no other housing in view.

Mum, Dad and I at Eastville, Lincolnshire

Con was eager to buy a house, but Bill was not enthusiastic. He worried about becoming unemployed and being unable to pay the mortgage. Con managed to persuade him and, in 1937, they bought Hazledene on the opposite side of the road. Hazledene was a typical semi-detached 1930s house, which later was named 84 Peterborough Road. The cost was approximately £500, and Bill and Con obtained the mortgage from the Abbey National Building Society. The repayments were made monthly to the bank, which, for Con and I, meant an outing to Peterborough. We went by bus, which was initially operated by Bill Hales, a village businessman, and later by the Eastern Counties Bus Company. At the bank Con filled in a pink form for the amount, which was about £3 17s 11d, a sum which is minimal in the 21ˢᵗ Century but was then difficult to find and in order to augment the family income, Con took on some cleaning work. Bill and Con expected Hazledene to be their permanent home, but early in the 1970s my brother, Leslie, changed career. He decided to leave Perkins Engines and to stop repairing motorcycles and to take over a fish and chip shop at Bourne. This was not a successful move, and he became the owner of Longthorpe Garage. The property included a bungalow which if sold to strangers may have caused difficulties for the running of the business. Bill and Con felt that the best course of action was for them to purchase the bungalow. The removal to 347 Thorpe Road in 1985 began a very happy time for Bill and Con, they both loved Longthorpe. Bill was delighted to be a knowledgeable garage assistant and Con made many friends and was a well-known resident.

Con's sister, Bill (Florence), was employed by Dr. Harkness, a local GP, to help with his six children and Con obtained a few hours of work each week at the doctor's house. I went with Con and had a little adventure on one occasion. Con was cleaning a fire-grate and I decided the hob would make a seat and used it as such, not knowing that the fire had only recently been extinguished. My bottom was somewhat warmed, but fortunately not badly burned. I cannot remember how old I was when I went into hospital, but the reason was that I needed the removal of my tonsils. It happened to many children at my age because doctors believed the operation would aid the health of young children. I hated being left without Con, but that was hospital rules. I do not remember being taken to the operating theatre or seeing the doctor or nurses, but I do remember looking up and seeing a large ceiling light. I remained in hospital for several days and Con brought books for me but at no time was she able to come into the ward. I was happy when I was permitted to go home.

Bill and Con made regular trips to Peterborough in order to pay bills and do shopping, but Con was particularly eager to see her sisters and I was very happy to see my aunts. Con's sister Win worked at Neaverson's café and cake shop in Long Causeway, a business which was owned by Gertrude Neaverson nee Garfield, Albert's sister, and her husband Herbert Neaverson. There were also two sweet shops belonging to the Turner family, one in Broadway and the other in the Arcade. Bet worked in the Arcade with her colleague Win. The shop had high counters piled with all kinds of confectionary and it was dark behind them, but I was always plied with sweets, so I was happy in the gloom. Bet was unfairly dismissed from this post. She was responsible for closing the shop and delivering the 'takings' to the owner, who estimated the time it took to walk the distance to make the delivery. One Saturday Bet was taken by car to deposit the money and as she was earlier than usual, the owners of the business accused her of closing early and sacked her! Luckily, Bet quickly found employment in the cash office at the International Stores, a grocery shop, in a row of shops built in the façade of the Town Hall. The shop had walls of black and white tiles and a cash system that operated between the assistants and the cash office on a wire across the shop. When customers purchased groceries, the assistant put the bill and the money in a container hung on the wire, pulled a lever and the container sped across the store to the cashier, who returned it with the correct amount of change.

A similar system operated at Barrett's which was on the corner of two Peterborough streets, Long Causeway and Midgate. It was a long-established business, very old fashioned in the 1940s, and on the upper floor the wooden floorboards squeaked as people walked across them. Goods for the home were sold there and I loved the china department and continue to love every china department in every shop. Glasses/Glass, a ladies dress shop was on the opposite corner of Long Causeway seemed very upmarket, while Trollope's, another outfitter, was the supplier of Fletton Grammar School uniform, but I considered Mrs Dale's shop the most interesting. This small establishment was near the river bridge and was approached through an archway and courtyard. There was no display window on to the street but inside the shop the lighting seemed very bright and there was a particular smell of new clothes and materials. Mrs Dale supplied goods on a weekly instalment basis, a convenient method of payment for those on tight budgets.

After the shopping was completed Con and I went to Woodston to visit Albert and Florence, her Mum and Dad. We took a double-decker bus to 'the fish shop', the name of the bus stop and the shop from which we bought our tea. Perhaps eating fish and chips ensured that everyone was silent while Albert listened to the football results on the radio and carefully filled in the scores in the newspaper columns and then checked his football pools. He made these checks by gas light as there was no electricity in the house and I was always fascinated by the way Florence lit the delicate mantle with a taper which then began to glow with a white light. It was difficult to be quiet if you were required to sit on the horse-hair sofa, which had been in the living room as long as I could remember, because it pricked your legs. I was also interested to watch Florence do the ironing; with no electricity she used flat irons heated on the fire. She used a holder to pick them up as the handles were hot, spat on the bottom to test the heat and then used them. I could not understand how she did not burn the garments.

Farcet

The Village of Farcet could never boast of being one of the most attractive villages in the country. Indeed, it would score well on a list of those being unattractive, but as a child I had no experience of other villages to be able to make comparisons and accepted it as it was. Many villages have interesting festivals, but Farcet had a Rhubarb Feast, held annually on the last Sunday of May, when sticks of rhubarb were affixed to telegraph poles! The reason for the feast is difficult to discover. It might be that it developed from an ancient rite of spring or perhaps rhubarb grew well in Farcet and the celebration came as the crop was ready to eat.

Farcet Village Sign

Certainly, the feast remained a high point of the year in the early 20th century, even during the First World War. In June 1916 the Peterborough Advertiser reported:

'Farcet Feast': On Sunday and Monday sticks of rhubarb were hung by wags at different points of the village. There was a constant stream of visitors at night. The Salvationists held an open-air service on the brow. On Monday the usual paraphernalia of fairs and feasts were present, but not in such large numbers. The trade was brisk and the conduct of visitors orderly and quiet. There was a large number of soldiers on leave.

Unfortunately, the village no longer celebrates the feast although rhubarb festivals are still organised in some parts of the world.

Hazledene, our home was situated on Peterborough Road which was lined on both sides by houses and bungalows of all descriptions and beyond the turning, which ran down hill into the village and continued as the Broadway southwards towards Yaxley. Gazeley Hall was the one large house in the village. It was on the western side of Peterborough Road about a quarter of a mile from the turning into the village and set well back amongst trees, with a large gate marking the entrance to the drive. The hall was built for Mr. Robert Bird, a wealthy farmer in the 1830s, but it was less than a handsome three storey mansion. Later the third storey was removed, and the house was given a flat roof with crenulations and painted white walls. The last owner, Mr. Burchnell, a local businessman, used the grounds to farm pigs and sadly after a serious fire the house was demolished in the 1960s when Gazeley Gardens, an estate of bungalows, was constructed. Other buildings of note on the same side of road as the Hall were Throstlenest Hatcheries, Driby and Storey's Garage. The Hardy family ran the hatcheries and sold newly hatched chicks. The Gilbert family, Mr. and Mrs Gilbert and six children occupied Driby, a large double fronted house built in 1929. Mrs Gilbert was a plump, but pleasant lady while Mr. Gilbert was a manager at Fletton's Limited Brickyard. The Archers owned a market garden between Driby and Storey's Garage and grew vegetables and fruit behind their house. Mrs Archer sold the produce at the door while Mr. Archer travelled around the area with horse and trolley from which he served a wider cliental. Jack Storey, the owner of the garage, was a well known 'character'. His sons John and Roland took on the business after his death and John was always a good contact for any necessary car repairs.

Two roads turned into the village from Peterborough Road, Back Lane, later renamed St. Mary's Street and Main Street while Middle Street was a branch off Main Street. At the top of Back Lane was a row of three very old cottages and a beautiful old Horse Chestnut tree behind which was a field with a pond. The cottages, the tree, the field and the pond disappeared in the late 1940s when Airey houses were built and St. Mary's Close constructed. These houses were prefabricated and built to alleviate the housing shortage at the end of the Second World War. Opposite Back Lane on the Peterborough Road a row of about six small brick cottages had been built at the end of the 19th century, these too were demolished as were some attractive white cottages which were at a right angle to the road and facing the church. A group of small bungalows for the elderly replaced them. A farmyard with large gates known as the 'boarden doors', where pigs were reared, separated the brick and the white cottages.

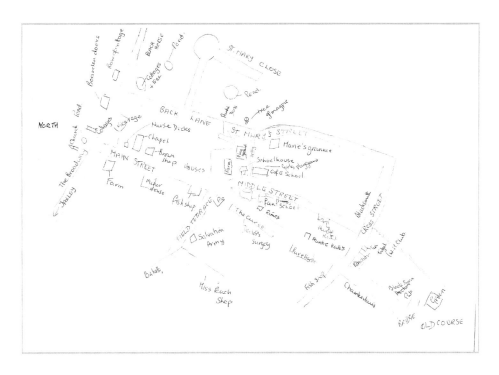

My sketch of the main village of Farcet

At the bottom of the village Cross Street linked Main Street, Middle Street and Back Lane, while Red Row and Field Terrace were unmade roads, turning off Main Street. Herbert and Doris Brown, Bill and Con's friends, lived in a small, terraced house in Back Lane. Bill had known Herbert for some years but when Herbert married Doris from Walton, the four became close friends. The toilet at Herbert and Doris' house was at the bottom of the garden. It was a deep pit and I was always afraid that I would fall down it. Mary, their first daughter was born four years after me and when Con was looking after Doris, I sat on the stairs guarding the baby. I wanted to ensure no-one came to steal someone who was to become a very special friend. Hobbs's farm was next to the terrace of houses and its boundaries went from Back Lane to Main Street, where there was a large barn. The Hobbs family were dairy farmers and delivered milk, but not in bottles. Arthur (Hobbs) came to Hazledene, he carried his milk can with a measure hooked on the side. He measured the milk into a jug, so there were no empties to return. Ecologically, this was sound, but the milk was not tested or pasteurized and could have carried germs. It did not, to my knowledge, and I liked it. Milk is no longer produced at the farm, its buildings have been demolished and houses built. The old C. of E. school was on Middle Street with a jetty beside it running to Back Lane, and the infant school was at the point where Middle and Main Street met.

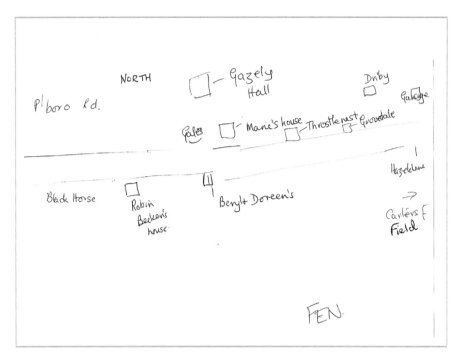

My sketch of the location of Hazeldene on Peterborough Road

Three public houses served the village, the Black Horse on Peterborough Road, the Anchor on Cross Street and the Black Swan which was situated near the bridge over a water way, known as the Pig Water, but which was actually part of the old course of the river Nene and formed a natural boundary between the village and Farcet Fen. In 2017, the last of the public houses was closed, thus meetings to have a drink of beer were no longer possible in the village. A tin chapel was beside the Anchor; it later became a working men's club. The blacksmith's shop was opposite the Anchor, but the blacksmith ceased work in the 1940s. There was a fire in the building and the damage was not repaired and the repair of horses' hooves ceased. Just beyond the bridge was a green where a fair was held annually. I went with Doris and Herbert on one occasion and my foot became trapped on one of the rides, my sock was torn, and my ankle hurt, but not seriously. Brown's shop, opened by Herbert's father, Charles Brown, was in Main Street. Charles was the village barber and Herbert followed in his footsteps until he joined the army. After the Second World War Herbert and his sisters, Enid and Lucy, ran the business as a general store and newsagents. I did a newspaper round and cycled to the shop early every morning to collect my bag of papers. Ivan Lock and I delivered the newspapers along the Peterborough Road, he did one half and me the other. Previously, Herbert had made the delivery along the whole length of the road and always finished at Hazledene for a cup of tea. He smoked Player's cigarettes, and I collected the empty packets from which I cut out the sailor's picture. It was possible to link these pictures together in a chain and eventually I had one that reached from the picture rail to the floor with some to spare. Next to Brown's shop was the Methodist chapel which was later to become the village hall. The house adjacent to the chapel was occupied by the district nurse. Nurse Dicks was stern but ready to advise or help in an emergency.

An old stone house and farm was opposite Brown's shop and on the same side was the oldest building in the village. It was, most probably, the Manor House. Above one door was the date 1662 and

Lizzie Parkinson, a rather grubby-looking old woman, occupied this part. The rest of the house was the home of the Hales family while the yard was used for the lorry business. This important old building has succumbed to the fate of so many, demolition and replacement with modern houses. By the early 2000s the old stonehouse had also been demolished for more new houses. A row of council houses was between Lizzie's cottage and the farm, and a cobbler operated from one while the Slack family lived in another. A small shop was situated in Middle Street and Pratt's fish and chip shop was opposite and an infant school with unmade Field Terrace ran beside it. The post office was on the corner of Field Terrace and the postmaster, during my childhood, would talk continually. I was told that he had been gassed during the First World War, but I did not understand the significance of the information, at the time I was unaware of the horrors of the conflict. The Salvation Army was a few yards along the unmade road, where meetings were held, and activities were available to anyone interested. The Army was well supported and played throughout the village every Sunday morning. Albert Woods was the baker, and his shop was situated on the next corner beyond the Salvation Army and a wool and haberdashery shop, operated by Miss Peach from her front room. In Main Street, next to the infant school, the Rimes family shop sold animal feed. I was sent to buy a substance to put with cooked vegetable peelings to feed the chickens, namely Karswood, a red powder, which was supposed to encourage egg laying. On the same side a general store was some time later owned for a short period by Kath (Con's sister) and her husband Charles Coppen. When they went on holiday I was left in charge with my assistant Mary (Brown). Once we had a panic because the ice cream freezer failed! A hardware shop owned by the Ketteringhams, was opposite. They had two daughters, Gillian and Shirley, the latter wore a leg iron and I always felt sorry for her. Previously, Mr. and Mrs Gasgoine were the proprietors and came to live next door to Hazledene on their retirement. Dr. Harkness held a weekly surgery in the front room of one of the houses in the Curve between the hardware shop and the post office. Frequently, I was sent to collect medicine for various people. Red Row boasted a second fish and chip shop and produced the most delicious scallops [potato slices in batter]. Beyond Red Row a butcher's shop was owned by the Chamberlain family. This business closed when local butchers were no longer permitted to slaughter animals as a result of European Union rules.

Hazledene

Hazledene or 84 Peterborough Road remained a typical semi-detached 1930s house. It had a porch with a glass fronted entrance door leading into the hall with the stairs to the upper floor. The hall floor was wooden parquet, and the stairs had a banister with open uprights which I was required, at times, to dust. I always hated the task. The stair carpet, specially made to cover the area on the treads where people walked, was held in place with triangular wooden stair rods. The pantry under the stairs had shelves and a meat safe, a cupboard with mesh sides and door to keep meat and dairy goods as cool as possible. Refrigerators were for people with more income than that of Bill and Con. The pantry shelves were lined with tinned goods, preserved fruit and vegetables, jams, and pickles. On the bottom shelf opposite the door stood Con's weighing scales with the pan holding the wrappers from butter and margarine. These were used to cover the individual sponges made in teacups without handles. Con's puddings were her 'piece de resistance' and no-one ever minded the colour on the top of the sponge which was left by the fat wrappers. The electric meters were below the weighing scale shelf and for many years the electricity was paid with shillings which were inserted into the meter. The electricity man emptied the meters and returned some of the shillings if there had been over payment. I liked watching him make the piles of shillings. Con made jam yearly and I adored licking the preserving pan after the jam had been put into jars. Like uncooked cake this just-made jam tasted the best. Sometimes when the jam had been kept for some months the sugar leached from the fruit and made the jam lumpy. I hated it then. Deep freezers were not available, so Con bottled fruit and vegetables in special 'Kilner' jars. She also salted runner beans; sliced beans were packed between layers of salt so that they could be eaten during the winter. Eggs were preserved during the Second World War in isinglass, a kind of gelatine, to ensure that they were available when there was a shortage. Powdered egg could also take the place of real eggs, if necessary, but it was disgusting. The pantry had one special use for Con. She hated thunderstorms and hid in it when a storm threatened and pretended that she was tidying the shelves.

The ground floor of Hazledene comprised of a front room, a living room with a French door to the garden which later became the door to a conservatory which Bill built, a kitchen and an outside toilet and coal house. Bill changed the outside toilet and coal house so that there was 'a back' kitchen with a copper to heat water for washing and bathing and an inside toilet. Upstairs there were two main bedrooms, a small bedroom and a bathroom. The floors were covered with lino and rugs; carpets did not arrive until the late 1950s. The living room was heated with a coal fire, which had to be lit every day with coal and sticks collected from the coal shed in the garden. There was no central heating, and the bedrooms were cold. In the winter, the windows were frozen with beautiful patterns and Con used to say that Jack Frost had made them. On those frosty mornings it was possible to see your breath as soon as your head was above the bedclothes and then it was imperative to get dressed by the fire. The front room had a blue leatherette three-piece suite, a bureau and a little gate leg table and was used infrequently. The fire was lit on high days and holidays and particularly at Christmas, but it never felt comfy and cosy like the living room. Originally, the living room had a Triplex grate which was a coal burning fireplace with two ovens on the side and a hob on which to stand kettles so that the water would boil. Later, Bill replaced this with a modern style grate, but still with a coal burning fire. An alcove was on each side of the fireplace with a built-in cupboard on one side and a tall free-standing cupboard on the other. The best china and the silver tea pot were stored in an upper part of the built-in cupboard which had glass doors and in the lower part all manner of items were stowed. The fire warmed it, so it acted as an airing cupboard for the bed linen, but Con's work basket had a place in it. She was not a great dressmaker but was a very good darner of socks. She continued her mending until she was 90, always using her darning mushroom but never a thimble. The tall cupboard was largely used for books. Bill loved technical tomes and was never happier than when solving a problem. Photographs, which I liked to look at, were kept in the lower part of the cupboard in a flower-decorated tin.

The table with its wooden dining chairs, which I disliked, took up much of the room. Bill's country style wooden armchair chair must have come from The Fens and although it was not valuable, it is sad that it is lost. I have memories of lovely dark winter nights when the fire was warm, the curtains drawn and there was time to do knitting but maybe my imagination is working overtime. It often did, especially when I was listening to the radio, and I was a great listener! My homework was regularly done to the accompaniment of Dick Barton, Special Agent. Television was not part of my childhood experience. Bet (Con's sister) and her husband Jess, who by that time were living across the road, acquired television for the Queen's coronation when I had already left Hazledene for college, but it was sometime later before television arrived at Hazledene. Even then the black and white set came from Grannie Dolby, Jess' mother. It was an elderly piece of equipment and any adjustment for better viewing was made with a knitting needle!

The back garden of Hazledene was long, and beyond it stretched Farcet Fen as far as the eye could see. In the distance the tall chimneys of the brickyards were visible and brick making was an important local industry. Visitors to Peterborough regularly commented on the smell of sulphur but those born near the yards were usually oblivious to the odour of the chemical. Bill grew vegetables in the garden and three blackcurrant bushes had been planted along the fence that separated it from the fields. The black currants tasted lovely but took much time to gather. The field directly behind the house was farmed by the Hobbs family and I used to watch the Hobbs brothers ploughing with horses: they also used horses when drilling (sowing the seeds) and to pull the binding machine that cut the corn and tied it into sheaves. The sheaves were then made into stooks, which resembled elongated wigwams. Two sheaves were leaned together with the corn end upwards so that they stood upright and a group of about four pairs made a stook. The farmer hoped for dry weather at this stage so that the corn would dry. Then the horses returned with carts which the men loaded with the corn by lifting each sheaf with a pitchfork. When the corn was back in the farmyard the threshing machines arrived and the corn was shaken out of the ears. I was always delighted to watch the threshing machine at Ponder's Bridge where Bill's brother, Fred, was farm manager. The straw was then built into straw stacks and thatched to keep for winter animal feed. Once the field was empty, and before the ploughing began again, gleaning was possible. The ears of corn that had been missed were gathered to be fed to the chickens which were kept in the chicken coop in the garden. Bill was an expert gleaner. No doubt he had had plenty of practice as a child, and he made beautiful, neat bouquets with the ears of corn. My collection was always very untidy. When Fred retired, he moved, with his wife Ida, to Farcet and unfortunately, he was driving his car when he suddenly died. There were no other people involved but such a death was an obvious shock to the family and friends.

St. Mary's Church, at the top of the village, is where I attended Sunday School, sang in the choir and was married. At Sunday School, a special stamp illustrating a story from the Bible or marking a festival or a saint's day, was given on each attendance. Prizes were awarded annually for a complete number of Sunday school attendances. Each year the church congregation joined the Sunday School outing. Hunstanton was the destination, but the coaches stopped at the halfway point on the journey: the seaside was a long way in those days! However cold it was, and it was usually breezy, the young people changed into costumes under a towel on the beach and went into the sea. Mothers and grandmothers kept their coats and hats on!! On one Hunstanton outing I sat on the back seat of the coach with Cedric Slack, I was somewhat smitten by him!! On Ascension Day, after a church service, an outing was arranged, and school children and parents travelled to Wicksteed park. Mothers packed huge picnics because we were always hungry, and we did not go into cafes. They were too expensive! As well as Sunday school, I went to regular church services. In those days, we used the Book of Common Prayer, the language was very formal, the sermons long and noise was not permitted. The church key was huge and ancient, and it was necessary to collect it from the vicarage when the church flowers needed arranging. The vicarage, opposite the church, was big, uncomfortable, and cold but had a large and extensive garden where church fetes were held. At these events there were stalls selling whatever had been donated, collected, or made. Teas were available and games of chance in evidence. Bowling for the pig attracted me but I didn't try my luck so didn't win the pig. Much of the garden has been sold for housing, the vicarage replaced with a more modern building and the old building redeveloped as apartments. The church has, in 2015, been renovated and is extremely improved.

When I first went to Sunday school the Rev. Mr. Gurnhill was the vicar, but he left the village almost immediately, hopefully not because of my arrival. The reason was more likely that his son Christopher who was in the Fleet Air Arm was killed in the Second World War, and he did not wish to stay where there were painful memories. However, it is possible that the move was necessary under Church of England rules. Mr. Jackson, Mr. Maloney and Mr. Boxall followed the Gurnhills in order. The Jacksons married late in life and seemed old from their arrival. Mrs

Jackson's favourite occupation was embroidery, and her needle work was excellent. She worked a tablecloth as a wedding present for Arthur and me. The Jacksons each had a memorable feature. He always clutched his surplice and her bottom teeth protruded over her top teeth. Looking at her could be disconcerting. The Maloneys had six children and were always on the verge of poverty. Mr. Maloney had been a 'Bush Brother' in Australia and Mrs Maloney was Australian. He was regularly on a short fuse and could break out in a temper if things upset him. On retirement the Maloneys went to live in Walsingham and one of Con's last outings was to see Mrs Maloney. David Boxall was a particularly difficult man and his time at St. Mary's was not the easiest for some of the congregation. Arthur was the vicar's warden and therefore a member of the Parochial Church Council and often needed calming words from Alf Couzens, the people's warden, to prevent him from losing his cool.

My Childhood

I was an only child for six years and precious to my parents. They did not have a great deal of money to spend on me, but they made sure I felt loved in special ways. I was the centre of attention of not only Bill and Con but also of my aunts. When I was about two years old Bill and Con with Bet and Marg as well as Herbert and Doris took a holiday at Hunstanton. They stayed in a caravan and enjoyed a very simple but extremely happy time. I am on all the photographs of this holiday with a retinue of adoring adults, all wearing the most attractive swimming costumes!!! They were shapeless, striped and knitted. I had the added extra of rubber sand shoes; no doubt I disliked walking on the shingle. I was particularly indulged each week when Herbert and Doris made their regular visit to Hazeldene. Doris arrived earlier than Herbert who always brought fish and chips for supper. I was already in bed but was permitted to get up to sample the supper because I formed the habit of getting out of bed, sitting on the stairs and calling, 'I can smell chippies!' These evenings came to an end very soon after the war began, Herbert was called up into the army and Hazledene had its extra residents. Bill's employment at Flettons' Limited Brickworks also ended at the outbreak of the Second World War when brick production ceased, but up to that time he regularly worked at night. This meant he ate his main meal in the late afternoon. He particularly enjoyed egg custard, not cooked in the oven but steamed in a basin, and he always left some for me. I adored the watery bit in the bottom of the basin.

INTERNAL MEMORANDUM.

From:-

W.G. Mells.

Date:- 14th February 1939.

To:-

Mr. Boyden,
Kings Dyke

I have recently received several complaints from Haulage Contractors to the effect that loading at night is considerably delayed because they are unable to find you. Following up these complaints I understand that on many occasions you are to be found in the Machine Shop. As to what you are doing there would seem difficult to explain, since according to my instructions you should be either attending to the Pumps or supervising the loading of vehicles.

I have also complaints as to the manner in which you address Haulage Contractors. I know, of course, that you have always been short-tempered, and in fact have had complaints in the past from employees. I had hoped, however, that experience in the position which you held up to the time of closing down the night shift would have taught you that you must learn to control your temper, and to speak to people as you wish to be spoken to.

I also learned in enquiring into these other matters, that during last week there were two quite unnecessary mistakes in the writing out of tickets.

Taking the sum of the matters which I have detailed above, I think you will agree that in the ordinary course of events I should have been justified in discharging you without further consideration. As, however, you have been with me for a number of years and I think it will probably only be necessary to bring these matters to your notice to to ensure that there will not be a recurrence either of the complaints or the obvious inattention to duty, I propose to allow thematter to end with this letter, to which I do not expect a reply.

If I have cause to write to you again, my letter will be exceptionally brief and equally require no response.

WGM/ET

A reprimand Dad (Bill) received while working at the brickyards, I think Leslie inherited a bit of his spirit!

Although I was a girl, Bill wanted me to know what he did when he went to work and I could have been no more than five years old, when I was taken to the brickyard to see the making of bricks. I watched the clay being dug, formed into bricks, and being stacked into the kilns. I must have walked on the kilns because a 'burner' showed me into one of the chambers where it was possible to see the fires burning. At about this time, Bill had a brush with the management at Flettons' and received a warning. The incident, it seems, was over a lorry driver's inappropriate way of addressing the brick workers to which Bill reacted strongly. It seems difficult to imagine but he could get into colourful language if he was sorely tried.

Pets at Hazledene

On my third birthday, my cousin Billy brought me my first pet as a gift. It was a white kitten with black and tan patches. Billy carried it in a paper carrier bag and hung the bag on the doorknob of the living room before he permitted me to see the animal. Tiddles became part of the family for many years, so much so that, when I refused to eat my meals, Con gave the food to Tiddles but then I went into the back yard with her and knelt on the ground and tried to share the food from the cat's dish! It must have had a more appealing flavour at low-level.

Leslie holding our cat and showing early interest in cars, with me at Hazledene

Like Tiddles, Whiskey was also a memorable cat. He was an intelligent animal and learned to obey the instructions of John, my grandfather, to 'roll over'. Both Tiddles and Whiskey were hunters and always brought home their prey, good if it was a mouse or rat, bad if it was a bird, to show Con before they ate it. Unfortunately, Whiskey ended his life as a result of being caught in a trap or finding poison. He returned one morning limping badly and very ill and died soon after. Dogs were also pets at Hazledene! Leslie and I pestered Con and Bill until they allowed us a dog. We called him Monty and we thought he would be small, but he had big feet and grew large. He became an escape artist and caused crisis and confusion. He decided some young bullocks in a field would be wonderful playthings. The farmer did not agree and neither did Bill, who was afraid that he would be summoned for not keeping Monty under control. There was no choice, Monty was put down. Mick was the next dog with a longish black with some white coat and with a major peculiarity. He hated Bet (Con's sister). The reason for his dislike was never obvious, but he bristled if he detected that she was near the house. She, however, learned the way to evade him and could have become a good burglar! She could get into Hazledene without Mick or anyone else knowing she was coming. Sadly, Mick died after getting a bone wedged in his throat.

The Second World War

With the advent of the Second World War, sleeping space became at a premium at Hazledene. Con's sister Bet and her husband, Jess, were married in March 1940 while Jess was still in the army. I was a bridesmaid and wore a shiny gold silk dress. Soon after the retreat from Dunkirk in which Jess was involved, the need for skilled workers to produce necessary equipment for the armed forces was paramount. The army called for volunteers to perform this work and Jess volunteered. He was accepted but did not become a civilian. He remained a member of the army while working at Brotherhood's making turbines for ships until the end of hostilities. Bill also worked at Brotherhood's as part of his war effort. The brickyards closed as soon as the war began and the workers either followed Bill into factories or joined the forces. The Brotherhood's factory was approximately ten miles away from Hazledene and there was no public transport to correspond with the irregular working hours which were necessary to ensure 24-hour production. It was not possible to use either motor bicycles or cars because petrol was unavailable, and so Bill and Jess cycled 20 miles everyday for many of the war years. The result of the closure of the brickyards was an end to building and houses were not available either to rent or buy and Bet and Jess were unable to find anywhere to live. Bill and Con offered the newly-weds accommodation, and they occupied the front bedroom, while Bill and Con slept in the back bedroom, which had the most fantastic view over The Fens. I did not appreciate this vista as a child, although I spent time in the room when I had chicken pox and measles at the same time and was really poorly. My eyes were covered with rounds of lint because there was a fear that my sight would be affected. Thankfully, I survived without any damage and was able to return to the small bedroom.

Building an air raid shelter at 96 New Road, Woodston

When Leslie was born, he joined Bill and Con in their bedroom in his cot, and when Emma and Albert, Bill's sister and brother arrived to live at Hazledene other sleeping arrangements were necessary. Their arrival was as a result of the eviction of my grandfather, John, from his tied home. Albert and Emma had lived with John, thus Bill and Con felt it their duty to give them a home. Albert slept at Granny Lant's house and I shared the little bedroom with Emma. It was in that room that I had an experience which is indelibly on my memory. I saw an angel, or I saw something that I believed was an angel. I was about six years old and remember it more than sixty years later as clearly as if it happened last night!! I was alone in the bedroom, Emma had not come to bed, and I must have been asleep because I suddenly opened my eyes and there it was, standing at the head of the bed. I find it difficult to describe but it is in my mind's eye and strangely, I wasn't afraid although I was very easily frightened. I was scared if my pet cat, which I loved, came upstairs. Yet I didn't call out and went to sleep again quickly so what did I see?

The crowded household meant that Con had the responsibility of the cleaning, washing and cooking for six adults and the care of two children, one of whom was a baby and not strong. It is not surprising, then, that the one chastisement of my childhood occurred at this time, and I deserved it. Washday was on a Monday, and it was a day of hard physical work, as there were no automatic washing machines or dryers to make light of the work. Con began by lighting a fire under the copper to obtain sufficient hot water for the job in hand. The household linen and heavy garments were then 'dollied' in a 'dolly tub' with a 'posher' and afterwards put through the mangle. A mangle was a large piece of equipment with two wooden rollers which were turned with a metal handle on the side. The washing went between the rollers, the handle was turned, and the water squeezed out. On the day I describe extra problems were imminent because it was raining heavily. Rain on washing day meant that nothing could be pegged on a washing line out-of-doors, but everything needed to be draped on lines inside. Ironing usually done in the afternoon would have to wait until the next day which probably meant a disrupted weekly timetable. While the trauma of a wet morning was going on I was getting ready to walk to school and was told to put on my mackintosh and Wellington boots. I decided that I did not want to wear the boots and continually argued that I wouldn't put them on whatever Con said. My final thrust was that Pat O'Donnell (a school friend) did not wear her boots if she did not want to do so. At this assertion Con lost her temper and smacked me very hard. Bet intervened on my behalf and the smacks quickly stopped but I do not think I refused to wear Wellingtons again, although I know Con was sorry to have resorted to the action. The stress of crowded conditions and housework for so many adults as well as the children took their toll on Con and soon after the war she succumbed to a depressive illness. At the time people spoke of it being a 'nervous breakdown'. She was unable to be left alone and often went into fits of uncontrollable shaking. She was in hospital for a period, and it was quite a few months before she recovered, but thankfully she did completely. In later years, Con spoke very little about this episode, but once when reminiscing with Bet she said it was the one time in her life when she cried for her mother.

To a child, six years is forever, and I became so used to the Second World War being part of life that I believed it would go on for always. When I heard Vera Lynn singing 'There'll be Blue Birds over the White Cliffs of Dover' I had no idea what peace would be like or if it would make any difference to my life. Despite my inability to have the concept of life without war, I have vivid recollections of newspaper pictures as the war was coming to an end. One was the first images of concentration victims when Belsen was liberated, and another the picture of a dead member of the Dutch resistance. She was in her coffin but was beautiful and was holding three tulips, they were orange for Holland and in my mind, I can see the colour, although I am not sure if it was a coloured picture or if the colour was merely reported. When 8th May 1945 actually arrived, it was a day to be remembered, but my memories are not of holidays from school, but of the evening of VE Day when there was a grand celebration in front of the Black Horse Public House. Con believed I should be part of this extraordinary day and she and Bet took me because I was only 11 years old. It seemed that the whole village was there. Everyone was ecstatically happy, singing loudly and dancing wildly and an American serviceman asked me to dance. I refused because I could not believe that someone wanted to dance with me. The request, however, made me feel I had grown up! Between VE Day and VJ Day there was an interval of about three months, and it felt like living in limbo. When VJ Day arrived there was a feeling of anti-climax which makes it easy to understand why the forces in the Far East felt marginalised. National celebrations followed with parades in London, church services and street parties. Houses in Farcet, in concert with all other areas, were decorated with union flags and bunting, and everyone smiled. The opportunity to watch the celebrations throughout the country was at the cinema where pathe or movietone news was shown. The programme at the cinema included a main film, which was the one that you went to see. Then there was what was known as a B film, usually a short and not well-known production, as well as the news and trailers for the next films. The programme was continuous, and it was possible to go in at any time which meant you often saw the end of the film before the beginning! With this non-stop show, usherettes were available to conduct you to the correct seat and to sell ice creams in the short breaks between the films. At this time, the cinema was tremendously important to those interested in fashion! The first post-war Parisian fashion collections of Christian Dior were shown to astonished film audiences. Gone were the austere clothes of the war and in came small waists, flared and long skirts. Criticism came from some quarters because the clothes required much material. When I first saw the 'New Look' I had the idea that long skirts might mean a 'turn back' to times when women were forced to obey men, but once disabused of that idea, I loved the new fashion and Con bought me a brown coat with all the fashion details. I felt very grown up.

Neighbours

Good neighbours, Bill and Rose Scotney with their children Brian and Hazel lived in the house which formed the pair with Hazledene and beyond the Scotney's house was a piece of empty land and the shell of two houses, the building of which had begun in 1939, but not completed until the Second World War ended. During the war these unfinished houses became a much-loved playground for Brian, Leslie and Hazel (known as littl'un or lit!) and their friends. At the time that Bill and Con moved into Hazledene the neighbours on the opposite side were a very elderly couple, Mr. and Mrs Welfare, and she gave me some little Victorian pottery dolls which I played with in my doll's house, and they are no longer perfect. Many had their heads glued back when they had unfortunate accidents. When Mrs Welfare died, I was intrigued by her death and demanded to see the body. Con agreed that I should go into the front room where the coffin was standing and be lifted up to see inside. It was the first dead person I had seen but I was not perturbed, although I can see the scene in my mind now and Mr. Welfare gave me a silver horseshoe brooch in her memory. He was unable to live alone and after he moved Mr. and Mrs Gascoigne moved in with their lovable grey dog, Bambi. They stayed a relatively short time and went to live in Ramsgate in Kent.

The Kirkpatricks arrived next, Tom, Ethel and their daughter Enid. They came from Totnes in Devon where they had worked for a wealthy couple. Tom had been a chauffeur/handyman and Ethel the housekeeper. Ethel had elegant tastes and the house was never without flowers, but strangely she always cooked on her primus stove in the conservatory/garage, which was built on the side of the house. I loved visiting the house and admired the many 'objets d'art' that decorated every shelf and cupboard. I would have liked to have been given her spirit kettle, but my memento is a gold edged plate. Tom worked at Ford Motors in Peterborough and was one of the first in Peterborough Road to have a car when the war ended. It was a Ford and the design retained much of the 1930s with the doors opening away from the front column. Leslie and I always made a special annual visit to the Kirkpatricks on Christmas morning. After breakfast when we had opened our presents, we went to show Tom, Ethel and Enid what we had received. This tradition continued until 1954 when on that occasion one of the small diamonds fell out of my engagement ring! Luckily it was quickly retrieved and later replaced, and it has never fallen out since!! Christopher (my grandson) gave it to Philly, and I am very happy. When Enid married, she and her husband emigrated and went to Southern Rhodesia, but the marriage ended in divorce and Enid married a Rhodesian tobacco farmer, Keith Green. Tom died in Farcet, but Ethel went to Southern Rhodesia/Zimbabwe when she could no longer care for herself and died there. The Plowrights (father-in-law and daughter-in-law) occupied the next house until their deaths, while beyond them was a detached white house which also served as a butcher's shop. Alfred Carter was the butcher and Mona, his wife, served in the shop, but regarded herself as somewhat sophisticated. Alf, as he was known, was an amateur musician and played the saxophone. Peter their only child also went into the music business.

A small general store, situated opposite the butcher's shop, belonged to Ivy Wass. She lived at the shop with her parents and brother who had Down's Syndrome. In 1945, Ivy married, sold the business and relocated with her family to Woodston. Bet and Jess had just been allocated a council house in Croyland Road Walton, and I had stayed with them and helped to remove wallpaper from the bedroom walls. Con, however, knew that Bet harboured an ambition to own a shop and as soon as she picked up the local newspaper and read the advertisement detailing the sale, she dropped everything and rushed to Peterborough. Bet and Jess very quickly made all the arrangements to buy the business and returned to live in Farcet.

Bet (Con's sister) in her shop

Bet was devoted to her shop and ran it for 30 happy years, one of her happiest came in May near the end of my third year at the grammar school when Barbara Elizabeth was born. Bet and Jess had been married for eight years so she was a very welcome addition to the household but her birth being on a Sunday caused some hilarity. It was said that the baby had to choose Sunday for her arrival so as not to inconvenience the customers. Con became the temporary shop keeper as she did many times in the future to allow Bet, Jess and Barbara take a holiday. I was delighted with my new cousin and when she was christened at St. Mary's Church became her godmother, with Mollie and Jim, Jess' brother, being the two other godparents. I took my role particularly seriously. I hurried home from school each day to care for her. On one occasion we were playing, and Barbara hurt her arm. A trip to hospital was necessary and I was very scared in case the arm was broken. Thankfully it was not.

At the beginning of the war, Hazledene had a new look. The windows were crisscrossed with wide adhesive paper tape to prevent the glass flying out of the frames should a bomb fall on or near the house. Extra curtains of special blackout material were made and hung at the windows. At night, these curtains were tightly drawn so that no light was visible to guide enemy aircraft to buildings. It was at the time of Dunkirk when Bill expressed his concern about the outcome of the war. The fall of France was a very black moment and Bill expected an invasion almost at once. The Battle of Britain, with the 'dog fights' that were so well observed by many people, ensured that his fears were unfounded. Planes in action were not so obvious over Farcet although The Fens were ideal for airfields, and, in the immediate surroundings, there were those at Alconbury, Upwood, Wittering, Polebrook and Wyton, from which hundreds of aircraft flew very low over the Farcet fields immediately before D. Day. Peterborough was generally fortunate, and few bombs were dropped on it, despite the presence of the airfields and the fact that it was an important railway junction. The cathedral was slightly damaged by a firebomb and the brickyards were targeted briefly. The bombing of Coventry, however, made an impression on my memory. The bombers were visible as they flew over and the explosions were audible. Bill drew out the big free-standing cupboard and Con stood behind, with Leslie in her arms and me beside her. Bill went outside many times to see what was happening and came back and reported that 'someone is getting it tonight'. I do not think I was afraid, I had my parents and felt they would protect me from anything. Bill built an air raid shelter in the back garden, but it would not have proved a real sanctuary because it flooded, so if the bombs didn't get you the water would.

Bet became a fire warden/watcher and patrolled at night making sure no firebombs had fallen. An absolute black out was the order of the day and as a result, on one occasion, she fell into a dyke full of stinging nettles which caused her some discomfort, but the marks were regarded as the badges of war. Road signs were removed so that 'spies' were not helped to know their location. Those who needed to travel on official business were able to have maps, but generally families like mine did not travel great distances. Even if you wanted to visit a place at a distance, cars were not widely owned and petrol was only available to those who had absolute need for individual transport. All fuel was required for the war effort. Con's sister Kath was able to hone her driving skills; she was a WRAC chauffeur for high-ranking army officers. Bill was not called upon to rejoin the army, but was a member of the Home Guard, and as he owned a motorbike became a dispatch rider. The Home Guard was put through regular training exercises and some of Bill's stories were as amusing as those told on Dad's Army. On one occasion Bill took Bert, Con's brother, on the motorbike to a lonely outpost to be on guard duty. Bill returned to retrieve him at the end of the exercise but met Bert walking back. The reason was that he was too scared to stay in The Fens alone. Good thing there was no invasion that night.

Members of the Peacock family in The Fens, Jim and Johnny and friend

Con's sister Marg as well as their mother, Florence, also did their wartime duty. Each week they spent an evening at the railway station providing refreshments to the servicemen who travelled through the city. My cousins Jim and Johnny Peacock were more actively involved. Both were in the Royal Navy and Jim served on the battleship King George V. Once he brought Leslie and me a banana each, but they were very green, and we needed to keep them until they ripened. During this time of ripening, we regularly showed them to visitors because bananas were rare fruit.

Despite the lack of petrol, visits to relatives were possible and one which I enjoyed was to Wistow to see Bill's sister, Elsie, and brother-in-law, Jack. I had six Peacock cousins; the youngest Pansy was about my age, and we enjoyed being together. I was excited when Dot, the eldest, chose me to be her bridesmaid. Bill, Con, Leslie and I went to Wistow on a double-decker bus and the journey seemed very long. The fen roads were uneven, but I liked sitting on the top deck at the front of the vehicle where there was an unimpeded view across miles of flat land which gave the impression of flying, it felt like a true adventure. We always visited on a Sunday and Wistow was not on the bus route, so we got off the double-decker at Bury, a village about two/three miles from Wistow and walked to our destination. Shellow Hill, a steep incline that required much effort to climb, was between Bury and the turn into Wistow and I was always pleased that it was down hill into the village. Luckily, the walk for the return bus was not so long, although it was up hill to the main road where the bus stopped. It was possible to see the bus almost as soon as it left Warboys, a nearby large village so you knew how much time you had to wait or that you must hurry to the bus stop. Elsie's house was always full of people and there were many animals, which I liked to pat. Once a puppy died the day after I had visited, and the tragedy was put down to my continuous handling of the small animal. Jack and my cousins Jim, Johnny, and Nip, from an early age, went shooting and guns were in evidence. When they had been out with their guns, dead rabbits and game birds were everywhere. I was often teased about being wary of these dead animals which were waiting to be skinned or plucked and eaten. Shooting at Wistow was not mainly for sport but the animals provided much needed food. Autumn was an especially good time to visit Wistow. We went to pick blackberries. There were endless fields surrounded by blackberry hedges and we collected huge baskets full of the fruit. I ate more than I picked but Con made jam and pies when the fruit she and Bill had picked was carried home. The pies were eaten very quickly but the jam lasted into winter.

It was not possible to go on holiday at the seaside during the Second World War, the coasts were protected to stop enemy invasion. At Skegness there were huge rolls of barbed wire making the possibility of playing on the sands impossible. Con and Bill took Leslie and me to Eastville in Lincolnshire to stay on the farm with Amy and Reg, special friends of Bill and Con and aunt and uncle to us. It was possible to go by train because it was in the pre- Beeching days and there were hundreds of little stations where trains stopped. A drain ran through the middle of Eastville and on one occasion Bill rescued a child who had fallen into the water. A wooden bridge spanned the drain which was crossed to reach Reg's parents' house. Reg's mother was an enthusiastic plants woman and crammed her conservatory with every sort of plant. Blue plumbago is a constant reminder of her. Reg and his father ran Station Farm and had many horses to do the work in the fields. At night the horses ran free of bridles, collars, and reins and in the morning were clustered together, waiting for Reg. They knew they would be fed, and that the day's work would begin for which they appeared ready and eager. Later, when mechanisation arrived, Reg let me ride on the tractor with him. The machine had no cab and I just stood beside him - health and safety was not a consideration! Amy was a fantastic cook and even in wartime the table at Eastville always groaned. Hanging from the ceiling were sides of ham wrapped in muslin – pigs were killed on site and the meat cured in brine so that it could be eaten over time. The ham could be rather fat for my liking, but Bill loved it. Amy turned some of the ham into a Lincolnshire speciality, known as chine; slits were made in the skin side of the ham and filled with a mixture of herbs which percolated the meat and gave it a particular flavour. Puddings and cakes showed Amy's extensive expertise very well. One favourite was treacle sponge which she made in a huge bowl because everyone wanted more than one helping! At tea-time the cakes came out of seemingly never-ending tins. There were jam tart, lemon curd tarts, small and large sponge cakes of various flavours, fruit cakes, flapjacks and more. A two week stay at Eastville was a recipe for putting on weight. The downside of Eastville was the toilet facilities. They were the outside pit/ bucket type and hated by me! Reg and Amy had twin daughters, Pat and Ann and I saw them at a very early age, not long after they left the hospital. They had been separated in cots and would not settle. Once they were put into one cot, they quickly settled and for their lives always felt for one another. During their childhood the family left Eastville for New Leake and holidays transferred to that village. Leslie and the twins had good times together, especially one year when they played a record, 'Down on Misery Farm', continuously for the complete week. Pat and Ann married brothers and produced their families while Con and Bill visited Reg and Amy many times with enjoyment. Sadness was felt deeply when Pat's husband died and was felt again when Pat followed and left her only daughter. Jono and I attended Ann's special birthday and saw her with Peter her husband at Pam's (Leslie's wife) funeral. Unexpectedly, Ann died in January 2016 and Peter died in 2021.

Schooldays in Farcet

I went to school in 1939 and from the day I started I enjoyed it and attended regularly. The village had two schools. An infant school, built in 1912 by Huntingdonshire Education Authority when the number of children increased, stood on land which had previously been a farm, but the extensive playground was bereft of any notion of countryside. It was a bare expanse of concrete without trees or flowers and certainly without play equipment. Schooling for the children older than seven years was in the Church of England School, a Victorian building, established by the 'National Society' in 1840, just eight years after the Government passed legislation which provided grants for schools. Both these schools became redundant in 1974 when a new building was constructed; the 1840 building was demolished, and the infant school became a factory and took on a dilapidated look. I was enrolled at the infant school, which was about a mile from Hazledene when I was just over five and a half years old. I walked the distance four times a day because no school dinners were provided by Huntingdonshire and most pupils went home for a mid-day meal. I grew to dread the walk, not because I found the distance tiring but for two reasons. The first was that Robin Beeken lived near the Black Horse, a public house, which was on my route. Robin found it amusing to threaten girls as they passed by, and I reacted as he hoped. I was scared of him! Secondly, if I walked via Back Lane, I passed a hollow tree by which there was an aggressive magpie. It persistently flew at any passer-by, and it petrified me. Luckily, neither obstacle caused me to become a school phobic.

The infant school was typical of the time. It had three classrooms divided by partitions which could be moved back on noisy brass fittings to become a hall and one individual classroom. The roof formed the ceilings, so the rooms were high with exposed rafters. The desks and chairs had been purchased when the school was built and were not Victorian iron desks but wooden tables and chairs of differing sizes to accommodate the age groups. Those in the reception class were small, too small for the five-year-olds of today. The teachers arranged the furniture in groups and the children in ability sets. A wide corridor ran from the front door to the back of the building where the boiler room was situated. The door was often open, and it was possible to see the flames of the furnace. It is surprising there were no accidents. A cloakroom with a concrete floor was near the front entrance. The basins were in two back-to-back rows in the centre with a channel for a drain serving all the basins. The water was cold and the towels always wet and horrible. The bucket toilets, situated well away from the building, were open to the elements and disgusting. I often ran all the way home to avoid using them. I think this school toilets' experience began my anathema towards all public toilets. Mrs Rowe was the head teacher and two other teachers – Miss Steeper and Miss Crick - completed the staff. Mrs Rowe taught the 'top' class, children who were seven years old, and sat at a table covered with a green cloth on which inkwells and pens sat prominently. At the end of each day the green cloth was carefully folded, and the writing equipment put away. Miss Crick, the reception teacher, wore high button boots to travel to and from school. At the conclusion of the afternoon, the class sat cross-legged on the floor and listened to enthralling stories of her life. Miss Steeper, the middle infants' teacher, lived in Fletton with her sister and mother to whom I took flowers when she was ill and received a special thank you letter. Miss Steeper appeared to favour me although she once punched me in the back during a lesson and I do not know, to this day, what I was doing wrong. I was very upset because, throughout my school life, I never deliberately disobeyed a teacher and was a hard worker who learned reasonably easily. Every morning and afternoon the registers were very carefully marked in red and blue ink and each Friday the attendances and absences were totalled with the requirement that they balanced so that the percentage attendance was accurately recorded. I learned to read with the Beacon reading scheme and had two favourite stories from these books. They were about Chicken Licken who believed the sky fell on her head and the little engine that struggled to pull the trucks up a steep hill! Letter shapes were perfected using seashells on sand trays and writing was done in books, cut in half, with blue lines for lower case letters and red ones for tall letters, tails and of course capitals. We had lots of plasticine which was brightly coloured but with daily use the colours became mixed, and the modelling material finished as a dirty grey. I was not greatly enchanted by plasticine. It made my hands smell.

Empire Day was an important event in the Farcet schools and one year the infant children went in horse drawn farm carts for a picnic and games in a field along Broadway. It was, for me, an exciting expedition. Later in the 'big' school the event was celebrated with a concert and an Empire tableau which included Britannia and children from all the nations. The inevitable map of the world on the school wall displayed the very extensive redness of the British Empire. I believed entirely in Empire! I thought the countries that belonged to it would be proud of their membership and was totally convinced that it would last forever. May Day was also special; a maypole stood proudly in the big classroom but was taken outside so that it could be danced around to celebrate the coming of summertime. To us village children the day had nothing to do with 'workers'! We danced singly or in pairs and held the ribbons which were fixed to the top of the maypole and hopefully wove patterns with them. In order to weave and undo the patterns the dancers were required to remember the movements, and when, not if, a mistake was made, the ribbons became tangled much to the annoyance of the teacher. May garlands were also a factor in making the day special. I once made a garland in Con's clothes basket; it was a summer scene with many flowers. I covered the basket with a cloth and asked for payment in return for viewing my masterpiece.

In April 1940, I went to school as usual and when I came home Granny Lant and her daughter, Phyllis, were there and I could hear a baby crying! Granny Lant had been the licensee of the Plough Inn in Farcet Fen and neighbour and close friends of John and Liza my paternal grandparents. My brother Leslie had arrived without me being given any hint that a new addition was expected! What was worse no-one let me see 'my Mum' and I was packed off to Woodston to stay with Albert and Florence (my grandparents). I objected and made an outrageous fuss until I was taken back to Farcet by Les, Con's brother, and his wife, Joan. They chose to walk from Woodston to the village via Buntings Lane, a pathway through the brickyards, but I refused to walk and demanded to be carried, and I was six years old. No doubt I was angry and jealous! Leslie was not a healthy baby and was frequently ill, sometimes Bill and Con needed to watch over him all night. At one point, his cot stayed in the living room so that he could be kept in a constant temperature. He also developed whooping cough and I went with Bill to take him to the factory where tar was used, and Bill held him over the container of steaming tar in the hope it would help his breathing. I don't think it did. He grew, however, into a beautiful toddler with gorgeous blonde curly hair and was the apple of his parents' eyes. He developed arthritis but it was not properly diagnosed (even doctors talked of growing pains) and in his teenage he was given gold injections. These helped the problem but were not a cure and arthritis has affected him all his life. Leslie began school just before I went to secondary school, and I was given the responsibility of taking him. He did not like school, and I was daily embarrassed by being told that my brother was crying at the school gate and wanted me. He did not follow me to the grammar school but attended the 'school on the bridge' at Fletton and achieved well. He won a special prize as he achieved high marks for his work.

Ballet Classes

The head teacher of Farcet Church of England School was Mr. Whitticase. He died early in my school life and Mr Grant took his place. Mr Grant was a gaunt man, who enjoyed amateur dramatics. I remember him in 'The Mikado', wearing thick black tights, kneeling with his back to the audience and waggling his legs. The Grants had two sons, Keith, and Ian; Ian sat beside me on his first morning at Farcet Infants School. The family lived in the thatched schoolhouse, which was perhaps the most attractive house in the village but has since been spoiled by being roofed with modern red tiles. The school had a bell above the roof and every morning it sang out its discordant note to encourage dawdlers to hurry. Inside, coke burning stoves had been installed in the large room and an adjacent room, (these rooms were separated by wood and glass partitions) while the two other classrooms had open fires. The fuel, on which the children often played, was heaped in the playground. Some desks were locker type with chairs while others, heavy iron affairs with lift-up seats and lids, remained from earlier times. The windows were well above eye level to ensure the pupils were not distracted from their work by the everyday activities outside the building. However, I watched certain of my peers who misbehaved and thought they were fortunate; they were made to stand on their chairs as punishment which enabled them to see outside. I decided that I wanted to look out of the windows and eventually I achieved my goal. My disobedience was to continue talking when I had been told to be quiet. I was delighted and could hardly wait to give Con the news of my achievement. She did not share my pride and I did not try the same trick again! Standing on a chair for misbehaviour is no longer possible as a new school was built and the old building demolished.

The boys' playground was a fenced square area of concrete, situated away from the school along an alley, known as 'the cut'. Their games invariably consisted of much rough and tumble and loud shouting. The girls played in the yard around the school and amused themselves with certain games at particular times of the year; the skipping season meant either individual skipping or collective games. The latter needed one or two long ropes, often clothes lines, and two people, one on each end, turned the rope or ropes. Those who skipped used the rope in turn - running through without jumping or jumping a specified number of times and then running from the rope. The child skipping was out if she stopped the rope turning. Another group game was 'The Big Ship sails on the Alley Alley Oh' and needed a long line of girls each holding a hand with the leader making an arch with her free arm and a suitable wall. The girl at the end of the line then led it under the arch and in and out arches made by the linked arms to the singing of the big ship sails on the Alley Alley Oh on the last day of September. The captain said it will never, never do never, never do, never, never do on the last day of September. When everyone found their hands crossed the game ended in a melee of falling down and laughing. Hopscotch was popular in its turn and different grids, drawn on the ground, varied the pattern of the hopping. Balls could be used in varying numbers: individuals could bounce one or two balls against a wall and three people could play 'piggy in the middle'. In this game two people threw a ball to each other while the third stood in the middle and tried to stop the ball as it flew overhead. Games with 'conkers' had a time slot in autumn, with marbles, yo-yos and cats cradle having their particular timeframe.

Mr. Grant taught the top class and at times Mrs Grant came to be with the class. She was not a qualified teacher but acted as an unqualified supply teacher. She was a fussy woman, but likeable even though she felt she had status as 'the village headmaster's wife'. Mr. Johnny Bull was the school musician as well as being a class teacher. One teacher made a big impression, she was very smartly dressed, and her hair was always tidy. It appeared she often went away at the weekends because, on a Friday afternoon, she opened a case and got out a silk head scarf and carefully tied it on her head before taking her register to the head teacher. Mrs Dane, the fourth member of staff, walked in an unforgettable fashion. Her legs seemed too thin to carry her rotund body which appeared to be pushed forward. While at the Farcet schools I had just one significant absence. I was hospitalised for a tonsillectomy, an operation performed on many children as a cure for continuous throat infections, and it was in the days when parents were not permitted to enter the children's ward. I hated being left and was frightened about going into the operating theatre! Con tried to visit me but was only permitted to leave a comic with a nurse! I was promised that after my tonsils had gone, I would be rewarded with ice cream. Unfortunately, in war time ice cream was not readily available so I missed out on my reward! Indeed, the war was significant in every aspect of my school life. Every member of the population was issued with an identity card indicating their personal identity number. Mine was TECI 3 and was engraved with my name on an identity disc which I wore round my wrist as a bracelet. I liked my 'bracelet' and did not understand that it was meant to identify me in the event of an accident or death!

Evacuees arrived in Farcet early in the hostilities and, initially, the influx of children made difficulties for the schools. Lessons were organised on a two-shift system and some of the older children accommodated in the infant school. My home life was not affected by the evacuation. Bill and Con had difficulty in making room for all the family residents and could not take in any of those driven from London. Everyone, including school children, was involved in the war effort. The collection of wastepaper was deemed essential, and pupils were asked to take as much as possible to school and received a coloured badge depicting an army rank as a reward. A specific amount was required for each rank, an extra amount for a higher rank. To be a field marshal represented piles and piles of paper. I managed to achieve this rank because Bill sacrificed his carefully preserved technical magazines and I had many relatives who helped to increase my collection. The issue of gas masks began as soon as war broke out but immediately after distribution an additional filter was added. No doubt it had been found that the first filter was insufficient to reject the strength of the gas that may have been used. The masks were contained in cardboard boxes with a string long enough to go over the shoulder for ease of carrying, but special gas mask bags could be purchased, and they gave a more up-market appearance. Leslie, being a baby, was issued with a large appliance and he would have been put entirely inside. We practised putting the masks on as quickly as possible, but thankfully we never had to wear them for real.

War time meant food rationing, and everyone had a ration book so that each person received weekly the minimum amount of food necessary to keep healthy. When compared with 21st century expectations, the individual allocation of butter, cheese and meat was very small. No noticeable shortage was obvious at Hazledene where Con always managed to feed everyone well. We had no tropical fruit, but gardens became the places to grow local fruit and vegetables. The vegetables could be used in unusual ways, marrows became an ingredient for sweet dishes as well as an accompaniment to meat, and rhubarb was often added to strawberries and raspberries to increase the amount of jam obtained from limited amounts of soft fruit. Rabbits, hares and game birds were available in the country and Fred often supplied a pheasant. Con rationed the cakes. She permitted Leslie and me one each at tea-time and no more. It was at this time that Brian Scotney gave me some comics and amongst them was one from Australia. I had long wanted a penfriend and I chose the name of a competition winner and wrote to June who became my penfriend. Soon after the correspondence began, June and her family started to send food parcels as a reaction to the news 'down-under' which obviously painted a picture of a hungry Britain. Yet, there was no news, as far as I was concerned, indicating that Australia lived in fear of a Japanese invasion. However, many years later, I learned that the Japanese did raid Australia and attempted to occupy parts of the country, with those people living in the areas having very difficult times. Despite this activity, the parcels continued until 1945, and the contents were exciting: the packages were so different from those in local shops.

Prisoners of war were a regular part of life for school children. Many of the prisoners were set to work on farms to take the places of men away fighting. Lorry transport dropped them off at their place of work in the morning and collected them in the evening and they were not supervised, other than by the farmer. The prisoners were distinguished by their uniforms of dark brown serge with different coloured circles and triangles sewn on them but that did not prevent friendships developing with those with whom they worked and members of the community. An Italian prisoner worked at Gazley Hall and he waited for his evening transport near the gate. After school my friends, Beryl, Doreen Smith, Marie Stocker and I stopped to talk to him. It is interesting that our parents did not object to this activity, they had no animosity towards the prisoner and did not think we were in danger. I became somewhat jealous of Marie because 'our' prisoner made her a belt from cellophane paper from cigarette packets, but he did not make me a similar belt! Even though there was only limited time to walk to and from home at midday, the four of us managed to waste time by calling at the house of Marie's grandmother which was near the school. We waited while Marie ate pudding; it always seemed to be rice pudding with prunes. I don't think she shared it with us, but I would have refused because I hated the skin of rice pudding. This dawdling restricted my mealtime but once a week I had a shorter walk to Beryl and Doreen's house where I ate my dinner. Con was cleaning at her sister Mollie's house each Thursday. I adored Mrs Smith's baked dumplings, but I detested pineapple jam (I have no idea how this particular variety was on sale because pineapples were not available) and once Beryl, Doreen and Mrs. Smith tricked me into eating some. Mavis Allen was also a friend but being an only child, she went straight home when school closed. Much later, I met her when she was returning to England from Australia but then lost any contact. Immediately after the end of the

Second World War, I went to Fletton Grammar School. I was 11 years old, and I lost touch with these early friends, although not permanently in the case of Marie.

Grammar School

At Farcet School practice tests for the 1944 scholarship for secondary education and the 11+ in 1945 were very important and we laboured over them every day as the great examination drew near. I was unsuccessful in the final scholarship examination and Con wanted to transfer me to a school in Fletton. This school had been built as an elementary board school and had three storeys, infant on the ground level and children up to 14 in the upper storeys. Con, however, decided against this option when Mr Grant pointed out that I was only 10 years old and changes in education were imminent. Towards the end of the Second World War a nation-wide determination emerged that once peace returned every child would have equality of educational opportunity and receive secondary education. The 1944 Education Act was seen to achieve the desired equality and a secondary school, also in Fletton, attended from 1910 by fee-paying and scholarship pupils, became a grammar school. In the 1960s, Fletton Grammar School moved to Orton Longueville, occupied a new building, and later was amalgamated with the nearby Secondary Modern School to form a comprehensive. Places at the grammar school were allocated by the 11+ test. Keith Wilson, Ivan Lock and I were successful and became the first three pupils from Farcet to gain grammar school places: a significant achievement for a small village school. The night before the first day of the September term 1945, I slept at Betty's Stores with my new gym slip hanging in the bedroom awaiting the grand adventure.

**Four Fletton Friends: rear Barbara Bullimore and Megan Cameron,
front me and Sylvia Smith**

The head teacher, when I arrived, was Mr. Rumsey, but he retired almost immediately and was replaced by Dr. Gaught, a most objectionable man and disliked by the majority of pupils. Miss Stott was the mistress in charge of the girls and taught Geography. She drove an Austin 7 car and whispers reached our ears that her fiancé had been killed in the First World War, which seemed highly likely, but she did not satisfy our curiosity. Mr. Ridgard, my French teacher, later became the first principal of the newly formed Brook Street College of Adult Education, where his photograph continued to be displayed for many years. Mr.Irwin, an upright unsmiling man, took his place and I was frightened of him. He had the nickname, Satan, because 'he could always find something for idle hands to do'. Mr. Legge taught mathematics very thoroughly but was subject to asthma and on his retirement moved to the south coast away from the fumes of the brickyards. Mr. Weston and Mr. Winfield joined the staff in 1945, the former was appointed as the music teacher and the latter the PE teacher for boys, but he also taught the occasional lesson of R.E. Mr. Weston, an excellent musician, raised the profile of the school with musical performances. I was in the choir, although with no singing voice it is difficult to believe. At Christmas the choir performed a programme of carols at many churches and chapels. Mr. Winfield became a Peterborough legend as an energetic and enthusiastic city councillor and remained a teacher when David and Jono became pupils.

The distance from Hazledene to the grammar school was about four miles and at first, I travelled by bus, but Brenda Jackson was in my form, and we soon became cycling companions. Each morning I called for her at her house near Whittlesey corner and we rode to school together. During the winter of 1947, memorable for the extreme weather, we pushed our cycles. Snow was piled shoulder high along the roads while the road surface was too dangerous for cycling, but we did not miss a day and the school was never closed. After the snow came floods in 1953 which soon covered much land and Con and Bill took Leslie and me on a double-decker bus to witness the extent of the inundation around Wisbech. It was an unbelievable sight with Wisbech an island surrounded by water as far as the eye could see. At Hunstanton the sea was very dangerous and a number of those on a particular boat were drowned and people were moved from their homes. Before this incident Auntie Doris took her niece and me to Heacham where we stayed in a houseboat on the sand, but the houseboat disappeared when the weather was so dreadful. My non-cycling friends were Barbara Bullimore, who lived in London Road, Sylvia Smith who lived off High Street Fletton and Megan Cameron from Yaxley. Unlike my friends, however, who stayed at school for their lunch, I refused to do so. The provision of school meals was part of the 1944 legislation, but I was not prepared to try them. Instead, Florence, Con's sister (Auntie Bill), fed me every school day for seven years. She made all kinds of fattening puddings such as suet pudding and treacle, spotted dick, and jam roly poly and I adored them. It was during one of these dinner times, when I was in the third year, that I heard the news of the assassination of Gandhi, (30th January 1948) the great leader of India. He had featured prominently in newspaper reports about Indian independence and, although, I was interested in the events in the sub-continent, I mainly wondered if he was warm enough as he wore only a loin cloth! Con hoped that I would become an expert piano player and paid for my lessons. I practised everyday at 96 New Road. Unfortunately, neither lessons nor practice ensured Con's hope. I did not manage any kind of expertise and Con's sister Kath learned to hate 'American Patrol', the piece I played constantly.

Fletton Grammar School, which had become a school for children up to 11 years of age, was a two-form entry school of 60 children, 30 in each class with the classes being named A to E and 1 to 5. I was allocated the letter route. The subjects which all pupils studied were Mathematics (geometry, algebra and arithmetic), English (literature and language), French, Geography, History, Art, General Science, Music, Religious Education, Physical Education, Games (hockey and tennis) and Domestic Science. I did well in the academic subjects, but not those which needed physical prowess. My biggest rival was my contemporary from Farcet, Keith Wilson, and in the annual examinations we vied with each other for the top places in the class and we received prizes at every speech day to the fifth form. At the end of five years of general study, everyone faced an external examination which, from 1911, was the School Certificate. Matriculation, which represented the necessary level of attainment to enter university, was linked to this examination and I managed to matriculate. Nineteen fifty was the last year of the School Certificate, making me one of the final students to achieve this certificate. A new examination regime had been developed and the General Certificate of Education (GCE) was introduced in 1951. I did not leave school after the examination as many of my class did but went into the sixth form and serious decisions about the future needed to be made. I had had no idea of what I wanted to do but was certain that I did not want to be a teacher. In the primary school I planned to be a missionary! I remember writing about teaching the little black children about God. To me the rest of the world consisted of savages waiting to be saved by the 'righteous British'! I had also thought I might try aeronautical engineering but was not invited for an interview. No doubt the reason for no interview was the fact that I was a girl. I should have made an application for university because grants for higher education were available to all who had the ability. Students were not prevented in their ambitions by lack of resources or the fear of debts to be repaid. Universities were not in my experience, however, and no-one spoke to me about them. Others in the sixth form were sending for teacher training college prospectuses and I think I was seduced by that from Whitelands and decided to apply for a place. I also applied to Homerton at Cambridge and Dudley. Why Dudley when I do not like the Midlands! Perhaps the prospectus was especially attractive.

I was going to be a teacher after all. Con and Doris accompanied me to my interview on a November Thursday in 1951, the day of the Lord Mayor's Show. I was interviewed by the Vice-Principal and must have performed well because I was offered a place. I accepted. I remember reading a passage containing difficult words and was asked to explain my reasons for wanting to be a teacher. I waffled but somehow gave the right impression. Earlier in the year, an important excursion to London was arranged for everyone in the school to visit the Festival of Britain. The Government had determined that this event should prove to the world that Britain remained a country to be reckoned with and to cheer up the people who were still living a life of austerity six years after the end of the hostilities.

The site of the festival was on the south bank of the Thames, and we found the buildings and exhibits amazing. The Skylon, a tall, slender, cigar-shaped steel structure was the most impressive which we all admired and which, had it been retained, may have become as iconic as the London Eye. The Festival Hall was the only permanent building and more than half a century later has been renovated and updated and remains a centre for music.

I made my first trip to Paris during the second year in the sixth form. I had saved some money from my Saturday job at Woolworth's and my daily paper round but to earn extra cash for this excursion Anne Prior and I worked at the Gables Maternity Hospital. We did a variety of tasks; most would no longer be permitted under health and safety legislation. We enjoyed carrying two babies, one in each arm, up and down the stairs from the nursery to their mothers but scrubbing the labour ward did not appeal greatly. On one occasion Anne cycled to Thorpe Hall to fetch the forceps because they were required for a difficult birth. The poor mother obviously had to wait!! I wore a new green coat and a hat and carried a new leather handbag for the journey to foreign parts! We travelled by train and ferry and stayed in a school in the Latin Quarter. Every day we walked along the famous Boulevard St. Michel to attend sessions at the Sorbonne; we were there to improve our French, but we did not miss the sights of the city. We went to the Ile de la Cite and Notre Dame, the Sainte Chappelle and the Louvre where the Mona Lisa was just another painting on the wall. It had no extra protection and no crowds surrounded it. Naturally, we walked the Champs Elysees and visited the Arc de Triomphe with the grave of the Unknown Soldier. We took the lift to the top of the Tour Eiffel and went to the famous shops in the fashionable boulevards where the girls bought wide elastic belts with metal fasteners. These belts were 'a la mode' and we all wore them with pride. Despite this trip being only seven years after the end of the war, Paris seemed to be very sophisticated and was without wartime scars. I learned that Hitler ensured the city was not destroyed because he wanted, when he had won the war, to use it as his capital.

Once back in school there was very little time remaining before the next stage of life beckoned. Whitelands insisted that students went into a local school to observe classroom organisation and watch teachers giving lessons before they began training, and I observed at Fletton School in the infants' department, a separate establishment with its own head teacher on the ground floor of the three-storey building. Although the observation was useful, the most important event before going to college was the 'A' level examination and I had, to my undying shame, the one failure of my academic career. I was successful in the History and French papers, but only gained a GCE in English. I made a major error in recognising a Shakespeare quotation and thus answered all the parts of the question wrongly. Thankfully, I made up for this disaster at the end of my first college year by coming very near the top in the English examination, which every first-year student was obliged to sit.

Teacher Training

Whitelands College was one of the oldest teacher training colleges and a Church of England establishment, with 300 students, 150 first and 150 second years. The college building, situated on West Hill Putney, had been designed by Gilbert Scott and was an elegant building with real style surrounded by beautiful grounds. Every student who lived in college had an individual room along corridors named after streets in Chelsea where the college had originally been established. My first-year neighbour in Cromwell Road was called Isobel and she lives in my memory because she had thick black hair which was plaited and wound around her head. The second-year students chose their own rooms and, as a second-year student, I had a first-floor room with French windows opening on to a balcony. Some extra student accommodation was needed, and several girls lived in flats at the gate of the college grounds and others were in nearby private homes. The student body was arranged in god families and second years became mentors, known as godmothers, to first years who were the godlets, to be supportive and guide them in the ways of the college. There were eight in our family, Chris, who has died, Sheila, whose health remains poor (2017), Patsi, whose husband has died and me with our godmothers. Mine was Joyce Davies who lived off Midland Road (Peterborough) and now lives in Orton Longueville. When I became the godmother, my godlet was Ruth Fovargue from Whittlesey who died at a very young age. In the dining room the tables accommodated eight people, exactly right for our god family, to eat meals together. At one end of the room was a table set on a small platform. It was overlooked by portraits of previous principals and was used by the lecturers. Students were required to join the august body in turn to dine at this table and it was described as going 'on high'! When I joined the higher body, I talked in what I believed were sagacious terms about my passion for Jane Austen! As the college was a Church of England foundation the chapel was an integral part of student life with services held everyday and bells rung regularly. Despite this I regarded the college as liberal, but I was used to being obedient and had not given my parents any worries. Rules were not particularly strict when viewed in the context of the time. Men were not forbidden to enter the rooms as long as they left at a reasonable hour. Signing in at night was obligatory at weekends and, although it was necessary to obtain late passes if you were going to the theatre or attending some other event, they were generally granted. On two very particular occasions, I had a late pass. I went alone to the Festival Hall for a Wagner concert. No-one else joined me in my Valkyrie period! The second time was to see a ballet in which Margot Fonteyn and Michael Soames were dancing. It was a memorable experience.

Courses were arranged around the infant, junior and secondary age groups and students chose to concentrate on one of these groups. I chose the junior group for no other reason than I believed junior children were the most interesting. It is strange then that one of my particular interests has been the early years. At the time, however, I was not prepared to teach the basics to infants and secondary pupils did not appeal. Education lectures, taken by a junior specialist in the case of the prospective junior teachers, were, I suppose, intended to teach the students how to teach. I don't think this aim was successfully met. There were no clear guidelines about the way to do the job and it was a case of learning when you went into school. Maths and English lectures were largely designed to allow students to experience the work suitable for the chosen age group, but again did not help with lesson delivery, despite the college principal being Mrs Williams, a mathematician and author of books to aid teachers. The mathematics lecturer was, coincidentally, Leonard Cowie, the husband of Evelyn who was later to feature as my MA lecturer. Health lectures described childhood ailments and of particular interest were the sessions on head lice! We all knew they would, most likely, come our way. Child development was an important aspect of other lectures and a child study obligatory. The child who was the subject of this task was to be known to you. Like many others, my study included much information of doubtful accuracy so that it followed more nearly the features we had been taught. Other lectures were less memorable; I went to some biology sessions and spent time in the animal shed looking after the various livestock, and attended a gardening course which in no way enhanced my gardening expertise. Every student was required to choose a special subject and mine was history which I greatly enjoyed. The course was based on early history - Charlemagne and Frederick Barbarossa. I can always remember that Frederick died when trying to swim a river, the Rhine, I think!

In the first term of student life, it was school practice for all, and I was sent to Hoxton, and a school in the New North Road. The building of the latter was Victorian, three storeys high and with, even at that time, difficult children. They took no notice whatsoever of a young inexperienced girl from the sticks and made me wonder if I had chosen well in entering a training college. Two other school practices followed in due time; the final was the longest and mine was at Ealing. The children's behaviour and ability were reasonably good, and my class was of nine-year-old pupils. Project work was very much in vogue at the time, and I decided on the crusades. One child with her mother made an absolutely marvellous miniature crusader. School practice meant a great deal of lesson planning, collecting resources and dreading the supervisors' visits. My two supervisors were the peculiar biology lecturer and Miss Blackman the history lecturer and they allowed me to reach the final examinations. These were three-hour papers and success meant certificated teacher status, and I achieved certification.

Each academic year the college celebrated two important festivals. St. Cecilia's Day was in the autumn term when students and lecturers, dressed in their best clothes, enjoyed an evening of musical entertainment. The most important day of the year was, however, May Day. John Ruskin had been instrumental in the inauguration of the event which was based on a philosophy of aesthetics and 'beautiful young ladies' behaving well. Each year the first-year students elected a student to be their queen. A special dress was made for her, and she was crowned on May Day. Our queen was Vera who wore a Tudor style dress because it was the year of the coronation which was promoted as a contemporary Elizabethan age. New summery dresses were in evidence and the day was taken up with chapel services, celebrations and a procession with the newly crowned queen leading the many previous queens who returned for the day. In 1953, late 19th century queens appeared! The two years at Whitelands ended with a grand ball and a partner was essential. My beau was a willing or unwilling student from a men's establishment. The evening was enjoyable, but I was not over enamoured by him, and he certainly did not pursue me. The years 1952-1954 included some very important national events; both had a weather theme. The first was the great winter smog when London was shrouded with thick choking fog. It was impossible to see more than a few feet outside and the fog penetrated the buildings so that it was difficult to see from one end to the other of the corridors. The second was a joyous occasion but very wet – the Coronation. It had been a blow to everyone when King George VI died so suddenly, and I shared the country wide sympathy for the sad new monarch as she stepped from the aeroplane which brought her back from Africa. By the summer of 1953 sadness had turned to joy and Patsi, David (Patsi's partner), Chris and I slept on the street with millions of others and cheered the smiling Queen as she rode by in the state coach. Whitelands is now no more! The listed shell of the building remains but it has been converted into apartments; the dining room is a gym, and the gardens are a housing development. The name, however, is retained at the University of Roehampton. Several years have passed since I went to Roehampton with Patsi for a celebration of crowning a new queen. There were a number of attendees from our year, and it was interesting to meet them but, as yet, I haven't been to another special occasion. I had seen Patsi quite a few times over the years and after the death of her husband I stayed a weekend with her. It was good to catch up with her and hear all her family news. All of us met together at Chris' house just after the storm when many trees fell in 1987, and difficulties were everywhere. It was the 'long noted' storm when the weatherman assured the listeners there was no likelihood of there being a storm! Neither Patsi nor me, were informed of Chris' death and consequently we were unable to go to her funeral. Sheila, who was the one who did not have good health, remains reasonably well. Perhaps Patsi and I should visit again.

Life with Arthur, A Lonely Sailor

I came home from college at the end of each term, always travelling by train at the cost of 11s 3d, the fare of a single ticket from King's Cross. On one occasion, Con pointed out a report in the local paper headed 'Lonely Sailor'. The content indicated that a member of the ship's company of HMS Barfleur, who came from Peterborough, did not receive mail. I was persuaded to write to Signalman Arthur Chambers D/JX 865394, and some correspondence began. It did not last long! The reason for the curtailment was that I went to work at the post office. In those days, sorting and delivering the Christmas mail was a good money earner for students. During one period of sorting, I found a letter addressed to June Sayer, who lived in Churchfield Road, in a handwriting I recognised. I was quite upset! I went home and burnt all the letters I had received from Arthur Chambers as well as his photograph and decided my letter writing to a member of the armed services was over. I did not keep to this decision. Arthur wrote me more letters and I answered them and arranged to meet him on Paddington Station on Saturday 15th May 1954, the day the Royal Yacht on its maiden voyage brought the Queen home from Malta. HMS Barfleur had been part of the escort. Arthur had no idea what I looked like so it was necessary for me to describe myself and the clothes I would wear. I donned my tailored navy-blue pin striped suit which had been made by a tailor in Bridge Street Peterborough and pinned some lily of the valley on my lapel. We met romantically 'under the clock at Waterloo'! We spent the day together and ate a meal at a restaurant called Mario's in Putney High Street, where Arthur gave me an Italian jewellery box. On this first encounter, he presented himself as a 'Jolly Jack Tar' and wore his cap on the back of his head, turned back the cuffs of his uniform and smoked heavily. I was beguiled by him and excited by the naval connection, only later did it become obvious that Arthur lacked self-confidence, and frequently felt isolated in the career he had chosen.

Arthur on HMS Barfleur – my favourite photograph of him

When the evening ended, I went back to college and Arthur caught a train to Peterborough to his father's house at 124 Elmfield Road. Arthur senior had remarried by this time, but he later divorced. Unknown to me Arthur had continued his communication with June (in Peterborough) but decided, some days after his return to Peterborough, to end the relationship. Her marriage was reported in the local paper in November of 1955.

In June 1954, Arthur was 21. I returned to Peterborough for his celebration and in July my time at Whitelands College came to an end with my newly acquired status of teacher. Before leaving college, I had applied to Huntingdonshire Education Authority and Peterborough Joint Board for a teaching post. The interview at the Town Hall for the Peterborough post was an unforgettable experience. I sat on a chair in the middle of the horseshoe council table around which the panel of about five councillors and Leslie Tait, the education officer, was arranged. I must have answered the questions satisfactorily although I don't recall the specifics, but no doubt there were some especially for females about their marriage plans. I was offered a post but did not take it because I had already accepted one in Huntingdonshire, although any interview for that is less than a vague memory! The position was at Fletton School in the combined junior and senior department. Mr Plumb, the head teacher, gave me a class of very 'special needs' children but no classroom. I was in the hall onto which every other classroom opened and through which everyone walked. I am certain the children learned little during the year that I was their teacher with the constant interruptions and my inexperience. No-one asked to see any lesson plans or tried to find out what I was doing. Some senior pupils, amongst which was Leslie, my brother, were housed in a prefabricated building and I was put in charge of the senior girls' games. What a mistake! However, the previous teacher of the netball-playing girls had been a games specialist and the netball team had been extremely successful. As a result, I was able to maintain the situation and the team repeated its success. Fortunately, I did not stay more than one year, just long enough to celebrate my 21st birthday and my marriage. If I had, my lack of expertise would have become more and more obvious.

Marriage

After his leave Arthur returned to Plymouth and was then posted to Scotland to the Signal Station at North Queensferry on the Forth which is no longer a naval establishment and has become a domestic home. While serving at the Signal Station he decided that marriage was what I wanted and acted on the assumption by speaking to Bill who agreed with the idea. I do not remember an official proposal, but I was very naive and think I viewed marriage through rose-coloured spectacles. I certainly did not raise any opposition and was probably excited about being a bride. The wedding was arranged for 11th April 1955 at Farcet Church, a date less than a year after I had first met Arthur. Perhaps I should have been wary of marrying so quickly; I knew very little about many aspects of his background, his beliefs, or his aspirations and on the morning of the wedding I had grave doubts about what I was doing and although Mary (Brown) thought it was only nerves and jollied me along, I sometimes wonder whether I went through with the ceremony because it was expected. Even at the reception, at the back of my mind, I questioned whether marriage was what I wanted. Such a revelation is not easy to write because David, Jonathon and Alison mean more to me than life itself and despite these misgivings our marriage lasted thirty-two years during which we had some extremely interesting experiences. It seems more likely that my doubts were a premonition of the future. Arthur was caring and generous and there is no doubt that he loved me, but his love could be possessive; he became difficult to live with; he wanted to make my decisions, be involved in and control my every action.

Cutting the cake on our Wedding Day

Arthur's Family

Arthur's insecurity and lack of self confidence was increasingly apparent as our attachment to one another developed. He found making relationships difficult and constantly felt the need to prove himself. Over time his psychological difficulties gradually came to the fore, but the seeds of his problems were sown before his birth. The marriage of his mother Violet and his father Arthur united two families with troubled backgrounds. Violet's father, William Pollard, was born in 1871 in the Lincolnshire village of Carlton Scroop. Henry, William's brother, was a year older and Sarah Ann, his sister, was two years younger. The children's father died not long after Sarah Ann's birth and by the time she was seven their mother had remarried. Perhaps tensions within the new family led William to leave home; certainly, by the age of 19 he was lodging with six other young men in South Witham and was employed on the railways as an engine cleaner. Three years later, William had left Lincolnshire and had joined the Royal Navy. Violet's mother, Lavinia Mundy, was also from Lincolnshire and was born in Sleaford but the couple married in Portsmouth in 1902, where Lavinia was living, after William returned from the Far East. The wedding ceremony was conducted at the Register Office with, it appears, no family present. William had joined H.M.S. Marathon in 1898, the year Violet was born in Sheffield when Lavinia was only 19 years old and was away in the Far East during the Boxer uprising in China. It is only possible to surmise the circumstances.

If Violet was William's child and it seems likely she was, then Lavinia became pregnant when William returned on leave to Lincolnshire after serving on his first ship, H.M.S. Resolution. There can be little doubt that Lavinia's father was aghast at his teenage daughter's pregnancy; he was a local Wesylan preacher and no doubt his reaction was to send her away until Violet was born, and the marriage solemnized. The year after the marriage, Lavinia gave birth to twin girls, Mabel and Ethel. And in 1907, Robert William, described by one of his sisters as 'Mam's favourite', the only son and the youngest child was born.

Violet – Arthur's Mother

Two months after the beginning of the First World War, William, a stoker, left Portsmouth on HMS Kent and did not return until January 1917. During this long commission he kept a diary in which he recorded events both dramatic and mundane and his odd comment illustrates that the sailors that manned the fleet in the Southern Atlantic and Pacific felt they were forgotten. The lack of attention that the local Peterborough newspapers paid to these men so far from home gives credence to their feelings. The Battle of the Falklands did not appear in the diary of major war events published in December 1918! Yet this important sea encounter in 1914 prevented the enemy from invading the islands and was crucial to the transport of men from the Empire to fight for the 'Mother Country'. Although armed protection for the troopships continued to be necessary, without the sinking of the Scharnhorst, the Gneisenau, the Nürnberg and the Dresden, the enemy would have had control of the Southern Atlantic with refuelling, provisioning, and rearming on hand in Port Stanley and the difficulties of getting the much-needed troops to their destinations might have been insurmountable. Yet, the Peterborough Advertiser devoted just one small paragraph to the sinking of the four ships. Reading the pages devoted to the land campaigns and sea battles in the North Sea with full details of local soldiers and sailors must have caused Lavinia distress and led her to think that neither William's service nor her family responsibility was appreciated. It is possible that her resentment led her to become the strict and controlling parent she is reported to have been. Indeed, it seems that when William returned to civilian life, he had a very secondary role in family life and was a dutiful husband to the wife who told him what to do! He was employed by the London North Eastern Railway and was described as 'a kindly interesting old man who was most talkative away from the house'. William died in 1934 at the age of 63 years and Lavinia staged a great show of mourning! Her domination of the children continued; even after her death they were unable to escape her shadow and lived unhappy and unfulfilled lives with tragedy or illness never far away.

Violet is reported to have been a pretty young woman who, as she grew up, became rebellious and determined to have fun. Her behaviour displeased her mother, and she was frequently in trouble for being late home and in the company of the opposite sex. Battles were serious when Arthur senior began to 'court her' and it is reported that she was locked in her bedroom but escaped through the window to make her planned rendezvous. Lavinia expressed loud disapproval of Arthur senior, but Violet was not to be deterred and the pair were married in the first half of 1923. (Cert of marriage P'boro 3b.609). Marriage, however, does not seem to have lived up to her expectations. Despite her determination to escape her mother's control, Violet retained a naivety and wanted her life to be 'happy ever after'! Arthur senior was not the romantic hero she sought, but a railway worker whose hours of work were unsocial and whose spare time interests were trades union activities and politics. During the early days they were content and, in 1924, their first child, Eric, was born and he brought joy. He was the 'apple of their eyes' and Violet began to hope for a daughter so that the family would be perfectly complete. Ten years of disappointment followed before the likelihood of the 'perfect family' became a possibility and, in 1933, a new baby arrived. The new arrival was, however, not Amelia or Amanda, the longed-for daughter, but a second son, Arthur, who grew up convinced that he was 'second best' because he was not the daughter his mother wanted. As a result, he spent his life trying to prove he was a worthy son but was always compared unfavourably with Eric. During the Second World War, Violet gradually sank into depression; she was consumed with worry for the safety of her husband and her son. Trains were often the target of enemy action and Eric was in the Royal Navy. She could not be left alone, and Arthur was regularly kept at home to be her companion. Violet tried to escape from reality through romantic fiction; she became an avid cinema goer and wanted to believe that the great romances were true. Arthur accompanied her perhaps as many as three times each week, but Violet was not able to escape, and her mental and emotional stability became increasingly fragile.

Arthur senior's background was no less difficult. Betsy, his mother was small and bent in her old age and ended her hard life in St. John's Hospital, Peterborough, which had been the workhouse. Her father died just before her birth to Mary Lilley in Helpston in 1873. Betsy was a domestic servant before she married Thomas Andrew Chambers in 1896. Thomas was born in Orton Waterville in 1876; his father Charles was described in 1881 as a retired farmer and living in Orton Waterville, but by 1891, the family had moved to Fletton and Charles was a land surveyor while Thomas was described as a boat builder's apprentice. It appears that Betsy mirrored the pre-marriage experience of Lavinia in that Arthur senior's elder sister, Mabel, was born in 1894. His older brother arrived a year after the marriage and Arthur senior arrived in 1900. One year later, Betsy was recorded as the head of the family. Arthur senior believed that his father went to Canada and also said that his father promised to return or send for his family when he had made some money! Of course, he never did, and his wife and children remained in poverty. Betsy kept the family together and was employed by a local laundry well into old age. Arthur senior worked after school and at weekends to help support the family. When he was 11 years old, he was offered a scholarship to the King's School and a place in the Cathedral choir. Poverty prevented him from taking up the scholarship and he left school as early as possible to work at Baker Perkins. The factory was near the railway which held Arthur senior's heart. He had no interest in factory work and, after a very short time was told to go and get a job on the railway. He began as a cleaner, progressing to fireman status and finally reaching his ambition to be a driver. He was an able man and had ambitions to take a bigger part in politics but the pressures at home made his ambition impossible.

Arthur senior in his favourite position

Arthur and his Mother

Arthur had academic potential but did not reach it. Violet over protected him, perhaps it was a way of compensating for her guilt over her feelings at his birth. Any little cough or cold became a major illness; he was regularly confined to bed or kept indoors for long periods and missed the opportunity to learn to relate to his peers. Without friends of his own age, he spent time with a retired policeman, who lived nearby, and became interested in gardening. Arthur's absences from school through his own 'illnesses' were equalled by those caused by Violet's increasing obsession with her health. Although he learned to read before he was five years old, he left school having achieved little of note. Arthur senior did not have the time or the inclination to take an interest in his activities and he spent most of his time listening attentively to the stories which Violet wove about the life she wished she had. Arthur shopped for Violet and ran errands for his grandmother and aunts and saw very confusing models of women. He witnessed a domineering grandmother, submissive aunts, an unhappy wife and an over-protective mother.

Arthur tried to be the son Violet desired and obeyed all her whims. He also wished to gain the approval of Arthur senior by following in his footsteps and found work on the railway where he began on the lowest rung, as an engine cleaner, a very dirty job, and he failed on two counts. Arthur had not learned any practical skills and got dirtier than all the other young employees. Violet complained about the state in which he arrived home and also that her health prevented her from coping with washing overalls. Arthur and the railway parted company and he obtained work at a local sweet making factory, but with little more success. Violet made constant demands and despite the fact that there was not enough time, insisted Arthur return home for lunch every day. She did not want to be alone. The result was that he was frequently criticized for being late. Violet had no comprehension of Arthur's predicament; she was completely obsessed with her 'illnesses' and wanted medical attention constantly. She was insistent that Arthur collect her prescriptions even when it led to more problems over time keeping. Arthur felt he had no support from Arthur senior and decided to escape the situation by following his brother into the Navy. He applied in secret. He knew there would be recriminations if his plan was discovered. While Arthur was awaiting a reply, Violet's demands continued and, on one particular day, she told him that he must collect her pills as she needed them desperately. Arthur refused because of the warnings that his lateness would not be tolerated and said he would get the medication after work. Heated words were exchanged; Violet was tearful and accused Arthur of being unkind and uncaring. Arthur was guilt ridden and, after work purchased fruit as a peace offering and planned what he would say to lift her spirits.

On nearing home, Arthur was surprised to see it in darkness. Violet should have been there. He entered by the back door and put on the light. He looked at the clock, a clock he later wanted to destroy, and saw that his mother had been baking but she was not in the kitchen. He went into the hall. His mother was there. She was dead on the stairs. She had hanged herself with a scarf that Arthur had persuaded his aunts to give him. He had wanted it because its decoration with flags represented a naval connection. Arthur acted in a daze, he went to a neighbour who accompanied him back to the house, cut the scarf and contacted Arthur senior. Arthur was hustled out of the house, he was 16 years old, he had been with Violet constantly and yet he was denied any part in her death. He was thought too young to give evidence at the inquest and was not able to say goodbye. He concluded that everyone believed he had been responsible for his mother's death and never came to terms with the suicide. The day after Violet's death, the reply from the navy arrived and Eric took it upon himself to return the application forms with the message that Arthur was no longer interested in joining the service. This treatment added to Arthur's lack of self esteem. Perhaps Arthur senior thought he was protecting Arthur from bad memories, by preventing him from returning home but Arthur hated living with his aunt and had increased feelings of guilt. He decided that he must get away from Peterborough and reapplied to join the navy and was accepted.

On 15th May 1949 Arthur took himself to Derby after a brief and unhappy farewell from Arthur senior and was thence transported to HMS Ganges, the boys' training establishment at Shotley in Suffolk. He did not find naval life easy; his lack of self esteem made him the butt of 'the group'. He did not fit in well on any ship, although he tried hard to be 'jack the lad' on HMS Barfleur and perhaps achieved reasonable relationships during that deployment. Included in his mementoes, Arthur kept cards and menus on which friendly Christmas messages were written. His naval career began to be dogged by health difficulties as early as the Korean War, when he had to be removed from his ship which was due to proceed to the Far East. He had a severe chest infection. Not many years later, when serving in Scotland, his emotional condition was very delicate. He had financial difficulties which, had they not been solved, would have led him to serious thoughts of suicide.

11th April 1955

Arthur chose a naval colleague as his best man and was delighted that the wedding day had arrived. He did not have any doubts about what he was doing. The design of my dress was copied from the cover of an Australian Woman's Weekly and was made by Mrs Cree, a dressmaker, who lived in Willesden Avenue in Walton. She also made blue and white voile dresses for the bridesmaids, blue for Ann my cousin and Mary my friend, and white for Barbara, another cousin, and Clare, a cousin from Arthur's family. My veil and headdress were borrowed from Doris and the flowers ordered from Eames, a local firm of florists, whose service proved a disaster. I wanted camellias, which could not be supplied, and I had to be satisfied with arum lilies. Furthermore, the bridesmaid's floral headbands were forgotten which necessitated unsatisfactory ribbon headbands being hastily manufactured as a substitute. The reception was held at Farcet Infant School with the catering in-house! The horseshoe shaped cake, which we cut with Arthur's divisional officer's sword, was made by Fowlers, a local bakery firm where Arthur worked part-time when on leave. (I had also been employed by the Misses Fowler in the family grocery shop in Dogsthorpe Road during a vacation from college – Arthur had arranged it!) My 'going-away dress' was also made by Mrs Cree and was of sea blue turquoise brocade, over which went a pale greenish coat with tan hat, bag and shoes. We travelled by train to London and at the station Jess had beer in the back of his van and encouraged his colleague postmen to join in the celebrations. We stayed for the wedding night at Mrs Pratt's bed and breakfast establishment, where boyfriends, including Arthur, and families of Whitelands' students stayed when visiting Putney. Brussels was the city of choice by Arthur for the honeymoon and we flew on Sabena, a Belgian airline now long defunct. My choice had been Paris, but Arthur was not happy to agree because I had already visited it. We enjoyed the sights of Brussels, particularly 'le manikin', but Brussels doesn't have the same romantic ring as Paris.

A Slow Boat to China

After the Brussels sojourn, I was once again teaching the children with learning difficulties under the eye of everyone and constantly interrupted but supported by no-one, while Arthur returned to Scotland. I expected that this pattern of life would continue but later in the year Arthur obtained or wangled an accompanied draft to Hong Kong. It was, for me, the greatest adventure and I am very grateful that I had the experience of a long sea journey, but I am equally aware that Arthur wanted me to himself. He really believed he could mould me into the wife of his dreams. We left England on the troop ship H.M.T. Empire Clyde on 30th November 1955 just seven months after we married. The 30-day voyage began at the long-disappeared Peterborough East Station, but we nearly didn't get there! The taxi firm forgot to collect us, and the train was caught by the skin of our teeth. The luggage was thrown into the train compartment and then into RN transport in Liverpool to be taken to the docks. We took a taxi and boarded the ship early in the afternoon and the Empire Clyde sailed while we were eating dinner!! My homesickness kicked in at that point and lasted as we sailed southwards through the Irish Sea, passing the Scilly Isles and the flashing Bishop Rock lighthouse: the last sight of home for two and a half years. Sea sickness took the place of homesickness as the ship sailed into the Bay of Biscay.

Once food could be consumed again it was necessary to come to terms with the rigorous rank discrimination. On board there were officers and their ladies, non-commissioned officers and their wives and lower ranks and their women! We came in the last group, and I was put in a cabin with Mavis Beasley while Arthur was with the other 'low-level service personnel' which meant he could only access the third-class lounge which should have been named the steerage facility and was the evening venue. No entertainment was immediately provided, but after a week some was grudgingly permitted. It appeared to be the kind of activity that the officer in charge imagined the incumbents of this space would expect – tombola, whist, and films. Despite my low-class position and my limited expertise as an infant teacher, I was given the job of teaching this age group on board the ship. I continued in this role until we reached Singapore two days before Christmas and completed my employment with a Nativity play, the first of many down the years. The mothers of the children, I believe, saw my efforts more as a baby-sitting service than an educational experience and removed the children from the classes, probably rightly, if there was something more interesting. They were also less than enthusiastic for their children to attend classes when in the Red Sea. The heat inside the ship became so intense that neither pupils nor teachers had energy for schoolwork.

H.M.T. "EMPIRE CLYDE"

When the Empire Clyde turned left into the Mediterranean Sea, I expected clear skies, sunshine, and blue water but the weather remained grey and the sea choppy. Mist hid the Rock of Gibraltar, although it was possible to make out the coasts of Tangiers and Algeria. Luckily the Mediterranean gradually cheered up and I began to believe it was always blue and the sun always shone! The African coast, which appeared to rise sheer out of the sea into a range of mountains, remained in view briefly, and as we sailed eastwards my naiveté, and insular childhood and teenage began to show. I found the loss of a regular half an hour of sleep an enormous challenge and worried that I would not get my time back for more than two years! Port Said brought a welcome letter from home and I eagerly watched the pilot arrive on board to take control of the ship. From the first-class boat deck, I had a good view of the statue of Ferdinand de Lesseps and the headquarters of the Canal Shipping Company as the ship edged into port. My impression of Port Said was that a sickly smell hung over it which covered up 'filth' and that most of the inhabitants lived in ramshackle boats which they rowed in what, I described, as a 'typical' Mediterranean way. I was a real innocent abroad! The ship came alongside near the entrance to the Suez Canal beside the oiling berth and began to take on oil. Water was also taken on board, and I found it unpalatable. The local traders, whom I decided reeked of garlic, swarmed over the decks, and set up their stalls from which Arthur and I purchased the famous pouffe and which, in the fullness of time, became the container for the correspondence between us. I also bought a handbag and a brooch with a decoration of elephants, but refused to pay for the previous Sunday's English newspaper because the trader was asking 11 pence for it which I believed was extortion. Along with the traders a 'gully-gully' man began to do his magic tricks and the children, and I thought him wonderful.

The convoy through the Suez Canal moved off at about half past eleven at night and the Empire Clyde was the lead ship. I was excited as I watched the preparations get underway. A search light was high on the ship to light the way and members of the Egyptian army and police were on board for the duration of the passage of the canal to ensure the convoy was not impeded by any dissident groups. The people we saw standing along the banks were not enthusiastic spectators of a British troop ship but only one expressed his displeasure by exposing parts of his anatomy I did not wish to see. And I had believed that the world loved the British! By four o'clock the next day the ship was out of the Suez Canal, had dropped the pilot, the security guards, and the traders. The passage had lasted 16 hours which had included anchoring for three hours during the night and two hours at about mid-day in the Bitter Lakes to allow the north-bound convoy to pass. Port Suez at the southern end of the Canal, a smaller edition of Port Said with the same sights and smells had been left behind so had the Anzac Memorial, the British Consulate, and an anchored troop ship, which briefly brought on the homesickness. It was waiting for a convoy so that it could continue its voyage home. In the darkness, the banks of the Canal reminded me of Farcet Fen but in the day the desert, palm trees and camels and distant mountain ranges were much more exotic, although the people lived on small, cultivated patches and their homes I described as shacks and wrote that they were, 'disgusting, revolting and shocking'. The one big disappointment was that not one of the pyramids was visible, but the signal stations placed at intervals to ensure the convoys travelled at regular intervals could not be missed. An awful experience began at Port Suez. A woman came on board and joined my companion, Mavis, and me in our cabin. She was argumentative and regularly drunk. In the end she was removed from the cabin, but the episode caused me some distress.

The ship headed into the Red Sea and as it did, so the heat increased. It was essential to be on deck to feel comfortable and at half past six in the morning on 4th December 1955 we anchored in Aden. It was not possible to go ashore until nine o'clock, so we watched the oil pipe being attached to the ship and the refuelling begin with B.P. oil. That reminded me of home. Entertainment for the spectators began when the 'bum' boats arrived. I had never imagined anything like them. The boats were manned by traders who supplied everything of which you had no real need! You shouted down and asked the trader for what was of interest. He then passed up the desired item in a raffia basket for inspection. You, in turn, sent down the money or returned the item in the basket. At the prescribed time we went ashore, and Aden was a whole new experience. I had never imagined such a barren place, with sun baked rocks towering to great heights. Water was scare and we saw it being distributed by a camel-drawn water cart. We were told that it hadn't rained since 1933; I have no idea if that was true. The houses were very white and seemed to increase the barrenness as they reflected the sun's rays. The heat was intense and the men very black. They wore turbans and long brightly striped robes although those working for western firms were in overalls. Mostly they went bare foot or had rough heavy sandals. Many sat in lines on their haunches, no doubt waiting for work. Few women were on the streets, and most were completely veiled. We wandered the streets and looked at the shops which I found very strange, but almost resisted making any purchases because many items were imported from Hong Kong! We did, however, buy Christmas presents, a Ronson lighter for Arthur - he continued with his smoking habit and an elephant ornament for me. Before we returned to the ship, we sampled some beer and lemonade and paid with a pound. After a long wait we received our change! Things were cheaper then! Once back on board, the ship was soon heading into the Arabian Sea and for the next six days the sea was calm, the skies blue and the sun hot. The most north easterly point of Africa was just visible and there were some flat jungle, covered islands, one of which boasted a white lighthouse on the coast, but nothing else.

The arrival in Colombo in Ceylon was delayed until half past four in the afternoon on 20th December and we left the ship about half an hour later in a small launch which was not only difficult to get on and off but bounced across the very rough water. Once on land we found a guide, who took us first to the Army and Navy Stores to buy souvenirs. I was too innocent to realise that this was normal practice of guides everywhere. Take the punters to a place where rewards on their percentage spending are available! I bought a wooden elephant for five shillings, an amethyst ring for 30 shillings and some postcards - not a great return for the guide. The elephant survived but not the 'valuable ring'. A tour of Colombo followed, which included the Parliament House, the Town Hall, and the area where the European expatriates lived, obviously the smartest spot. The Buddhist temple was also on the itinerary, and I was surprised that I had to remove my shoes before we were taken around by a temple assistant. It was the first time I had come face to face with a Buddha and I found its colour and size overwhelming but not likeable. We were given a temple flower and told that the tree outside the temple was the one that the Lord Buddha sat under and received enlightenment. To stress the veracity of the story a coconut oil lamp was burning under the tree. Unfortunately, there are other trees in other places about which the same claims are made. Visitors can believe what they want. On the way to our last call, a café, we passed a group of carol singers, but it was almost impossible to believe Christmas was upon us. The meal was good but very English - steak, egg, tomatoes, and chips. Why didn't we take advantage of where we were and eat a local dish? I don't think I realised it was possible. Just as we were about to return to the ship, our guide presented us with bananas and a pineapple, which we enjoyed on the way towards the next port of call, Singapore.

Sailing time between Colombo and Singapore was five days and the first two brought unpleasant weather, a rough grey sea caused the ship to roll, and sea sickness again became a problem. The ship was decorated for Christmas which made everywhere look festive but made me think of home. I had never been away from my parents before at Christmas. The weather improved gradually and by Christmas Eve, it was warm and sunny, and, in the afternoon, the men dressed up as pirates for the children's party and a good time was had by all. Christmas dinner was served to the children and Father Christmas distributed presents with the help of the pirates. The evening was taken up by carol singing and celebrating. Some celebrated rather too much! On Christmas morning I received presents and Arthur, and I went to church. We had been regularly on the voyage, but this was a special occasion. The purser did not pray so excessively for the ship. I don't know if the reason was Christmas or whether he thought the prayers were being answered and Hong Kong was on the horizon. The lunch was disappointing being boiled beef and beans, but the evening dinner made up for it. Everyone dressed up and Arthur and I were permitted to eat together – the first time since leaving Liverpool – and the food came in mountains. During the meal Singapore was reached and the pilot came on board to take the ship in to the entrance of the harbour where we anchored for the night. Mail arrived with the pilot, and I had a pile but nothing from Con which was very disappointing. I consoled myself with mince pies, made by the baker with mince meat we had in our luggage and Christmas cake which had also been carried from home. Even after the huge meal we managed a few mouths full.

Boxing Day came early, breakfast was at six o'clock and Arthur and I were first to leave the ship, which was berthed by the quay, and were taken by army lorry to the Britannia Club, otherwise known as the NAAFI, where we ate a meal. Once again, we stuck to a grill and chips! Why? I found Chinese food revolting. I knew nothing about the world. We crossed the Singapore River, saw the Raffles Hotel, the cathedral and had photographs taken on the Padang. I found the living conditions of the poor Chinese whether on land or on the water difficult to accept. We were back on board by six o' clock when we sailed and headed into the South China Sea on the last lap of the journey. The day had not seemed like Boxing Day, and I wrote, 'How could it? Me riding in an army lorry in Singapore'! My experience had been so limited. The Empire Clyde took until New Year's Day 1956 to reach Hong Kong and New Year's Eve spoiled a voyage that was ending on a good note. The officer in charge would not permit us low class travellers to have the facilities to celebrate and sent the troops to bed. Such high-handed behaviour would have caused a mutiny today. Perhaps the most important legacy of the voyage to Hong Kong was Alison's name. I became fond of a little girl of about three years who was on board. Her name was Alison, and I chose to employ it nine years later.

Twenty-eight Peacock Road

On board the Empire Clyde, we became acquainted with Wally, who was in the army, and Dorothy, his wife, and, when we arrived in Hong Kong, we went to live with them. The arrangement lasted only a few weeks and we rented a flat in the same block at North Point, which, at that time, was a settlement separate from Wanchai and Shaukiwan. The colony was much less crowded than it was to become and low-rise buildings were in much evidence. The two tallest buildings were the Hong Kong and Shanghai Bank and the Bank of China, the latter slightly taller than the former because it was a later structure and China wanted to prove it was not to be outdone by the British. The only public transport to the Peak, the highest point of Hong Kong, was the tram and at the summit there were no tourist shops or stalls. Some countryside remained on Hong Kong Island and the New Territories were sparsely populated and farmed. A train service ran from Kowloon to the Chinese border and army camps were situated in the territories. Twenty-eight Peacock Road, our flat faced sheer cliffs where the rock had been blasted to create building space. It contained a living room, two bedrooms, a bathroom, kitchen, and an amah's room and was basically furnished. I was quite the dutiful housewife and made curtains and chair covers as well as cushion covers. We bought an American fridge of which I was inordinately proud. The purchase of crockery and pots and pans was essential, and we chose some green Pyrex-type tableware for every day. How could I have used my money for it, it was horrible! The 'best' china, white with a pale green rim, was elegant and I would use it today if it had survived. Breakage was not the fate of the Wedgwood tea set, however, and more than 50 years later it remains intact and almost unused. A 'lucky-lucky man' (a travelling salesman with a pack) called regularly and I bought far too many items, most of them non-essential! Camphor wood chests and carved furniture were obtained from local shops, and one wasn't enough for me, I had to have two and a table to match. Charlie Tseung with whom I kept in contact until his death worked in the local grocery store named Lin Chan's and where we shopped. Charlie liked to advise us on our purchases, but his wine advice was not expert because we regularly bought Blue Nun and thought it quite the height of sophistication.

Arthur's work at HMS Tamar was largely office bound and as well as the British naval staff a number of locally entered Chinese naval personnel were employed and Arthur made good relationships with them! Ships of other nations used Hong Kong harbour and at Christmas 1956, Dutch ships arrived and Hans, a sailor on one of them and his friend spent the day with us and from the brief acquaintance a long-term friendship developed with Hans. I needed to teach, I had no interest in the usual activities of naval wives – coffee mornings and chattering. I obtained a post at Victoria School, where I had the R.N. Commodore's daughter in my class and was slightly in awe of the rank. The staff were supportive and the head teacher, Leslie Hogan, easy to work with. Marion Peat and Maureen Clark were two colleagues with whom I have remained in contact since that time. A Black Watch Major was the education officer and I fell in love, not with him but with his tartan. As a locally entered teacher my salary was much less than those teachers who were employed from the U.K.

In one month, however, these second-class teachers received a substantial pay rise, and I bought my string of cultured pearls, with a real pearl clasp more expensive than the string! I always wanted pearls, but Arthur was unhappy; he believed they would bring tears. Perhaps they did eventually.

On 1st July 1957, David was born at the British Military Hospital. His impending arrival had been somewhat of a surprise to me because there was no discussion about a family. Indeed my 'family' was a blow-up doll and a little teddy bear, but Arthur took a unilateral decision and left me to cope alone with nights of sickness and school to face in the morning.   The pregnancy was kept a complete secret and everyone in England disbelieved the telegram, which was delivered, announcing the arrival of David William.

Contents of the telegram announcing the birth of David

Indeed, Jess checked with the Royal Mail to ensure the message was not a hoax. At the time of David's birth, children of naval personnel were registered in Hong Kong and did not have a British birth certificate. Fortunately, when he was about six years old the opportunity arose for him to be issued with a British birth certificate. Without the correct documentation he would have experienced all kinds of difficulties once Hong Kong reverted to Chinese control. David was baptised at Hong

Kong cathedral, wearing a long Christening gown. Arthur's colleague, Bill with John and Joan Taylor were his godparents. A celebration followed the service, and the Christening cake was complete with a stork. The worst experience of David's babyhood for me occurred when I awoke to find cockroaches running over him while he slept in the green metal cot we purchased for him and for which I dutifully sewed a quilted pale green eiderdown. I must have had a green phase during the pregnancy!!! His pram was provided by Charles and Vera Kuo, who we met through the Farcet neighbours of Herbert and Doris. Charles was the son of a Chinese industrialist who met Vera from Halifax while he was studying textile manufacture in the U.K., and they became very helpful and kind friends. It was strange having a baby to look after, but of course I went back to school and David was left with Lin, the amah. She cared for him excellently, probably better than I would have done. At Christmas 1957, David's first, we loaded him with gifts, and Eric, Arthur's brother, came from New Zealand on a visit. Arthur was beside himself with joy as the time approached for Eric's arrival, he seemed to worship his brother. I think, on reflection, that Eric was dismissive of Arthur, he certainly gave me to understand that he was the far more experienced and able brother. He definitely wasn't!

I regret that we did not take all the opportunities Hong Kong offered. Arthur was very reluctant to go to the beaches or the outlying small islands and we spent most of our time on Hong Kong Island, although we took part in naval social events and spent our leisure with a small circle of friends. I had teacher friends, but I was not able to socialise with them. We returned to England in July 1958 after two and a half years in the colony, rather longer than the usual naval posting but I would not leave school until the end of term. Packing began some months before departure because we had collected so many belongings. I deserted my beloved fridge, but we still needed 12 or13 packing cases to be returned to the U.K. by Sea. We travelled back to the UK by air on British Overseas Airways Corporation, a predecessor of British Airways. Life had moved on in two years and servicemen and their families were no longer moved by sea and we boarded the BOAC plane with few concerns about the journey. At that time planes had to make regular refuelling stops and we touched down at Bangkok, Bombay, Basra, and Frankfurt. Bombay was an overnight stop, and it was there that our worries began. Our room was burgled, and David was becoming unwell. On the Sunday before we left, we went to the beach and David probably put some sand in his mouth and acquired a bug. By the time we neared Basra, he was very ill, and the airline arranged for a doctor to meet the plane. David had developed gastro-enteritis and needed immediate medication. Without it he may not have reached Heathrow. The doctor was an Iraqi with the result that I can never feel antagonism towards the people of the Middle East. The medicine worked well and when we landed in London David was improving but we were whisked through Customs. Bill and Con met us in the old green van and Con had a flask of Horlicks; she gave David a good drink and he never looked back. However, I caused him some distress not long after we arrived back at Hazledene. The weather became cool, and I put socks on his feet to keep him warm. He continually kicked off one of the socks, so I fixed it with an elastic band! He cried loudly and long, and I decided he must see a doctor. I took off the sock and found the problem. The elastic band had restricted his circulation! What a mother! After this mishap, he continued to do well and celebrated his first birthday with Barbara on her birthday. Arthur was determined that he and I should go to the Channel Isles. Mum and Dad looked after David which we did, but perhaps it was not right to leave him when he had just arrived from Hong Kong.

Life with cars

Soon after arriving back in England, Arthur and I decided we needed a car although neither of us was able to drive. Arthur, innocently, went out and bought a grey car – make long since forgotten. Bill took one look at it and decided correctly that Arthur did not have enough knowledge to make a sensible choice and was insistent that, if we were determined to buy a vehicle, it should be reasonably up-to-date and reliable, and advised that NXL 788, a Morris Oxford, met the criteria, and indeed it did. Bill was the driver until Arthur and I had become qualified drivers. Arthur was determined to pass his test before me and applied for the examination long before he was competent. He had already tried to drive a van at Fowler's bakery and had crashed it into the doors and, not unexpectedly, failed his test. He passed the second time but never became a driver with any feeling for the engine! I also failed my first test, but I had an excuse. I took it shortly before Jono was born. My second test was a month later when he was about two weeks old, and I had problems. I had been to the hospital for treatment for a breast abscess and did not care whether I passed or failed. I passed! NXL proceeded to give very good service and never let us down despite the fact of our inexperience and ineptitude. My first long drive, very soon after gaining my licence, was to Portsmouth. I was taking David and Jonathon to the house at Eastleigh. Con was with me, and a funny incident occurred, although I was more embarrassed than amused at the time! Learning to drive in Peterborough meant there were few opportunities to practise the important skill of hill starts. Unfortunately, before the construction of motorways, the route to Portsmouth passed the Ascot Racecourse where traffic lights were situated at the top of a steep incline with an immediate right turn. I arrived at the lights, stopped and then, when I had the right of way, stalled the car at least three times! A lorry headed a queue of vehicles behind me and after the third failure the driver leaned out of his cab and in a tired voice commented, 'How many more b--- times!' I was most put-out, but it did make me get away on the next try!! At Eastleigh, we garaged NXL at a friend's house where it was difficult to manoeuvre into the entrance and one of us scraped the wing! NXL took us to Devon for a holiday at Budleigh Salterton, during which we visited some of the nearby beauty spots and other seaside towns. David and Jonathon were very young but enjoyed playing on the stony beach. When we left the West Country the journey to Peterborough was completed in very wet weather which made for difficult driving, but NXL did not falter. The worst event with NXL was my accident; I was driving along Palmerston Road when a child and a dog ran into the road and into the side of the car. Fortunately, he hit the body behind the front wheels so was not hurt, which was a great relief, but he spent the night in hospital, and I had a night of concern.

When we said goodbye to NXL, a blue A40, PEG128, took its place and I made my first drive north to Newcastle. Con and I took David and Jono to visit an auntie who I think was related to the first wife of Grandad Garfield. During our stay we went to Alnmouth where the boys loved playing with the huge seaweed. Just before Alison was born the blue A40 was exchanged for a second A40. This time the colour was white but its life with us was brief, it had to go before we went to Singapore. I sold it for less money than its value and the salesman gave me an IOU for £200 which was never redeemed because he was no longer selling cars when we returned home. Immediately, on arriving in Singapore we obtained a blue Cortina. It proved that Arthur and I were, indeed, bereft of car buying ability. It was a disaster! The car started only when it chose and most times the driver turned the key endlessly with no results. Bravely, we decided to drive it up the east coast of Malaysia; the bullock carts caused Alison great amusement. The road went through rubber plantations, pineapple farms and the jungle. On the return drive, the ill-fated Cortina skidded off one of the wooden jungle bridges. Luckily no one was hurt, and we travelled the rest of the way to Singapore in a lorry that was transporting huge trees from the jungles of northern Malaysia or Thailand. On reaching Johore Bahru, I needed to visit the toilet and resorted to the facilities at a garage. I hope never to use a toilet in that condition again! No where in the world have I experienced such a lavatory not even in China. The Cortina was not to be trusted and we purchased a mini which served us well until our departure from the Far East.

We acquired a dark blue Morris estate car when back in the UK but by the time Arthur was in Fulborn Hospital, the blue Morris had been exchanged for a green Morris 1100 saloon. This vehicle covered the distance between Peterborough and Cambridge two or three times a week. The roads were not as direct as they became later, but the traffic was much less. A14 nose-to-tail journeys were a future nightmare! On one occasion, however, ice and snow in Broadway Yaxley caused me to brush another car. No real damage was done but I was not happy until the minor scratch was repaired. After the 1100, a Maxi was the car of choice, and it took us to Devon. Two British Leyland Marinas followed; the first an acid green 1800 then a maroon 1300. The acid green vehicle was a TC with the kind of engine I liked while the second was not at all nippy. Both were problems. They were manufactured at the time when British Leyland workers were out on strike more than they were inside the factory. The green one was temperamental, and starting became a major problem. Once at St. Thomas More School when it refused to start, Bill came to the rescue, but he was saved major work. Indeed, he did not do anything; it came alive as he approached it! The maroon one was no more reliable, and Leslie advised that a Japanese make would prove more reliable.

My sluggish Marina in Coneygree Road

I felt a traitor as I felt an obligation to buy British but the Datsun F11 was a gem. It behaved as a car should. I had just one problem on a very snowy morning when I had taken Arthur to work and was returning to Whittlesey. I reached Horsey Toll, and the car would not hold the road and slid towards an oncoming vehicle. Some damage was the result but no injury to either party. The little F11 was changed at Sycamore's in Stamford for a white Datsun Bluebird with a brown roof. It was the workhorse of the century. It did everything it was asked, and even after several years hard use, it made the journey to the south of France four times without a blip. Sycamore's Datsun franchise came to an end and the next purchase was made from a garage at Fenstanton. It was a second white Bluebird, E128GEG. On a journey to Reading from Petersfield, we came to a halt to allow a car in front to turn right and another vehicle, being driven from the airport by a tired driver, hit us in the rear. I was most perturbed, but the repair work was covered by the driver's insurance. The next car was a white Nissan Primera which was purchased in 1987 in the hope it would interest Arthur. Unfortunately, he was ill at the time and showed no interest. Indeed, he did not really understand what he was being told. In 1994, the Primera was changed, not in make or model, but in colour. British Racing Green was the choice, and I was delighted to purchase my personal M60BMC registration with my last expenses from Cambridgeshire. M60BMC was then attached to a third white Primera and Jono bought an old white BMW for his station trips, which was replaced by a red BMW and then by his very worst purchase of all, a red box of a VW Polo. I hated it so much! At this point Jono's habit of disappearing for hours on a Saturday began and a whole melange of vehicles came and went: a red BMW, a black Mazda, a black BMW, a silver BMW Estate, a blue BMW Estate, a red Mazda Estate, a black Mazda Sport, two black BMW Coupes and a stormy blue Mazda 6 Sport with a second stormy blue Mazda 6 Sport appearing after a year. Eight months later the stormy blue Mazda was abandoned and replaced with the same model but in black. A White Mazda 6, sport arrived but was quickly replaced by another white Mazda 6 sport which was taken to the Palace and used for Nicola and Alex's wedding.

In the Quad at Buckingham Palace about to receive my MBE from Prince Charles

Very quickly replaced by another white Mazda which was disliked from the arrival as it had a diesel engine, therefore a further Mazda 6 came, it was a good deal, but very soon was changed for an unwanted grey Alfa Romeo Giulietta. It was undesired and had noisy brakes, also it was backed into a wall. It was not kept long. A red Mazda 3 hatchback came next but at Christmas 2015, I hit a bus and Jono hit Alison's car when reversing at home. The vehicle was repaired but on its collection one of its wheels was not tight and the drive home was frightening. In February 2017 a bill arrived for the payment of the repair of the bus. A new version was obtained in September 2016, but has a little button to operate the usual handbrake. In November 2016, Jono set up the team at Sycamores BMW to allow me to collect a beautiful new BMW 440 car and I drove it home with much 'after' work around me. Fortunately, it was not harmed.

Portsmouth

On our return from Hong Kong, Arthur was posted to Portsmouth where he began a course in the hope of obtaining promotion to Yeoman of Signals. He worried consistently about his progress, but after many trials and tribulations his work was rewarded, and he changed his uniform from bell bottoms to a suit. I accompanied him to Portsmouth, and we lived in Twyford Avenue next door to the Portland Arms in North End. We were lodgers in the home of Mrs Pratt, a widow, where our accommodation was a bedroom, a sort of sitting room and a kitchen, which was really a conservatory with a leaky glass roof. We shared the bathroom with its ancient hot water geezer, and it scared me. It always seemed ready to explode and lighting it became a task too far. I did not enjoy cooking either. I was unused to gas cookers and this one was not only decrepit but unpredictable. Cooking difficulties were increased by the drips of rain through the leaks. I was lonely and did not enjoy being solely a wife and mother. I walked every day with David to the green area that overlooked Whale Island, the RN gunnery school, now the location of the roll on, roll off ferries. Sometimes I took David to meet Arthur at the dockyard gate from where we could see HMS Victory and it was then that I taught him the details of Nelson and the Battle of Trafalgar. After some miserable months, an opportunity arose for us to move to a detached house in Cosham, but the stay was barely a month; the owners wanted the house for themselves. We moved to a flat in Cosham where we met Mary and Peter. Although I had a friend in Mary and together, we enjoyed many activities, the life of a housewife did not suit me! I wasn't made for shopping and getting meals for the home-coming husband. Arthur on the other hand liked the idea very much. He believed I should be content with no more stimulation than that from television soaps and comedy shows!

At the end of 1959 Arthur joined the Royal Yacht and sailed to the West Indies with the Princess Royal. I returned to Peterborough where Jono was born in the Gables in Thorpe Road on 10th March 1960, a day when I had been cross and smacked David. I suffered terrible guilt because I left my sad little boy and came back with a new baby. I imagined David would hate me and reject his new brother! Arthur returned from the West Indies when Jono was about a month old and an unusually difficult time for the marriage ensued. I met Arthur at the station and thought that he would be pleased to see me and would want to know all about his new son, but he wasn't, and he didn't. He was totally off-hand and had no interest in anything concerned with family.

Jonathon (Jono) with my Dad (Bill)

I am certain that he had had a brief affair, but I was never able to find out the exact details. In May 1960, Arthur sailed again for the West Indies. This time Princess Margaret and Anthony Armstrong Jones were on board Britannia. It was their honeymoon trip. While the yacht was in the Thames, I tried to contact Arthur, and the operator did not believe that I had a legitimate reason for telephoning. After the completion of the honeymoon cruise, we went back to Portsmouth but not before Jono had been baptised at Farcet Church with Jess and Leslie as godfathers and Mary as his godmother.

We lived in a naval house at Eastney, complete with regulation furniture and bedspreads with an anchor design woven into the material. Arthur continued on the yacht and went on the annual autumn royal cruise to Scotland. He recounted, with some pride, that the crew had entertained the Royal

Family and he had presented Prince Charles with a lollipop. Bet and Jess made a short visit, and we enjoyed several excursions, although, during one to the New Forest, Arthur had one of his unfortunate moods, a precursor to many difficult periods. Florence, by this time known as grey granny, also came to stay which was a pleasant interlude. In October 1961, Arthur joined HMS Mercury, the main establishment for naval communications, in the heart of the Hampshire countryside. Memories of the many events at Mercury, were revived by a visit, in 2007, to Petersfield. Unfortunately, by this time Mercury was no longer a working establishment, but a sad, unused, and lifeless building, a sure sign of this country's shrinking naval power. Arthur was next on-board HMS Blake and I took David and Jonathon to Plymouth for a short stay while the ship was in port. We stayed in the most disgusting bed and breakfast. We couldn't eat the breakfast; I hid it in Jono's pram and disposed of it in a litter bin. Arthur was then drafted to HMS Corunna, and I left Portsmouth and returned to Farcet. We had decided to buy a house in Hampshire, and I needed to earn money for the purchase. At the time, Mary, Sally and Joan, my cousins, were pupils at All Souls' School in Manor House Street. Their mother, Auntie Bill spoke to Mr. Rogers, the head teacher, and before I could blink, I was teaching at Eastfield in what was a three-classroom extension of All Souls'. My class numbered 36 third year junior pupils. On my initial visit, I looked at some stories displayed on the walls, and was interested to read the beginning of one. It said, 'My name is Cornelius and I am a Roman centurion.' I thought that there were some imaginative children if they could think of names like that. I had not realized that I was in a Catholic school with many children of Irish parentage and Cornelius, the Roman, was Cornelius O'Sullivan.

All Souls' School

Life at school was more stimulating than life in Portsmouth and I felt a member of society again and David and Jonathon were content in the care of their grandmother. Despite class numbers, I recall the days being fulfilling, the teaching enjoyable and the stress imperceptible. Memories are of particular events and amusing incidents. When I first arrived, school dinners were cooked at St. John Fisher, the secondary school, adjacent to the three classes, and transported from the kitchens to be eaten in the classrooms. This was far from satisfactory as the smell of food was present for the afternoon and, it was decided that we must eat in the secondary school. Each lunch time teachers and children trooped to St. John Fisher and one day we arrived in the foyer to find that some mischievous student had put a half-smoked cigarette in to the mouth of the bust of St. John Fisher. It caused great amusement even for the teachers who should have known better. I hope that my arrival was not the cause, but the deputy head teacher announced his departure a few weeks into my first term. Brian Foy replaced him and as Brian was unable to drive, I picked him up each morning at the bus station. Brian was an excellent colleague as well as a brilliant musician and made school life more interesting. We became good friends and Arthur, and I, spent many enjoyable evenings with him and Margaret, his wife. While we were in Singapore, they moved to Somerset and on one of our visits to Frome where they settled, we had an adventure. I was driving on a dark wet November evening and somehow, I missed the way and ended up in a farmyard with straw blowing all around the car! Consequently, we were late for the Mediaeval Feast! During other visits, Arthur and I enjoyed the festivals of light, which are a winter feature in the west of England; there is nothing to equal them in East Anglia.

The Christmas concert featured highly at All Souls' School. It was staged in the Elwes Hall, a Catholic Church building, and it gave Mr. Rogers the opportunity to take on the persona of a theatre impresario. Every teacher swung into action to ensure that no child missed being a participant in the grand theatrical production. Each class was dragooned to do something: perform a play, sing a selection of songs, or give a display of some physical activity. These individual efforts continued for a seeming eternity, but they merely presaged the top-of-the-bill extravaganza – the Nativity play. It took the same form year by year! Angel Gabriel stood on a pair of steps, draped with white material, to announce his message, shepherds wore dressing gowns and head-dresses made from tea towels, while the fire that warmed them was a torch under red tissue paper. Mary and Joseph disliked one another and stubbornly refused to walk close together. The finale had the stage crowded with angels, singing an off key 'Gloria' and arranged precariously on P.E. benches leaning at angles with material clouds pinned to them. Baby angels from the reception class were in the crib and almost asleep because of the lateness. Inevitably, one made a puddle and became distressed, a situation which added to the delight of the performance. I was the director on more than one occasion, but Mr Rogers thought he was the fount of all knowledge where the Nativity was concerned and any of my ideas were very quickly rejected. I didn't know the story properly!!

Coneygree Road

Life at All Souls was much more preferable than the housewife role and, by September 1962, a decision about the future was necessary. David was five years old and had not started school. Arthur and I had already had doubts about the practicability of the house in the south, decided that it was a non-starter and cancelled the option and David began school at All Souls where he was settled and happy. It was, therefore, time to find somewhere to live near Bill and Con. One evening we were looking at bungalows being built in Stanground when a man appeared and said he knew where there was one for sale. When asked for details, he pointed to the bungalow nearby and said that he was the owner. Eventually, we purchased 243 Coneygree Road although getting a mortgage was difficult with only Fletton Urban District Council being prepared to loan the necessary finance. Large numbers of rabbits had lived in the area which resulted in the name Coneygree but, since childhood, I had always believed that it was synonymous with 'dirty' families! Living in the road taught me much about being non-judgemental! Arthur was delighted to be a homeowner and we planned the decoration and furnishing. One major task was to put coving in the sitting room, and during the work a part fell and hit me on the head and an obvious join remained as long as we lived in the bungalow. Arthur built a bookcase and later a bar, although he wasn't an expert handyman. The bar was my idea; I imagined it expressed sophistication! During one summer holiday I tiled the bathroom but I was not an expert tile cutter and the edging half-tiles were never to my satisfaction. A conservatory was added, the kitchen tiled, and the units painted pale blue and white, always my best colours. The furniture, chosen from shops that have long since disappeared, was of the time and had I not changed my ideas, it would have been desirable 'retro' in the 21st century.

Equipment which is considered essential in the 21st Century was not in 243 Coneygree Road when we moved in. There was no fridge and eventually when we purchased a very small model, I was excited. Telephone connections were not standard in every house and the way in which a telephone was obtained could be frustrating. An application was made to the post office and then a long wait ensued until an allocation was made. It was some months before we received an allocation and then the line was a party one, meaning we had to share with another household. It could be very annoying to pick up the receiver and find it was already being used. An unusual aspect of the bungalow was that locks were fixed to the tops of all the interior doors to protect the house, not from intruders but from Jono! He was a determined child to whom obedience was not his first thought. Early every morning, he was out of his bed looking for mischief and the locks prevented him harming himself or doing too much damage. He also refused to stay in his bed in the evening and a contest of wills developed between him and me! In the end, I put his reins on and fixed them to the metal frame of his bed. They defeated his wandering but in the high-profile days of child protection I might have been in trouble. Major changes to Coneygree Road came just before we returned from Singapore. Con and Bill constructed a room in the roof for David and Jono so that they had plenty of space in which to sleep and play. Stairs to the new room went from what had been a bedroom and became a dining room. Alison had the small bedroom and when a baby everything was pink including the cot which was decorated with a big rabbit. After Singapore, she developed very definite tastes and demanded an all-mauve colour scheme.

Alison Constance Chambers

The year Alison was born, 1964, the summer was beautiful, and the sun shone daily. Con and I took David and Jono to Hunstanton where we stayed in Bet and Jess' caravan. The boys had a really good time, digging in the sand, paddling in the sea, and becoming bronzed. Arthur senior visited and remained sartorially dressed in three-piece suit and leather shoes when he went on to the beach with his grandsons. In September, it was odd not going back to school, but Alison was born on 11th September. I was not eager to go to the Gables for the event and had determined to drive myself at the last minute. 'Oh', I said, 'I'll leave the car in the car park and Dad can fetch it'. Sylvia Bridge, a friend and wife of John Bridge who was my brother Leslie's friend from Perkins Engines and had been invited by Mum and Dad to live at their home in Farcet while I was in Hong Kong, arrived at Hazledene because it was her daughter Tracy's birthday and Sylvia insisted that she drive me. On arrival at the maternity hospital, I sat in the entrance hall and a visiting vicar came down the stairs, went to the door of a ward, stopped, turned around, came to me, and said, 'Be of good cheer!' I did not feel cheerful, and it was fortunate that a nurse came to me otherwise the birth would have occurred by the front door. Since that time Alison has always had definite ideas about what she should do and where she should do it. David was seven years old when Alison arrived and decided that on this auspicious day no-one was going to meet him from school and that he should walk home. Bill and Con were desperate when they discovered he was missing but he managed to negotiate the town and walk about three miles before he was found in Fletton Avenue. Arthur also had a memorable day; he was on HMS Troubridge in Malta and won at tombola. When the ship returned to Portsmouth, Alison was christened on board in the ship's bell. I went back to school as quickly as possible, and Con took on the care of Jono and Alison. Jono developed a great attachment to his grandma, which lasted to her death, and he loved their daily coffee breaks at Betty's Stores. Con accommodated his curiosity; he always wanted to know how things worked and his toys were taken apart very quickly. Maybe his destructive tendencies helped him towards his career.

Alison, David and Penny in Singapore

Singapore

In 1965 just before Alison had her first birthday, we flew to Singapore, which was then part of Malaysia, where Arthur was given a two-year draft. As a result, we were on the island at a momentous time in its history. In 1966, Prime Minister Lee Kwan Yew declared Singapore's independence from Malaysia. I was driving in the city at the time on my way to the dentist and there was no indication that anything out of the ordinary had happened. The city was as calm as on any other occasion. Many people in England believed this action would create problems and that Singapore would not survive separate from Malaysia. It was an opinion completely erroneous; Singapore has gone from strength to strength. We soon found a house in Jalan Bangau, next door to May and Joe Byrne, an RAF couple, with whom we became friends. Arthur's job included trips to sea as well as office work in the dockyard. His first trip to sea was just as we had unpacked and I was left to organize all the tasks connected with settling in a new country, which also unexpectedly included moving house. This situation meant that when Arthur returned, he did not know where he lived and had to search for his family! The situation caused him much distress and as time went by, he began to show signs of being unable to cope with the ups and downs of daily life. He began to complain of various physical problems and on several occasions was returned from the short exercises at sea because he was 'ill'. The new house was one-storey and detached with a living room, three bedrooms, kitchen, and dining room. A good-sized garden, completely grassed, surrounded the house and a 'garden boy' cut it regularly. A bougainvillea was growing over the front door, and it flowered continually for the two years we lived there even though Jono dug down to the poor thing's roots. The house was situated in Jalan Kechubong and backed on to the Yio Chu Kang, which was then a main road. The traffic was, when compared with road conditions 40 years later, light and it was very easy to hear the approach of a lorry, carrying a lion dance troupe as it travelled from venue to venue. The musicians beat out a loud rhythm on the drums and we ran to see the lion as it was held high and made to sway from side to side.

Naturally, I soon returned to school! I obtained a post at Nee Soon, an army school situated in the camp where the gurkhas were based and several gurkha children attended the school because they spoke English well. The building surrounded a central quadrangle where classes could enjoy outdoor practical activities. David and Jono did not come with me but went to school at RAF Seletar. They wore a clean school uniform every day, fawn shorts and white shirts, white socks, and sandals. The poor amah had plenty of washing! Most of their classrooms were open tappas, huts with roofs made of coconut leaves, which were cool. David was a well-behaved pupil whereas Jono was a problem child. His head teacher wrote notes, from time to time, describing his pranks. He particularly disliked Steven Sizeland who lived next door. Steven was an only child and spoilt, and Jono was frequently in trouble for poking or hitting him. Jono made friends with other boys, however, and Mr Knapp, a neighbour, became his hero. Bicycles were inexpensive and we bought one for each of them. Jono learned to ride very quickly. David took longer and fell into the monsoon drain many times before he became proficient. Later when he was riding his bike from Coneygree Road to Hazledene, he decided to read a book at the same time. Not a particularly sensible idea and he fell off once more but this time into the path of a double-decker bus. Good thing the bus had good brakes and an aware driver, or he might have been a squashed boy. A bad time for both boys was when they were in the hospital at RAF Changi for minor operations. Jono was a poor thing when he came home, and David was miserable because he was kept longer than expected; his wound was slow in healing. Alison was too young for school and was looked after at home by an amah. She adapted to Singapore weather and walked bare footed on the hot concrete, perhaps the cause of the size of her feet. Clothes were inexpensive and she had many pretty dresses, she was a dainty little girl at the time. Her prettiness did not extend to her behaviour at the church at RAF Seletar. She became famous for talking to the extent that the padre regularly took her out of the services.

In the summer of 1966, our Mini took us to Penang, an island on the northwest coast of Malaysia and on the way, we visited Malacca an old colonial town and very quiet! The ancient cannons remained pointing out to sea and David and Jono used them as climbing frames. As we drove through Kuala Lumpur, Arthur had one of his famous moods and threw the car keys at me. I believe I commented on his driving. We then reached the Cameron Highlands which in the days of the Empire were a retreat for the planters and administrators. The Highlands also proved a retreat for us from the heat of Singapore and we stayed two days at the government rest house and enjoyed the cool temperatures and misty mornings. We visited a tea plantation and watched the women nip the tea leaves off the bushes. What a task for a cup of tea! A ferry crossed the channel between the mainland and Penang, which, at the time, was rural and quiet. The sea and sand were beautiful and the hostel, run by the NAAFI, had a swimming pool. Jono persuaded us to buy him a blow-up plastic lobster which he loved and named Lommy. One day he and Lommy disappeared, and crisis mode set in. We imagined that he had gone to the beach and was lost in the sea, but he was by the pool giving Lommy a swim! We left Penang on the earliest possible ferry on the day of the return to Singapore so that the journey would be completed in one day. It was quite an achievement to cover 300 miles in a Mini with three children. Later at Christmas, Bill, Con and Arthur senior came to visit. We had almost a month together and it was most enjoyable. The time was filled with sight seeing and pleasurable activities. The latter included making the most of the excellent swimming pool at RAF Seletar. David and Jono had already learned to swim, although at times Jono could not go into the water because he had developed his ear problems. Con actually wore a costume and went into the pool but she did not learn to swim. Arthur's brother Eric also came from New Zealand, and the two Arthurs were delighted to see him while he again tried to portray himself as more worldly than any of us. At the end of their stay Arthur senior was delighted to return home. He was living at Easton-on-the-Hill with Muriel, who he had recently met, and wanted nothing more than being with her. Con did not, however, have a good homecoming. The day after she arrived, her mother Florence died in January 1967. She had been ill for some time with what must have been Alzheimer's disease which wasn't widely understood at the time and the last years of her life caused pain and frustration for her family.

Whittlesea/y

I will never know why an urge to move took over, but some time in the early 1970s we decided that we would sell 243. We looked around but could not find anything suitable. The answer should have been to stay where we were, but Leslie told us about a house for sale in Whittlesey. We looked and decided to buy, and, in the end, it was sensible because the Stanground area now has hundreds of newly built houses. The house was at Whittlesey and perhaps I was pulled there by my past although the connection to the town was much shorter than I believed; between 30 to 40 years rather than the generations I had imagined, although we attended St. Andrew's Church close to the street where John Boyden lived as a boy and where his funeral service was held. One hundred and eighty-two Peterborough Road was a house with four bedrooms on the first floor and space in the roof for more. On the ground floor a lounge and dining room with connecting louvred doors and a conservatory, a kitchen, utility room, a toilet and an integral garage provided living and parking space. Once again, we undertook extensive alterations; teak wardrobes were built in all the bedrooms, most of the roof space became two extra bedrooms and storage cupboards. An arch was constructed between the kitchen and dining room, a breakfast bar built in the kitchen, and bookcases in the conservatory. Alison went to Sir Harry Smith Community College (secondary school) and found a very successful niche. Unfortunately, the house gave me a strange sensation; I always felt as if I had not unpacked, was staying briefly rather than living there. Perhaps the awful spell of weather that prevented us from getting from Peterborough to Whittlesea was the last straw. We stayed at Longthorpe while Alison was alone in Whittlesea, and soon I was looking for another place to live. We moved to Alwalton on 19th November 1979.

St. Thomas More School

Mr Rogers wrote to me while I was in Singapore and asked me to return to Manor House Street to act as head of the infant school. The junior department had by this time been transferred to Eastfield in a new building, which incorporated the original three classrooms and named St. Thomas More School. This was an interesting interlude and children and teachers continued happily in the old building until, some two years later, St. Thomas More Infant department opened. Everyone transferred to Eastfield and the old All Souls was closed. A particularly sad aspect was my disposal of the two large statues which had dominated the corridor for most of the building's life. Once in the new building, life revolved around the wooden floor. Mr Rogers had become obsessed with maintaining the floors when he took over the junior school. No child was permitted to wear outdoor shoes, all were to have plimsolls. This situation caused footwear problems; either the children walked in sock feet when they lost their plimsolls, or they continued to wear them when worn out which put them in imminent danger of injury. Mr. Rogers was never persuaded to change his attitude towards footwear and even teachers were governed by the plimsoll rule. High heels, particularly those known as stilettos were banned. On one occasion I thought my heels were safe, but they were not, and I marked the floors and was never forgiven. Mr. Rogers had equally strong rules over boys' trousers and refused to allow them to wear long trousers. However cold the weather was or however red and chapped legs became, Mr. Rogers had no sympathy and resisted every request from mothers to permit legs to be covered. It did not matter if the 11-year-olds were as tall as the male teachers they were obliged to continue wearing short trousers. I think that he believed junior boys were children and should not be dressed as adults. Mr. Rogers' quirks extended beyond rules about pupils' dress and caused difficulties for teachers when they required particular materials for lessons. Stock was ordered and delivered on Fridays and had to include all the necessities for the following week and the issue of new pencils was based on the number of stubs returned! I caused displeasure by breaking longer pencil stubs into two to get a double issue of new ones. Once the deliveries had been made, stock cupboards were locked, bolted, and barred and the keys firmly attached to the key chain which hung from Mr. Rogers' belt where they remained unused for the next seven days.

Mr. Rogers and his wife, who was the school secretary, always ensured that they lost none of the school holidays. They left school on the day the term ended and did not return before the morning of school re-opening. Mr. Rogers had worked at Tamworth in Staffordshire and he spoke of it as if it was the centre of the world but Tamworth was out shone by Blairgowrie in Scotland, where the Rogers spent their holidays; that was heaven. Unfortunately, Mr. Rogers always came back with some educational idea to initiate; his most famous was perhaps the introduction of the Colour Factor, a development of the Cuisinaire system. Colour Factor came in the form of rods which were to revolutionise the teaching and learning of maths. The rods were of different lengths; each set was coloured differently and represented a digit from one to 12. The children were supposed to memorise the colours but were not to think of them as numbers. It was a nightmare! Even more of a nightmare was packing away the material. Each box had to be checked and any missing rod found. The major problem was the white rods, they were one-centimetre cubes and every time the lesson ended some had disappeared and every child dived on to the floor to look for them. It meant immediate death for the teacher if one remained lost! Topics were a popular area of the curriculum and Mr. Rogers was enthused to include all the classes in a travel theme. I was encouraged to become the sewing teacher and make a wall hanging depicting the history of aircraft. Examinations were part of the Rogers' educational philosophy and twice a year the children were subjected to them. The papers were properly set, and examination conditions imposed even for the young children. Included in the tests was Mr Rogers reading and poetry check. Every child read to Mr. Rogers and recited a poem. This latter had to be an individual effort and there was much muttering before the testing day arrived. The children had a cunning plan. They found a poem that was not too long to learn but not so short that Mr Rogers would criticise it for its brevity. Liking the poem was of little importance.

St. Thomas More School's morning assembly obviously had a Roman Catholic slant, but the children entered the hall in the same manner as the majority of schools, class-by-class. The school, however, had an up-to-the-minute sound system connected to the classrooms, about which Mr. Rogers was particularly proud and thus the entry had a musical accompaniment. At the end of the religious section, Mr. Rogers took on the role of quiz master and asked mathematical puzzles. They were the kind that began with 'think of a number' and continued with various numerical activities and the expectation that someone would arrive at the correct answer. Perhaps at times he ought to have asked the teachers because they all groaned inwardly at this part of the proceedings and hoped they would not be asked the answer. Mr. Rogers was also an enthusiast for whole school annual outings, but he was not enthusiastic over their organisation and handed that task over to other members of staff. These expeditions were in the days when charging was possible, so everyone went and paid for the pleasure. One year the school travelled to York, and everyone walked the wall in long crocodiles and visited the Minster. Eating was the most popular part of the day and filled much of the time; it began almost as soon as the coaches left the school and continued until the outing ended. My most memorable expedition was to Wicksteed Park; memorable because two of us took 80 infant children to a park which was then full of possible hazards. Legislation since that time would prevent such high numbers of pupils with so few teachers. Thankfully, there were no accidents. Either the children were more obedient than now, or the teachers had more control.

David

On the return from the Far East, David went into the Junior 4 class with Mr. Kuras as teacher, and during the year he did an 11+ examination and was allocated a place at Orton Longueville Grammar School. Coneygree Road was in Huntingdonshire, which still retained the 11+, although Peterborough had abandoned the examination. Arthur and I had grand ambitions for him and thought he should attend a public school. The attempts to obtain a place at such an establishment were unsuccessful and he began at Orton in 1967. He was a good average student but did not achieve the expected grades at A level and his desire to go to Trinity College Dublin was thwarted. He settled for a place at UEA and obtained a degree in European Studies, although it should have been in Guinness drinking. He had various jobs to earn money to supplement his meagre student grant one of which was as a grouse beater in Tomintoul in Scotland but that lasted about a day and a half. He did not find walking over grouse moors to his taste. He maintains that he hated his time at university and that he has learned more of value since leaving higher education, although he agrees he enjoyed his time at the University of Vienna doing a language course. Despite his low opinion of his education, I was proud of him when we attended his graduation. Jobs were in short supply at the end of his student days, but he found work at the post office in Whittlesey and then in Peterborough before he entered the civil service. As a result of his civil service post, he went to live in London and remained there until he moved to Reading.

**Jonathon playing with David and Alison in the room Bill and Con built
at 243, Coneygree Road**

In London, he joined the Royal Naval Reserve and met Jenny in the service. They married in April 1984 and Nicola was born in July 1989. Christopher followed in July 1991.

Jonathon

Jono also attended St. Thomas More, and his main claim to fame was acting as the caretaker's right-hand man although he enjoyed his time in Mr. Kuras' class where he got his first taste for electronics. Sister Anne was also a favourite teacher. The 11+ examination had ended by the time Jono was 11 and he followed David to Orton Longueville where he performed abominably. His peer group comprised of a large percentage of Italian heritage boys who were totally disinterested in school, and he took on the same attitude. His behaviour was questionable at times, and he played truant explaining that his class had been sent home as the result of teacher absence. I went to every open evening but not one teacher indicated that his attendance and work were abysmal. He served petrol at Longthorpe garage at the weekends, which increased his knowledge of cars and motor bikes and, most importantly, kept him away from his school contemporaries. He obtained two GCSEs and said his life's ambition was to be a chef. One day in a kitchen changed his heart's desire and he went to the Regional College where he managed to retrieve his failure and gained a number of GCSEs. The railway beckoned him once he had successful examination results and he went into the travel centre at Peterborough station, where he improved his knowledge of geography and became interested in accountancy. British Railways agreed to sponsor him on an accountancy course at the Regional College, but he applied to join the Royal Navy and was accepted although his hearing was doubtful.

Jono was an enthusiastic entrant to the senior service, but the enthusiasm disappeared quickly; physical activity was not his metier and he found that he enjoyed very little about the life. Academically he was successful. He received a captain's commendation for his work as an artificer apprentice which was fortunate as it gained him a place at the Polytechnic of Central London when he was discharged; his hearing was not good enough for the work for which he had trained. He obtained a first-class BSc. degree in 1985 with the award for the best student. He remained at the Polytechnic as a lecturer for a year but realised he would not complete a PhD if he continued to lecture. He gained a place at Peterhouse Cambridge in September 1986 but one year into his research he was forced to become Arthur's carer. After the emotional stress of that task, he could not return to Cambridge and worked at the TSB until he went to finish his course at Imperial College. He was awarded his PhD in 1990 with the graduation ceremony at the Albert Hall. He was elected as a Fellow of the Royal Academy of Engineering in 2012. In February 2014 Jono was awarded a Higher Doctorate from Imperial College with the presentation at the Albert Hall, David, Alison, and I were at the ceremony. Cubs and Scouts had played a big part in David and Jono's childhood. David became a cub in Singapore and after the return home the two of them joined Stanground troops. They camped regularly in England and in Europe, and took part in gang shows at the Embassy, an activity which meant many rehearsals in various venues where I waited for hours outside. David toyed with Venture Scouts, but Jono was unable to do so because we moved home. David's interest in football began in his teenage years and he travelled distances to see games. On one occasion he came home with a damaged face, an opposing team supporter had taken a dislike to him and hit him. One night he did not arrive home at all which put the family into a dreadful state of worry. The police were alerted, and he was found asleep in a railway carriage in a siding in King's Cross. Jono did not become a football spectator, he was too busy earning money to buy a vehicle, and at 16 purchased his moped and began the ownership of a long, long line of two-wheeled and four-wheeled modes of transport. He has come to enjoy football to an extent but can miss a game if there is a necessity.

Alison

Alison's school career began at Caverstede Nursey School where she lost her butterfly purse and holds, to this day, Betty Hay guilty for its disappearance. When Arthur was admitted to Fulborn Hospital at Cambridge, however, Mr. Rogers agreed she should attend St. Thomas More although she was not quite school age. Alison was always a social child and eager to make her mark. She fitted into any group except in Mr. Evans' class. He acted as if she had had special treatment while I was at St. Thomas More and that such a situation would not continue when I was no longer there. She continues to resent him. At the end of each school day, she walked from St. Thomas More to Eastholm Infants a stroll for which she had little enthusiasm. The streetwise children of the area gave her a hard time. In 1975, she transferred to Sir Harry Smith School where she blossomed. Her abilities were encouraged, and the problems of dyslexia were not allowed to knock her self-esteem.

Outside Hazeldene in Peterborough Road Farcet with Alison and the blue Morris estate

Her stated ambition was to become a WREN, but she excelled at all things practical, particularly sewing and after two years at the Regional College changed tack and gained a place at the London College of Fashion where she studied between 1982 and 1984. She then set up her business at Longthorpe in Con's back room. She specialised in making wedding and ball dresses and her work was excellent. A relationship with Richard Kaye changed the course of events, particularly as it ended at the time of Arthur's death. She closed the business, left Stamford, where she had lived with Richard and went to work in London immediately at Jeffrey Rogers and then at Coppernob. Redundancy followed with an economic downturn, and she returned to Peterborough where she worked at the Gordon Arms and at Sky TV until the local paper advertised available positions at BT. Her determination never to work in an office was changed and she became a Peterborough BT person where she was offered an opportunity in London and her BT career took off. She became a property owner and had working contracts in Madrid, Amsterdam and Dublin. In 2005, her BT life ended dramatically in voluntary redundancy. She had already purchased a 500-year-old cottage in Ashwell, Hertfordshire, and over time continuing to renovate it. A post at T-Mobile materialised which she then left. The end of the regular employment was somewhat 'pleasurable' and she started baking from home but this had financial limitations. Another possibility in Human Resources occurred which was at Papworth Hospital, and she later moved to the Lister Hospital in Stevenage. I thought she would not stay long but it has turned out interesting and enjoyable work.

David, Alison, and Jonathon, whom I referred to as D, J & A

Eastholm/Abbotsmede Infant School

During my time at St. Thomas More, I decided that I ought to further my career and, acting on a whim, applied for a head teacher position at the village school at Clare in Suffolk. I made the application on the assumption that no-one was ever offered the first post for which they tried but the interview would be good practice. Naturally, I was offered the post and was in a quandary. There was no way I could go to Suffolk, and I refused the offer! Then came one or two unsuccessful applications in Peterborough until my fate was sealed and I was appointed to Eastholm Infant School! I was to serve my time in difficult schools. On my first day in charge, I faced a baptism of fire when a child had an accident and received some nasty bruising. Fortunately, the parent was not difficult, and I was able to placate her. There was no special training or certification for head teaching in those days and I learned on the job. My mentor was Maurice Watson, the head of the junior school. He was very individualistic in his head teaching so perhaps I absorbed his bad as well as his good habits. I was so inexperienced that I found it difficult to understand that I could make changes. I even believed I could not dispose of the stick insects! A jar of these peculiar things was on a table, covered by yellow wipeable cloth outside the office, and I imagined I would have to look after them forever. Eastholm was opened in 1940 at the beginning of the Second World War and, indeed, it was fortunate that it had been near completion in 1939 or it would have remained unopened until 1945. The building was expansive with a long wide corridor running from the front door to the back. The classrooms opened off the corridor, and an extension at the rear consisted of three extra classrooms and a dining room. Towards the end of the 1970s I set up a nursery in a mobile on the field. From time to time, when there was need of an extra member of staff, Barbara came to fill the space and Rebecca was able to play with the children. It was an experience for her! The nursery was later incorporated into the main building which made it much more part of the school. Pre-school provision was essential in the area and rescued approximately 50 children annually from their favourite playground - the gutter.

The Eastholm catchment area was one of deprivation and the children were not well-nourished. They were generally smaller than their peers and often unkempt. Some parents were feckless with unusual lifestyles, and they were not averse to resorting to aggression. The children did not generally find learning easy but were mostly engaging although some resorted to low level petty crime in and out of school. Social workers were involved with the families daily, and case conferences a regular feature in my diary. On one occasion I went on a visit with social workers to the home of Verdun and his numerous siblings. Verdun was small, scrawny, scaly-skinned and was named after the First World War battle. The house was, according to the social worker, in an improved state, but it was largely without furniture and had no floor coverings, except dog faeces, and food was not obvious. In our comfortable life it is difficult to realise the way in which some children live. One Monday morning news was received that a pupil, a six-year-old girl, had been killed by a car in Hunstanton. It was a sad event and I found it strange to fill in the details of the accident in the admission register, but we managed the emotion that the death caused. Counsellors were not deemed necessary at the time. Educational outings, particularly those giving children experience of other cultures, were part of the curriculum and visits to different places of worship were arranged. One mother, who was also Mrs Chambers, came to protest about a visit to a Sikh Gurdwara and, after a long discussion, she asked me if I was a Christian. I replied that I tried to be. She stated, 'Oh! I thought you were a Catholic!'.

My office was a large room and, when appointed, I shared with the secretary which was not the most satisfactory of arrangements. Later, it was divided into two offices and redecorated in pink with floral curtains. Unfortunately, it was always cold; the radiators were not as big as they should have been, and the hot water was cool when it reached them. I purchased a picture of ploughing with shire horses. I liked it very much, but it did not last long; the school was burgled, the picture stamped on, and my fortune written on the walls. Life had not become technical or electronic; there were no computers and when I obtained the first photocopier it did not work properly! There was one telephone available in the office of Pat Rate, the secretary, and she typed everything that needed to look official. Eastholm could dull the brain and towards 1977 I decided that I needed some stimulation, and applied for a seconded year and gained a place at Kesteven College of Education to do a B.Ed. degree. Mrs Clarson who was a teacher at St. Thomas More had the same idea and we went together. I drove to the college at Grantham two or three times a week and we attended lectures, wrote essays, and finally sat examinations. It was difficult being a student again. I had become too used to being in charge and having my office and my facilities. I did not take easily to writing essays which were criticised and marked but I gained a 2.1 degree from Nottingham University. Bill, Con and Arthur came to the University for the Graduation Ceremony.

Later, in 1981, I began a part-time course at King's College, London for an M.A. in History of Education. The lectures were held in the evening, so it was necessary to travel to London after school. I discovered through these late evenings that chocolate was the cause of my frequent and bad headaches. I stopped eating it which was a sacrifice but worth it for the end of the headaches. The course lasted two years but computers had not become household equipment and Arthur typed out my dissertation about the formation of the Peterborough Education Committee. He did not have an easy time because every time he made an error, usually at the bottom of a page, I insisted he re-type every word. He did my bidding, despite some impatience. On the day that the course ended, he and I went to the Savoy for afternoon tea, which was a luxury reward. After the tea we travelled down to Dorset to visit Sheila, a friend from training college days, and her husband Derek. They took us to visit Portland and I saw the Chesil bank for the first time. Derek told us the story that Portland people never mention the word rabbits but always call them underground mutton. The examinations followed and were conducted in the examination halls near the Institute of Education. The weather was hot, and the windows were open, and the hours of writing were measured by the chimes of St. Pancras Church. I achieved the M.A., and the degree presentation ceremony was held in the Royal Albert Hall. The gown for the event was collected from the top floor. I thought I would never get my degree because the climb up the steps was hard. Princess Anne, the Chancellor, did not attend which was disappointing but Con and Arthur came to applaud me.

Soon after I returned to school, Dave Mcleish, the new head of Abbotsmede Junior School, and I had a discussion about the fact that deliveries were regularly mixed between the various schools because all the names and addresses were similar, and drivers made constant delivery mistakes. After some discussion, as well as thought, Dave and I decided it would be sensible to change the names of the infant and junior schools but retain that of the secondary school. It was not a straightforward decision as there were several groups which had to agree to the request. We were fortunate as agreement came reasonably as there were not too many 'decision makers' who were required to agree. At the beginning of the next school year the name of the school was Abbotsmede, and the explanation was that Peterborough Cathedral had an Abbot in the days before all monks were driven from their abbeys and an abbot was no longer the leader of holy men, and the name of the river was 'mede' which completed the new name. I have no idea if there remains an explanation of this name in the school. Soon after this change of name I moved to Welland School. I visited Abbotsmede in 2012 to see all the changes to the school. It was both interesting and outstanding. There had been no lack of money.

Silver Wedding and first visit to Australia

Arthur and I celebrated our Silver Wedding anniversary at Valla Beach in Australia on April 11th 1980. Arthur organized a two-week trip. We flew via Muscat, where we were not permitted to disembark despite the heat, and Singapore where we were delayed. A Bangladeshi air liner crashed, no-one was injured but the runway was damaged and required repair. June, my penfriend, and David met us and were determined that we saw as much as possible and almost immediately took us to Kaola Park, where we were introduced to various Australian animals, then to see the Heads, which mark the entrance to Sydney Harbour, the yachts in Pitt Water, and the Hawkesbury River. After the sightseeing we returned to Epping through French's Forest. The next day Arthur and I crossed the famous Sydney Harbour Bridge, toured the Rocks area where the convicts first settled, and viewed the monument commemorating all early settlers. I noted the Sydney lace, wrought iron work, brought to Australia by the wool clippers and used to decorate buildings. A walk around Circular Quay gave views of the wonderful Opera House and a trip on the ferry to Manly completed the day. The programme continued with a visit to the Blue Mountains to see the famous Three Sisters Rocks. We ate our lunch at Evans Lookout and made use of the 'bush loo', then returned to Epping via Richmond and Windsor. The next excursion was to June's parents at Palm Beach, where we boarded the Jensen cruiser and sailed up Smith Creek, anchored and ate lunch, after which June gave us a quick outing in a rowing boat. The afternoon cruise took us up the Hawkesbury River, across the Harbour, through the Heads and back to Palm Beach from where we admired the spectacular view. A second day in Sydney included visits to many famous buildings and landmarks and included St. James' Church, the Barracks, the Mint, which was being renovated, Sydney hospital, the mosaic at the Mitchell library, the botanical gardens, St. Martin's Plaza, and Centre Point where we went up the tower for a panoramic view of the city. An excursion to the historic Vaucluse House, the home of W.C. Wentworth, the father of the Australian Constitution, was interesting. It was amazing to think of all the objects travelling so far in an age when the only means of getting from Europe to Australia was a voyage of at least six weeks! Life in the 19th century was the subject of 'My Brilliant Career' an Australian novel which was adapted into a film and being shown in Sydney at just the right time for us.

Our itinerary then included a 600-kilometre drive to Valla beach, where we stayed briefly. Valla is on the Pacific coast of NSW where June's mother had a holiday home. During the drive, we called at Newcastle, an industrial city and saw Loret and Lake Macquarie. Arthur and I celebrated our actual anniversary with a walk along Valla Beach and a visit to Nambucca. During the drive we passed the Big Banana; a banana plantation with a visitors' centre, topped with a huge banana. We also saw, to our delight, dozens of kookaburras perched on various buildings. David flew to Coff's Harbour airport, a real local facility, which he opened for us. After such a hectic schedule, we spent a marvellously hot day on the beach; the sea was cool, and the most energetic activity was collecting shells. Dinner followed at the Nambucca Island Golf Club, and I chose Balmain bugs - fish not beetles. On the return journey to Sydney, we noticed unusual names like Bulahdelah, crossed many creeks, saw the lakes around Forster and viewed Lake Macquarie again. Once back in Sydney, the stay in Australia was at an end and we were soon aboard the plane bound for Heathrow. Once in London, we did not head for Peterborough but caught a train to Plymouth for Jono's passing out parade at HMS Fisgard, where we were proud parents. Our Silver Wedding celebrations were completed near the end of the year when we held a large family party at Eastholm Infants School. Everyone was invited so we needed the school hall!

Australia: Visit Two

In July 1986, less than a year before Arthur was hospitalised and 15 months before his death, we paid a second visit to Australia. The flight made two stops, Bahrain and Singapore where Changi Airport had changed out of all recognition and impressed me considerably. Arthur appeared well for most of the time, although occasionally his behaviour verged on the unusual. I continued to justify his eccentricity but, with hindsight, I think June found him difficult. He insisted on going swimming even when plans had to be altered to allow him to do so, he was terrified that he would find a funnel web spider in the house and showed real fear at the top of Centre Point. The first few days in Sydney made us realize that July in Australia really is winter. Despite the coolness, we spent the days renewing our acquaintance with the city. We went to the Art Gallery and the Botanical Gardens and followed the Queen Elizabeth Walk to the Opera House where we took a guided tour of the building and admired the impressive architecture and the fantastic views from the foyer. As we had done before we ate lunch overlooking the water, and then revisited the Hyde Park Barracks which since our previous visit had become a museum depicting the lives of the first convict settlers. The Mint's renovation had been completed and had become the Museum of Australian History with interesting examples of Australian antiques including furniture, ceramics, and silver. June took us to Berowra Waters, a beautiful spot with lots of boats and water, and to Elizabeth Farm at Parramatta, built by John MacArthur, famous for introducing merino sheep into Australia. The house has been beautifully preserved and has a lived in feeling of old Australia with French doors opening on to a large veranda. A log fire was burning which was very welcome as the weather was cold. Indeed, after we had visited Hamilton Cottage, the house built for the MacArthur governess and containing beautiful antique furniture, the wind became strong, the temperature fell, and snow began. It lasted briefly but was the first snow in Sydney for about 20 years! The cold was severe enough for us to borrow warm coats to go to the Sydney Entertainment Centre to see the Olympic ice dance champions Torville and Dean. A visit to the cinema to see the film 'Crocodile Dundee' was possible before we set off northwards on our adventure.

Joe, June and David's son-in-law, lent us his car and our first stop was at Newcastle at the Oak Milk Bar where we rekindled our memories of six years before. Harrington was the overnight stay, and we viewed the Pacific surf rolling in and fishing boats in a small harbour from the vantage point of Crowdy Head. When we reached Valla Beach, it was like coming home, nothing seemed to have changed. After a brief rest, we resumed the northwards road and travelled through places that were like the Australia I imagined. Balina had wide streets and low houses and Ulmarra was also a typical small town. Miles of sugar cane skirted the roads, and we crossed beautiful rivers as we headed for Byron Bay to view the lighthouse which marks the most easterly point of Australia's mainland. We encountered a 'tick gate' where two livestock inspectors with proper Australian hats were waiting to inspect the next load of animals. Massive concrete pineapples denoting pineapple producing farms and a huge concrete cow outside the dairy farming headquarters were not enhancing sights. A stop was dictated by a signpost! It was to King's Cliff, and we turned off the main road and headed for it. The river Tweed empties into the Pacific at King's Cliff and the coast is the Tweed Coast with miles of golden sand and rolling surf. We travelled northwards all the next day, through Brisbane, Nambour, Gympie, Maryborough and reached Gladstone in the late afternoon. Gladstone was not stunningly interesting and the motel at which we planned to stay was full. We returned to the Bruce Highway by which time it was getting dark, and Rockhampton was 126 kilometres distant, so we headed back towards Tannum Sands along a very narrow road. It was completely dark when we reached the village shop but there we found help and kindness. The lady in the shop rang the Boyne Island Motel and led us to it. We were most grateful. The stars were very bright, and we saw the Southern Cross. Northwards again next day and by mid-morning we reached Rockhampton, the heart of the cattle country and guarded by concrete cattle at its entrance and exit. Here we crossed the Tropic of Capricorn, but there was little sign of tropical weather. Mackay was our destination and the road from Rockhampton was soon covered.

Mackay was where we planned to take a boat out to the Great Barrier Reef, but no boats ran on Sunday, and we had arrived on Saturday. Fortunately, the tourist office assistant was helpful and booked an air trip for the Sunday. Food was the next requirement and we found it in a sports club/ tavern. It was crowded and noisy, a place where the locals were enjoying their Saturday social life. Beefy Australians in check shirts were playing guitars, and the raffle prizes consisted of very large trays of meat   Food when we collected it from the counter came in huge helpings. The trip to the Barrier Reef was everything of which I ever dreamed. The weather was marvellous, and the day went well, despite one hitch. We drove to Shute Harbour, stopping at Airlie Beach to buy sandwiches and after the purchase, the car refused to start. Panic! A motorist rescued us; he noticed the lead had fallen from the starter motor, a problem that was quickly repaired and we went on to collect our tickets, eat our sandwiches and admire the view until it was time to board the sea plane for the flight to the Reef. From the plane, there was a great view of the Whitsunday passage and the islands with the wonderful beaches, and we saw three whales. We landed in a lagoon near a reef which had been uncovered by the tide and headed to the reef in a glass bottom boat and saw a cuttlefish swimming beneath us. The atmosphere on the reef is eerie; there is absolute silence except for the odd sounds from the reef itself. It must be remembered it is a living entity and is 600 feet deep. We walked on the coral and went snorkelling, which I managed after a few false starts. It was a wonderful experience with the multi-colours of the coral and the fish. I saw the edge of the reef but wasn't prepared to go past it. The ocean was too vast, too deep and altogether too awe inspiring. Arthur was not prepared to snorkel but viewed the reef with a special viewing glass. After two hours we returned to the boat although it was more difficult to walk back as the tide had turned and the reef was becoming submerged. We reached the airstrip by early evening and after eating set off back to Mackay and saw a kangaroo feeding by the roadside. It was dark so not the easiest of journeys as some parts of the road were narrow.

Next day, Mackay was left behind when we began the trek southwards and drove 678 kilometres to

Bundaberg. This part of the continent was sparsely populated with small settlements of traditional houses, large cattle stations, stud farms, forests, and mountains in the background. Much sugar cane was growing in the area and, at dusk we saw it being burned before cutting began. The whole sky seemed to be on fire! Just north of Gladstone we stopped at a heritage site where old Queensland buildings were being preserved, a pleasing innovation. Bundaberg was the next place, and we parked the car in the middle of the main street, Australian style, and headed for the Rum Distillery for a conducted tour. Next, we stopped at the avocado groves; it was interesting to see avocadoes on trees. Once on the Bruce Highway again we drove via Goodwood to Buderim, just north of Brisbane where we made another overnight stop. This time at the Fiesta Motel; Arthur had promised the owners, Mary, and Colin McDonald, that we would call, and they welcomed us with open arms. We were their first real guests! We hit the road early in the morning heading for Brisbane. On this part of the journey, I was stopped for speeding by an Australian gun-toting policeman. Arthur pleaded my innocence of 'Oz' motorway speeds and I got away with my crime! We parked at Zillmere station and went into the centre of the city on one of the comfortable and clean electric trains. We took a bus tour on a mini coach with just two other passengers, two new graduates from Cambridge. The tour gave us a good impression of Brisbane and afterwards we went to the Botanic Gardens and the Lone Pine Koala Sanctuary, where there were not only koala bears but kangaroos, emus, and a duck-billed platypus. I had my photo taken with a koala. There was just time for a brief look in the Hall of Memories before we sped back to Zillmere, collected the car, and headed south. We reached Valla Beach late in the evening.

The next two days were spent recuperating and planning the next trips. Winter had really arrived, a gale blew, and the ocean was grey. The rain fell in sheets and Nambucca swimming pool was too cold for swimming, the solar heating had had too little sun! We set out again the following day and headed towards the rain forest through farmland and reached Bellingen where we looked around the Yellow Shed, an arts and crafts outlet, full of the things you don't need. In the Dorrigo Forest we saw a scrub turkey and had a picnic. Rain began again and we set off on the mountain roads. The forest, the countryside, the views, and the waterfalls were spectacular. We stopped at Thora, where the sun shone, and we ate a massive Devonshire cream tea on a café veranda. Once back in Valla we ate at the golf club where we were alone in the dining room. In 1980, it had been difficult to get a table, but the waitress explained that people were too scared to cross the causeway because the previous day it had been flooded. We had crossed without a thought and our bravery or bravado ensured we had special treatment. Next day was Sunday and at the local church service there was an appeal for people who had been affected by the floods in Sydney! Our stay down under had been beset by unusual weather. Floods in Sydney were almost beyond living memory. The beach called in the afternoon and the weather turned gloriously sunny and warm. We walked beside the blue ocean with huge surf, and we made it to Wenonah Head and back in a rapid two and a half hours despite the stretches of soft sand. It was an exhausting experience.

Bowraville, a town that was just as I wanted it to be, was reached by a drive through rolling hills and farmland. The town had wide streets with palm trees growing in the centre reservation, verandas to give shelter outside the shops, two old hotels and a post office. We bought stamps at the post office and then went on to Bellingen via the Bowra Nature Reserve through the rain forest with tree ferns on either side and along mountainous unmade roads. Some places were hairy, tight bends with a sheer drop and muddy surfaces. Tea at the Boiling Billy Coffee Shop was welcome but not the comment, 'What you came by the mountain road! Good thing you didn't meet a logging lorry!'. Next day we headed towards Coff's Harbour, but first made a 14-kilometre detour to the Russell Lake and the Russell Gallery, where the art made the journey worthwhile. At Coff's Harbour we watched the surfers, and afterwards visited the Honey Place. Interesting but I hate honey! When the sunny days returned, we watched a kookaburra sitting on an old gum tree and nearly sang the song but instead went to the station which we had discovered at the end of a forest road. We did not intend to travel any where but watched the XPT, a fast passenger train. We had not expected a fast train in that area. We also climbed the rocks at Valla to see what was round the headland. It was more beach and ocean!

We took advantage of Education Week and the Education Minister's invitation to visit the local schools. We found Nambucca Heads Public School, a large primary establishment and were welcomed by the principal who took us on a conducted tour and explained the school system in Australia. A three-and half-hour cruise on the Nambucca Princess along the Nambucca River was an excellent expedition after the school visit. Before boarding the boat, we viewed some units, being built by the river. Arthur was tempted to put down a deposit but resisted. The Princess went as far as Mackville where lunch of a smorgasbord of hot and cold dishes, sweet and coffee was provided before we turned back and headed for Nambucca. There we read the graffiti on what was called the Vee Wall. We made one last visit to Coff's harbour and on the return drive stopped at a beautiful spot by the Bellinger River for a picnic. The next morning a complete change of weather was obvious. The television noted a temperature of minus two at Kempsey and we decided to go to Mary Bolton's Pioneer Cottage. Mary Bolton is a third generation Australian and her grandfather was a 'cedar getter', one of the men that stripped the continent of much of its cedar. Mary has collected many historical artefacts and has displayed them in a replica pioneer cottage. Despite being interesting, the displays were rather jumbled. Daffodils, roses and camellias were flowering together in the cottage garden! Afterwards, we drove to Scott's Head, another attractive coastal settlement and then inland as far as Taylor's Arm where the pub with no beer was to be found. The vastness of the country and its sparse population was obvious. We managed a visit to Mt. Yarrahapinni, a not to be missed place. We reached it by driving through banana plantations and the state forest on very rough winding and climbing roads. When we arrived at the top the view was fantastic, north and south across the vast country to the mountains and eastwards to the coast. Afterwards, we picnicked by the Nambucca River for the last time, and next day we left Valla Beach and travelled southwards, stopping at Macksville to buy post cards and Telegraph Point because I liked the sound of the name, but it was not noteworthy. A further stop was at Wauchope and Timber Town, a reconstruction of a 19th century settlement, where we watched a demonstration with a working bullock team. We needed more time, but it was necessary to reach Karuah on the point of Port Stephen, where there was another beautiful river, to stay overnight. We arrived back in Sydney the following morning.

Sight-seeing was not at an end and next day we set out for Canberra. The Woolwich Ferry passed under the Harbour Bridge on its route to Circular Quay, where we boarded the express coach, which took four hours to reach Canberra. Once at the Development Centre, a film showed the history of the city after which we ate lunch at the High Court. Next on the itinerary was a brief visit to the Parliament House and then on to see the progress on the building of the new Parliament. The Foreign embassies are attractive as they are built in the style of the country which they represent. Sadly, one of the least interesting is the British High Commission. From the top of the Black Mountains Tower the view was amazing. I was delighted to see the Brindabella Mountains; I had just read Childhood at Brindabella. Finally, the tour went through the grounds of the National University to the War Memorial where the exhibitions were extensive and there was too little time to see everything. On the way back to Sydney we saw kangaroos feeding at dusk and Lake George with its water returning, during the day the lake is dry. We stopped at the 'Big Merino', a restaurant with a huge concrete ram as a landmark; it was a tourist trap with expensive food and 'tat' for sale. In the last days in Australia, we went to Kurrajong to visit Joe's mother. She lived in a small cabin beside a big house built on a hill with a view towards Sydney. A huge log fire was burning by which we all sat to warm ourselves. Joe's mother was an amazing person; she had been an antique dealer and retained much of her interesting collection. David also took us on a tour of his factory to view the manufacture of soft drinks and finally we ate a formal dinner in the 'lounge room' at David and June's home. Then Australia was left behind as we headed for Hong Kong.

Cho met us at the airport and Hong Kong hit us with a bang. It had changed out of all recognition from the time we lived in North Point. The hotel Lee Gardens was in Causeway Bay, and we were given a suite because double rooms were full, and we decided to take full advantage of the luxury. What a disappointment! A power cut lasted all night, and a workman constantly came in and out the room and climbed into the roof to attempt a repair. We could not use bath or shower and went to bed by the light of the night watchman's lamp! Next morning, we collected our money from the Hong Kong and Shanghai Bank, a building which had been transformed. The well-known classical building had changed into a 40 plus storey space-age establishment. Indeed, the whole of Hong Kong had gone upwards with skyscrapers or underground with Kowloon and the island being linked by a tunnel. Roads had been constructed on reclaimed land that made many areas unrecognizable. We visited Peacock Road, but number 28 had been demolished and new flats were being constructed on what had been sheer rock. I achieved my desire to go to Macau and, although it was extremely hot, we did all the touristy bits. We went to the casino where the gambling was well in action, walked over the bridge to the Hyatt Hotel to buy an ice cream and returned to Hong Kong by jet foil.

We stayed with Maureen, a schoolteacher colleague, and Wilf for the rest of the time in Hong Kong and briefly enjoyed colonial life; we drank gin and tonics while overlooking the Harbour. We visited the cathedral but were unable to see the baptismal records and took the tram up the Peak where all had changed with buses running to the top. It is a real tourist trap. Charlie Tseung was overwhelmed when we met him and, sadly, it was the last time we saw him. We used the Mass Transit Railway, a fantastic innovation, to reach Kowloon and shopped at the Ocean Terminal and Harbour City. Old memories were revived by using the old Star Ferry to return to Hong Kong to meet Vera and Charles for dinner. We ate Peking duck for the nth time! The evening ended in the luxury of the Mandarin Hotel while the beggars slept outside on the pavement. There was just time to take a tour of Shaukiwan, Sheko, Stanley, Repulse Bay and Happy Valley before returning to Central to pack and go to the airport. Cho organized a first-class check-in, although we had to travel steerage! On our arrival in Gatwick, David was there to drive us back to Peterborough.

Arthur's Problems

Arthur's emergency admission into hospital in 1987 was the culmination of a life of problems which had accelerated after our return from Singapore in 1967. He enjoyed the first weeks in Peterborough, but at the end of his leave he was not well enough to return to a naval establishment and was sent to Netley Hospital for treatment for his anxiety problems. Improvement was slow and, in 1969, he was discharged from the Royal Navy as 'below the physical level required'. He was fortunate to find employment at Perkins' Engines as a security officer. It was a uniformed position and very suitable for an ex-serviceman but was short-lived when one morning he collapsed as he was about to set out for work. In the weeks leading up to the collapse, Arthur had pursued his long-held determination to become a freemason. Sponsorship was essential to achieve this ambition and he contacted a naval officer, under whom he had served, for support. The negative reply not only disappointed Arthur but disturbed his thinking processes and he began to believe that he was being watched. He became convinced that the dustbin was being searched for information about his life! His mental state deteriorated seriously, his collapse followed, and he was admitted to Fulborn Hospital in Cambridge. I was interviewed by the psychiatric social worker, something I found unsettling as he was a colleague with whom I had regular professional contact. Arthur was hospitalised for some months during which visits could be difficult, particularly when he exhibited strange behaviour. On one occasion he produced an out-of-date woman's magazine which, he said, had the answers to all our problems. I did not agree! Improvement occurred when the doctors decided, as a last resort, to use electrical convulsive therapy. This procedure brought improvement and he was able to spend weekends at home and finally was discharged. The downside of the treatment was the obliteration of key memories. He was never able to remember David's confirmation at Ramsey Abbey Church.

After the illness, work was difficult to find but he was fortunate to obtain a post in the laboratory at the sugar beet factory, where two supportive colleagues assisted him when he could not manage his specific tasks. He remained for two sugar campaigns after which Marshall's Car Sales employed him as a petrol pump attendant and he appeared well-suited to the work. A scheme of monthly bonuses based on sales of oil was in operation and Arthur proved himself a good salesperson and collected some significant sums. The settled period ended abruptly when he was asked to transfer to Dogsthorpe where Marshall's had acquired a second filling station. At first, he showed pleasure and regarded the proposed change as promotion, but suddenly for no reason, decided that the move was discrimination and demotion and he resigned; an indication that his mental state remained uncertain. Luck was again with him and an opening at the British Rail parcel terminal occurred. The work was primarily loading and unloading trains for Freeman's the mail order company, which at the time, was a large employer in the city. The physical work suited Arthur and he improved enough to apply for more interesting work with British Rail which entailed recording the movements of freight trains on a computerised system. His application was successful, and the work brought him into contact with Arthur Pateman. The two became 'soul mates'; both had distinctive opinions and odd philosophies on which they agreed completely.

Employment with British Rail brought travel concessions and Arthur and I took the opportunity to visit Venice. Our hotel was on the outskirts, and we became expert travellers on the vaporetto along the Grand Canal. It was February and the weather was particularly cold, and we needed the very thickest clothes; it was not gondola season. The visit coincided with a festival, and everyone was in their Sunday best. Many women were wearing fur coats and I admired them. I was not as aware of the awfulness of wearing animal skins then. The buildings were as beautiful in the cold as they are in the sunshine and at one palazzo an old Italian man became an unofficial guide. He spoke no English but managed to make us understand with actions and, of course, demanded payment at the end of the tour. We visited the impressive Doge's Palace but were only able to admire St. Mark's Cathedral from outside. My greatest wish was to be invited into one of the houses on the canals, but my wish did not come to fruition, although I managed, at dusk, to catch a brief look through a lighted window as we passed by on the canal. The railway travel concessions also allowed us to take Bill on a day trip to Edinburgh. He must have known the story of Greyfriars Bobby from a young age as he frequently expressed a wish to see the little statue. At the time of the visit, I did not realize that Edinburgh would become a much visited and favourite city!

Arthur achieved his Masonic ambition during the British Rail years. He met Francis Beeton who proposed him, and initiation followed. Arthur was delighted to be part of lodge activities and gained a position in the hierarchy but did not live long enough to reach his desired aim of being worshipful master. He believed that being a freemason gave him status, but he took the ritual too seriously; he copied everything he was required to learn and believed implicitly that he would be subject to the various punishments listed in the handbook if he told anyone about the lodge ceremonies and, gradually, his emotional wellbeing deteriorated. He began to complain of having various illnesses and was certain that colleagues and management were discriminating against him. When his agitation was severe, outbreaks of temper resulted. He was frequently difficult to persuade to go to the office and many times, often in the night, I drove there to cool a problem. In the summer of 1985, Arthur, Jono, and I went to Arosa in Switzerland, a picturesque mountain town where we were able to enjoy long walks and good food. Arthur needed very careful handling to avoid incidents of high emotion. He was reluctant to do anything too strenuous and gave the impression of being much older than his years. His one real interest was 'talking' to a German pastor, which was interesting as neither spoke the other's language. The certainty that he had some major illness grew after the holiday and he often visited the doctor. He took time off work and regularly said that he would not live to old age. Soon he was unable to work a 'shift pattern' and was away from the office for several months on doctor's orders.

In November 1986, British Rail was unable to find him suitable work and he was retired on the grounds of ill health which meant that he received disability benefit. The retirement came into being in February 1987 and appeared to be the best outcome. Arthur seemed happy and had decided that he would be content and useful. He announced that he would spend time gardening and would relieve me of some household chores. I was not about to join him in retirement. The plan was put into action and appeared to be working well, particularly when he decided to go swimming regularly. He said that this exercise would be of benefit in relieving the arthritis which he was certain was one of his problems. He swam two or three times each week, and on Sunday mornings I went with him to encourage him in the activity. I was too optimistic, paid little attention to Arthur's increasing concern with his health and laughed at his insistence on taking as many pills and potions as possible. I was cross when he catalogued his ailments to those who, in a cursory fashion, asked about his health and tolerated, as I had done always, his desire to know exactly where I was at any given time. I did not notice, perhaps I did not want to, the fact that the garden was not weeded and that I was doing the housework and preparing the meals. I certainly did not realise that he was sitting alone staring into space. The doctors did not observe this rapid deterioration either.

During the summer half-term holiday in 1987 Arthur and I went to 'cat-sit' at Petersfield and the week proved pleasurable. Arthur's problems seemed less obvious although he was not exactly 'his old self'. We enjoyed many outings, including one to the Isle of Wight, but on the day we were due to return to Peterborough we left abruptly. Arthur could not be persuaded to do otherwise as he had made a telephone call home and knew that there was a letter from the DHSS asking him to attend a review of his health and ability to work. The communication struck fear into him; he regarded it as a slur on his integrity and did not accept that regular medical examinations came with the receipt of a disability allowance. Arthur's depression increased and he spent the following week planning what he would say and making copious notes. He wrote 'in spite of medication, my health is not improving, and I am becoming aware of physical limitations on my body' and 'the medical world informs me that for three of the complaints I have the future is not good'. He was assured at the examination that he was unfit to work, and his allowances were secure, but he was told that his GP would receive a letter of explanation. Arthur decided that the letter would indicate that he could undertake some kind of work and he was so worried that I suggested he make an appointment to see the GP and talk about his fears. There were no immediate available appointments, but one was made for the morning of Tuesday 9th June.

I left home at eight o'clock as usual; Arthur was already dressed for his appointment. He came to the door to wave me goodbye and managed to bring Beauty, the old dog to wave her paw!!! He looked tense and unhappy, but Arthur had a face that often-displayed worry, he did not smile easily, and I consoled myself that the doctor would put his mind to rest, and he would soon be ringing to tell me his news. School was very busy; I was showing groups of children around the building in preparation for school in September. When I returned to my office at about twenty minutes to twelve, I answered the telephone. It was Alison who enquired if Arthur had had dental treatment. David had rung her to say that he had spoken to Arthur who 'sounded funny' and now the telephone was consistently engaged. I told Alison not to worry and that I would telephone. I rang a number of times with no success. That did not raise any concerns as Arthur was a telephone addict and should have had a receiver permanently fixed to his hand. I wonder what he would have done with a mobile telephone. I thought, 'No problem, he's talking again and then will complain when the bill comes in'. I rang a few more times with the same result and decided that I would make a last call and if there was still no reply would go home to check the situation. This time there was an answer but it was a policeman who said, 'Your husband is still alive'. At first the import of this speaker did not sink in, and shock was delayed for some minutes. The policeman told me to go to the hospital and Alison and I went together. When we arrived, the receptionist had not heard of Arthur and for a brief moment it was possible to believe I had got it all wrong! Almost immediately, however, we were treated to the arrival of the ambulance with flashing blue lights and police motorcycle escort!

At 'Accident and Emergency' Alison and I were put into a side room and were asked about the availability of pills at home. Arthur's unconsciousness did not seem to indicate heart attack or stroke. Alison went to look if there was any indication of him taking an overdose but returned saying that all the medication was intact. We waited, with no explanation, for almost three hours until a nurse came to take us to the ward. She warned us that we must expect all the trappings of someone deeply unconscious and indeed when we saw Arthur, he was linked to heart monitor, drips and various other pieces of paraphernalia. A nurse was beside him to check his condition every 15 minutes. We spoke with the registrar and discussed the possible causes of such an unexpected collapse. He seemed to accept that Arthur had not made an attempt on his life, but his state did not make medical sense. I had a feeling of unease. Later, a second doctor said that Arthur's coma was very deep and advised that we should tell David and Jono and ask them to come to Peterborough. They arrived shocked and worried, and we sat around the bed not knowing what the next turn of events would be. Remaining at the hospital was a possibility but we went home to get some sleep, which was, in reality, impossible. Jono and I returned to the hospital at about seven o'clock next morning and Arthur's condition was unchanged. About an hour later, the nurses asked us to wait outside the room and as we stood by the door there was an unexpected sound – Arthur's deep voice. He had regained consciousness and the following day he was questioned about what had happened, but he remained confused and unable to converse properly. Later, some of the medical paraphernalia was removed and we were able to go home for a night's sleep.

Thursday 11th June 1987 was again spent at the hospital attempting to encourage Arthur back into the world, but he was not interested. Visitors came and we tried to joke about him being unable to vote. Usually not voting would have caused Arthur dismay but on this occasion, he had nothing to say. The doctor came to the ward and as he left, he commented, 'as I suspected'. I knew at once that Arthur had attempted suicide, although, like Alison, I found nothing when I carried out a second search. I was desperate to get away from the hospital and the implications of what I had heard. At home the implications became reality. In the toilet, I pulled the toilet paper, heard a rattle, and found an empty pill bottle secreted inside the cardboard roll. So, he had had pills and the reason for a mug of water on the window ledge was explained. Jono and I returned immediately to the hospital, the doctors needed to know with what drugs they were dealing, and remained until after midnight although Arthur's conversation made no sense. I felt I had failed him and wanted to keep the suicide secret, but next morning he confessed that he had wished to kill himself and had had the pills for ten years! (Alison overheard the doctors discussing them and had indicated they were indeed ten years old) He was saving them in case of nuclear war and Arthur's nuclear hell was, obviously, 9th June 1987. Arthur also explained the barbecue skewer that was out of place and the small cut on his chest. He had intended to stab himself and later he believed he had done so. He was never, however, able to explain the breakage of a large glass bottle in which small change was kept or the fact that the police were called.

Once a suicide attempt had been established, Arthur was seen by a psychiatrist and as the next day was his birthday, we felt that the worst might be over, but 12th June did not end on the expected positive note. When we reached Longthorpe, Con had received news of Arthur senior's death. He had had a series of heart attacks over the years and, fortunately, Arthur had visited him the previous weekend. On his birthday, we told Arthur of his father's death, and I was surprised that he did not seem distressed. Indeed, he seemed indifferent to everything, even his birthday cake evoked no pleasure but when he heard a visitor's voice he was suddenly greatly agitated. He was certain that it was a former colleague who had come to spy on him. Arthur was discharged from hospital on 16th June but continued in a very delicate state of mind. He attended his father's funeral and went to the graveside but during the return car journey he began to fantasize about being sexually assaulted as a child. This was a distressing turn of events, but I thought a new interest may help him and suggested that he help with the boys from Welland at the regional pool. They needed a man with them in the changing rooms. He was not enthusiastic but was persuaded to agree.

Tuesday 25th June was the first day on which he was to help at the pool, but he did not arrive. On the parkway he crashed his car and tried to jump over the railway bridge on to the rails. He was restrained by a lorry driver and was readmitted to the hospital on the decision of the psychiatrist who had seen him previously and a consultant from Cambridge. According to Arthur, this latter doctor was only interested in his loose-fitting false teeth! By the weekend Arthur had become very 'high' and tried to escape from the ward. We restrained him but the staff advised against physical contact. They asked us to coax him into the office, where a sedative was administered, and then to leave him. During the next days the drugs kept him calm, and the psychiatrist decided that Arthur's problems were entirely of his own making, and he could choose to free himself of them! Consistent with this diagnosis he was taken off the sedatives and sent home for the weekend. At home, his behaviour was totally inappropriate. He followed me about and needed to be prompted to do everything and required continuous watching. I took him to church, but he was childlike, he could not relate to the members of the congregation. He was reluctant to return to the hospital where the psychiatrist's reaction was that he should stay at home until Friday when the consultant would discharge him completely.

Jono was alone caring for Arthur who became increasingly difficult to manage. By Wednesday, the hospital agreed to readmit him but two days later the consultant was insistent that Arthur could solve his own difficulties. It was 'Arthur's problem'!!! Jono took him home again and suggested he do some gardening and when I arrived, I was delighted to see him weeding. It appeared that the consultant was right. Such a belief was short-lived! A blue van drew up and Arthur immediately decided it was a police van. He was extremely distressed and soon after the van left he began to walk to the police station. It was difficult to know what to do, we followed him but were unsure whether to confront him or to wait and let him tire himself. We decided to contact the hospital. It was quickly obvious what the staff thought. Arthur was playing tricks and should be scolded like a naughty child. He was almost at the police station when we caught him up. We bundled him in the car, and I lashed him with my tongue. This incident was a precursor to a deteriorating mental state with bizarre behaviour during the day and at night. As a last resort a call was made to the GP who was unable to have a rational conversation with Arthur and telephoned the hospital. A conflict of opinion was obvious; the GP believed Arthur was suffering from a serious depression, but the psychiatrist stuck to the diagnosis that the problem was for Arthur to solve alone. The compromise was that Arthur should stay at home until Friday when the consultant would see him once more.

Jono made every effort to pacify Arthur at home; he took him for drives which seemed to calm the agitation but attempts to visit friends failed dismally. Arthur quickly became unsettled and withdrawn and he could not cope with visitors in the home. He prayed out loud, sang funeral hymns, would not eat, and looked at Jono with pure hatred. On Thursday 16th June, he again decided to go to the police station, this time dressed only in his pyjamas and a mackintosh. Jono managed to dress him and, in despair, tried yet another car ride but without success and once he was out of the car was insistent that he go to the police station. Jono told him that the police did not want him, but he was adamant and, because the door had been locked to prevent him escaping, tried to dial 999. Jono replaced the receiver at which Arthur became annoyed and aggressive. There was no alternative but to ring the doctor who agreed to make an immediate visit. During the telephone conversation Arthur went into a bedroom and appeared to be looking out of the window but had covered his spectacle lenses with toilet paper. He determined once more to go to the police station despite the fact he was unable to see where he was walking. Jono could do nothing but lead him around outside until the doctor arrived, who, without delay, telephoned the hospital to say that Arthur must be readmitted. It was difficult to get Arthur into the car and at the hospital, the staff were seriously unhelpful. The porters gave no assistance with parking the car and would not help with Arthur, and Jono was left to struggle single-handedly with him to the ward where a non-interested negative atmosphere greeted them. Five members of staff in the office took little notice of Arthur's arrival; one had the decency to say he was not to be readmitted and must go to the Gables. Jono was left with the arduous task of returning to the car, driving Arthur along Thorpe Road, and coaxing him into the Gables!

The psychiatrist at the Gables was sympathetic and seemed to grasp that Arthur had a considerable problem, and during the first few days his behaviour was more settled but yet another rapid deterioration followed. He tried to escape, wandered down the drive towards Thorpe Road and attempted to climb into a delivery van. Jono, Alison, Simon and I had planned a holiday in France and while we were away, friends and family visited but as soon as we returned, we went to see Arthur and found him standing in the corner of the entrance hall looking up at the ceiling. He had no interest in anything, and it did not appear he understood that we had been away. He had not been seen by the consultant psychiatrist because 'he didn't visit the Gables – just the hospital'! Arthur was, eventually, transferred back to the hospital but his behaviour became even more worrying. He disturbed other patients, fell down, refused to settle in his own bed and had some severe bruising that wasn't satisfactorily explained. He was put in a single room on a mattress on the floor for his own and other patients' safety. On one day when we visited, we found him locked in a room painting his false teeth with an art brush. He was heavily sedated and spent the next three weeks deteriorating more markedly than before. He ate little, walked with difficulty and lost weight. His condition was so concerning that I rang the psychiatrist to ask what more could be done, and a period of electro convulsive therapy was planned. After five treatments and the reduction of drugs, his movements were better, and he showed signs of improvement. Visitors noted the improvement but then our old dog Beauty died, and Arthur was noticeably affected by the news. He talked about the dog with visiting friends who found it necessary to restrain him from leaving with them. He telephoned me and wanted to know why I had not visited him, and I tried to reassure him that I would see him later, but then he asked a fellow patient when the ship sailed and soon after walked out of the hospital unobserved. The first we knew of the absence was a call from the hospital asking if Arthur was at home. He wasn't and he was missing for a week. During that time searches were made everywhere, his disappearance was publicized but he was not found until 30th September 1987 by children playing in the disused sewage farm at Stanground. He was in a disposal tank the contents of which were similar to quicksand. If his body had not been found, then it may never have been discovered. It is likely that he was walking towards Coneygree Road, had crossed the river at Stanground and wandered into the sewage farm at a point where the fence was broken. A policeman brought the news. David first identified Arthur at the mortuary and after identification, the coroner released the body, and the funeral took place at Alwalton. Donald Warne, the vicar, gave the oration and spoke about Arthur, warts and all. Following the funeral, an inquest was called. I found it very difficult being questioned closely. I felt I was being blamed! Arthur's life was found to be worth £1,000, the amount Anglian Water paid as compensation; the fences were unrepaired which allowed Arthur to wander into the dangerous area. Alison later used the money to buy a car!!

Dogs

The reason for Arthur's attempt to return to Coneygree Road was that the death of Beauty reminded him of where we had lived when he adopted her. He was working at Marshall's Garage when he saw Beauty in a car. She was being taken to be 'put down'! Arthur refused to allow the killing of such a lovely little animal and brought her home. My reaction was that Arthur, David, Jono and Alison had a choice between me and the dog! Their resounding reply was that they would pack my case!! Beauty became a part of the family!!! She was totally obedient, lived until she was 17 and was sadly mourned. She was not our first dog; we had been given Penny in Singapore by neighbours when they returned to England. She (Penny) was a small and loveable little animal, and we were devastated to have her destroyed but we had promised not to leave her to the fate of many dogs owned by service people. They were deserted, became part of wild packs and usually died as a result of injury or hunger. After Beauty's death Jono went secretly to a dog pound and found Minnie. Con, Alison, Jono and I collected her, and on the way home she was named. Alison suggested Winnie after Winnie Mandela because she was black but after some discussion about its suitability, Con came up with the idea of Minnie after Minnie Louisa and everyone agreed. In the first months, Minnie was a handful. She was not only a thief but was boisterous and knocked a cup of boiling coffee over Jono which necessitated many hospital visits. Once she had settled into a routine, however, she followed in Beauty's footsteps and became a faithful pet, caused no problems, and lived happily until 2000. Again, Jono was determined to have a replacement, went to Wood Green Animal Shelter and chose an apology for a German Shepherd. Alison chose Star as the name. What a travesty! She could not be less like a star. Her learning capability was poor, or she resisted training and was determined to do what she chose. She was most happy in kennels where she could run free. She could, at more than eight years old, climb the garden stone wall but her climbing abilities gradually deteriorated. She, however, retained a desire to run away and ignored all calls if the freedom of the road beckoned. Age prevented any kind of running as her back legs became very weak and she needed a support, which was obtained from the south of England. The contraption kept her going for a while, but she deteriorated to the extent that she became extremely ill. Jono eventually understood it was unkind to keep her and a vet came with her nurse and together they put her to sleep. She was buried with the others and very quickly we were on the road north to collect India. She is an entirely different animal despite her being a white German Shepherd; her Labrador ensures she is intelligent and obedient.

My lovely India – she isn't sharing the sherry!

Her only behaviour problem is that she does not like being left alone and is never happier than being on the back seat of a car and is content to wait, while if left at home she searches to find something to amuse her. Health can be a difficulty as she has a number of recurring problems which need a visit to the vet, a somewhat expensive occupation. She does not run away although she was once shut outside when the wind closed the door, and she was lost. Thankfully, she was found, and she loves the finder's dog. In the hot summer of 2016, she disappeared again, and I was desperately worried. I thought she had wandered outside and had reached the A1 which would mean disaster. I was in despair and several people tried to help find her. I returned home and there she was! She had found a cool area, gone to sleep and had not heard her name. She has made some 'doggie friends' to stay with from time to time. They are two lovely animals, one has done her duty as a guide dog, the other acts as a guide everyday and is always clever when guiding. A further problem arose with India. On two occasions she has scratched the doors and Jono has had to undertake repairs. The second time the problem included her knocking the internal bolt so that the door could not be opened! Jono had to come home from work and kick the door to gain entry!! Thus, we decided she must be left in the garage with the external door open when she was left. She quickly accepted the garage when she is left at home and sometimes uses her time to dig up the bush in the back area!

Life after Arthur: Welland School

Welland School was a saviour when Arthur died, despite its location in a deprived area. No-one can think of out of school difficulties when surrounded by 300 lively children. The school, built to serve an area of Peterborough where the population was on the increase, had been planned to be twice the size, but the expected number of children did not materialise, and a junior building became a primary school. Adaptations were necessary for the infant children, although like all schools more changes became essential as education philosophies developed and altered. Perhaps the most unusual aspect of the building was that the interior walls were of black bricks; an advantage in that decoration was unnecessary, but a disadvantage in that they were depressive on dark days. Initially, these walls were hosed down each holiday by the rather unorthodox caretaker! He would have preferred the school without teachers although he acknowledged their existence by constantly demanding that they carry out his orders. He believed that he was an excellent carpenter and handyman. Unfortunately, his hands did not substantiate his opinion. He had lost the end of one thumb and several fingers! After he retired a succession of replacements proved unsuccessful. When a suitable candidate came on the scene, he wanted a post where accommodation was provided and thus left when offered a post at a different school with a caretaker's bungalow. My final appointment was a hardworking, pleasant, reliable, and adaptable man who proved the point that it is possible to run a school for some time without a head teacher, but not without a caretaker, not even for a day. It is also difficult to be without a secretary as good administration is essential for the successful running of a school. At Welland, the secretary was excellent, but I sometimes felt that she believed she was indispensable, and I was surplus to requirements.

Life as a head teacher at Welland was always testing, but there were particular challenges when I took up the post. A nucleus of excellent teachers existed. It included a gifted teacher, who was small in stature but controlled any class with a look, and an excellent class teacher who was also an able football specialist. The boys admired her and defended her if any pupil from another school criticised her knowledge. Another professional teacher returned to the school after a break in service and was warmly welcomed. She was experienced and tough and one year the pupils had severe behavioural difficulties. They each needed an individual teacher, and she required every ounce of teaching ability to engage the class daily. Unfortunately, difficulties at home added to school pressures. She offered a daily lift to a colleague, who had car problems, and suggested her husband could repair the vehicle. Colleague and husband became much more than 'a damsel in distress and a knight who could repair cars', and her kindness brought hurt and enragement and frequently a loss of emotional control. Once she marched out of assembly, heels clicking on the wooden floor with the children watching open-mouthed. Later, she was found beating a filing cabinet and had a pressing need for tea and sympathy.

I was initially unwilling to consider one excellent teacher because she applied through a government initiative which aimed to increase the numbers of qualified teachers. I decided that the scheme was not for Welland, but quickly realized that I must not miss the opportunity of adding her skills to the staff. She had gained her qualifications in Zimbabwe and was a superb professional. She worked with a newly qualified colleague and together they produced and directed an opera with support from the education department of the Royal Opera House. The children wrote the words and music and performed extremely successfully for parents and visitors. Indeed, its success far exceeded any expectations and was a demonstration of what children from deprived areas can achieve.

Unfortunately, there were those teachers who did not meet expected standards and yet sadly held long teaching carers and sincerely thought themselves capable and competent. At the time it was more difficult for independent action and so they remained in post.

The opportunity to institute new ideas arose when a new deputy head teacher was appointed and proved an asset to the school: she was an excellent class teacher, managed difficult children easily and inspired her colleagues. I asked the only male teacher on my appointment to change his teaching group to younger children, and he seemed devastated but whether the move caused his heart attack and subsequent death I will never know. I was stunned by the outcome, but all experiences add to knowledge. A younger male, who had glowing references and performed well at interview, found the Welland children difficult and stayed only briefly, but went on to be a successful teacher in service schools. Finally, one newly qualified teacher produced inspirational paper plans for lessons, but the actual teaching rarely reached the aspirations, another did not like the children she taught and a third had a propensity to be absent after a social evening! Life was indeed a rich tapestry!

During my career, changes to classroom practice were numerous. Philosophies ranged from individual subject teaching to working on cross-curriculum topics, from learning through discovery to using formal schemes and from concentrating on phonics for reading to using 'real books' for learning to read competently. Accountability and inspection were less than rigorous and during my career I was inspected just once by Her Majesty's Inspectors of Schools (HMIs). The Education Reform Act arrived in 1988 with its attendant National Curriculum, detailing the subjects to be taught. It was the beginning of prescriptive methods of teaching through governmental innovations which were required to be followed. A new designation of school years was instituted and immediately after the files containing the National Curriculum arrived, Standard Assessment Tests (SATs), league tables and Office of Standards in Education (Ofsted) inspections jumped on to the agenda. I had long been involved with the National Association of Head Teachers (NAHT) and clearly remember a meeting when the area representative spoke of the efforts by one local authority to have greater control over the curriculum and to institute regular testing. I found it impossible to believe that such a situation would ever happen, but it did! I became keen to be part of the resistance to league tables, but the opposition was to no avail. These tables have not been good for Welland School; since their inception the school has regularly occupied a near the bottom position. Part of the reason for this situation cannot be divorced from the fact that some children lacked care; family relationships could be unstable and parental interest in their children's achievements was not always consistent. One of the saddest children, a boy, seemed very disturbed and exhibited inappropriate behaviour. Social services and other agencies were constantly involved, and case conferences held. In September 1994 he was found murdered and there was much media coverage. Sadness surrounded a young girl of a varied family background who was born with a degenerative disease of the nervous system. She came to school able to walk but gradually lost the ability, became tragically weak and needed constant assistance, but never complained and was loved by her peers. She gained a child of courage award which was presented at the Queen Elizabeth Hall in London. I was invited to the award ceremony and the many special children made it a very emotional day. I aimed to keep her in school for as long as possible because I believed she felt comfortable with her peers. Towards the end of her life, she spent time at the Cambridge Children's Hospice and a visit there was a humbling experience. She died in 1994; her funeral at Dogsthorpe Church was attended by a large congregation, which included many of her fellow pupils. One girl cried bitterly and said, 'I didn't think she would really die'.

Two boys who shared their name were memorable. One had a mother who seemed fond of alcohol and was prone to aggression. On one occasion, she arrived and demanded to see her son: he was in the care of social services at the time and visits were supervised. She was abusive and threatening towards the teachers until it became essential that I shut them safely in the staff room and attempt to placate her. She hurled various insults and informed me that she would be glad to dance on my grave! Eventually, she was calmed and left, leaving a rather stunned staff. The second appeared certain his mother was a lesbian and broadcast the fact loudly. He was a capable child but one who was frequently in trouble. He used his abilities in negative ways, an example of which was when, during a lesson about caterpillars, he suggested that they must have a very sad life as they did not have sex. When David announced the birth of a new baby boy, my grandson, but would not divulge the name, I knew it would be the same as the two boys and it was! One other troublemaker was confined in my office to prevent class disturbance. Soon after he was installed, money began to disappear from the safe. He was taking the key from my desk and helping himself whenever I turned my back! One little lad deserved sympathy; he had a range of difficulties; he was severely asthmatic, had dreadful eczema, wore glasses, had a squint and was very small and thin. Poor child! A teacher described him as being made by god with left over bits. Two girls deserve mention to illustrate that they can be as difficult as boys! One could become almost uncontrollable when displeased and once threw a drawer at me but the most notorious was used to the seamier side of life. She was a one-off, older than her years and not prepared to accept discipline. She had no fear of sanctions and controlled the area out of school to the extent that she brooked no disobedience from the teenage boys.

Despite the ineffectualness and the occasional aggression, life at Welland was never dull. Many parents were supportive and were willing to give their time to enable the children to have exciting experiences. One grandmother determined that the school should have a uniform and sourced a supply at a price that parents could afford. The children voted for their preferred colour, which was naturally red, a good socialist colour exactly right for Welland! As a result of my Whitelands' training, I had always felt I should institute May Day celebrations and I succeeded at Welland although I was certain they would soon be discontinued. I found out they were not ended immediately but, no doubt, the education changes finished them. A maypole was constructed, and maypole dancing became part of the celebrations. Teaching the dancers to plait the ribbons without tangling them was a frustrating occupation but on the display day they usually gave a good account of themselves. The children elected a May Queen and her attendants, and a special dress was made for the queen. She wore it proudly as she and her attendants processed to the throne, a chair with a colourful cover, for the crowning ceremony. A mass of flowers and the excitement brought some colour and prettiness to the lives of the children. Sports' Day and Parents' Evenings were important, and all classes enjoyed school expeditions. A favourite for the older children was Wicken Fen, near Ely where they stayed for the weekend. The area is open, and late-night walks were possible and during the day pond dipping was a much-enjoyed activity. A trip to Calais to see the work on the Channel Tunnel was a special outing and a great adventure, not only for the children but for the teaching assistants. They had travelled so little that everywhere south of the town bridge was a foreign country. The children found the visitors' centre at Calais a place to spend their money and were amazed to see some of the huge machinery used to make the tunnel. The day was a great success, although there were some mishaps, such as seasickness and the coach driver losing his way. It is to be hoped that some of those who went on the grand trip have the opportunity to use the tunnel or the Eurostar.

Lighter moments and amusement were caused by my 'bad taste' collection which consisted of ugly ornaments gathered on my travels and displayed in the office. A plastic copy of the statue of David from Florence produced much giggling from any group. They sniggered and whispered, 'Mrs Chambers has got a naked man on her cupboard'. In 1993, the school celebrated its 21st birthday with special events. A competition to design a souvenir mug was held and a girl from a very disadvantaged home won the prize. The mayor agreed to judge the fancy dress parade and to perform the presentation of the prizes and mugs. Fortuitously, the mayor was Con's sister Kathleen (my Aunt), who, when elected, expressed her pride in being a very ordinary Woodston girl who had become the first citizen of Peterborough. A visit to the Fitzwilliam Museum in Cambridge was enjoyed but not without moments of concern for the adults. Touching the artefacts might have been a disaster; particularly as some years later a number of valuable vases were broken. Book weeks and Christmas concerts were enjoyed and well attended. A visit from the local Member of Parliament during his time as Secretary of State for Northern Ireland during the troubles was a different experience. The school was searched for bombs and the protection force remained in the building during the visit. In all the years I spent in school, pupils came and went and just one remains in touch. Michelle was nine when I went to Welland and has faced many vicissitudes but has become a caring and hardworking woman, always with a smile.

China with Wisbech Grammar School

Early in 1994, I visited Wisbech Grammar School to support a boy of Pakistani parentage, who was academic and hardworking and an obvious candidate for a grammar school education. While there, a notice about a trip to China attracted my attention. I asked if I could be included and at the beginning of the Easter holidays the great adventure began. We flew by Pakistani Airways; the flights began with prayer and the planes have the direction of Mecca displayed on the television screens. The most interesting part of the journey was flying over the Himalayas and seeing the huge snow-covered peaks. We spent the first part of the trip in Beijing and visited many renowned places. Tiananmen Square was overwhelming. We remembered the students' demonstration and the way it was cruelly crushed but it was impossible not to be impressed by its sheer size, and feel it was a friendlier place when it was being used as a kite flying arena. It was surreal to walk through the gate under the picture of Mao into the Forbidden City. The city covers a huge area, and the pavilions are impressive, as are the marble carvings and statues. The magnificence of the interiors with wonderful furniture, brocade hangings and upholstery is outstanding. On this visit we were able to go into the pavilions and get close to the exhibits. Ten years later, many more restrictions were in place, and the buildings were rather shabby as a result of thousands more tourists. The Summer Palace was equally impressive with vast beautiful buildings and a huge lake. The Empress Dowager Cixi had a marble boat built and we were able to walk on it. Again, on my second visit it was out of bounds for the mass of tourists and the long promenade was showing signs of too many visitors. The Temple of Heaven is where the emperors prayed for good harvests. At the very centre is a circular mound which is built on the base of 9, a number regarded as lucky and is likely the place where the prayers were offered. The Ming Tombs did not thrill, they were interesting but chilling both literally and figuratively. We walked on the Great Wall and had photographs taken, but the Wall is so impressive that we didn't need anything to remind us of the experience of being on it.

After Beijing we travelled by sleeper train to Xian and the journey was an adventure. Beijing Railway Station was crowded with people; each one appeared to be carrying a large, checked plastic shopping bag so loved by the Chinese. Most were sitting or lying on the ground, and there didn't seem to be a timetable. When a train arrived, everyone pushed! We found it almost impossible to find our train and were greatly relieved when we did. The washing facilities were minimal, the toilet primitive, just a hole in the floor and the sleeping arrangements bunks. The 'Red Guard' train attendant ungraciously gave us pillows, and these almost caused a diplomatic incident. When we arrived at Xian, she accused us of stealing one of the pillows! We thought we would be incarcerated. Thankfully we were not. The skyline of Xian is dominated by the Big Wild Goose Pagoda part of the great Benevolent Temple. The Huaqing Hot Springs with an imperial palace and a bathing place are particularly associated with the Tang Dynasty but the room from where Chiang Kai-shek escaped to Taiwan is also there. The main reason for visiting Xian was to see the terracotta Army and when we arrived at the Exhibition Hall, we were staggered by the immensity of the area and the number of the warriors. Although the exhibition of the warriors at the British Museum in 2008 gave a different perspective, there is nothing to compare with seeing them in situ. Most of us fell into the tourist trap and bought model warriors. The visit to China was completed by an evening at the theatre where we were entertained by gymnasts and musicians playing Tang Dynasty music. Among the travellers in the plane on the return journey were a number of what appeared to be tribesmen with cooking pots and stoves. I just hoped they would not begin to cook! The aircraft made a stop at Istanbul where the turbulence was severe as we came into land, which was disconcerting for some of the students. Later, I made a proper visit to Istanbul and the feeling that it is a bridge between Asia and Europe is tangible, particularly when walking on the promenade beside the Bosphorus or sailing into the Black Sea. The Blue Mosque and Aya Sofya are huge and impressive and the Topkapi Palace with the furniture and fittings and the Harem gave an atmosphere of the lifestyle of the Sultan. Perhaps the most interesting was the Basilica Cistern, a Roman underground reservoir from which the water was used to supply important buildings. The Grand Bazaar was crammed with stalls, and every stall holder was determined to sell something to everyone. The dried fruit and nuts were the only things I wished to buy, although at a carpet maker's showroom Jono fell for the salesman's patter and purchased a small silk mat.

Leaving School and Other Celebrations

In 1994, I packed my cane and left teaching. I had always entertained the hope that my successor would be someone I liked but I handed over to someone with whom I, unfortunately, had no affinity and her time as head teacher was short. Before I set the burglar alarm for the last time, I was given an excellent send off and received many bouquets and gifts. The children performed a specially written play of Noah and the animals and after the performance I was presented with a Noah's ark. The story of Noah had always been my 'fall back' assembly subject! A party, arranged by the staff with input from Alison, was much more than a buffet with sandwiches and sausage rolls! The school dining room was changed into an elegant reception room with blue and white flowers, proper waitresses and strawberries and cream. Many colleagues, friends and family were invited, and necessary speeches made. Once school closed, I spent two weeks sorting out the office. At times the piles of papers almost reached the ceiling. When everything was completed, it was time to hand over my keys. That was the most emotional experience. I felt I no longer had any authority. What is interesting is that I was invited to the Brownies' special celebration twenty-two years later, the building had changed completely, and the present head teacher is successful.

On retirement from school, my picture of Noah's ark

At the beginning of September 1994, Jono, Alison, and I went to Corsica on holiday so that I could drink champagne on the morning I would normally be beginning a new school year. Alison was responsible not only for the retirement celebration but has been the organizer of all my special occasions. At the time of my 50th birthday, Leslie and Pam were living in Thorpe Road where the house had a large semi-basement room which Leslie had turned into an 'events' space. Alison and her friend, Karen, regularly disappeared and explained their absences with excuses which I gullibly believed. On my actual birthday, Arthur colluded with them and fabricated a story to get me to 'visit Leslie and Pam'! There I was faced with a big party complete with birthday cake. Ten years later the birthday party was shared with John Stephenson at the Crown Inn at Elton. His wife Patsy has been a special friend to me. In 2004, Alison took me to Hambleton Hall at Rutland Water for a very expensive dinner and later friends joined us for a lovely Sunday lunch. She then arranged an occasion in 2013, again at Hambleton Hall. We had dinner and stayed the night in luxurious surroundings. In the morning we tried to find Somerby which was a difficult task, but Alison had booked me in for 'a go' on a horse. I had always wanted to ride. It was the start of a long task, but, in 2016, progress is interesting! I had no idea it would be such an effort for me. The year 2014 marked another special birthday. This time it was my 80th, I could hardly have imagined me reaching such an age. Alison with Jono's support arranged an expensive celebration at the Talbot Hotel at Oundle. Many family members and friends came, the food was good as was the service and plenty of amusing talks entertained all present, particularly one delivered by my brother Leslie. Auntie Marg came and was carried up the stairs by Jono and Harry on a chair. She enjoyed herself which was pleasing: it was her last real outing as she died in January 2015. The evening slipped by rapidly and the party was over all too quickly. In 2017, a meal at Hambleton Hall was enjoyed by Alison and me! The horse riding continued.

Post School Life

I needed a project after school and decided that I would attempt to gain a PhD. I already had a booklet of available courses at London University and decided to write to the Institute of Education and make enquiries of Professor Gordon. By this time, he had retired, but Richard Aldrich replied positively, and I was fortunate when he offered to be my supervisor. I began work in January 1995. I had obtained an MA at King's College, but referees were still necessary and formal registration was also required. The latter involved taking my certificates which I had had framed, and they were heavy and bulky. Initially, I was under the illusion that my ideas for a thesis would be accepted but Richard was tough. Every aspect was thoroughly discussed and reviewed, and it was some time before my particular research was agreed. The thesis was to be entitled 'Provision, Personnel and Practice in Schools for Children under 11 Years of Age in Peterborough'. It necessitated interviewing past pupils and teachers and was time consuming. Indeed, it seemed to go on forever. The monthly meetings with Richard ensured I knew my 'stuff'; his questions were always searching. My seminar talk for transfer from M.Phil. to PhD was memorable! The seminars were and are always held in the Senate House, but on the day of my talk the building was flooded!! Cancellation was a high possibility but after much deliberation, the seminar was held in the Institute, and I survived the ordeal. Jono bullied me to complete the writing of my tome and, in 1999, the work was complete, but I had written more than the allocated number of words. I had no option but to apply for permission to include the excess. Six weeks passed before a positive answer came and only then could the thesis be submitted, with relief.

Christmas 1999 was a fraught time. I worried about the examination, while trying to enjoy the many millennium celebrations. We partied at Langtoft and Con, being the oldest person present, shared the cutting of the special cake with the youngest child. 6th January 2000, the day of my viva, eventually dawned and I faced my examiners, Evelyn Cowie, and Peter Cunningham. Thankfully, I was successful and can say that I was one of the first to get a PhD in the 21st century. Jono, Alison, Simon, and I went to Brian Turner's restaurant in Chelsea for dinner and we drank 'Bolly'. Jono did not join the toasting, he was 'proper poorly' but he doesn't drink champagne anyway. The graduation ceremony was more than a year later, but when it arrived, Con, David Jono, Alison, Barbara and Rodney came, and we all attended the celebration buffet. Afterwards, a second celebration, prepared by Simon, was ready at Alison's flat.

One of the most positive consequences of the studies at the London Institute of Education is the friendship of Anne Allsopp. Since about 2004/5 we have been meeting regularly to attend the monthly seminars at the Senate House, some of which have been interesting, others have not held the attention and have induced closing eyelids. Before the meeting we have taken the opportunity to utilise the day culturally and have enjoyed visiting exhibitions of antiquities, museums, art galleries and buildings of historical interest. We especially enjoyed visiting Apsley House, the home of the

Duke of Wellington, which is full of the objects that were presented to the Duke for his successful battles and his Parliamentary life. The illness and finally death of Anne's husband meant we were unable to meet for some time, but we are now meeting, but irregularly. We managed, in 2014, to visit the Tower of London for the Poppy display which marked the centenary of the beginning of the 1914/1918 War. Unfortunately, both Evelyn Cowie and Richard have died. Both were excellent and helpful 'teachers'.

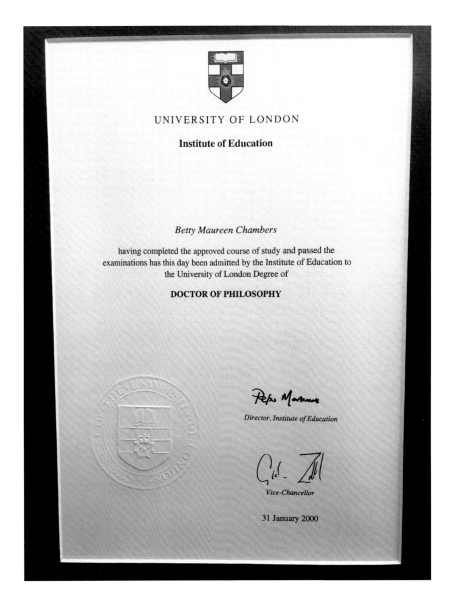

PhD Certificate

Australia: Visit Three

In 2000, with the successful PhD behind me, I flew to Australia for my third visit, and I did so alone. Alison gave me the ticket as a Christmas present and I boarded a crowded plane at Heathrow bound for Singapore. I was very impressed by the cleanliness and efficiency of Changi airport and was soon on my way to a friend's flat. We spent the day visiting the Botanical Gardens and going to the Long Bar at the Raffles where we drank cocktails and threw our peanut shells on the floor as is the well-established practice. After dinner at an open-air restaurant, we studied the map to find out the best way to Jalan Kechubong and next day I set off on the MTR. I was going to Yio Chu Kang, a name I remembered well! At the station I found a knowledgeable taxi driver, who, by chance, took me to Jalan Bangau, which had hardly changed in 40 years except that the trees and bushes had grown profusely, then to an almost unrecognizable Jalan Kechubong. The road was much narrower than I remembered, and many more and larger houses had been built with two impressive residences on the site of our house. Two original houses remained but looked in need of renovation, and, no doubt, demolition not renovation was their fate. Nee Soon, previously a British Army base, had become a Singapore Army facility and I was not permitted inside, but I took photographs from the gate before returning to Singapore City. There, I visited some of the places with which I was familiar from previous years. The Cathedral remained impressive, but the Padang, where I had my first Singapore photograph taken 45 years before seemed much smaller than I remembered.

I completed my journey to Perth the next day where Helen Farran, Con's friend, met me. Almost immediately she took me to King's Park, from where there is a magnificent view of the Perth skyline and where there were preparations at the war memorial for the queen's imminent visit. A drive beside the Indian Ocean ended at the Hillaries to visit the Underwater World. This centre is almost a carbon copy of Under Sea World at Queensferry in that it has moving walkways through the tunnel-like tanks with the fish swimming all around. In Australia, the crocodiles were being fed and, although small, were aggressive. It seems that once they grow too big for the tank, they go on to a crocodile farm. I did not get an answer to the question; do they end up as products, such as handbags? Turtles and seals were in the bay but no dolphins; they had all died, probably as a result of pollution or global warming. Very early on the following morning Helen and I set out southwards; we reached Pemberton for lunch and then went on to the tree walk, a suspended walkway at the level of the canopy of the great Jarrah trees. It is exhilarating to be so high but could scare anyone with a fear of heights, as the walkway is mesh and sways as you walk from one platform to the next. We also sampled the low-level walk, a path through the amazingly colossal roots. We passed the night in a peaceful log cabin set amongst the huge forest trees and boasting a spa bath and a log fire. It would have been lovely to stay longer but we headed south to Cape Leeuwin, an area which the Dutch explored in the 16th Century. The Indian and Southern Oceans meet off this coast and we climbed the lighthouse for a magnificent view. Turning northwards we headed for the Jewel Cave and took a fantastic tour underground, before going to the Cave Works to see the exhibition of the formation of the caves as well as their discovery and exploration. We called at a winery on the return and once in Perth went to the theatre. One performance was a comedy and the second a play about growing up in Western Australia which was entertaining and illustrated that children and young people are the same the world over.

Fiona who had been a teacher at Welland School and Rob, her husband, took me to a Wildlife Park where I fed kangaroos, emus, and alpacas, after which I did the real touristy thing and had my photograph taken with a koala. The keeper asked me to continue to hold it while she cleaned an injured and infected ear; a male had become aggressive. The animal became heavier and heavier, and Fiona was worried that its claws were very near my throat. I handed it back with relief. My first lone Australian trip was next. I caught a four-wheel drive vehicle for a drive to the Pinnacles. The first stop was at the Yanchep Wildlife Park where a fault on the vehicle was discovered which caused a wait of more than an hour for a replacement. Once we were underway, we did not stop until we reached Cervantes, where we paddled in the Indian Ocean and had a picnic lunch. Then on to the Pinnacles, thought to be the fossilized remains of tree trunks which once formed a huge forest. I had gained the impression from the pictures that all the fossils were large, but their sizes vary, and it is easy to get lost in the huge area they cover. The next part of the journey was to the beach on non-tarmacked roads, so the tyres were deflated. The dunes are gigantic and despite the wind the daring raced down them on improvised sledges.

One of many highlights of the trip came next when Helen and I drove to Rockingham Bay where we took a boat to go swimming with the dolphins. We donned the required clothing, wet suits and snorkels and were allocated to our access-to-the-sea group which was denoted by a particular-coloured belt. The search for dolphins began immediately we left the quay and when the first pod was located three groups entered the sea satisfactorily. We were in the last group, and I was at the front, but was asked to allow a woman to go first as she couldn't swim! Disaster almost resulted, she panicked and began to roll over, so that I could not grab her belt and was pushed and splashed. Behind me, her husband who was also a non-swimmer started to panic and shout and we returned to the boat immediately. Fortunately, we went back into the water at once otherwise I might have lost my courage, but the dolphins had disappeared, and we returned a second time to the boat. A search for more began and this time we were fortunate enough to experience being in the sea with dolphins and a stingray. The chase continued for more pods but our last attempt to go into the water was cut short by the choppy sea. At the harbour, the two non-swimmers were purchasing, somewhat ironically, T-shirts bearing the logo 'I swam with dolphins'!

My planned tour to the Wave Rock was cancelled owing to lack of clients so I chose a wine cruise on the Swan River and the wine flowed from 10 am as the cruise began until 5 pm when the boat returned to Perth. The journey along the river was relaxing and the crew pointed out places of interest including the area of Rolf Harris' home. It was at the time when Rolf was everyone's favourite entertainer and an admired painter of portraits. Indeed, he had painted the Queen and received a knighthood. Unfortunately, illegal actions were discovered and at the present time (2016) he is in prison. Sandalwood and Houghton, the two wineries we visited, each proffered eight or more wines to be sampled. Mulberry Farm was the venue for lunch; the food was excellent, the other tourists friendly, wine flowed continuously and after the meal the crew entertained us before the boat turned back. After a wine-filled day, a lazy day in the garden was welcome and it was followed by an evening at the theatre for a performance of 'Don't Dress for Dinner', a comedy staring Dennis Waterman. Next on the agenda was sight-seeing around Perth and Freemantle. A coach tour of Perth took in the buildings of note, and at Lake Munger we watched the pelicans and black swans. Cottesloe Beach is a pleasant spot on the edge of the Indian Ocean, and we stopped briefly to enjoy the sunshine and afterwards travelled along the coast to Freemantle. A leisurely cruise transported us back to Perth, where the film 'American Beauty' was showing and Helen and I took the opportunity to see this unusual production, before meeting Helen's family for a specially arranged dinner. My last Perth days were spent with Fiona. I saw aboriginal art as well as work by local students at Perth Art Gallery and visited London Court, a shopping street in Tudor style full of gift shops waiting to ensnare tourists. Finally, I entered Freemantle prison! This edifice, built by convicts, has become a tourist 'must'. The guide was, I'm certain, an ex-guard and very proud of the prison, and thoroughly enjoyed showing us the most gruesome artefact - the gallows.

I bade a sad farewell to Perth and was soon flying towards Ayres Rock. The airport at the Rock is small, despite a constant flow of tourists. On the way to the Sails in the Desert, my hotel, I saw the Olgas, a spectacular rock formation, and got my first glimpse of THE Rock. The hotel proved to be good but, surprisingly, the evening was cool with heavy rain, and I went to bed early in order to be ready to depart for Ayres Rock at 6am. After some confusion about which bus I should board, I was directed to the group for the aboriginal walk. At the 'viewing place' we watched the spectacular sunrise. The Rock changes colour from almost black, through purple to the red that is always pictured. A drive around the base of the Rock followed and the driver pointed out particular formations and areas of significance for aboriginals. Breakfast was eaten at the Aboriginal Centre and our guide for the walk was Andrew Uluru, the brother of the Keeper of the Rock. Andrew told us many fascinating and interesting facts and was insistent that the Rock is called Uluru, the aboriginal name. The desert was unusually wet with flowers blooming, so I saw the Red Centre in rare circumstances. I did not need to make a decision about climbing the Rock. It was closed owing to the possibility of storms. In the evening I ate a solitary celebratory dinner as it was 11th April and, coincidentally, a couple in the restaurant were just married.

The journey to King's Canyon, my next expedition, was very long and required an even earlier departure than that to Ayres Rock. Breakfast was eaten at an ex-cattle station where the owners had diversified into the tourist trade. They had a collection of kangaroos and to make extra income, they rounded up wild camels for export to the Middle East. At King's Canyon, I decided against the walk around the top, there were 400 steps to reach it and the heat was 36°C. Instead, I took the walk at its base, which was cool with the many quick-flowing streams. A few weeks before, the Canyon had been cut off by floods and people marooned! I did not miss the view of the top, however, as I took a helicopter ride, which was a new experience. On the way back to the hotel we stopped to view Mt. Connor, which is yet another rock formation and looks rather like a flat-topped Ayres Rock. I left the next day. The plane to Alice Springs departed in the late afternoon and the little airport was almost empty as was the small plane. I had three seats to myself and an excellent view of Amadeus Lake with water; usually it is only a salt flat. I had always wanted to see Alice Springs, since reading A Town like Alice, but the airport is well outside the town and my only achievement was to change planes. The walk to the departure lounge was long and, by the time I reached it, the last calls for the Melbourne plane were being made. The aircraft was crowded and at Adelaide everyone had to disembark - not certain why but we dashed back because it was pouring with rain. Janice and Matthew, who had lived in Forge End, met me at Melbourne but not until I had collected my luggage and panicked in case they had forgotten me. Coffee and cakes in the city followed before we went to their house.

The first excursion in Melbourne was around Port Philip Bay. The countryside of Victoria seemed similar to some parts of England but on a bigger scale. We ate fish and chips on the ferry and admired the views. Our destination was Queenscliff and the return journey to Melbourne was by road, during which we visited a number of beaches, saw the places where Janice would like to live and visited Haileybury, Matthew's school. Haileybury is obviously an excellent school and Matthew chose it because he wanted his abilities to be fully extended, but whether his brittle emotional state will allow him to achieve his aims remains to be seen. The day finished with a tour of the waterfront to see the lights and eat a Chinese meal. I discovered that Melbourne is famous for its food. The last day included a trip to the business centre where one small dwelling house remained hedged in by huge skyscrapers. The owner had refused to sell or move. Big business, no doubt, eventually succeeded in obtaining the site. I saw the Yarra River and enjoyed the impressive war memorial. Then it was off to the airport for the flight to Sydney. It seemed a very short stay. When I left Melbourne, I did not know that Mathew would be married when I next saw him, but now he and his wife have two children. I hope to see them during this year 2017 – he did visit with his family.

June met me and we drove to her house which has an impressive view onto the harbour. There was no time to enjoy the view, however, because plans had been made for a seaside break at Molly Mook, a little coastal resort south of Sydney, with Helen, Joe, Nina, Lucas and the 'boss' Eliza Rose. The holiday home, belonging to June's cousin overlooks the ocean and is less than a stone's throw from the beach. For three days we walked or sat on the sand, fished in pools, swam in the sea or just enjoyed the sun. On one afternoon we managed to pull ourselves away from the beach to venture into the small town to take the young ones to the cinema. On leaving Molly Mook, we set out for Jindabyne, stopping on the way at Tilba, a heritage village full of old buildings and craft shops, crossing the Monaro, extensive hills with no trees, and the Snowy River before arriving at Silver Top. My bedroom had a view straight down to Lake Jindabyne and next morning we searched for kangaroos near what is known as 'the big dam', but there were none just numerous possum holes. I saw kangaroos, however, as a number appeared on the lawn. On a day when it was very cold and snowy, we set out on a 'great expedition' to scale Mount Kosciuszko. Australia is a very flat continent and Kosciuszko, said to be the highest point, is situated in a protected area. Thredbo, the Alpine centre of Australia and where there had been a serious avalanche, is on the way to the ski lift which we took to the start of the two-and-half-hour trek. There were times when I wondered if I would make it, particularly the last ascent to the summit, but I was very pleased when I succeeded. Easter Day brought excitement on the egg front and later June took me in to Jindabyne to the visitors' centre to see the story of the Snowy Mountain Scheme and the creation of the Jindabyne Lake. On the drive back to Sydney, June, David and I stopped near Lake George for a picnic, bypassed Canberra but called at Berrima to visit friends. There I met a visitor to Australia and was most surprised to find it was Miriam Margolyes of TV and theatre fame.

Back in Sydney, June and I climbed the bridge. Great preparation for this event was essential, a video was watched, a disclaimer signed, a breathalyser test given, watches and other droppable items put in secure storage, one-piece suits, safety belts, warm and wet weather clothing, radio and earpiece provided. A check with a metal detector and practice stair climbing followed before we made our way on to the bridge, up the ladders to the main structure and then the climb to the top. All the time we were on the bridge we were anchored to the structure by a chain to prevent any accidents. We were higher than the opera house and the view was marvellous and the feeling exhilarating. Once the climb was over, we were disrobed and had all the technical bits removed, given a certificate, and encouraged to purchase a photograph before being sent on our way to recuperate with tea and cakes. Afterwards I watched the never-ending Anzac Day parade on television; Gallipoli has a high profile in Australia and people exude patriotism. Pride in the country was as high at the Royal Easter Show which was held near the new Olympic Site. The regional displays exhibited every Australian fruit and vegetables and the Great Australian Muster - the story of the Man from Snowy River - in the main ring was cheered and cheered and cheered!!

I took myself to Sydney by ferry, and spent time at the Art Gallery, in the Botanical Gardens, at the Hyde Park Barracks and Government House. The latter was a new attraction and one which I found fascinating. I went to the top of the Centre Point Tower as I had done on a previous visit and the view made me realise how much of Sydney I had not visited. The day finished with a meal at an Italian restaurant at Mossman. A concert at the Opera House was special and a visit to the Olympic site gave the opportunity to visit the main stadium, the aquatic centre and the sports centre where the Hall of Sporting fame was located. After a search we found the details of David and his success at the Munich Olympics. On my last day, June suggested a trip to Bradley Head to see the memorials to various ships all named HMS Sydney and several guns from the 1860s and afterwards my final dinner was eaten at Café Sydney which overlooks the Harbour Bridge. The morning of my departure gave time for a brief look around Hunter's Hill before heading for the airport and boarding the plane. I arrived back at Heathrow at 5am on 1st May 2000.

Volunteering

Although I retired from Welland School, I did not desert education completely and became a Bishop's Visitor to Church of England schools. I was interviewed formally before being accepted as a visitor and then trained for the role. I was licensed at the Cathedral by Bishop Bill and looked forward to the challenge of this task, but my tenure lasted no more than two years. I did not feel that the schools welcomed what they perceived as extra inspection. They had enough with Ofsted! I also became a governor of Caverstede Nursery School and maintained my membership of the Early Years Partnership. The former was interesting and satisfying but came to an abrupt end. The head teacher moved to work for early years in the education office and a new appointment was necessary. The deputy head teacher was regarded by many as an ideal candidate, but the chair of governors was not supportive. I felt this unfair, wrote a reference for her and acted as a mentor. When she was not appointed, I voted against the appointee and decided I could not continue as I would be an embarrassment to the new head teacher. It was not an easy decision as I was very interested in nursery education. I held the position of chair of the Quality Assurance Committee of the Early Years Partnership and led the members in the work to ensure that parents could be confident that their children were receiving quality care and education. Guidelines were produced detailing the factors that would give that confidence and the pre-school providers produced evidence that they were meeting the requirements. An official ceremony was held at which successful establishments were presented with a Peterborough Quality Assurance Certificate. I resigned from the Partnership when I felt I could no longer do the job efficiently. I was not in the day-to-day hurly-burly of the work.

I was persuaded to become a governor of Walton Junior School and continued in the role until 2007. During the years of service, I took an active part in the work designated by the Government as being the remit of governing bodies, but my particular role was preparing the improvement/development plan for the governors and was involved in ensuring they attended regular training. I had planned to resign in 2006, when the head teacher completed his career, but agreed to remain for another year as plans to amalgamate the junior and infant schools were afoot. The local authority left much of the enormous workload to the governors and was slow in completing the necessary administrative details. Thus, to keep to the timescale the new head teacher was appointed on 21st March a few days before the amalgamation was officially sanctioned. The summer term was filled with the practicalities of amalgamation, and sometimes it appeared doubtful if everything would be ready, but the new Discovery Primary School opened in September 2007, when I finally resigned from school governing. Educational appeals feature on my list of voluntary activities and are an interesting but sometimes boring occupation. An appraisal pilot of appeals panel members was introduced of which I became part. It involved co-operation with Essex and Suffolk and attending training in London. The innovation proved too expensive to be continued but having had this extra training I usually find myself chairman of the panel. I continued this task for many years but decided to end being a panel member in 2017 when my son David was 60 [Jonathon (2023): Mum didn't write this, but a trigger for this decision was also that a fellow panel member highlighted that Mum had repeated a question, perhaps this was one of the first outward signs of the onset of dementia.].

I was encouraged, actually bullied would be a better word, by Marjorie Stone to become chair of the Peterborough Alzheimer's Society branch, a volunteer role very different from educational tasks and one in which I served for 10 years. I needed to learn a whole new vocabulary and understand the needs of people with dementia but felt it a valuable charity in which to take a part. Over the years, however, the Society changed its management structure and developed the philosophy of big business where volunteers seem to be less valued. At one event, a Tai Chi group gave a demonstration of the exercise, something in which I had long been interested and I decided to join the group. Tai Chi exercises both the mind and body and learning and improvement are continuous. I initially thought I would never be able to remember the sequence of the moves, but eventually it was committed in my memory. I continued my role as secretary to St. Andrew's Parochial Church Council, a task I acquired by accident! Arthur was a member of the council from the early days of living in Alwalton and on one occasion I waited for him until a meeting finished. No-one was available to take the minutes; I volunteered and recorded the meetings for 25 years before I was able to put away my pen. Despite this accomplishment, I acquired various roles one of which is to ensure the flowers are in place for services and particular festivals. I am not a good flower arranger but on one occasion agreed to do, for me, the impossible task of decorating the church for a wedding. Thankfully, Simon came to the rescue and the church looked magnificent. Since my school days and my first French lessons I have always wanted to be proficient in the language and continue to attend classes. Unfortunately, I seem not to have an aptitude, although I make real efforts to improve. I went to Normandy in 1994/95 on a most enjoyable course and later stayed with a French family. Through the Adult College's exchange arrangements, I met Marie Therese and went to visit Bourges, a most beautiful city, and she has been to Peterborough. After life in school, I realised that exercise was important to maintain a level of physical health and I joined the leisure club at the Swallow Hotel in September 1994 and have used the swimming pool regularly since then. The hotel name was changed in 19/20 to The Marriott and swimming remains a special exercise but in October 2016 the pool needed some attention and there was no swimming until 2017.

Forge End

Once the decision to leave Whittlesea was made, a search for a new home was essential. A variety of houses were visited but none felt right until, after weeks of scrutinising the local newspaper, I found the advertisement for a house in Forge End, Alwalton. The immediate reaction to the bungalow was that it was exactly what was wanted. I haven't changed my opinion since, although soon after our move we thought we had made a huge mistake. Much of the floor was excavated before the cause of an under-floor leak was discovered. Once we were properly installed, we began to consider changes and the first major alteration came in 1981 when we altered the main bedroom and the bathroom. Wardrobes and a chest of drawers were built in the bedroom and the bathroom given a complete makeover while the sitting room was carpeted, and the kitchen given new worktops and new appliances. Unfortunately, the sitting room remained an odd shape and the in-line position of the entrance doors caused problems in the kitchen and the dark colour cupboards and worktops were depressing. Thus, after Arthur's death changes became inevitable and significant. Richard Kay prepared the plans and Alison took on the management. The weekend that Alison and Jono made preparations for the work they dropped a huge, heavy box. Minnie, the dog avoided death by a whisker! We then vacated Forge End; Jono and I as well as Minnie went to Longthorpe, and Alison moved in with Brenda and John South.

The work of transformation lasted about three months. The living room took on a better shape, the kitchen and entrances were completely renewed and the wooden floor reinstated. During the time away from Forge End, Jono and I went to New York for Easter Weekend. A helpful taxi driver took us to the hotel on Fifth Avenue, from where we had a view of the Empire State Building. New York is renowned for shopping, but we did none, the shops were closed for Easter. There were queues but for church, particularly outside St. Patrick's Cathedral. We obtained theatre tickets from the cabin on the Avenue and enjoyed two shows. We booked a bus tour and saw something of New York, but the guide ensured we spent much time in China Town with the purpose of relieving us of our money. A boat trip to Liberty Island gave the opportunity to walk around the Statue of Liberty, but the weather was absolutely freezing, and we did not want to stay long. We passed Ellis Island where immigrants were processed but the most memorable part of the weekend was going to the top of one of the Towers in the World Trade Centre, something that is now impossible! The view was spectacular, but I was unhappy during the descent. There were crowds and the direction to the lifts was poor. I remembered with horror that downward journey on the day the towers were destroyed.

Working in the garden at Forge End

A second trip to America, in May 1997, made a break when the second session of Forge End renovation was taking place. This time the alterations included the construction of a large new bedroom, changing a bedroom into an office, the bathroom into a bedroom and constructing a new bathroom and shower room. This time Alison and I crossed the Atlantic. We loved New England and I think I prefer Boston to New York. We stayed in 'bed and breakfast' establishments which in America are known as inns. The one in Cape Cod was elegant. In Boston we followed the Freedom Trail and saw the many buildings associated with the American Revolution and War of Independence. At the State House, while looking at a collection of old flags, we listened to a teacher talking to his students about the revolution. I just had to say, 'We are not really that bad!'. At the Charlestown Navy Yard, we went on board the U.S.S. Constitution, Old Ironsides, which is the oldest commissioned warship afloat. The Museum of Fine Arts has so many exhibits that more time was needed to appreciate even a fraction while the Isabella Stewart Gardner Museum contains an eclectic collection that could be described as bizarre. Boston extends into Cambridge and like the original city of that name houses a famous university, the Massachusetts Institute of Technology (M.I.T.) at which I have suggested Jono gets a post so that I could live in Boston for a time! We hired a car to drive to Cape Cod and stayed at Falmouth and toured extensively, making sure we viewed the Kennedy properties! Excellent fish meals were available in a very American caravan-type restaurant. At Princetown we looked at the spot where the Pilgrims landed and visited the Heritage Plantation, which has extensive gardens and a vintage car museum and as it was the American Mothers' Day, I was given free entry. Every mother who was with her child/children was given the concession. We loved Martha's Vineyard, particularly the coloured Victorian holiday cottages, known as Oak Bluffs. On the journey back to Boston we stopped at Plymouth and went to the Plymouth Plantation, a place of living history. The Pilgrim settlement is an authentic reconstruction of a Pilgrim village, and the inhabitants re-enact Pilgrim life. The last night in Boston was spent in a car park waiting for the airport to open. Alison would not find a hotel for a few hours!

Con at Alwalton

Bill died in 1979 after a very brief period of feeling unwell. One week before his death, he was climbing on a roof making repairs and soon after the work was complete, he began to develop symptoms of a cold. In the early hours of 9th March, he got out of bed, had a heart attack and did not survive. In all respects the rapidity of the event was what Bill would have wanted. He would have hated a long period of incapacity and would not have been able to tolerate time in hospital. He was greatly missed but Con built a life without him. She was a continuing asset to Leslie and Martin, retained her interest in village activities and enjoyed many holidays in England and abroad. Not long after the alterations to Forge End were completed; however, Leslie began to think about leaving the garage. His ability to cope with his increasing stiffness made the work of car repairs more difficult but he was concerned about what would happen to Con if the business was sold. The only answer was for her to come to Alwalton, where the increased space meant a new bedroom was available for her and her furniture and personal possessions. She had been extremely independent at Longthorpe and I expected her to continue her enthusiasm for activities, but it did not happen that way. Perhaps I took her independence from her, perhaps moving her away from Longthorpe took her away from all she knew or perhaps she wasn't as well as I thought. At first, she seemed her old self, and her 90th birthday party was the celebration she loved but little things began to demonstrate her slipping abilities; she wasn't able to manage the tasks she had, throughout her life, done without a thought. One example was when a large number of plums needed to be stoned for freezing. Con said she would help but she was unable to remove the stones. Previously the plums would have been finished with ease.

Unfortunately, it was not long before carers were needed if I went away and, at first, she enjoyed being looked after at home, but the arrangement ended when one carer was without understanding or sympathy. A new arrangement was made, and Con stayed at Werrington with the manager of the day centre which she attended. Con had, at first, rejected out of hand the idea of going to a day centre, but once she was persuaded to try, she enjoyed the activities and the companionship until the day she became ill. On the particular day, Con was unable to eat her breakfast, but I insisted she went as I was certain that she was being difficult. She wasn't and during the day the worries of the staff mounted, I was asked to collect her, and her health became steadily more concerning. The next day, the doctor called an ambulance to take her to hospital. On the journey she was very ill, and I had doubts about her survival, but after being admitted to PDH she was transferred to Edith Cavell where she remained for seven weeks. She deteriorated during those weeks, and I attach much blame to the staff for her losing the ability to feed herself and for her becoming incontinent. Care was very patchy. She was assessed a number of times, but it was totally impossible to find out the result of these assessments and no plan for future care was properly discussed. Suddenly, two days before I was due to go to Mallorca, I was told she needed a residential nursing home and needed it 'like yesterday'. Fortunately, Primrose Hill at Huntingdon, a new care home, had rooms and Con lived there and was looked after very well until she died. Her popularity was illustrated by the number of friends and family at her funeral at Longthorpe Church. She is buried beside Bill in the churchyard under a big horse chestnut tree. Some years after her death Alison met a carer, who worked at Primrose Hill care home. She remembered Con as a lovely lady. Even after 10 years people remember her fondly.

Mum's (Con's) 94th birthday with Pam (Leslie's wife), me, Alison, Jono and Leslie

Visits abroad and at home

Alison was responsible for us venturing into gîte country when she persuaded Jono to go with her to Provence to visit Richard Kaye, and, in 1987, the south of France called us as it did in succeeding years. On this first occasion, we left immediately school closed in a car that was loaded to the gunnels. John South delivered Simon with food, prepared by Brenda, another of my special friends, for the journey. We crossed the Channel by ferry and shared the long drive. I drew the short straw, as I did many times on subsequent drives, and drove from Paris to Lyon during the night, while the rest of the car occupants slept. The return journeys were mostly less fraught, and we usually stopped at one of the many interesting towns en route. Once at Orange, we watched the preparations for a rock concert by Kid Creole and the Coconuts in the almost perfectly preserved Roman amphitheatre with its acoustics making it a perfect venue. The destination for three years was 'Monsieur Rouvier Land' otherwise known as Brenon; a tiny hamlet situated up a steep track at the summit of a mountain in the Var Department. Whether we travelled the Route de Soleil and looked out for Mont St.Victoire, the mountain always associated with Cezanne, or went via Grenoble and the Route Napoleon, the road taken by Napoleon after his escape from Elba, we joined most of the French and Dutch population in heading to the sun. The 'gîte', a rustic cottage, was far from the crowds and its facilities basic. Simon found the beds caused a problem for his back and slept on his mattress on the floor. The cooker was hardly state of the art, but we managed to cook much local produce, purchased from the market at Draguignan. The favourites were ratatouille and roasted tomatoes. Grasse, famous for its perfumeries, was on the route to Cannes, which we considered our seaside despite the crowded beach. The film festival was long over when we were holidaying, so we had no celebrities to ogle.

Nice with its Promenade des Anglais was a reasonable drive from Brenon and the flower market was always a blaze of colour while the open-air restaurants with their spectacular arrangements of sea food were an evening interest. St Tropez, just along the coast, has a wonderful setting but the traffic jams and the crowds did not encourage more than one visit. An excursion to Monaco was made for Simon to see Princess Grace's tomb and for me to stand outside the casino in Monte Carlo waiting for a rich 'sugar daddy'! I was never fortunate enough to find one. The old university city of Aix-en-Provence provided the opportunity to be self indulgent and drink chocolate and eat gorgeous chocolate cakes. The area of France north of the Riviera is mountainous with rocky gorges and the Gorges de Verdon is one of the most famous with a sheer drop into the gorge and towering rocks above. The drive around its rim with the hair pin bends causes the heart to beat faster but, at least, safety barriers are in place. In years gone by a sure-footed mule would have been essential. Perhaps not so well known is the Gorges du Loup but there, wonderful glace fruit is produced, and we regularly purchased some of the sticky, sweet mandarin oranges. Across one of the ravines north of Brenon, at the village of Moustiers-Sainte-Marie, a star is suspended on a chain. The village is famous for its blue and white faience and all kinds of useful and useless objects are displayed in every street. The tourists love such opportunities to buy mementos and we were tourists!! Alison insisted that we visit the grave of

Le Corbusier and finding the cemetery was difficult, but once there she made a beeline and found the grave immediately. Picasso was a famous resident of Provence and produced much of his ceramic work in Vallauris. In 2007, Nicola insisted we visit an exhibition of Picasso's ceramics in Edinburgh, and much from Villauris was on show. In nearby Vence the Foundation Maeght is a modern building with changing exhibitions which we always found worth a visit. Renoir's studio remains much as it was in his lifetime with his painting materials and easels on show while photographs portray him working with brushes tied to his hand. Arthritis prevented him from holding the brushes in his fingers.

Every summer holiday Nicola and Christopher came to stay at Alwalton. When they were very young I was still at school, but when I had finished my teaching life they had begun school. Thus August was the time for the holiday. The activities were going to the swimming pool, picking strawberries and spending time with Hannah and Ellie, and going to the seaside. Hunstanton with the amusements was the most popular but Brancaster and Wells-Next-The-Sea were also enjoyed. Going to the top of a new windmill at Swaffham, from where it was possible to see large areas of the land, was exciting. Visiting Ann and John (my cousin and her husband) was always pleasing but the swimming pool was too cold for Christopher and John found other enjoyable activities and praised Christopher for his behaviour. London's visit was special, as it included going to the Palace, but after a time Christopher found the inside somewhat boring. We, therefore, went to see as many famous places as possible, including the Crown Jewels at the Tower of London. Most important was going to Scotland to stay with Barbara and Rodney. Once we went on a plane because Nicola and Christopher had not flown at that time, but usually we had a train journey and during one journey Christopher left his bag on a train. He was very unhappy, and everything was done to find it but with no luck. In Edinburgh it was the special time of the year for all kinds of activities. Nicola and Christopher hoped there was the possibility of seeing the hanger man, he had a coat hanger and performed tricks which amused all those watching. The most memorable 'Tatoo' was the one when Christopher was 'young and small', the weather was awful, and he was soaked. Whether he went again is questionable. Over the years we visited the seaside, saw the rescue boats practising, and regularly ate fish and chips outside. We visited the Royal Yacht and Concorde; and saw the way boats were lifted up on water on the Falkirk Wheel. The gallery of modern pictures is interesting but for Nicola and Christopher the garden with its grass and water was more interesting.

I also had holidays with Jono, Alison and Simon. One year when we were based in the South of France, we took a drive to Italy along the road high above the Italian Riviera through many unlit tunnels which was exhilarating and made possible a stop at Pisa to see the leaning tower before continuing to Firenze. There we stayed in a grand hotel on the corner of St. Mark's Square. Our luggage consisted of a few belongings in plastic carriers! The day of sight seeing in Firenze was far too short. There is so much to see. The journeys to and from France were on toll roads but those in Italy did not seem to be standardized. The charge was different each way although the distance was the same and the route consistently via Genoa. A holiday at Pegomas brought us a whole new aspect of 'gîte' life! The drive to the south included a visit to Versailles where we admired the magnificent palace in brilliant sunshine. On arrival at our destination, we found the accommodation was part of a family home and the owners gave us a warm welcome. Friends joined us for the first week of our stay and found the heat difficult. They were probably relieved when the day came for their return home. When I arrived back from seeing them off at the airport, I was given a 'tonic and gin'! Not long after finishing the drink, I collapsed and from my bed could hear mutterings from Jono, Alison and Simon about my condition and the need for medical attention, but I was not able to utter a word to stop their concern. Thankfully, no medical intervention was necessary, and I had recovered by morning when we went to visit the Dominican chapel in Vence which was decorated by Matisse. It is small but the brilliant yellow and blue glass is breathtaking. The owners of the gîte cooked us a meal on our last night which began with fried courgette flowers, but at which they informed us that they were going to levy an extortionate excess because of our extra guests. So the next morning we escaped like thieves in the night, although we did pay for our visitors but through Gites de France and a reasonable amount!

Jono and I then decided to go on a 'fly-drive' holiday which turned out to be a near disaster. The St. Etienne near Lyon was not the one where we had made a booking and the planned holiday could not continue! We went on to Nice and after some unproductive phone calls (no mobiles at that time) we decided to stay. The 'fly-drive' was arranged to finish in Paris, so we had a long drive to catch the plane home! Another near disaster occurred when we drove to Italy with an overnight break along the Italian Riviera. Unfortunately, the whole population of Italy had had the same idea and we were forced to sleep in the car. Arrival at the destination also produced a near calamity; the holiday cottage was already occupied. Fortunately, the cottage belonged to the proprietors of a nearby hotel with vacant rooms and we spent a holiday in the sun and then took an interesting return route. As we drove along the Route du Soleil, we turned left and went to Barcelona, where we promenaded along the Ramblas. I did not like the fact that birds are sold from small booths which are closed up at night and over the weekend with the birds inside. We walked on the pavements with their Miro paintings and visited the cathedral which seemed very dark. Most important was to see the buildings, designed by Gaudi, particularly the unfinished Sagrada Familia. From its top the view is marvellous; we noted the site of the Olympics. When we had retraced our journey into France, we headed towards Brittany with a stop at Carcassonne. I had always wanted to visit this Medieval town but my desire was dampened by pouring rain and low temperatures. Simon was working at La Baule with its famous long beach, and he took us to see the church with its outside pulpit. We set out at midnight to drive across the north of France to Calais for the return to Peterborough.

Despite the Italian experience, Jono and I returned to Italy but faced weather which was autumnal and wet. The hotel was an isolated converted monastery, near Perugia, beautiful, like so many ancient Italian cities. The hotel, unfortunately, had no comfortable sitting room in which to relax and there was nowhere nearby to go in an evening. The food was also disappointing and, one evening, the dining room was invaded by passing travellers and the needs of the guests were hardly considered. The swimming pool was too cold for swimming, and as a result we drove many kilometres and covered every inch of Umbria and the Marches. At Assisi, we saw the places special to St. Francis and his girl friend St. Clare! It was fortunate that we chose to go in 1995 because the next year an earthquake damaged the domo, meaning extensive and expensive repairs became necessary. Tremendous thunderstorms spoiled an excursion to Spoletto but at Orvieto the sun shone and lit up the superb front of the domo. Now every purchase of white wine from Orvieto reminds us of the visit. We saw the caves at Montepulciano where the bottles of the famous red wine are stored and in Sienna we noted the banners of the rival communities as the preparations for the Palio, the famous horse race, were made. We did not see the actual race, perhaps as well as it is reputed to be dangerous, but no doubt the spectacle outweighs the danger. We reached San Gimignano, the most famous preserved Medieval fortified Italian city with its many towers overlooking the countryside so that approaching enemies could be easily seen.

Jono had seen the ferries going to Corsica from Nice, so as I looked towards my last year in school we booked to go to the island. It was a late booking, and our accommodation was in what could be described as a skiing chalet in the sun. The arrangements were unusual but acceptable. We hired a car which upset those in charge of the chalet; they wanted everything to be negotiated through them. Perhaps they made money that way. Corsica was still on the wild side with bullet-holed road signs and distances that were measured in time because of the poor surfaces. Driving from Calvi to Porto was hair-raising: the road passes amazing cliffs and climbs and twists over the Col de la Croix. I could not miss Ajaccio because I wanted to see the house where Napoleon was born. Later, in Paris, we went to Les Invalides to view Napoleon's place of 'burial'. There are many more cities connected with Napoleon. Maybe I should make a list and make it a mission to visit each one. The best experience for me on this holiday was making a scuba dive. I wore a wet suit, belt with weights, flippers and mask, and had my air tank on my back but it was still strange to find breathing was possible under the water. I did not roll off a boat as is usual with scuba diving. It was possible to enter the sea down steps at the research station and, of course, I was accompanied by a 'buddy'. Corsica proved a hit, and we went back the next year with Alison.

After years of spending summers in Europe, the decision was made to travel farther afield, and the choice was Penang. The journey was long and tiring, particularly for Jono who had just been to Bangkok to work at the university. On arrival we found the hotel was the Raza Sayang, which was superb with beautiful grounds, lovely accommodation, good restaurants, and excellent service. We spent much time relaxing in the grounds and swimming in the pool but could not miss some sight seeing. We took an excursion around the island and went to the snake temple and were photographed covered in snakes. In Georgetown, Penang's capital, I was pleased to see the ferry going to the mainland. It brought back memories of service life. In fact, I wanted to find other places I remembered but it was impossible. In Georgetown we also saw the famous colonial hotel, the Eastern and Orient, which was closed and dilapidated. I was sad! At the top of Penang Hill, a second hotel from colonial times, the Bellevue, used no doubt by expatriates in years gone by was elegantly faded with few guests. We revisited Penang later and stayed at the Raza Sayang again. The hotel showed its age, and it was good to know that refurbishment was planned. Penang had become more urban, with towering apartment blocks in which many Chinese, who had moved from Hong Kong when it reverted to Chinese control, lived. We were delighted to find that the shabby Eastern and Orient Hotel had been splendidly renovated and regularly enjoyed coffee and cakes in the restaurant. An 18ᵗʰ century house, built by a rich trading Chinese family on Fung Sheh principles and called the Blue Maison, had been restored by the Penang Society. Many of the original features had been retained; the stained glass had been obtained from Britain and appears to have been designed by Rene McIntosh. Accommodation in the Blue Maison is now available for tourists, and it must be interesting to stay in this historic residence. A visit to a tropical fruit farm included a fruit tasting and one of those to be sampled was a durian. Despite it being described as the 'King of Fruit', it tastes and smells disgusting. Batik is not another fruit, but a fabric widely used in Malaysia; the female cabin crew of the country's airline wear sarongs made of batik and the men shirts. At a factory, it was possible to watch the production of the fabric and the way in which wax, and heat are used in the design of the patterns. Crossing to the mainland by bridge was an experience that I could never have expected when I first went to Penang but Butterworth on the mainland was no more beautiful than when it was an RAF station.

Jono was keen to holiday in Santorini, a Greek isle, where he had attended a conference. The journey included a change of planes in Athens and, although the terminals are a short distance apart, the taxi driver took advantage of our lack of knowledge of the city and made a long detour to increase the fare. It was not a good start and in Santorini things did not improve; the hotel was the worst in which I have ever had the misfortune to stay. The rooms and facilities were primitive and the food and the dining room appalling. The weather, however, was hot and we hired a little box on wheels and circumnavigated the island many times and admired the gleaming white buildings with their blue roofs. Santorini is a favourite stop for cruise ships, but the quay where passengers disembark is at sea level and the coaches need to climb the winding cliff roads to bring the tourists to the sights. Luggage and some goods are carried up the steep cliffs by the ancient form of transport - sure footed donkeys. Minoan archaeological sites at Akrotiri have remains of the buildings and artefacts of these ancient, civilised people which illustrate the way in which they lived. Santorini is famous for its caldera, an almost complete lagoon caused by a terrific earthquake, after which the Minoans seem to have disappeared. The people who re-colonised Santorini chose to live in cave houses which were warm in winter and cool in summer. Caves continue to be used as holiday apartments in Oia, a village very popular with tourists. Oia attracts crowds every evening; people arrive eager to watch the spectacular sunset over the sea and are so impressed that they clap as the sun disappears below the horizon. When watching as tourist I did not applaud because sunsets over The Fens are as impressive.

In Fira, Santorini, overlooking the caldera

The year after the Santorini visit Jono and I with Alison and Simon went to Crete where there were more opportunities to see Minoan remains. The island of Crete has numerous sites, but the discovery of Knossos was a major archaeological event and the ruins have become an important tourist attraction. Knossos was an important city, and some historians are of the opinion that the tsunami from the Santorini volcanic eruption overwhelmed the Minoan fleet, shattered trade and brought hunger and death to the Minoan civilisation. Crete also has many sites connected with the Second World War including war cemeteries. The German burial ground is sombre with regimented dark stones but the allied one is in a beautiful spot beside the sea and very peaceful. One of the major walks is down the narrow St Maria Gorge to the sea. We did not take the walk because if difficulties occur, rescue comes in the form of a donkey. On a second visit to Crete, the accommodation was in a small apartment in the grounds of an hotel. The hotel terrace had a sea view and faced the small island of Spinalonga, where the last leprosy colony in Europe was situated. The visit to the island was made poignant by the recent reading of Victoria Hislop's novel 'The Island'. A third visit to Crete was made in 2009 when Jono rented a villa near a village named Plaka. He, Alison, Simon and I lazed in the sun by our own pool for most of two weeks. Most evenings we ate in the garden when it was cool and the bats were beginning to hunt for food. We very occasionally ventured into a small family restaurant for different dining and once ate by the harbour in Chania. Excursions were limited but we made one visit to the

178

south coast to swim in the Libyan Sea and the sand burnt my feet! The museum at Iraklion was a must as the Minoans once again called. As a child, I read the book called The Bull of Minos and I really believed it was just a story not real history. On the morning of our departure, we called at the Souda Bay British Military War Cemetery which remains as peaceful as ever.

In February 2002, I went to Mallorca to dog sit for friends and found it odd being alone in a house that was not my own, but I enjoyed the experience and repeated it for three winters and two summers. The summers were frequently hot but with the advantage of a private swimming pool were to be preferred. Mallorca is a beautiful island with mountains, lovely countryside, beautiful beaches and a sophisticated city in its capital Palma.

Two years later, a conference for Jono was held in Nara, a city which preceded Kyoto and Tokyo as the capital of Japan. We flew via Hong Kong as it was planned that we should stop off on the return journey. Unfortunately, Asian flu caused problems and the planned Hong Kong event was cancelled. Nara is a compact city but full of temples, shrines, and pagodas. I had a guide who gave me an individual tour, told me about the various buildings and took me to a Japanese restaurant for lunch. The Naramachi is the old area of the city, and I went to the Koshi-no-le, a replica of a traditional merchant's house. It gave me some understanding of the way the Japanese used to live with its sliding doors and tatami floor covering. The visit coincided with the cherry trees being in full bloom; everywhere was beautiful and it is true that news reports detail the spots where the blossom is most luxuriant. These reports are important because people have tea under the trees. We took a train from Nara to Kyoto and saw the imperial garden as well as the geisha area. Perhaps the most memorable event happened at Osaka airport. We drank tea and it was served in fine china teacups with saucers! What luxury.

A Special Trip 2005

The following year Jono was part of a delegation to China which meant visiting Hong Kong, Shenzen, Nanjing, Shanghai, and Beijing. Shenzen was built to rival Hong Kong when the latter was still a British colony. It has vast parks where famous world buildings have been replicated and settlements depicting different cultures built. The museum of minerals had displays of jade in all colours as well as numerous other precious minerals. I wanted to buy a lacquered screen; they were newly produced but by ancient methods. Hotels have also been built and at the one where we ate dinner a lake had been constructed surrounded by Italian style houses and apartments. From Shenzen we flew to Nanjing, a very old city with walls from the Ming Dynasty but now known primarily for the massacre that took place when the Japanese invaded China in the late 1930s. The memorial of Sun Yat Sen, noted as the father of modern China, is on the outskirts of the city. Leading up to it is a massive flight of steps which needs lots of stamina and breath to climb. At the Nanjing Museum, I saw a vase that I had seen in an exhibition in London and met a famous Chinese painter who was exhibiting paintings for the year of the Cock. The journey from Nanjing to Shanghai was by coach and it was possible to see that there are remnants of the old China in the countryside where peasants were working in the fields. Shanghai is a city to be seen! It retains some pockets of the old international areas; the house where the Communist party's first meeting was held is on the edge of the remaining French Concession, and a few old buildings still stand on the Bund but modernity has taken over. The Oriental Pearl Tower gives wonderful views but is becoming overshadowed by taller hotels. A model of Shanghai has been constructed which has become a fantastic tourist 'must see'. A boat trip along the Huangpu River gave a sense of the growing industrial might of the country and its continuing use of coal; the piles were mountainous!

Visiting the Summer Palace in Beijing

We also visited the huge bridge over the mighty Yangtze and I remembered the Yangtze Incident and understood that it was easy for a warship to travel up it. The statue of Mao, built to commemorate the opening of the bridge under his regime, is dominating. The last stop for the delegation was Beijing. Jono climbed the Great Wall. I did not get to the top on this visit, because the section to which we were taken was extremely steep. While in Beijing a reception was held in the British Embassy; the décor was a mixture of British and Chinese with a very English garden. Jono was the star of the evening; he gave the speech to the assembled crowd.

New Year 2006 found us in Vienna, staying at the Hotel Sacher, where the very chocolaty delicacy, Sacher Torte was invented. We found Vienna everything we had hoped and wanted to visit every possible wonderful building and managed a good number. We went to the cathedral and the Hofburg Palace, which was the centre of the Austro-Hungarian Empire, and the displays show the diversity of the peoples and the opulence of the regime. I was interested in the exhibition about the Empress Elisabeth; I knew little about her. Around the Rathaus, the Christmas Market was still in full swing, and at the Kunsthistorisches Museum we viewed a Goya exhibition as well as the usual displays. The National Library had some Mozart scores on show, and we attended St Augustine's Church to hear his Requiem; 2006 was Mozart's two hundredth anniversary year. The Sacher is situated opposite the Opera House, and we bought tickets for a performance of The Barber of Seville. We also went to the People's Opera to see Hansel and Gretel. Many children were enjoying a Christmas treat. Theatre going in Vienna is a civilised occupation; outer garments must be left in the cloakrooms and the audience dresses elegantly. The coffee houses were exactly as I expected, very cosy and very Viennese. The main reason for the Vienna visit was to attend the New Year's Concert, an experience to remember annually. Each New Year we can watch the television and say 'I've been there!'. The celebrations for New Year's Eve were somewhat disappointing; there was no official firework display, people just let off their own fireworks in a haphazard way, which could have been dangerous! The only good thing was drinking champagne in the street.

Jono's next conferences were held in venues that I either liked or wanted to visit, Singapore and Hawaii, so I could not miss them. Singapore had developed since my previous visit with even more things to buy. I used the underground to go to China Town and the Chinese Museum. The museum showed a Singapore exactly as it was when we lived there. The same was true of the Singapore Exhibition on Sentosa Island, it displayed the old port and Chinese workers as they were in the 1960s. The small island of Sentosa is a recent development and the fountain display is impressive and the garden of orchids outstanding. The visit was in November, and I had just sold the poppies for Remembrance Sunday, so I took a trip to Kranji to visit the war cemetery and memorial. It was hot but very peaceful and I found a Chambers on the memorial wall. Jono and I sampled the Long Bar once more and from Raffles went to the concert hall for a music performance. Jono insisted on taking a rickshaw. I was embarrassed! The journey to Hawaii was broken in Las Vegas. I had decided that we must visit Cho Ming Fai (Manfred) and Ivy, friends from Hong Kong days. We went to the

Hoover Dam and although it is restricted because of the fear of terrorism we took the tour and saw the huge turbines, which Bill would have been excited to see. A new bridge is being built over the gorge and when it and the new road are completed, I would like to drive over it. After the Dam, we went to Lake Mead, formed to feed the dam, and threw popcorn to the hundreds of carp which live in it. The journey through the desert gave an impression of what travelling across the country a century ago was like. The casinos in Las Vegas are huge. The Venezia is memorable with its canal, gondolas, and gondoliers as well as replica Venetian squares, buildings, and bridges. I felt cheated when we left as we had not seen the Strip at night.

I had always wanted to go to Pearl Harbour and it was one of the first things we did when we arrived in Hawaii. At the visitors' centre we looked at the many artefacts from the USS Arizona, after which came a film. Before it was shown the audience was asked to indicate if they remembered Pearl Harbour. I didn't know whether to be pleased or sorry to be in the minority that remembered! Then we were taken by launch to the Arizona which now has a quiet and peaceful memorial built on the sunken hull of the ship. The remains of the ship are still visible in the sea, and it is possible to watch oil that continues to seep out after more that 60 years. Remnants of Battleship Alley are a further reminder of the fateful day in December 1942. I went whale watching but saw no whales; it was too late in the season. An excursion around Oahu gave a good impression of the whole island. Jono and I took a flight to the Big Island to see the volcanoes and to walk on the lava. A king and queen ruled Hawaii before the Americans annexed the country and the kingdom had connections with Britain which is the reason for the union flag being incorporated in the Hawaiian flag. The Iolani Palace is now a tourist attraction which is particularly worth visiting; it is small but beautiful. The conference dinner was held on Waikiki Beach outside the first hotel to be built on the beach in 1928. The setting was all a tropical beach should be and the entertainment, given by members of the Polynesian Cultural Centre, exactly right for the venue. The fire dancer from Samoa was breathtaking and the buffet more than satisfactory.

A summer visit to another island was primarily for relaxation. Jono chose Malta, and we found the hotel when we arrived late at night by luck and instinct. Between sitting by the pool and visiting the health club, we did the necessary sight seeing. Malta has massive connections with the Knights Templar and Knights of St. John and in every ancient city there are the artefacts to remind visitors. Mdina with its narrow streets and ramparts calls to mind battles. Cathedrals and castles are full of memorials to knights and the decoration for which they were responsible. In Valletta we viewed Sliema and walked in Straight Street, about which Arthur used to talk when describing the days when Malta was a Royal Naval base. A war memorial near the bus station had the names of members of the Royal Air Force who perished during the siege of Malta. We searched for the name of Kath's (Con's sister) airman, Jimmy, who was shot down over the island, but we could not find it. One evening we went to the Verdala Palace for an army band concert hosted by the President. After an enjoyable evening of music, we went into the Palace to view the restored frescoes. These wall paintings had been covered with white paint during World War II when the palace had been used as military headquarters. We counted ourselves fortunate because the palace is not open to tourists; it is a presidential residence in regular use. We took a trip to Gozo, the small island neighbouring Malta and went to the fort, where we almost sizzled on the ramparts.

I did not expect to return to Las Vegas, but, in 2008, it is where I found myself. Jono's conference venue! He worked and I went sight seeing. I visited as many casinos as possible without playing any of the millions of machines and took a two-day trip to the Grand Canyon. I stayed overnight at Williams, a town on the old and famous Route 66, and went up to the Canyon on the re-established and renovated Grand Canyon Railway. It was a most pleasant experience, and the Canyon was spectacular. At one stop on the bus tour of the northern rim of the Canyon we (the tourists) were able to see the Colorado River and it appeared like a tiny brook. We were fortunate enough to see three Condors flying over the rocks and with their six feet wingspan, they appeared to be as small as a blackbird against the vastness of the place. Caesar's Palace on the 45th floor overlooking Las Vegas was our accommodation. The view of the Strip with the lights was as colourful as it had been described and we could watch the regular impressive display by the famous fountains outside the luxurious Bellagio. Paris Las Vegas with its replica Eiffel Tower and Arc de Triomphe was nearby and easy to see. On the last evening we had tickets for the Coliseum to see Elton John's Red Piano Show, something to be remembered. The Americans go in and out to the bar during the performance to replenish their drinks and do not save standing up to the end of the show. They stood up, clapped, and cheered as Elton walked on and he hadn't played a note!!

Summer 2008 was one of those summers that do not encourage taking holidays at home; the weather was abysmal, but Jono and I chose Scotland. Luck was with us for the Edinburgh Tattoo which was as enjoyable as ever with a fine and fairly warm evening. At the very north of the country, the day was, luckily, also fine and sunny but otherwise the rain fell in torrents, and it was cold. The drive to the north was through magnificent, beautiful, and dramatic countryside, but the lowering clouds brought memories of Scot's novels and kilt wearing heroes. The hotel in a small village west of Thurso overlooked a deserted beach and the Pentland Firth, not places to sunbathe, or paddle. When we reached John O'Groats we behaved like tourists, went into the souvenir shop, and almost purchased something that would have been exactly right for my bad taste collection, if I had still possessed it. John O'Groats is iconic but is spoiled by a run down and empty hotel. Dunnet Head, on the other hand, has no real marks of the tourist industry but is by far the more interesting. It is the most northerly point on the British mainland and has commanding views of the Orkney Isles. The Castle of Mey should not be missed; the Queen Mother did a service to the area by rescuing the building and it is the perfect place to visit with its wonderful position, and its non-regal atmosphere. After the castle, I toured a croft which had been a family home until recent times and showed the way the people lived and survived in isolated hamlets. The final visit was to the east of Thurso to a village called Betty Hill; I thought it should be my very own property. It was built after the Highland clearances to accommodate some of those who were evicted from their homes. The Duchess of Sutherland was responsible for the construction of the settlement and her name was Betty, hence Betty Hill. On the return journey, the weather at Inverness was so appalling that there was no opportunity to leave the hotel until it was time to drive southwards. An improvement in the weather allowed us to go to Loch Ness and visit the Loch Ness experience which presents in an interesting fashion the formation of the loch and theorises the possibility of there being a resident, in the form of a monster, known as Nessie. The ride along the edge of the loch made us realise its huge size. After leaving Scotland, we made our way to Hadrian's Wall, a place I had long wanted to see. We climbed to the top of the Peel Crags and understood the achievement of the wall's construction and imagined the feelings of the Romans who garrisoned the forts. The Vindolanda Museum has exhibits that are fascinating; I wonder if modern shoes will be exhibited in the way the Roman sandals are! Further detours were made before we drove into Alwalton, the first to Whitby to see the ruined abbey, then to Scarborough and finally across the Humber Bridge. Some of the Yorkshire Moors over which we drove were covered in early morning mist.

Just before Christmas 2008, I went to Paris with Rachel, (the granddaughter of my penfriend June) who stayed at Alwalton for some time while she was enjoying travels in Europe before going to university. We rescued her from a small hamlet near Reading where she was very unhappy and ready to return home. Once in Alwalton she began to enjoy herself and during her stay she and I undertook many enjoyable expeditions. We went to London, Liverpool, Edinburgh, Leeds and Stratford-on-Avon (Jono came to this venue) and finally took Eurostar to meet Rachel's parents, brother and boyfriend (Steve, Vicki, Mitch and Joel) at Charles de Gaulle airport on their arrival from Australia. We stayed in an apartment in the Latin Quarter and went to museums and art galleries and walked the streets viewing the various famous buildings. I left the family two days before Christmas Day and it was a sad farewell, particularly as I had also had to say goodbye to June who came briefly to stay during October when we went to Sissinghurst to see the gardens. Once back from France, there was little time to make the final preparations for the festive season and in reality, Christmas became a little unreal. On Christmas Day Jono and I were called to Wentworth Croft Residential Home. Uncle Jess was having a recurrence of his ill health and we decided to ask Barbara and Rodney to come immediately. They arrived on Boxing Day and late in the evening he died. New Year 2009 was a calm time and on 3rd January Brenda's birthday was celebrated at Ashwell, where the transformation of Alison's house was making progress.

The venue for Jono's 2009 conference was in Taiwan and after much consideration he decided to attend so I went as well. The journey included a change at Hong Kong to a small local aeroplane and it was a relief to land at Taipei. Our accommodation almost at the top of the hotel, with an exceptional view over the city, was excellent. As in previous years, Jono attended the conference, and I went sightseeing. The National Palace Museum was the objective of my first venture, and it did not disappoint. The backdrop to the building is a range of mountains and was designed to house the huge number of artefacts from mainland China. Ancient treasures were taken from the Forbidden City to a National Palace Museum when there were stirrings of revolution at the beginning of the 19th Century. At the outbreak of the Sino-Japanese war the objects were moved to various cities and finally the Chinese Nationalists packed the treasures and sent them to Taiwan in the face of China becoming a communist state and eventually built a new Palace Museum for them. The beautifully displayed artefacts are so extensive that it is impossible to view them all in a day. Sun Yat Sen is regarded as a founding father as much in Taiwan as in mainland China and I made my way to his Memorial Hall. It is built of marble with a yellow pagoda shaped roof. The large, seated statue of Sun Yat Sen is high above the heads of the visitors, and on arrival I imagined that the two soldiers on guard were also statues, but they were not, and the guard was changed with a distinctive ceremony. A display detailing Sun Yat Sen's life were labelled in Mandarin, so I was unable to read them but in the art gallery I met the artist of the exhibition being staged there and he presented me with a disk containing all the displayed pictures. Chang Kai Shek followed in Sun Yat Sen's footsteps, escaped from the Chinese Communists and was instrumental in setting up the Nationalist Government in Taiwan. A second marble Memorial Hall was constructed, this time with a blue roof and without a display space or gallery, to commemorate his life, but surrounded by an expansive garden at the entrance of which are two distinctly oriental buildings, one a concert hall, the second an exhibition space. The changing of the guard ceremony was a repeat performance of the former with extreme marching and gun twirling. Taipei, the capital of Taiwan, boasts the 101 tower with 88 levels and I took the lift, which takes less than a minute, to reach the top and about 33 seconds to descend. Yet, there is no unpleasant sensation while travelling up or down. The views from the viewing area can be spectacular but the day was long. I appreciated, however, all I could see. I flew to the Taroga Gorge, a most beautiful area with mountains, rivers, and rocks. There was much walking and climbing, and the day ended with a visit to a marble factory. Taiwan not only produces marble but many other minerals including beautiful jade and coral. The return journey was by train and immediately before going to the station there was a brief stop at the Pacific coast where I picked up two attractive small rocks, two was the permitted number, to carry home.

At the beginning of 2010, I was considering if I really wanted to go to Dallas. The name Texas conjured up in my mind desert, 'cowboys and Indians' and George W Bush while my knowledge of Dallas was limited to the assassination of President Kennedy and the long-running television soap opera. The city, however, proved to be a cultural centre with landscaped gardens and friendly people in abundance and very much worth a visit. Dallas was founded in 1841 and on Founder's Plaza a representative shack of that lived in by the first settler, has been constructed. Since that time, Dallas has benefitted from cotton growing, being situated on the route of the cattle drives, oil production and electronic development all of which have helped to make it a rich city. Native Americans are not obvious as the early settlers agreed that they would restrict themselves to a specific area if the 'Indians' withdrew from it. The settlers reneged on the agreement and claimed more and more land. Quanah, the last great Comanche chief fought against the injustice, but eventually realised that, if his people were to survive, peace must be negotiated, and he became an important peacemaker. Dallas has impressive museums, a concert hall and an opera house, soon to be joined by a theatre for ballet and a huge area devoted to art and the arts. I visited the Museum of Asian Art, the Dallas Museum of Art as well as the Sixth Floor Museum. The first of these was built to house a collection of Eastern art, particularly jade, donated by one rich Dallas citizen. The Museum of Art contains paintings, furniture, and artefacts from many parts of the world, but of particular interest is the Reeves Collection. This is a reconstruction of a Provencal villa (French) with all its contents which include beautiful furniture, many valuable works of art, amongst which are three by Winston Churchill, silver, porcelain, and sculpture. A special exhibition at the time of my visit was of a series of painting by Jacob Lawrence depicting the part played by Toussaint Louverture in the emancipation of slaves in Haiti. It was not only interesting but informative as I knew neither artist nor subject.

The Sixth Floor Museum is in the Book Depository from where Lee Harvey Oswald is believed to have fired the shot which assassinated President Kennedy and the exhibits are of that event. I went early in the morning and attendance was impressive. JFK has become an idol not only in America but around the world. The grassy knoll remains as it did in 1963 and nearby is the Kennedy Memorial an unexpected large concrete structure. The doorway where Jack Ruby shot Lee Harvey Oswald can be viewed but not used and Ruby's nightclub has become a public house. The Red House Museum was built as a courthouse and was due for demolition before it became a museum. Dallas boasts a statue of Robert E. Lee, the famous general of the Civil War with a reproduction of his southern mansion on the site. It also has the Mansion House Hotel, previously a private home, where President Roosevelt stayed, and an extensive house owned originally by the owner of the local newspaper but at one point in its history became an undertaker's establishment where the bodies of Bonnie and Clyde were exhibited. The Dallas memorial of the cattle drives is a bronze life size representation of a drive with its attendant cowboys, and it was good to have seen it before visiting Fort Worth, where the stock yards were situated and where the cattle were housed and sold. Now cattle are auctioned over the internet, and one was in progress on our visit. Fort Worth retains much of the atmosphere of the cattle era with many of the buildings connected with the old west. Sundance Square is dominated by a mural of cattle and near the old fire station is the site of the studio where the photograph of the Sundance gang, which was used on the famous wanted poster, was taken. At the Welles Fargo office, an original stagecoach is exhibited, and it is difficult to imagine that it could accommodate the 18 travellers that it is reputed to have carried.

The Rodeo Stadium was large and smelled of horses and cattle and, unfortunately, there was no action on a Saturday morning, but the re-enacting of a cattle drive is a tourist attraction that happens every day and long horn cattle are driven down the road by the cowboys as happened in the past. A fact I learned about the long horn cattle and indeed the horses so closely connected with Native Americans is that neither animal is native to America. The first European explorers left the cattle and horses behind after their early forays into the country. The native people took to horses. Riding made hunting and travelling easier. They were not interested in the cattle which developed their particular characteristics and were not valued until the settlers arrived. Mounted on a wall in a bar were the heads of three buffalo which were the real animals of the American plains, and the herds of these magnificent animals must have been impressive. The Texan men who were drinking at the bar were also impressive; they wore ten-gallon hats and cowboy boots, were broad shouldered and towered above the visiting tourists. Perhaps the most famous shop in which to buy handmade and decorated boots is in Fort Worth and it displays a photograph of Prince Charles and Camilla each being presented with a pair of boots. I wonder if they wear them? The store uses a wide variety of skins to make the boots and the decoration ranges from restrained to 'over the top' but the price range is only expensive. Restaurants were numerous and world-wide food obtainable but Mexican was the most enjoyable and on one evening it was possible to eat outside, but the warm weather that was expected in Texas disappeared after two days and was replaced by a bitingly cold wind and snow. Texas has a history of change and has shown allegiance to six flags, the Spanish, the French, the Mexican, the Union of Southern States, the One Star and finally the Stars and Stripes. Under the One Star, Texas was independent and despite choosing to join the United States, continues to be known as the lone star state.

Birthdays

In 1997 David celebrated his 40th birthday in Reading. It was difficult to believe he had reached such an age and was married with two children. His party was very enjoyable, and I think he may have had a headache the next morning! Peterborough was the place of celebration for 50 years and once again it was a very enjoyable get together. Jenny had celebrated her anniversaries just before David's but there wasn't a number on a cake because ladies do not wish to broadcast their age. Just before the journey to Dallas, Jono celebrated his 50th birthday. He wanted very much to mark the milestone by hiring a coach and taking his guests to Hunstanton to play the 'penny' machines on what remains of the pier. After the session of excitement there was to be a fish and chip meal followed by the return journey with songs. Jono's favourite seaside has always been Hunstanton, and many birthdays have been enjoyed at 'Peterborough-by-the-Sea, but the half century spectacular did not follow the planned route. Too many of the proposed guests did not relish a day at the seaside in March. As a result, the venue was changed to the Crown at Elton where everyone enjoyed an excellent meal and then, when we returned home, the cake was cut and eaten, speeches were made and funny stories about the 'birthday boy' were remembered and laughed about. The decoration of the cake was of Alfa design as at that time he owned an Alfa Brera which pleased him, but as Jono has, over the years, had a series of different makes of car he changed his allegiance once more and returned to the BMW marque! Alison was 50 years old in 2014 and it was quite a time before she decided the way in which she was going to celebrate on the birthday. The actual day of celebration was excellent, it was in her home. She had a small 'orchestra' to entertain the guests as they arrived, a fish and chip van produced the food, and it was good. Ice cream and a celebratory cake were also available. Speeches were delivered to wish her well and everyone obviously enjoyed the occasion. She certainly has a lot of friends in Ashwell. Simon had celebrated his 50th birthday at the beginning of the year. It was a Sunday lunch at the White Hart at Ufford. It was enjoyed by all who attended. Norfolk featured in holiday plans for the summer but a plan to stay in a holiday bungalow went wrong owing to cold, wet weather and an unheated dwelling. However, the various villages linked to the Boyden history were visited and photographs of the churches taken. Lincoln Cathedral was also on the itinerary as well as Sutton Bridge where we drove to the lighthouse. Peter Scott began painting birds at that point and his work encouraged the care of birds. Then Jono decided he wanted sun, and we went to Gozo for the second time where we stayed in the Kempinski Hotel which was excellent and swish. There was time for relaxation and some activities such as early morning walks with a local resident, a boat ride to see the corals and the spectacular rock formations and to visit Neolithic remains. We also climbed the 'Way of the Cross' Stations of the Cross arranged up a steep hill. We had to do this climb during the late afternoon as earlier we had tried but the heat was too intense.

November and December 2010 became hectic months. Firstly, it was Jono's conference in Singapore, and we travelled there in a plane which we only just caught!!! (Always be sure of the flight number you are booked on!) Singapore had more smart shopping malls than on previous visits and Orchard

Road was packed with people day and night. The cheaper stores are in the basements while the upper levels have the outlets of top fashion designers and extremely expensive jewellery shops. The crowds are immense and local income permits the spending on luxury goods. Our hotel was the Shangri-la and it was just what I like with a lovely pool and much comfort. The President of Singapore and the Vice-chairman of China attended a dinner while we were there, and the building was surrounded by police. Our sightseeing was limited but planned that way to ensure relaxation, and we went to Kranji War Cemetery on Remembrance Sunday, and during the week Canning Fort, the Armenian Church and the Botanic Gardens. At the end of the week Jono returned but I went on to Sydney and stayed with June and David. I had an excellent week with a family dinner on the Sunday, a visit to Manly, a lunch at David's sister and brother-in-law's apartment, which overlooks Manly Beach, lunch with Helen after June's patchwork class, dinner with Phil, Sarah (Mary's daughter) and Caitlin, a visit to the aquarium, the art gallery and the opera house for the ballet. The week was completed with a breakfast at a nearby restaurant and a long flight back to Heathrow where the winter weather was already in action. While I was in Sydney Jono learned he had received his Fellowship of the IEEE, which was extremely well deserved and very satisfying.

I managed to fit in a weekend in Scotland just before Christmas and went to a Royal Marine band concert and a performance of Hairspray in Edinburgh, but the weather was atrocious, and Alison and Simon did not make it and I had to leave early and experience a somewhat delayed journey. Christmas was celebrated at Ashwell in the renovated house. David Jenny, Nicola and Christopher came and we had to take Star!! Brenda, John and Karen came with Simon on Boxing Day and John served me the port as it was his challenge when he returned from hospital after his long illness. Unfortunately, his death followed in a most sad way. While having his dinner he swallowed a piece of meat without chewing it properly which blocked his throat and he sadly died. Jono and I had just left for Prague, but we managed to return home in time for his funeral.

The conference of 2011 was held in Prague, a beautiful city with many spectacular buildings. Jono had been very involved with the organisation of this event and was busy every day ensuring that all was proceeding properly, particularly as numbers of attendees were very high. The flight was short, and we arrived on a Saturday and were faced with a wait in the hotel reception. The computer was not working which meant the allocated room was not known. Luckily Jono's organising profile meant he was 'important', and the room was soon found. On Sunday we met one of Jono's fellow organisers - a particularly nice person and accompanied him to a Mass at a church next to the monastery which is still in use. The service was interesting, the altar boys minute and the incense heavy. We learned that the Archbishop of Canterbury was visiting the next week – following us, no doubt. Afterwards we had lunch at a nearby restaurant and ate good Czech food then enjoyed an afternoon and evening of sightseeing, made more interesting by being shown the City by Ales, who is a native. We went into St. Vitus' Cathedral, which was very crowded, visited the castle and saw the President's residence, many of the public squares and the bridges. We walked over the Charles Bridge and saw the famous clock. A grand organised tour of the city was my first solo event, and I met an American professor, Janet Baker, with whom I spent the day. She was an attendee at the conference, and we got on well. A walk around the castle, including the Vineyard, was the first stop on the expedition and included another peep into the Cathedral which was again crowded. A river trip was next and that was a pleasant interlude – we turned around near the weir. Afterwards came the clock again and we behaved like tourists and waited for the time of the performance. That was the end of the organized tour, so Janet and I walked through the city streets to St. Wenceslas' Square and returned to the hotel by underground.

On the Tuesday, I managed to understand the underground ticket machines and went into the city. I walked from the National Museum in St. Wenceslas' Square to the National Theatre and found my way, by chance, to the Old Town Square (and the clock), had coffee and watched the world go by. Then walked to the river and found the old synagogue and afterwards walked back to St Wenceslas' Square and back to the hotel. Instead of going into the hotel I decided to walk towards Vysehrad, an important area of the city, but turned back and then retraced my steps all the way the next morning. I went into the church of St. Peter and St. Paul which has two spires with impressive brightly coloured doors with coats of arms edged with gold leaf. The village has other interesting buildings, St. Martin's Rotunda and is said to be the oldest building in Prague and the Leopold Gate which is the entrance to the village. After walking back, I caught the coach for a trip to Kutna Hora. This involved a journey of five and a half hours. We stopped at the Ossuary Church with its bones and skulls arranged in piles or strung up as if they were decoration. I thought it the most bizarre and horrible place, particularly as it had a peculiar smell. I was happy to leave! When we arrived at Kutna Hora we went immediately to St. Barbara's church. This town was the centre for silver mining in the Medieval era and as St. Barbara was the patron saint of miners the church has many unusual frescos depicting mining and associated activities. We then walked along the bridge passed a building which was a monastery and then on to the town square and the castle known as Italian Court; its construction began in the 13th Century and became the Royal Mint because of the silver available. Kutna became the centre of economic power with the King visiting regularly. The Prague Goshen was minted in the castle and became an important coin. We waited in the courtyard for our tour and the guide carried keys and locked each room as we passed through.

In Prague with Jono and friends

On the return to Prague, it was time to go to the Czech Evening which was the conference celebratory event and held in the Zofin Palace. The evening began with a musical performance which was excellent, but the 'hungry hordes' when the buffet began made it difficult to obtain a fair share of the immense amount of food available. On the Thursday there was an early start to get the tour to Konopiste Castle. This building is set in wonderful grounds and surrounded by beautiful scenery. The castle was the home of Franz Ferdinand, the Austro-Hungarian Emperor's nephew and related to Ceci, the Empress. Franz Ferdinand is the person who was assassinated in Sarajo an event which started World War I. The castle contains a huge collection of weapons, and the furnishings are in excellent condition. I did not like the fact that they have a bear pit and as the old animal had died it had been replaced with a young animal. Not a good idea in this day!!! Friday morning found me in the swimming pool on the 25th floor, wonderful view and a brilliant pool. After the swim I went to IP Pavlova to find Dvorak's Museum, had some difficulty but it was interesting when I did find it. In the afternoon I went to see Janet Baker's part in the conference and after Jono's last duty we went to Vyšehrad to an Italian restaurant for an enjoyable meal. Took my last swim on Saturday morning and then went into the city via St. Wenceslas' Square and Old Town Square, then on to the Castle and went into St. Vitus Cathedral and paid to go into main area but St. Wenceslas' Chapel was closed! Visited St George's Basilica and were to visit two more palaces, but it was not possible because time was limited.

Prague was visited again in October 2015; the flight was from Stanstead and Ales met us and took us to a hotel, both comfortable and interesting. Prague has a 'look alike' Eifel tower, and I almost reached it but the little railway which carried visitors was out of action. I did not realise I could have walked to it! However, I found the area I knew well from the previous visit, where it is possible to overlook the city. I went to see the paintings that were displayed in the same building as the conference was held. The pictures seemed to be quite dark and not ones that enthused me. When the conference attendees finished their session, everyone was shown around the monastery library but at a great speed which meant there was not enough time to admire the building or the books. Afterwards it was time for snacks and meeting people. The next day I walked to the cathedral and saw the statue of the first president with many wreaths beside it and found out his service was being marked. Changing the guard took place and attracted huge crowds, I watched from a distance and afterwards walked around the grounds. In the evening, opera called, and we saw Rigoletto, the orchestra was large and extremely good while the actors improved as the story continued. The following day, a walk to the cathedral was unsuccessful. There were queues and I wanted to visit Wenceslas' Chapel, but once again visitors were not permitted to go in. It was suggested a visit might be possible on Sunday if a service was attended. That was not possible as we accompanied Ales to the service in the monastery church. Lunch was eaten in a restaurant with both an excellent view and enjoyable food. The evening meant a visit to the theatre, which was enjoyable and returned on a tram, fortunately we managed to get the right stop! The return journey was a disaster, the plane was very late and back at Stanstead there was no one to unload the baggage, thus the return drive was not only late but fog bound. Events had not been good during our absence; Pam, my brother Leslie's wife, had had another fall and was in hospital and visitors were not permitted because an infection had invaded the ward. Leslie and Sheran were able to visit but no-one else. However, Pam did not seem to be improving and I was able to visit just a few days before she died. The funeral was very well attended, and the weather was exactly what Leslie wanted, it was pleasantly warm and everyone able to follow the hearse to the church did so. An action which is not often practised today. The church was full and friends talked of Pam and I read the lesson which Christopher had chosen and on which the vicar preached his sermon. After the service all followed to the crematorium and then to the Masonic Hall for refreshments and give everyone the opportunity to reminisce the memories of Pam. The burial of the ashes was three days later.

Trans-Mongolian/Siberian Railway Journey

Mil and I spoke about taking this journey in about 2008/9 and planned to go in 2010, but Mil realised she had booked to go to Scotland with Alzheimer's Society on the dates we needed to choose because our wish was to go to the Naadam Festival in Ulaanbaatar, the capital of Mongolia. It was therefore decided to delay the trip until 2011. The booking was made and in the early months of 2011 I made my first visit to London to get visas; the Chinese visa office was at Holborn Viaduct and the process was much easier than when the Chinese embassy processed the applications. After I had collected these important documents, it was necessary to wait to apply for the documents for Mongolia and Russia as I was going to Prague with Jono and could not part with my passport. The wait was fortunate as Mil had mentioned that she had been diagnosed with a kidney problem but was certain that she would be able to wait for treatment until she returned from the trip. It did not happen that way and she needed an operation almost immediately. Thus, I was left to go on the journey by myself and I made my visits to the Mongolian Embassy and the Russian visa office with less enthusiasm, but I knew I had to go. Before departure it was necessary to have health checks, purchase necessary pills and potions for all eventualities and decide on clothes and luggage; the latter was somewhat concerning as the instructions stressed that the case was not to be too heavy to be carried up and down stairs and lifted on to the trains.

1st and 2nd July 2011

The day before leaving Jono tried to book my seat on the aircraft but it proved impossible and panic began to arise, but it turned out well. I had been upgraded and travelled business class to Beijing. Julia Flack with Boris, the dog, collected me at about 9.30am and drove me to Heathrow-Terminal 5 - on 1st July David's birthday. The journey was easy, traffic reasonable with some signs of queues along the M25 but no hold-ups. We found a parking place without a problem, went into the airport, and had coffee. When Julia left me, I handed in my case, went through the security without being stopped or frisked and went to the business lounge where food and drink was available. I read the papers and sat for a time and then wandered around the shops with little eagerness. At 3.30pm, the gate was announced, and I took the shuttle to gate 34. Marvellous to be first on the plane and go up to the top deck where there was comfort, properly served good food, and the ability to sleep. Indeed, it was possible to say the flight was enjoyable - business class for me forever! Arrived at Beijing on time on 2nd July and collected my luggage - had a few panics when I thought it might not be on the plane. Miao, Jono's student, his parents, and 'brother' met me and took me to the hotel, which was very 3* but adequate and clean. Without Mil I had a room to myself. Once I had registered, we had lunch and the dishes just kept coming. Miao's mother Li Li had presents for me, so it was a good thing I had something to return the compliment - a Royal Wedding vase and a book. In the afternoon, we went to the Temple of Heaven and spent time there, but I needed to get back to the hotel for 5pm in order to meet everyone. They were all nice people and understood I must spend two days away from the group. After the meeting, Miao and family took me to a restaurant where once again the courses came in a never-ending line. I slept reasonably well although I woke up and thought it was much later than it was. I decided the alarm may not have worked.

3rd July 2011

I saw my people ready for their day trip, but I had breakfast with Miao and family - too much to eat again! Li Li and I had our photographs taken dressed as empresses and walked through gardens beside a lake known as a sea of Beijing. I decided I would prefer to go to the Olympic Park rather than the Great Wall as I had been to it more than once. The site takes up a tremendous area, but I do not think China lacks space - YET. We went into the Bird's Nest, which was very interesting, but I was careful not to mention the architect (he is anti the regime and was prevented from leaving China not long after our visit). Saw the Water Cube, other buildings, and the torch. I could not believe the torch was so big! After the Olympic area, we went to a 'real' Chinese restaurant! It is difficult to believe it is possible to get such food and service in an area where we might turn up our noses! The food was superb and the waitresses demure and caring. And the toilet facilities were lovely! After food we went to Prince Kundi's Palace, a smaller edition of the Forbidden City, very interesting but crowded beyond its capacity. An exhibition of beautifully made wall hangings was colourful but the subjects were not consistently to western tastes, while an exhibition of photographs had captions only in Mandarin which made things difficult. The funniest episode was trying to get into the hall for tea and entertainment. There were so many people that it was a mad, heaving, pushing mob that went through the door. Thanks to Li Li who grabbed chairs we were able to sit down. However, the entertainment lasted all of 4/5 minutes during which we managed to grab one sweet each but had no time to drink any tea because the women attendants were slamming down new tea bowls for the next performance, and we were quickly ushered or pushed out. We came out of the grounds at a different gate from our entry where rickshaws were parked, and we travelled back in them to the car. I am against riding in rickshaws, but I had no way to object in this instance and the 'vehicles' are severely regulated. Miao and I had a knowledgeable cycle rider and as we went through the hutong (old living areas which are fast disappearing) he stopped to point out interesting items. Once the car had been found we returned to the hotel and had another meal!! Afterwards we went to a shop which sells very expensive Chinese goods made of gold and jade. I did not buy anything. Once back at the hotel I repacked my case and decided this activity will be an on-going chore.

Enjoying time in Mongolia

4th July 2011

Miao collected me at 8am as previously and we had breakfast together. Then we went to Beihai Park; another huge area with two lakes - North Sea and Middle Sea. The story is that there are eight lakes in Beijing which were believed to be seas by Mongolian raiders when Mongolia and China were at war. The raiders had not seen such large expanses of water and believed they were seas. The large building is a Palace comparable to that of Prince Kundi with long painted corridors like the Summer Palace. One building became the repository of the best of ancient calligraphy; both the building and the calligraphy blocks need some tender loving care. Crossed the lake twice in the 'royal' barge and climbed the steep steps of a temple situated on one of the islands. Music and dancing were going on for anyone who wished to join in - western dance music and dancing. A water lily show was also in action. We went to a restaurant near Tiananmen Square, which was very poor, when compared with other eateries. Miao, his father and I planned to go to the National Museum, but it was closed on Mondays, but we were able to see the huge red hammer and sickle monument which is there to celebrate 90 years of Russian Communism, which I hope is not a permanent fixture. Instead of the museum, we wandered along the main shopping street where everything was decorated with red - streamers, lanterns, flags, all recognizing the 90th anniversary of communism. Met Li Li and went to a tea house which had been the first cinema in Beijing. After some more walking and looking we went for a celebratory meal. It was a real banquet, with huge amounts to eat and included Peking duck which was succulent and carved by the chef! Drink was also plentiful. Afterwards it was back to the Hotel where I bid farewell to Miao and family somewhat sadly. Packed quickly but did not make proper provision for the train. Did not sleep well either!

5th July 2011

Ready for the off with my companions, had not arranged things well and really was short of some necessities. I shared a compartment on the train with Elizabeth and John who were kind and helpful. Amelie, our travelling companion also came into our compartment. Despite being careful with what I brought my case seemed heavy. The Chinese attendants were awkward which made going to the toilet difficult. Of the two toilets on the coach, one was kept locked, no doubt for their own use and well before a station was reached, they locked the other! The reason was that sewage went straight on to the line. Went with Elizabeth to have supper in the dining car and it was reasonably eatable. We arrived at the border between China and Mongolia at about 8pm and we started the long wait. The exit permits from China were collected as well as our passports and we were required to stand up for the officer to give us a general 'look over'. Then we went into the workshop for the bogies to be changed because the gauge of the tracks is different in the two countries. The carriages were lifted while we were inside, one set of wheels was removed, and the other set pulled in - we felt very little despite the exercise being quite significant. At the end of some four hours or more we were taken back to the station and given back our documents. Then on to the Mongolian border where the exercise of documents proceeded again and after two or so hours they were delivered back, and sleep could commence.

6th July 2011

I awoke with a start and thought I was late, but all was well, and we had a long way to go. Elizabeth and I walked along to the dining car and found it had become completely transformed. It was completely Mongolian an absolute delight of wooden carving. We had breakfast but I could eat very little - I think I was still full from the weekend. The journey continued until about 1.30 pm when we arrived at Ulaanbaatar, where Odka, (proper spelling was Odgerel and means Star of Light) was on the station awaiting us. She was going to be our guide while in Mongolia and we were taken by coach, which was driven by Tsoodol. He was a good driver in a country where rules of the road are something that are rarely referred to. On the drive to the hotel, we stopped at a bank to change money. I changed some of my American dollars and then it was onwards to our hotel where there was a grand mix up with the room numbers, but when that was resolved the rooms were clean and comfortable. We had a very brief time to get ready for the next activity and I misheard the time to meet and was late, which was out of character for me. I am usually too early for everything. I had to perform a forfeit in the bus for my apology for lateness. We travelled to the very large main square of the city and walked across it. A huge statue of Genghis Khan dominates the Parliament buildings and the square itself; Genghis Khan is of course a Mongolian hero who conquered much of Asia. We next went to the National Museum, where a very good guide took us through the galleries and explained the exhibits well. For me the one I most enjoyed was the costume display. There were examples of the many individual tribal clothes, all very colourful and in marvellous condition. I next had a small disaster! The museum was closing so I nipped hastily to the toilet, but at a very delicate moment the lights were switched off! I had real trouble fixing my trousers and my money belt and had to cling to my bits and pieces as we walked across the square to the restaurant. We had to wait for a table as the place was full, the Festival being near but we enjoyed the Mongolian barbeque, which was a new and interesting concept for me but very tasty. You choose your own meat, fish, and vegetables and it is then cooked by expert barbeque cooks on a large hot plate which has a large wood fire in the middle, I enjoyed it very much. Afterwards we walked back to the hotel, and I sorted out my cases. Booked an alarm call and went to sleep.

7th July 2011

The alarm call did not happen as expected and I awoke with a start and once again thought I was late, but I wasn't, and I had plenty of time for breakfast. After this non-waking up signal, Carly or Andy rang me every morning. The coach departed at 7am and I had been checked out by whoever carried my case. Once on the bus, I realised I had left the camera battery in the charger in the case. I needed help to retrieve it and was in trouble for walking about the coach - should always be sitting down but I wanted to take photographs! As we left Ulaanbaatar, the coach encountered a problem with road works. The road we needed had been closed but there was no diversion. The only action left to the driver was to take a short detour which was through mud, down a slippery steep incline and then up the other side. Although he made valiant efforts it seemed the coach would not succeed in the climb upwards and it was not until we all alighted, the engine was revved, and a run was taken at the upward slope that success was achieved. Once we were away, we were driven about 370 kilometres before we stopped at Erdene Zuu Monastery, which was the first Buddhist centre of Mongolia. During Stalin's time, the building was badly damaged, but monks are now back, and visits can be made but our visit was arranged for the following day. We were able to view the stalls which were set up opposite the main entrance before we set off for Karakorum where there was an encampment of gers with one very large one that operated as the dining room. We had our meal and were allocated a ger and sleeping companions. I was with Elizabeth and John again and we had some free time in the afternoon when it was sunny and fairly warm, and Maggie and I did some Tai Chi. I have to admit my brain was not in as good a shape as I would have wished. Perhaps it was an indication of the night's events! We had our dinner in the dining ger and talked about the coming activities. I tried to get a shower, but the water was cold which did not thrill me, but I booked a camel ride!

8th July 2011

I did not get my camel ride because I had a disturbed night. Despite my care, I had developed a stomach upset - others had already succumbed - and I felt terrible. I needed the toilet regularly which wasn't a matter of going into a nearby bathroom but entailed an outside walk in the dark across the ger encampment to the toilet block! After my interesting night, I had to face the return visit to the monastery and at one point as we stood and looked at a particular building, I began to feel terrible and moved into the shade only to fall gracefully down in a faint. I'm sure that I have never before fainted but there's always a first time for most things. Rosemary, Frank, Alan and Amelie were very kind and managed to revive me with tea and rest. I missed the monastery, but I have visited many Buddhist shrines. I decided camel riding better be given a miss and slept in a ger while others were riding horses or camels or walking. The ger was the home of a nomadic family which we were visiting and where the mother had had a baby, which was tightly cocooned, two days before. Yet, she served various Mongolian tit bits which I took but dare not eat. There were other children, one the brother of the baby was eight years old and would take part in the Naadam Festival horse race. There is free education in Mongolia for children up to 12 years of age and he was attending school. Secondary education, however, is fee paying. Students usually board and the cost is equal to US$700 per year on an average salary of US$200 per month. When we returned to the ger encampment it was time for dinner after which we played a Mongolian version of Five Stones, known as Knuckle Bones and actually using pieces made from animal bones. We had hoped for a hot shower this evening but once again only cold was available!

9th July 2011

My night was better so my problem seemed to be improving. We started on a long drive after breakfast, during which we had a toilet stop at a garage. The building looked as if it was up to date and hygienic but inside there was just a hole in the ground. We continued to a National Park where we had lunch and prepared for a trip to see the wild horses. These animals were almost extinct when a breeding programme saved them. We travelled to the area where we were likely to see them in 4x4s and the drive was along rocky tracks at a considerable speed. The walk up the hills gave us the opportunity to see the interesting flora and fauna and we managed to see the horses but only just, as the distance between us and the horses was considerable, and we had to share the binoculars. The journey was not enjoyed by some as it was bumpy, and people felt thrown about but I did not mind as I was in the front seat. However, we thought our vehicle would not get us back as it would not start and when it did, the driver decided he would become a Formula 1 driver!!! Our next stop was a considerable distance and meant going through Ulaanbaatar with its magnificent traffic jams and pedestrians who consistently took their lives in their hands. We arrived fairly late and while we were eating the owner came for a conversation, although, officially, his wife is the owner in order to be the right side of Mongolian law. This ger encampment had certain extra features which were absent at others, but during the night it had something no-one wanted. Rain arrived and it poured so much that some of the gers were flooded and there was some hasty moving around. Our ger was fortunate and remained dry and Amelie joined John, Elizabeth and me when she became a refugee.

10th July 2011

We drove back to Ulaanbaatar via Turtle Rock and beautiful scenery. On the way we stopped at the Zaisan memorial, which celebrates Russian Mongolian co-operation in WWII as well as the space program with colourful murals and a statue of a Russian soldier at the top of 200 steps. I climbed to the top from which there is a magnificent view. Then on to Ulaanbaatar passing River Hatan Tuul where the water was high and running fast and seeing activities we did not wish to see - sheep tied tightly to lamp posts by the roadside and then being slaughtered ready for Naadam celebrations. Made me feel that I should reject meat, but that is somewhat difficult in Mongolia. We passed the area where astronomic research is carried out and where the army has missiles. The Police Academy looked very shabby, and the university building was not special. Perhaps Jono could look for students from it!! We also noted the stone monument which celebrates the fact that Mongolia is second to Africa in archaeology finds and thus information on the development of man. We stopped at the cashmere shop, which had a great array of garments, and bought Alison a scarf. Back at the hotel I had time to sort out things, after which we went to a local restaurant for dinner.

11th July 2011 Opening Day of the Nadam Festival

The Nadam Festival celebrates the three favourite activities of the Mongolians — wrestling, archery and horse racing. We started our day at about 8.30am when the coach took us to the stadium. There we became part of the crowds moving towards the correct gate to find our seats. We managed to find ours fairly quickly and sat on the allocated benches; there was very little comfort. It was obvious that some people had arrived early and seated themselves on other people's seats, hoping the owners would not arrive. Thus by the time of the opening of the Festival at 11am there had been a few altercations and, as 'health and safety' did not seem to exist all the steps were occupied and if you wished to get out it was necessary to climb over bodies. The opening ceremony began with the arrival of the army in colourful uniforms and a number of the soldiers surrounded the dais on which the president would make the opening speech. The arena filled up with the arrival of dancers in colourful dresses, Mongol hordes, and of course hundreds of horses. We were just able to see the President as he walked to the dais and made his speech. There was a big screen for a better view and the speech was on a loudspeaker but there was nothing we understood! Once the speech was over the cavalcade began around the stadium and as well as the dancers, the Mongol hordes, and the horses there were advertisements and people in their colourful clothes. The Festival is a time when the Mongolians wear the dress associated with their area and tribe, thus the mixture and the differences are spectacular. Of course, there is an element of modern dress, with some people completely dressed in western styles or others who don a mixture of both. After the ceremony we watched the wrestling for a while, but we were too far away to appreciate properly and we left the stadium, queued for the toilet and considered food but most of us were not hungry. The archery was most interesting, and we watched for a time. Both men and women take part and they are all skilful. The bows have come down from Genghis Khan's time and need much strength as well as skill to fire them with accuracy. We watched two people having to wrestle with getting the 'string' across the bow! Later, we watched what seemed to be a sophisticated form of 'Knuckle Bones'. The game appears to be a team approach with the players sitting on the floor and everyone present 'singing' a sort of noisy tune. The players have a piece of box-shaped wood which is used to hold the knuckle bones to enhance the flick by the player of the bones. Before leaving the stadium, we had a last look at the archery and then we made our way to the theatre, although we stopped for a drink on the way. I was cross about the amount I was charged and, indeed, I did not pay the amount demanded. The show was at the Mongolian National Theatre and the performance was spectacular with an orchestra, singers, dancers and individual musical performers; the horses' head violins were brilliant. A contortionist had a rubber body; a few months later I saw her on the French television. When we left the theatre, it was pouring with rain and it had been a very sunny day! Despite the wet we walked to the restaurant for the Gala Dinner. The starter and soup were good, but the main course was questionable, and I couldn't eat the pudding, it was chocolate ice cream. I asked for some other flavour, but chocolate came a second time!! A show of old Mongolian costumes was followed by a modern array of evening wear, both were most enjoyable. Thankfully the coach took us back to the hotel.

Horse riders after the Festival

12th July 2011

We had breakfast early and started out immediately so we could get to the races. The location was out of town on the hills, which resemble the Downs so it's a sort of Derby Day. Many families had camped overnight and everywhere there was kite flying. The day was not active for those who had come to watch the races. There was much waiting about, but the crowds were interesting and there was an exhibition of Mongolian activities and crafts. Horses remain central to Mongolian life and the people are natural riders, many do not have saddles or stirrups and they and their horses intermingle with the people, but it is not sensible to get too near as the horses may bite or kick! There are two races on this day and are for young boys between five and 12 years, after that your racing career is over. The number of riders is in the hundreds and the youngsters ride bareback. The races are over 15 kilometres, and we watched the end of both, we had a view from a stand for the second race and both times the winner was well ahead. There are special songs for both the winner and the last to reach the finish. A few falls are inevitable, but unfortunately one fall resulted in the death of the horse. Whether the child jockey was hurt I did not find out. The return to the hotel was very slow with a traffic jam to beat any traffic problem. The cars came from the races in their hundreds but did not keep to the road! To get ahead they went off road, across tracks, through roads works and anywhere else that it was possible or impossible to drive a vehicle. At one point there were seven or eight or more lines of traffic on a three/four lane road. And nobody gave way! We had dinner in the hotel in the evening with the grand session of working out who owed what!! Counting and re-counting went on for ages and the waitresses wanted to go to bed.

13th July 2011

Our first call was to the local monastery and Odka told us that her grandfather was important in the hierarchy of Buddhism and there is a prayer wheel on which both her grandfather's and grandmother's names are inscribed; a memorial like a gravestone. We all spun the dozens of prayer wheels and outside there were hundreds of pigeons and they are regarded as precious! Inside the temple, the Buddha was huge, 25 metres from floor to ceiling and made of gilded bronze. After the visit the group split, some stayed to rest and shop while I joined the rest to go back to the Festival on the Downs. It was more like a fair day with less queuing for the toilet (5 minutes as opposed to half an hour). We walked to the wrestling ring, where the officials did much discussing, children ran into the ring and some boys exhibited their skill as miniature wrestlers. Crowd was fairly large; I was given a chair (poor old dear) and we waited about an hour before the show began. It was preceded by a musical performance and the officials changing their robes to different colours to be the supporters of either the blues or the reds. It was also preceded by a 'punch up' in our growing crowd. I thought I was going under because by this time I had been inveigled to sit on a very low stool. However, I stood up to watch some wrestling. Soon after it was time to walk back to the coach via the horse racing and the food tents, I bought an ice cream, but it was horrible, and I disposed of it. The journey back was not a repeat of the previous night and once back at the hotel, it was shopping time for a cup. We went to the supermarket, but I did not get a cup but was able to borrow one when necessary. At the hotel, we collected our passports and made sure our luggage was ready before going to a Russian restaurant for dinner.

The coach was then loaded for the journey to the station. It was at this point I left the money for the Festival DVD, and at the station we bid farewell to Odka and driver and boarded the train. Then it was off towards Russia and the interesting episode of leaving Mongolia and entering Russia.

14th July 2011

I awoke about 5am and our two coaches had been abandoned by the rest of the train and it was soon time for the Mongolian 'border control' to collect passports and exit forms, then for the custom officers to inspect and search the train. We were then able to get off the train and go to the toilet - the ones on the train were locked 20 minutes before we arrived at the station to prevent unpleasantness on the lines. We then waited some time before we could return to the train and have our documents returned to us. The train then moved into Russia where entry forms were filled in. The 'lady controller' told me in no uncertain terms to ensure both parts were filled in the same. If I made an error, I imagined I would be thrown into a gulag! The compartments were then searched; our searcher was a large but agile lady who eventually smiled. Funny thing we had a smuggler in our compartment. She only travelled 'the border bit' but brought bottles of alcohol, duvets, clothes, knickers (some of which she wanted Rosemary to hide and others she put down the seats, stuffed others into her bra) into Russia. She managed to conceal her contraband all over the coach and was not discovered so she will live for another smuggling journey. After the passports were returned, we had to play a waiting game. We walked through the village, went to the small market and went into the only shop. Eventually, our two carriages were attached to another train and the numbers changed, but it was not until 4.45pm that we eventually left and began the journey to Irkutsk. Thus, we had two nights on the train and at times it travelled fairly speedily and made up about 5 hours. It was very hot when we left but during the night it cooled down considerably and I put on a jumper. I did not want to use the horse blanket of the previous night. I quickly got ready to arrive but felt grubby.

15th July 2011

We arrived about 7.30/8.00 am but no time for washing and were met by our new guide, Stas, and a driver. This was the station where there were steps, both up and down, but Carly insisted on carrying my case. The machine for changing dollars into roubles was out of action, so we went to the WWII memorial and the church of the Epiphany to await the opening of the banks. Changed my dollars and then we went to the Listvyanka village, which is an interesting tourist spot and where we had our first view of Lake Baikal. The village is built in wood and shows the way in which the people from the Siberian nomads to the pre-revolution lived. The revolution changed the country from being agriculture based to urban living but perhaps all change is inevitable; we wouldn't want to live as they did, particularly the women or the old. An interesting fact is that living beyond 60 was not expected and if anyone achieved that age, he/she was abandoned in the winter without food or heat. No-one could survive a cold Siberian winter. This action kept the population fit and healthy with no old people to support. Lunch came next, and then we went to the guest house, which is in a lovely position overlooking Lake Baikal but with many steps to climb. My double room had a fantastic view out to the Lake. After showering and changing, we visited the Baikal Museum which details all aspects and information about the Lake. It is the largest freshwater lake and could provide the world with all its water for 40 years. The main attraction was the two seals. Then it was back to the guest house for a cup of tea and relaxation. Then out to a restaurant overlooking the Lake for dinner and walked back to the guest house. It was 10pm and still light.

16th July 2011

Woke up too early when breakfast was not served until 9am, but I managed to use the time to tidy my things. After breakfast, the guide arrived, and we walked to Lake Baikal to take a boat trip. I paid my 300 roubles to be in Russia and a second 300 for the boat trip. It was breezy as we sailed out of the quay, but the return was smooth, warm and sunny and indeed the day became a perfect summer's day in Siberia. It seemed that every Siberian was on the stony edge of the Lake. After getting off the boat we walked to St. Nicholas Church, where an old Orthodox priest was chanting a service which turned out to be a baptism of a number of children. All were stripped of clothing ready for immersion, and some were not 'happy bunnies'. After leaving the church we went to a scrap yard full of old cars and motor bikes - Leslie would have been happy. Quite a number of bits of scrap had been used to make amusing sculptures. We then walked to the restaurant we had visited the day before. I had an apple turnover, but it was more pastry than apple. It wasn't my favourite lunch. We walked along the 'front' i.e., the edge of the Lake where there were many people enjoying the sun. We saw a wedding and had our photos taken with the bride and groom. We looked around the markets, but largely souvenirs on the stalls, and we returned to the guest house for a rest after a hot walk. In the evening there was a special dinner which celebrated Mick's birthday.

17th July 2011

Next morning everything was packed ready for the next step of the journey. The coach picked us up after we had taken our cases down the steep steps. We travelled to Irkutsk and were given a conducted walking tour around the town. Irkutsk has interesting buildings, many very old wooden houses, wide streets and gives the impression of Paris and once it was known as the Siberian Paris, but with the names of two of the streets - Marx and Lenin. That tag is no longer applicable. Near the river is a large statue of the builder of the Trans-Siberian Railway and opposite it the house of the Governor of Siberia. We visited the museum near the river, which was very interesting, but we really did not have enough time to see every exhibit as closely as we would have liked. Afterwards we had spare time which we spent by the river and saw the work going on to improve the heating of the city and then to wander back to the centre and look for a place for lunch. We found a pleasant little restaurant and after eating had a second look at the poster display which illustrated the history of Irkutsk, which has a diminishing population as does Russia generally, the exception being the big cities. We met at the designated hotel and caught the bus to the station. Stas the guide carried my case and once on the train our watches were put back 5 hours to correspond with Moscow time. We tried to keep awake as long as possible, but it was difficult. At least this train is more comfortable and modern with toilets open all the time.

18th, 19th, and 20th July 2011

Three nights and three days spent on a train is more than enough, especially as the scenery was similar for much of the way, miles and miles of tall pine trees. Some fields and plains but few animals and I estimate we saw only about three herds of cattle. The villages for the most part seemed to be somewhat run down with dilapidated houses, with everywhere that had been planted seeming to be with potatoes. At least we saw the post which marks the crossing between Mongolia and Siberia. As we got nearer to Moscow, we passed over some very big rivers with huge iron bridges and all the way where we stopped at stations of the bigger towns we were able to get off the train to buy necessities from the stalls and take some exercise. We arrived in Moscow at about 5.45pm where we did not have to negotiate steps so there was no need for anyone to help me with my case. We were picked up by a new guide, Sashia, and a bus but no help with cases by the driver - Russian drivers don't do loading of cases! We were taken to the hotel - the Vega, a pleasant surprise. It belongs to the Best Western chain and very much the kind of hotel we expect. All our party was accommodated on the same floor and the breakfast was a very good buffet.

21st July 2011

A sightseeing tour began the day. The first impressions of Moscow are that a large number of people are wearing crucifixes and weddings are everywhere! Our first call was at the Cathedral of Christ the Saviour which is not old but is a replica of the original building which was destroyed in the era of Stalin. The reconstruction was paid for by public subscription and we spent quite a time looking at everything. Then on to the area near the Novodevichy Convent, we were unable to go into the building but the gardens around it are beautiful. Many of the nuns used to be daughters of noble, even royal, families who had brought shame on the families! The Convent remains well endowed with money. Then it was on to Red Square (red because of the red of the bricks, not because of any connection with the Revolution) and a visit to St. Basil's (pronounced as St. Baysil's by our guide to whom I did not take). We climbed to the top of the cathedral and saw all the chapels, some of which are being renovated. Those wall paintings with too much damage are just preserved in their present condition. At the top some excellent male singers performed, and I bought a CD. Had lunch at the GUM store, which is a brilliant store, we had pancakes, and they were super. Afterwards I went with Carly, Andy and Amelie to the Gulag Museum. It is a very interesting place but not comfortable. However, it is good to remember what happened to those who opposed the regime. When we returned to Red Square, we noted Lenin's Mausoleum and then saw that firemen were at St. Basil's. On our way back we passed the Bolshoi Theatre, but it is still under renovation and not yet open for performances. Thankfully, there was no fire, but someone had released a smoke bomb inside, a somewhat stupid thing to do. The next event was a cruise along the Moscow River and saw a girl accidently fall in the water; she was not hurt, and her boyfriend helped her out and the day was warm. On landing, we went to Arbat, a pedestrianized area and walked almost to its end when Amelie realized that the restaurant she was looking for was no longer there. There were complaints and mutterings, but another restaurant was found and peace was restored. Rain was falling when we came out and we hurried to the metro, but everyone arrived back at the hotel and bed called.

22nd July 2011

Registered out and put our luggage into store for the day, then straight to Red Square and the environs of the Kremlin. First, we saw the eternal flame and the monuments to the special cities of the country; those from which the largest number of soldiers died in WWII. Watched the soldiers on guard, they used to guard Lenin's tomb, and later saw the changing of the guard and the officer adjusting their shirts! Then on to the Kremlin, meaning Citadel and the guide pointed out all the particular buildings cathedrals, palaces, bell towers as well as the Tsar bell from which a piece broke off in its firing and the various canons.

Outside St. Basil's Cathedral in Red Square, Moscow

There was a Fabergé exhibition which was a fortunate accident, and it was wonderful to see so many marvellous pieces of jewellery in one place. The Armoury was equally spectacular with its displays of clothes, jewels, artefacts and carriages. We needed more time! In the afternoon I went with Coly and Amelie to the Pushkin Museum, but we queued for the special Dior Exhibition and during our time there I was interviewed and photographed for a magazine but have no idea if it was published because I did not ask the name of the magazine. Got into the museum eventually and had a good time looking at as many paintings as we had time. Our walk back to Red Square was quick and met with everyone else. The last expedition in Moscow was a tour of the Metro. The city is famous for its wonderful ornate (Art Deco) stations, and they are indeed something not to be missed. It was necessary to return to the hotel to collect the luggage and then it was on to the Leningrad Station for Train 20, Coach 10 for the last leg. The station was absolutely packed but there were no steps and we eventually departed for St. Petersburg at about 1am.

23rd July 2011

Arrived at the Moskovsky Station St. Petersburg very early in the morning and once again there were no steps and we immediately went on a sightseeing tour, saw the Church of the Spilt Blood, the canal of Seven Bridges, the Bronze Horseman, and the Battleship Aurora of Revolutionary fame. Nearby the ship there are naval buildings which fly the cross of St. Andrew, but the colours are opposite to the Scottish saltire. Went to a shop which sells Christmas decorations at which I purchased a few, then on to a small café for lunch. I had raspberry tart which was very tasty. Next, we were taken to our hotel which is more Russian than that in Moscow but comfortable and clean. I went out with Carly and Andy, and we visited the Kazan Cathedral, with its dome described as an ugly imitation of St. Peter's. The Soviets turned it into the Museum of Atheism, but it is now back as an Orthodox Church, and we saw a long queue to kiss an icon. Then we went on and visited the Armenian and then walked along the corridor on the outside of the Gostiny Dvor, the largest department store in the City and watched a wedding party having problems with their car. While we were looking at the shops Andy decided to buy a shirt and while I was outside a group of people performed a sort of ritual by standing still in a kind of trance and another joined them and suddenly the human statues moved, and I laughed. Even the bride was advising on what to do! Afterwards we took a tour boat around the canals. It was an interesting trip except the guide was Russian and on a boat that advertised that the commentary was in Russian, so we knew what we were in for. After the canal trip we joined those who had not gone to the theatre and after the show the theatre goers came to the group and some happy banter and laughs followed. Then the rain came so we returned to the hotel.

24th July 2011

It was the day to visit the Hermitage and it was wonderful and could not be missed, but, oh dear, our day was the one when every cruise ship arrived. The number of people made it impossible to move let alone look at anything. Our guide, Tatiana, did her best, but we only managed to see what she wanted to highlight. A rugby scrum would have been more pleasant. It seems the best time to visit is late November or February when the temperatures are very low. After a lunch Mick and Maggie, Alan and Denise and Frank and Rosemary as well as I went to the summer palace. The boat journey is quite long which surprised me. The palace is a stunning building in a wonderful setting we only had a limited time. We returned and hurried to get ready for the theatre with dinner first. Dinner was at a Russian restaurant and the owner thought he was a great entertainer and funny. Actually, he was just annoying, but the food was good. When it was time for me to go to the theatre, I was accompanied by five escorts to the Malinsky Theatre. When I went inside, I had some difficulty in finding my seat but did eventually. John and Elizabeth arrived Just before the ballet began. Swan Lake was excellent, but my seat was hard and had to sit on my hands for the second act. Couldn't clap!! Returned to the Shelford but Carly, Andy, Amelie, Colman and I were too tired to go out, but we went to an Irish pub and didn't get in until 1.30 am.

25th July 2011

Up at 8am to see everyone who was leaving early. Then went out with Joe who is staying one extra day and we walked for miles and miles. Walked over the river near the Hermitage but stopped to see the cruise ships and there were about nine huge vessels. Tried to go into St. Isaac's but the queues were immensely long, and it was not worth paying to go in if there were too many people to see anything. Went on to the church of the Spilt Blood but there were coaches and coaches and coaches of people all wearing numbered badges. However, the outside of the church is what you want to see. Joe insisted we had a subway lunch. I had not eaten one before and would not rush to have a second. In the early evening we went to our Russian friend's restaurant, but he wasn't so over the top and the meal was good. I had fish but could not eat it all.

26th July 2011

Joe left at about 9.15am and I had planned to go to the Russian State Museum, but Tuesday is the day it closes so I walked to the Hermitage and went to the tourist information caravan and bought two fridge magnets; they are the best and the cheapest! I walked back along the river to the cruise ships and my legs said they had had enough. They have been muttering for a while. Once over the river, I sat in the little garden for about half an hour and then went to Nevsky Prospekt and bought a Russian doll for Nicola from THE shop but nearly did not because the salesperson had certainly not recently attended a customer service course. Had to pay for the bag!!! When back at the hotel, I completed this diary and because legs said no more walking, I ate my last bar and ordered tea from the hotel and found out I had Colman's exit permit and worried that I might not get out of Russia.

27th July 2011

Woke up and got all my luggage organised, had my last breakfast and then walked to the river and road beside the metro and worried about getting out of Russia. Taxi came on time and was early at the airport and was made to wait before being given admittance to the departure area. When permitted, chaos reigned; there were queues everywhere, few explanatory signs and departure gates in unusual areas. I became so frustrated that I made a fuss and when I pushed to the front I was able to leave my bag because Jono had registered it for me. The passport person asked me for my exit permit and laughed when I began to explain, left her little office and when she came back let me proceed. Then the plane was delayed for two hours but the flight was good and Jono met me at Heathrow.

It had been a remarkable journey with treasured memories. Fortunately, I understand Mil recovered from her illness and was able to enjoy the same experience later.

The end of the year of excess travel became even more than ever expected. I gained an MBE from the Prince of Wales on 18th November 2011 at Buckingham Palace. It was a day to be remembered for ever. The prince spoke to each person who gained an honour as if he knew every individual. It was extremely satisfying. David, Jono, and Alison were the only ones permitted in the palace with me. Photographs were taken outside the palace and cars were parked inside the gates.

Afterwards we ate at Brown's Hotel in a very pleasant dining room with a good number of family members,

February of 2012 was not a good month for weather. I went to Scotland in the first week and it was very cold. Rodney met me at Waverley Station, and we were soon at Dunfermline. Barbara and I walked to the shops the next morning and had coffee at Abbot House while the evening was one of music. On Saturday we went to Pitlochry where Neil Oliver was speaking, and I enjoyed the evening greatly particularly as I obtained his signature and had a photograph taken with him. Fog was a nuisance on the way back to Dunfermline, and, on Sunday morning the radio reported that the weather in England was not good, so we went to church and then Barbara and Rod took me to Waverly for the train home. The weather continued cold and snowy, but it was possible for me to go to Sheffield to see Christopher and we had an enjoyable day. I saw where he lives and some of the city, particularly as I had not visited it before. In actual fact it was much more interesting than I expected. In early March, Patsi and I took a lady from Alwalton to London, she had never been to the city before, so we went on the Eye and took a river trip before having a lunch and a look at some of the shops before returning home.

Israel

Israel was the venue of Jono's conference in March 2012 and the day before we set off, we met Karen and Archie in London to go to the Cambridge theatre to see Matilda; it was Archie's birthday treat. The flight was from Luton and arrived at Tel Aviv, which is on the coast, and from the hotel there was a good view of the sea and the beach. The weather, however, was cold, with huge waves crashing on the shore, showing that the Mediterranean is not always calm and warm! Tel Aviv is a city which has grown since the end of the Second World War when settlement by Jewish people was in large numbers. My first visit was to the Art Museum where the collection was excellent and huge. Impressionist pictures were numerous, but visitors were sparse. The next day, a tour began and proceeded along the Kidron Valley where Gethsemane was pointed out as was the Mount of Olives which was just in view. We arrived at Jerusalem near the Lion Gate and entered the old areas, the first was the Armenian Quarter and we walked through it and the other quarters. The Via Dolorosa had the stations of the cross marked and the place where Veronica wiped Jesus' face particularly attracted a group of people. It was fortunate that it was during Lent and a number of young men were carrying a crucifix. The Church of the Holy Sepulchre was impressive, and many people were present, but most probably, the tomb was not that in which Jesus was placed. The 'Wailing Wall', which is the remaining part of the wall of the second temple of Jerusalem, destroyed in 70 BC, where all can pray but not everyone together. Men and women have their separate areas, but all can leave a note pushed into the wall with a prayer written on it. A sign with a direction to Samuel's Tomb was interesting but there was no time to visit it. The Holocaust Museum was the next stop, but time was limited which was disappointing. It has an aura of peace, but the memories of cruelty to Jewish people cannot be forgotten.

The following morning the second tour began with a brief view of Armageddon, but a stop was made at Nazareth, now the largest city in Galilee, and the Church of the Annunciation and St. Joseph's Church were both visited. Under the two buildings were remains of Jesus' time and the guide particularly pointed out the position of Joseph the carpenter's shop. Whether it was accurate was not discussed! What seemed to be correct was the information that there were probably only 20 families living in Nazareth in Biblical times. Cana in Galilee, where Jesus turned water into wine, was viewed from the bus and we continued to the Sea of Galilee which is 200 feet below sea level. A visit was to the Church of the Multiplication of Fish and Loaves which is shaped like a boat and built on the remains of Capernaum, where the guide said that Christ lived with St. Peter's mother-in-law who was the customs officer and controlled the road to Nazareth and Samaria. The ruins of a synagogue may have been one in which Jesus had preached and while we were looking around the weather became dull and grey with the Sea of Galilee becoming quite rough so we experienced the way in which it can change as depicted in the story of Christ walking on water. The next place of interest was the Jordan River where many people were putting on special clothes and being baptised. I decided my baptism as a baby was sufficient.

Mountains had surrounded us - the Golan and Jordan Heights - as we drove to the river. We were just able to see the place of the Sermon on the Mount and Mount Taber, the site of the Transfiguration. The return to Tel Aviv was greeted with cold wind and Jono had gone with other conference attendees to Jerusalem where the weather was also bitterly cold. The final full day of the stay in Tel Aviv was grey and cool. The Mediterranean was showing its capabilities, huge rough seas, rain and bitter coldness! I walked along the promenade to Jaffa and looked around the town, saw the harbour and other notable buildings before walking back to the hotel. The weather was changeable on the last morning so only a short walk was possible before we went to the airport. The plane was on time and the drive to Alwalton was good.

Japan

We set off to Osaka on 25th of March 2012 and the journey to Dubai was good. We were going upper class but there was a problem with the A380, and we were put on an old type of plane which did not provide the expected comfort, particularly as we were bussed to the plane, and we carried the luggage up the steps   Jono could not rest and was changed to first class but not for every inch of the way. We thought about complaining but the cabin crew made sure that the service was good which helped a little! We arrived at the Kansai Airport and took a train to Kyoto from where we were taxied to the conference centre. The latter was expensive because the distance was long, but the area was quiet. Tiredness was with us, but I did not sleep because I had to be in Kyoto early for a trip around the city. It was an expensive taxi journey again but there had been no time to work out the underground route. The trip was well organised with seats allocated and good guides, very Japanese. The first visit was to the residence of Njo-Jo, who was a shogun, and the walls were painted while the floors were squeaky in order that any interloper was heard and dealt with. Shoes were required to be removed and it made the floor cold to walk on. The Golden Pavilion (Kinkaku-je) with its spectacular gardens was next. It was then on to the Imperial Palace, the gardens had been visited the last time we were in Japan, but this time we saw the rooms but there was no permission to enter them. The throne room was seen from a distance and the throne and other important artifacts had been removed to Tokyo for the coronation of the present Emperor to the disappointment of Kyoto citizens. A garden had been turned into a 'seaside' for the emperor.   After this visit we went on to the lunch which was organised very much like that in Israel. There were long tables for the crowds and the food was the same for everyone! Japanese food was good to sample, and I liked some but not the soup with bits of chicken. After the meal another coach picked us up, again the guide was helpful. Immediately, we went to a Shinto Shrine (Helan-Jingo) with its orange and white walls and its gate as copied by our door shapes (at our home in Alwalton). The garden was beautiful and used in the film, Geisha Story. Then on to Sanju Sangen-do temple with its 1001 statues of the extremely impressive Buddhist deity; shoes had to come off and photographs were prohibited. The last visit was to Kiyomzu temple, overhanging a valley with a waterfall. The water was thought of 'a cure all' for illnesses. The walk up to the temple was steep but lined by shops.   After this visit it was back to the hotel, the taxi was a little cheaper because the guide helped to arrange the price. By the time I had reached the hotel, tiredness had set in. I had sandwiches which were not the best I had ever tasted.

The next day was less hectic, and Jono finished his work at about 12 noon, later than expected with the reason/excuse his conference responsibility. We went to Kyoto by the subway and found the railway station confusing but eventually found the hotel from where the tour began. We then met Jono's Welsh friend and had a meal although he was in difficulty, the food hardly suited Jono. The next day was very warm in Kyoto where I went once again had to find the way out of the station to street level. Easy from the front of the station but difficult in a maze of shops.I walked to the area near Gion where ceramics are on sale everywhere.I bought two small dishes one of which I broke later.

I saw several women of all ages wearing kimonos, seems a popular thing to do. The following day, I found the tour hotel very easily and had a long wait. We then went to Hiroshima on a super express, in other words a bullet train. At Hiroshima, we first went to Mimaya Island with its religious aspect and the wooden statue in the middle of the water. Afterwards we went to the Peace Park and Museum, very interesting to see but impossible to imagine the terror of the actual events. A spot was pointed to where the person disappeared completely, and he/she was not the only one. Perhaps disappearing was better than being terribly burned. The city has now been re-built and lives go on as usual. Back to Kyoto was fast and comfortable and the next day we left the city with rain falling. The journey was long, but sleep was possible and the drive back from Gatwick reasonably fast, and Star was collected (from kennels).

Nicola and Alex's wedding

Three weeks later we were off to Reading for Nicola and Alex's wedding. It seemed impossible that the little girl, who came year by year to stay at Alwalton and enjoy everything including going to Scotland and Hunstanton, was getting married. The wedding present had caused some concern because my idea of completing the patchwork quilt was a near miss. The quilters needed it ready for the quilting on Thursday 23rd March and it was at their door 10 minutes before closure. Thankfully, the quilt was ready for presentation on the day. Jono and Rod were the chauffeurs for bride and groom and bridesmaids. The service was excellent with family members having the opportunity to do something special. Mine was signing the register to prove that Nicola and Alex had become wedded on 21st April 2012. I wore my palace dress, a memory of that occasion, and memories of the wedding will have the same importance. The reception was some way from the church but was special because it was in an ancient barn and the food was good. Alison made the cake and Patsi decorated it beautifully, but it was not cut at a good time. Dancing and talking completed the event before everyone needed to think about sleeping. Two other special events to remember in 2012. In June, the Queen's Diamond Jubilee was celebrated with the church decorated with a beautiful display. A special service was well attended and the parties in the church and the village hall were successful despite all the previous concerns! Unfortunately, the rain came down in absolute sheets for the Thames Pageant, which had been carefully planned with a special boat for the Queen and Prince Philip and the Royal family. There was an immense number of water vessels and, of course, crowds of watchers. The weather was almost a winner! Most of the river vessels sailed the route but some gave up, and the Queen and Prince Philip remained under cover which was perhaps a disappointment for both. The following day it was a 'watch the television' for all the events. Crowds were huge and the concert and fireworks very good. We were able to see the beacon on the hill at Chesterton.

On 3rd of July 2012 the Olympic flame came to Peterborough and Jono and I went to the railway station in Ferry Meadows and saw the train but no flame. It was in its little lantern, and no-one held it up. However not to be beaten, we went to Donald's Garage the next morning where we could put the car and watch the procession. It was really exciting to see the flame and to know it would burn during the weeks of the events. The Olympics began on 27th July and, on 3rd August Alison and I went to Greenwich Park to see horse jumping events.

A splendid day at the London Olympics, horse jumping at Greenwich Park

They were exciting, particularly when GB was so good   Alison and Simon managed to attend the final evening and saw the parade of those who took part, and the ending entertainment. At the end of August, Jono, Simon, Alison and I went to Gozo for a holiday. The first night did not indicate a good time as there were storms which left mud and floods. It did not stop us having a boat ride the next day despite the choppy sea and the necessity to wear lifejackets. Originally, we had looked at the inland sea and the window rock, but the boat went as far as Dweya Bay. The next day, Malta, and particularly Valletta, were on the itinerary, we viewed the harbour, the Cathedral and as many interesting places as possible. In the evening, we went to an outdoor theatre and saw A Midsummer Night's Dream before returning to Gozo. The next days were lazy and we sat by the pool or went into it. Simon decided to do a diving course so he was not available for Alison's birthday, but Jono and I went with her on a 'look around' trip. On the last day in Gozo, we visited the Neolithic remains, which are protected, and then to a windmill which was given to Gozo by the last miller.

In March 2013, Scotland called, the reason being that Alfie Boe was performing at the theatre in Edinburgh. Much of Scotland had booked seats so that we found it difficult to get a meal! The show was enjoyable, but I prefer Alfie singing opera while he appears to prefer a wider range of music.

He remains an excellent singer of course! At the end of May we drove to Heathrow, it was a very difficult journey, and we almost missed the plane. We were going upper class but there was little time to appreciate what was on offer. The flight for me was very good, I slept all the way to Vancouver. Perhaps it was the free drink that gave me so much comfort. On arrival we had the energy to walk all round Stanley Park - both sides of the headland - 8-10 kilometres. I was ready to be picked up by coach early on the Monday morning, but no coach arrived. Eventually, one of the receptionists realised my difficulties and contacted the firm. This meant we were kept on the move! Firstly, we went to Stanley Park, but in a different direction from our walk. and were immediately taken to the Totem Poles, which are both impressive and huge. Afterwards we made for Geville Island which has both a large market and shops and, on this day, a children's festival was in action which was interesting. Afterwards, it was a drive through China town and to the viewing column before being taken back to the hotel.

The next morning a repeat performance of no coach at the specified time but once one arrived, we were off to Vancouver Island by ferry. A tour of the island by bus took us about an hour; there were no stops and little chance of photographs! However, the driver was good with information and after he had completed the tour, we were given time to look at the shops. A lady from New Zealand, Shirley, and I inspected a few garments and then visited the Grand Hotel, an interesting building. The next point of call was the Buchard Gardens which were impressive and would have been marvellous if the weather had not decided to pour with rain. The gardens were originally an area where Robert Pim Butchard discovered rich limestone, developed a quarry and built a cement plant at Tod Inlet. Eventually, the limestone deposits were exhausted and Jennie, his wife, decided she would make an area of beauty. The gardens took many years to develop but are now world famous and remain in the hands of the Butchard family. After leaving the gardens, the bus returned us to the ferry via another interesting route which, when completed, we boarded the ferry and returned to the mainland. After renewing my energy by a good night's sleep. I walked along the waterfront where the cruise ships were being boarded and continued until I reached Gas Town and the railway station. I did not stop here but continued until I arrived at Sun Yat Sen's Garden. On the way back I stopped to watch the clock which smokes at particular times. As the weather was not at its best, I used the hotel swimming pool in the afternoon and then watched the float planes from the window.

The following day, the outing began with the bus being driven over the Lion's Gate Bridge, which previously I had only walked under. The journey was very scenic and was to Whistler which had just held the Winter Olympic Games. The coach stopped at a waterfall, and we all climbed up as far as we could. The arrival at Whistler was followed by a very interesting tour of the town during which the various areas of the Olympics were pointed out. In the afternoon a very small group decided to go for a flight in one of the tiny float planes. I sat beside the pilot, and we flew both through the clouds and in the clear air. We were over a forest, which is completely without any human habitation. Thus, I would not have wished to land or crashed in it. After what seemed a short time, we landed and visited the First Nation centre. Then it was back to Vancouver, with the sun in the sky for much of the journey. The last day in Canada followed and I went to the Art Gallery, and the next morning we finished the stay by walking around Stanley Park, saw the Stanley memorial and enjoyed both the gardens and the edge of the ocean on which a mermaid, like that in Scandinavia sits.

In July 2013, a clear run to Gatwick airport was expected but delays were on the A1 but the M11 appeared usable. However, there was no entry on to the M25 unless Heathrow was the wanted airport. Thus, the journey to Gatwick became annoying and the airline was not one to be chosen again. Fortunately, the hotel in Santorini was excellent and the pool encouraged me to sit beside it for most of the days. I managed to walk to Thera, which had grown and developed since the last time we visited. Evenings found us watching the sun go down over the caldera especially on the occasion when a cruise ship arrived with full lights. We did not miss the Minoan archaeology which is now displayed in a much more satisfactory way; everywhere is covered and walkways allow good viewing. Oia was the next stopping place which has excellent views, particularly of the sun going down. Apartments in the steep cliffs are popular with visitors. I visited the newly refurbished museum as my stay was moving to its end. It has real improvements, and the displays are much more interesting for visitors. In 2014 the visit was to Athens where my first activity was to try the swimming pool, but the weather was somewhat windy, and I decided on a walk. The evening was more interesting as there was a film, but not the usual one. The subject was about ancient people, particularly the Egyptians, the Minoans and the Greeks, but the screen showed it at all angles and drew you into it, so the feeling was most unusual. After the film we were driven to an area where we walked through a garden which had lights in the trees and bushes, and then into an interesting house which belonged to an artist. The following day I went on a walking trip which included the 'changing of the guard' by the soldiers wearing the distinguishing Greek uniforms and marching with their unusual step. We passed the memorial of the British poet, Lord Byron, the remains of particular buildings and then climbed up to the Parthenon, a building I have always wanted to see in reality. We spent time walking all the way round and seeing as much as possible. Looking from the top instead of looking up to the building was very interesting. On the way down, there was a museum to visit, very new and very interesting. The last evening meant a meal followed by entertainment by the students who attended the conference. It was enjoyed by all.

Launch of Mr. Mayor

It is difficult to remember when I began to write the book about Peterborough, but it was a result of my regular meeting with Anne who I met at the Institute of Education in London. She had already published two books about Luton, and I decided I ought not to be someone who did not do anything with the study of three/four years. For some months I went to the library and looked at books and newspapers about Peterborough during the 19th century. After some time, I realised Peterborough was late in having a council and that became the major part of the work although other topics which included the work house, the cathedral, water supply and sewerage were important. The book was completed by April 2015 and launched in the Town Hall. Unfortunately, there was a hitch, some of the volumes had not been properly bound and a whole new set of newly bound copies needed to be produced. They continue to be sold but whether all will be purchased remains to be seen. I intend to do some more research about the city but whether the work becomes a properly bound book remains uncertain. Almost immediately after the initial launch Jono and I went to Australia. We landed at Brisbane and were met by Mick and Maggie, who were with me on the Mongolian trip and had visited us after they had completed their European travels. They took us around the area, we had a meal near the ocean and Maggie explained she had become a 'sea rescuer' and was enjoying it. Australia, it seems, is in the process of building new homes which perhaps does not cause the concern it does in Britain. I left for Sydney the following morning and on arrival was welcomed by the most dreadful weather. Rain and wind were so intense that I hardly recognised where June and David lived, and it was cold with thick mist which made it impossible to see across the harbour. On the following day we went to see Helen and I was lucky that Nina was at home. Helen took us to see the surf, it was grey and huge. Trees had been uprooted, houses demolished, and flooding occurred in many places. June and I went to Sydney the next day and met Joe, Mitch and girlfriend as well as Rachel and boyfriend. After we had had a long 'talk' and eaten, June and I went to the art display which was interesting. The next day I decided to return to Brisbane, and it was a sensible decision; the planes can be cancelled without warning. The one I had chosen was cancelled and had it been the following day I might have missed the plane to London. As it was Anzac Day, and being in Brisbane, Jono and I were able to see the action and we ended the stay. In December, Nina was touring Europe and I met her in London, and we went to the Victoria and Albert Museum, after which it was back to Peterborough. The next day we went to Fotheringay and Stamford, the latter was very busy, but Christmas was near. In the evening we went to a pantomime, which had all the old jokes but was very enjoyable. Michele joined us on Sunday, we had a meal and then went to Chesterton Church for the carol service after which we went to see Brenda. Nina left for Prague the next morning.

At Chesterton Church with Michelle and Nina

Jono went to Harbin in July 2015 to work for six weeks at the university, and I went for the last week. I travelled with Air China, Alison came to the airport with me, and she knew I was not eager for the flight. We considered up-grading, but the cost was huge, and I was only going for a week. However, I experienced a journey from London which I would not wish to have again, but I was met at Beijing and directed to the plane for Harbin. I was pleased to arrive safely! The following morning, I took a walk beside the river. The weather was sunny and warm and there were swimmers in the river, but it didn't look very clean, so I decided to return to the hotel for an orange juice in the lounge. Next morning, I went to the swimming pool where the attendant was somewhat over the top with his 'service'. I felt like a poor old person who was unable to help herself in any way. Afterwards, one of Jono's colleagues took us to the tower which is one of Harbin's special highlights and we enjoyed the view and afterwards it was dinner with Jono's colleagues. The following day, sightseeing was on the plan, and we arrived at the museum without passports and were nearly refused entry. The building had been a church and I wondered if any of the locals knew anything about it or recognized the painting which was over the area where an altar had been. After leaving the museum we walked along the main street to the river where we had a boat trip. The next day, we set out early, crossed the river over the bridge, which could be seen from the hotel, and travelled to the tiger park. Once there, we had an 'armoured' bus to take us around the park where the tigers (and a few lions) were free to wander. They were magnificent creatures, a little smaller than African lions but no less strong. They jumped up the bus to reach the meat they were offered, and their strength and size of claws showed their killing potential. It was good to see tigers being looked after but there were areas where more care was needed. After the bus trip, a circus with acrobatics, motor bicyclists in a cage and performing dogs entertained us. All were enjoyed except the two small bears on leads. Afterwards we visited the gardens which had many houses, each with an individual design and an Eastern Christian Church which was also interesting. Lastly, we viewed a theatre show which indicated Russia still had some interest in that area of China.

**Taking an evening cruise on the Huangpu river in Shanghai with
Peng Ming's auntie and mother Yan**

In 2016 Shanghai was again visited and the reason was that Jono's annual conference was held in it, the largest city in China. We travelled in the 'upper ordinary class', and it was reasonable, but all long distant flights become tiring! We were met at the airport by Jono's student and his 'auntie' who drove us to the hotel. When we arrived Jono's insistence ensured we were allocated a room overlooking the river, on which there was constant traffic. It was also possible to pick out some of the buildings on the opposite side of the river which were built when Britain had influence in China, especially at night when all were illuminated. Peng Ming, Jono's student, his 'auntie' and his mother took us for a meal. Auntie chose it and it was really enjoyable. The next morning, I walked along the river while Jono was in a meeting with two of his former students and a present one. After lunch we went under the river by tunnel to see an old Chinese house. The crowds were unbelievable. The next morning, I took a walk and found myself near a huge traffic roundabout on which there was a high circular pedestrian walkway which was interesting to walk around particularly as the Oriental Pearl Tower is almost next door. The evening brought a real surprise! Just outside our window were two boats which were there to give visitors the opportunity of a river ride and we had such an evening trip and with all the illuminations it was spectacular. The next day Peng Ming's mother, Yan and aunt took me to a new area of the city, and I saw the sculptures outside the main entrance and visited the China Art Museum which was interesting particularly the spectacular wall of film. We had a Chinese meal at a good restaurant. Miao's Mother, Lei Lei had arrived when we returned to the hotel, and it was wonderful to see her. The next day we went under the river to the old area of Shanghai where we saw a house of an Englishman's daughter. It is now used as a hotel so it is only the entry that can be viewed. An interesting shop contained many attractive articles, but I did not buy! The hall used by early communists remains and I am certain that Mao Tse Tung attended meetings there. Then it was to an area of very old buildings and later we had a super evening meal in a very smart hotel and then it was back to our hotel. Unfortunately, the traffic was heavy getting back and Lei Lei and her staff left almost immediately. They had a long journey home. The next day Peng Ming's mother and aunt took me to a historic village which continues to be inhabited. We went for a journey on the river which gave a different view of the village after which we had lunch overlooking the water. From the restaurant it was possible to see a crucifix on a church, an unusual view considering the attitude to religion in China, but it was particularly right for me as it was Good Friday. We walked around the village and went into a most unexpected house with a garden and lovely furniture. The return journey was even slower than in the morning but eventually we reached the hotel where there was another marvellous meal with all Jono's associates as well as those who had had a day out. A birthday was celebrated at the end of the meal which really rounded off the time in Shanghai. In January 2017, Peng Ming gained his PhD, and I went to Newcastle with Jono to be at the presentation. His parents were also present, so it was good to be with them.

Christopher and Philippa's wedding

Jono went back to China in July 2016 for three weeks. I remained at home with India and the weather turned out to be very hot, which made me ill. The reason being that I did not wear a hat and did not realise the heat. Patsi came to walk India for several days because I felt really unable to leave the bed. Alison came to see my condition, which was improving, and we took India to Swaffham, and she enjoyed her outing, especially when she was supplied with a drink. When Jono arrived home, he was in time for Christopher and Philippa's wedding in August at which there was a large number of people attending. It took place in rural Suffolk and the bride was in white while the large number of bridesmaids wore different blues. There was plenty of food. Alison made the wedding cake which was very up to date - no icing - but it was not eaten on the day. It remained in one of our freezers until Christmas.

A member of the staff of the hotel, Jono and I in Oman

In November Jono and I set out for two weeks in Oman. We left India with Felicity (a professional dog sitter), and both were happy! The journey was reasonable, and sleep was possible. When we arrived at the hotel, we were somewhat taken aback as waiting for the room was longer than we expected but, when we were eventually directed to it all was satisfactory. Unfortunately, I had lost my reading glasses so, although the sun was shining and waiters provided all that was required, books were of no use. Luckily, Zenab (a previous PhD student of Jono now working in Oman) was able to provide some cheap glasses which made sitting in the sun much better - I was able to read. The next day television was very important, we watched to find out who had been elected as America's 45th President: it was Donald Trump, who has become determined to do what he believes is correct. The Opera House was visited the following evening, and the programme was not opera but a collection of musicians with mainly stringed instruments and a singer; all were excellent. The following days were lazy but very enjoyable. We regularly had afternoon tea, an evening walk and sitting on the sand watching the sea and waiting for the light to disappear. A visit with Zenab and her mother took us to 'the' souk they use. There was so much to look at that it was difficult to decide what we wanted. After some time, we chose presents for Christmas. Food ended the day! We saw the moon when it was nearest the earth, a so-called supermoon, and it was the hugest I have ever seen. As it was over the sea it was possible to see the movement of the earth clearly. A trip the next day included going into the central mosque where it is necessary to remove shoes and women must cover the head. We also went to the fish market which did not please me. The museum was the last building to visit, and it was very interesting. Zenab's friend was involved in arranging things. The next day was the celebration of the length of the Sultan's reign and decorations were everywhere. Before we returned home, we had a meal with Zenab and her family. It was most pleasant. Finally, we visited an area that was being changed from an old area of seaside into an area for new visitors.

Jono and I set out for New Orleans on the 4th March 2017, the journey over the Atlantic seemed longer than the last time we crossed it. We landed at Miami, as it was necessary to change planes. The wait seemed long, and the plane was small and full to New Orleans, but the taxi ride was reasonable as was the hotel, although the necessities were very reduced. The room, however, had an excellent window that overlooked the Mississippi river and the traffic on it was always busy and also very different in size. Those ships which carried holiday makers were absolutely huge and travelled speedily. On the first day of Jono's conference, I went on a bus trip and felt stupid because I thought I did not have enough money to pay what was owing to the bus driver. A very kind couple lent me some cash, but I had just enough and did not need to use the loan. However, after I returned their money, they bought me a drink and some eatables like soft scones. The bus driver was full of information, and we went through the French Quarter where there are smart houses built some years ago. Also, we were directed to the historic area (known as the Tremé Area) which is the birthplace of jazz first played by African Americans. Each year now, millions of people visit the largest and most outrageous festival in the world - the Mardi - Gras. I went to the area where the houses were flooded and most needed repair (some still not begun because of cost) which took a considerable time. The reason for the necessary work not being begun quickly was that those in charge refused to let people into the area. It took real determination to get the necessary people into the city to do the work. Those who refused entry found their explanation was not acceptable. Another interesting visit was to a cemetery which was large and the way in which the burial was undertaken. A number of bodies are interred in one grave but usually after they are bones only. On the last part of the trip the new flood control of water was pointed out, as was the production of gas and electricity with our last view being of horses in a field.

The following day Jono decided he must see the exhibition of the 2nd World War which begins with a short film, introduced by Tom Hanks the film star, with some actions, one particularly was of the seats being shaken as if there was an air raid. The display of fighting in Europe and the Eastern countries was excellent and made you wonder why the world is in turmoil and is world war possible again? The next day was a trip on the river and before I stepped on the boat, I had my photograph taken and travelled with a very nice couple. We went along the river which had many buildings on either bank, among which was one that produces sugar. The most interesting was when we stepped off the boat to visit the National Historical Park, which is the ground of the 1815 battle when the British were defeated by the Americans. The Americans are very pleased with the result, but the British do not seem to remember, probably because it was much the time of the Battle of Waterloo.

After the river trip, I went to look at the shops in the covered area but there was little that was good enough to buy except the cooking pans which I had already purchased and used. Instead of staying in the area I walked along the river and went to look at the cathedral from the outside. On the way back I had to cross the railway lines, but as a train was coming it was necessary to wait and I asked a man what the hugely long train was carrying. He explained it was mainly carrying sugar, but actually thinking about it, I decided that a train that was going towards a sugar factory must be intending to pick up sugar to be taken for use not taking it to the factory. The next day, I returned to the cathedral, and went inside so that I had seen the oldest holy building. I then went into the neighbouring Louisiana State building which was very interesting, and I spent much time looking at all the contents. At the gate of the cathedral there was a line of horses and coaches ready to take visitors for rides, which obviously needed payment! I saw the long, perhaps longer, train once again going towards the factory. All the trains used their very loud horn to warn of their oncoming because there were no methods of keeping people off the lines. The next day was the last day and Jono's birthday. We also had to get to the airport where we had a long wait for the plane to Dallas, which would not start. It was a long wait for the re-start, and we almost missed the connecting plane to London, our names were being called. However, there was a wait before we 'took off'. At Heathrow no cases arrived but they were delivered the next day.

Jono and I flew to Calgary in Canada in April 2018, but the hotel room was a small and dark place to stay in and it was not easy to find any place to shop. We were lucky, however, to see a particularly wonderful black gold tapestry in the museum which was inspired by the famous tapestry in France. We also took two days away from Calgary to visit the Canadian Rockies. As the winter had been long and cold there was a great deal of snow, and the lakes were frozen.

We stayed overnight at the Chateau Lake Louise hotel. Its very large lake was covered in several inches of snow, and we were unable to go across it. We also stopped at Banff on the bus journeys which was very pretty. Back at Calgary we visited the city zoo, and there were many things for young children to see, especially many animals and dinosaur models.

Ending in Tears...

Perhaps Dad (Arthur) was right to be unhappy when Mum (Betty) decided to buy the pearls in Hong Kong as the next few years did end in tears. After my uncle's (Leslie's) wife Pam died in 2015, Mum and I visited Leslie in Longthorpe almost every Sunday afternoon because, despite having many friends, he was finding it difficult to be alone in his house. We took India our dog with us for every visit and there was much humour in that on arrival India always wanted a drink of water and so Leslie claimed Longthorpe water must be better than that in Alwalton! After visiting Leslie, we would then go on to Brenda who similarly lived alone after the death of her husband John. Leslie was happiest when he was involved with car boot sales. He had become something of a Del Boy dealing with parts, particularly for old Jaguar cars. Steve who also lived in Longthorpe accompanied him to many events. They were great friends, as was Brian who still lives in Farcet and was born only one day apart from Leslie in 1940. Strangely, they both suffered from arthritis, could this have been due to their or their mothers' limited diet during World War II? Mum would be asked to make covers for bumpers which Leslie had had re-chromed. She also picked him up from the (chromium) platers on many Monday mornings after he had borrowed their van for a trip to a car boot sale, oftentimes in Newark.

First E-type that Leslie restored

During our visits to Leslie, he would drink a vodka and coke while I made tea for Mum and me. Unfortunately, it wasn't until he was extremely unwell in Peterborough City Hospital in December 2018 that Mum and I learnt that Leslie had very likely been drinking more than he should and during telephone conversations with Steve and his wife Margarette was slurring his speech. With hindsight I did recollect empty bottles of strong liquor in his kitchen, but at the time I paid little attention. As the years of visits went by, Mum did appear to start to find it more difficult to concentrate on the conversations and I did more of the talking. I wasn't sure why this was happening and put it down to Mum being tired as life at Forge End was becoming more stressful due to the structural problems with our house. Leslie had restored several vehicles during his life and had been very successful with his first Jaguar E-type. Regrettably, he didn't complete the second one as the engine work was much more significant and during 2018, he was finding it much more difficult to work in the limited space of his garage. I should have picked this up as a portent of illness. The last thing he did for Mum was to take her to the funeral of an old friend held near Nuneaton. After his death on New Year's Eve 2018, Mum wrote in early 2019 [this is typed verbatim]:

"Leslie was ill some time before being in bed. Unfortunately illness began and by illness he was ill and quickly dead. Jono was very good at getting things right. Jono became the person to do the briper things. He had missed?

By now two little ones. [great grandchildren]

Leslie managed to begin various ideas to keep his wish to go into looking his things. He did not keep his house properly. He went with me to go to a church for a school lady who I had. Leslie was good. He went to being dressed probably. I gave him for eating until he left them and was soon in hospital and was terrible for him! Dead very quickly. Hospital untelling Died quick.".

This was probably the last time Betty/Mum wrote with any level of coherence, dementia was clearly getting the upper hand as the mistakes in the above text would never have happened when she was well, and therefore her life story is concluded by me, her son and primary carer Jono. After a post-mortem it was discovered that Leslie had been suffering from lymphoma. It was extremely sad that despite Leslie seeming far from terminally ill on his first arrival in hospital, testing didn't happen possibly due to a disagreement between the ward registrar and the consultant, who could have performed a biopsy and thereby open a pathway to possible treatment; was it due to the impending Christmas and New Year break? A lengthy period of exchange with the hospital and coroner followed but little was achieved. Steve and I did much of the work in clearing Leslie's home in Longthorpe, which had to be completed by the end of January 2019.

I settled Leslie's financial affairs including gaining probate. I was given leave from my role as Head of the Engineering Department at the University of Leicester to do this.

Mum was extremely close to her brother Leslie and would do anything she could for him. Leslie's death clearly impacted her, and this was compounded by the problems of subsidence at our house in Forge End, Alwalton, which were growing [sic]. In July 2017 Alison noticed creasing of the wallpaper below the coving in part of our living room. This was accompanied by cracking in the parquet floor. Our insurance company was contacted, and a loss adjuster was appointed to examine the problems. The visit of the loss adjuster was at best brief. His report followed in the post with the conclusion that the problem was simply one of expansion in the parquet floor. I therefore asked a flooring expert to visit and after inspection, he concluded that although he could lay a new floor, he advised against it as it was his belief that we had a major structural problem. This was alarming and extremely worrying as we had no idea of the costs involved to rectify the problem and the insurance company appeared to be trying to evade any responsibility. The uncertainty was certainly not helpful for Mum. The next six-months were very difficult as it was necessary to employ our own structural engineer and builder to disprove the verdict of the loss adjuster. Countless emails were sent, meetings and telephone calls held, before it was agreed that the roots of the trees on the small strip of land adjacent to our property, termed a shelter belt, had caused the problem. Recent summers had been hot, and the trees had extracted moisture from the Oxford clay on which the property was built, causing shrinkage of the clay and subsidence of the house. It was the responsibility of Peterborough City Council to maintain the shelter belt. Fortunately, Mum had this in writing as she had previously tried to buy the land to expand her garden, her propensity to keep everything on this occasion was a real positive. A later visit from the loss adjuster representing Peterborough City Council was the moment when we felt that the insurance companies would accept our claim. When he saw the trees and the damage he said, "you have got us!". Our insurance company had been particularly difficult in accepting the claim and wouldn't accept the first report from our structural engineer. Only when chemical analysis was performed to verify the roots found under the floor were from the offending trees was the claim finally accepted. This happened at the end of January 2018, at the same time as I was concluding the business with Leslie's residence.

Repairs starting in the living room at home in Alwalton

The next 18 months included a protracted period of waiting for the trees to be removed as the resident feathered friends had to be rightly considered. In fact, the removal of the trees was very upsetting for Mum, and she rushed out towards the end of the process of their removal and put her body between a distant tree and the council workers and said it must not be cut down, it wasn't! A person with dementia can lose their inhibitions. We have since referred to this as "Betty's tree" and live-in carers we subsequently needed have told the birds that the tree had been rescued for them. After the removal of the offending trees the house was monitored for a year to ensure the ground had stabilized and heave wouldn't be a problem once the moisture in the soil was replenished.

Our structural engineer remained involved as we had little confidence that the company managing the repair work on behalf of our insurance company and provided the first loss adjuster, would do the best work. He proposed the repairs which were needed, and a programme of work was agreed. This didn't begin until the summer of 2019. Our insurance company did repay all the costs we had incurred to this point and offered £200 in compensation for the inconvenience we had experienced! A removal company was employed to pack and store our possessions from the area of our house where repairs were needed. Due to the magnitude of the work, Mum and I were asked to leave our home and Alison and Simon agreed that we could stay with them in Ashwell. This was far from ideal accommodation for Mum as the floors in their 15th Century cottage are uneven, with many steps between rooms and there was a real danger Mum could fall during the night when trying to reach the toilet. Needing the toilet often featured throughout the dementia journey and by now, as is often the case with people suffering from dementia, Mum was up and down to visit the bathroom very many times during the night. I slept on the floor next to her bed while I was at Ashwell to ensure she didn't fall when she got out of bed and a rota was put in place to look after Mum during my two-week trip to China and South Korea. Simon, David and Jenny, Nicola, Christopher and their respective families spent days with Mum while I was away. Paid carers had to be arranged to be with Mum when family members were unavailable. Mum had become more demanding by this time and accompanying her on visits could be problematic. Simon recalled taking Mum out in "her" car and she was very angry at him for driving. Mum's dementia also played its cruel tricks on Alison; on returning from work Mum asked Alison "What do you do?", Alison replied "I work in a hospital", to which Mum informed her "I have a daughter who works in a hospital". This was very upsetting at the time, but Alison now understands you must enter the world of someone with dementia, not try to use logic. On the day I returned from China my flight was delayed and Mum's anxiety level was extreme, she couldn't settle until I was in Ashwell. Dementia sufferers do become disorientated when they are in unfamiliar environments and being away from home due to subsidence was very unfortunate timing. It is said that subsidence is one of the most serious problems faced by homeowners but at least it would be resolved before the start of COVID-19.

On my return from the international trip, it quickly became apparent that I needed to get Mum back to her home as soon as possible. It took a lot of persuading to get the permission of the repair management company to allow us to do so. Although we had been told the work would take eight weeks, it ultimately took eight months! I was, however, successful and by October 2019 we were using two ends of the bungalow, catering at one and living and sleeping at the other. I therefore had to carry cooked food outside the bungalow to reach Mum. The new parquet floor was laid, decorating completed and the French window in the living room replaced. The work was signed off in January 2020 and I thought life would then become easier, but I was wrong. It was clear following the experience in Ashwell that Mum could no longer live independently, and I had already made the decision to take early retirement at the end of 2019 to look after her. I was almost 60 and had had an incredibly successful career as Professor in Signal and Information Processing and Mum had benefitted considerably from worldwide international travel as my companion at conferences. My success, however, was underpinned by her extraordinary support, so it was my duty to be there for her and meet my father's request the last time I saw him alive, just before he walked out of Peterborough District Hospital, to "look after your mother". With hindsight, how strange he said that at the time.

At the beginning of 2020 I had planned to begin my retirement by working on the house, relaxing and enjoying time with Mum travelling in the UK. I was already extremely tired after completing the handover of my role as head of a department with approaching 100 staff and 600 students, managing the subsidence problems for three years following supporting Mum through the death of her brother and clearing his accommodation. If we were to take trips in the UK I would have to drive of course as Mum had already had incidents of losing her way in Peterborough and a GP had checked she was no longer driving. I can't explain how difficult it was to remove the freedom to drive from someone who so enjoyed cars and driving. I remember well when she did the lion's share of the drive across France during the holiday trips to the South of France, so very sad but as I was to learn, dementia is like an indiscriminate robber and slowly takes everything that defines an individual. Although we did manage to get parts of our abode decorated there had already been indications that life was going to change substantially, and more difficulties followed. In December 2019 I had committed to examine a PhD at the University of Sheffield and (Auntie) Mary and (Uncle) Eric agreed that Mum could stay with them while I was away. The day went well until Mum suddenly decided I should be back by 2.30pm. Despite their very best efforts to assure her she was most unhappy when I arrived. In fact, Mary and Eric were so concerned about how she would be when I got her home, they rang and were ready to drive over to support me. Mum was also very disturbed when we visited The Crown Inn, Elton, near Peterborough to prepare for my 60th birthday. She was verbally aggressive towards the manager. Additionally, my trip to examine a PhD in Denmark had to be cancelled as Mum became very concerned that I was leaving, even though I had arranged for David to stay. I would soon be encountering such unpredictable behaviour multiple times a day, or at night, during COVID-19 lockdowns. The family carer is always on call and respite a rare commodity when the sufferer is aggressive.

As one of the live-in carers later said I was Mum's shield and without me she lost any confidence she still had. When David arrived, I therefore offered to drive him back to Reading with Mum. This wasn't a good idea as on our return journey Mum became very agitated and at times, I was forced to physically settle her to ensure we reached home. I had then to attend a colonoscopy at St. Mary's Hospital in London. I arranged for David to be with Mum while I had the procedure. Unfortunately, on the return journey Mum fell on the train as we were pulling into the station. A wheelchair was quickly found, and I was able to get her into the car. We did manage to return to London for one last time in February 2020 and saw La Boheme at the Royal Opera House, it was a splendid production, but Mum became more agitated during the second half of the production, and I had to restrain her in her seat. At this time, I read the book "Someone I used to know" by Wendy Mitchell which was an excellent record of early decline due to dementia. It was also the time when Brexit happened. Mum had been a staunch supporter of Europe but didn't appear to appreciate the gravity of events of 31st January 2020. Another problem for dementia sufferers is that medical visits can be difficult due to lack of comprehension of what is being asked of them. Mum had a difficult visit to the dentist in February and later such visits became even more problematic when Mum didn't always open her mouth.

However, we did meet a former school nurse at the dentists who knew Mum and went on to say that she was a "wonderful headteacher".

We had a trial of two staff from a company which provided hourly carers, but this was unsuccessful as Mum found their frequent arrivals and departures unsettling. This peaked on 28th February after one left. Mum was extremely agitated and wouldn't stay in the house. I was concerned for her safety as she walked out of Forge End and was crossing roads in the village oblivious to the traffic. My saviour was a lady from the village who noticed how Mum was behaving and allowed me to coax Mum into her home until Alison arrived. Alison had to drop everything in her office at the Lister hospital and drive up the A1 as proved to be necessary many times during the dementia journey. We therefore decided to employ live-in carers and met the care manager from a second care company, as the first didn't offer live-in carers, who was very professional and quickly grasped the challenges. As part of their assessment, Mum was asked where she wanted to be, and she was able to make it clear she wanted to remain in her own home. This became my objective. On 6th March, our first live-in carer arrived, she was of South African origin with a tough disposition, and she made a real difference during the ensuing months, particularly as we were about to enter lockdown and I would be mostly on my own with her and Mum.

My 60th birthday was on 10th March 2020 and celebrations were due to be a weekend in the Shangri-La hotel at the Shard, London. We had planned to attend the musical Mary Poppins and have dinner in the Ting restaurant with former PhD students who had since become professors. The following weekend a meal with family and friends was planned at The Crown Inn, Elton, near Peterborough. I did have some concern whether this would be possible with Mum's condition and found my answer in the form of COVID-19. Everything was cancelled and within a matter of days the whole country was in lockdown. A small party was held at Forge End and we ate a beautiful chocolate cake. Mum, the carer and I were on our own from the 16th of March just before the first lockdown started on 23rd of March. Mum was very disturbed the next night and I had to put locks on the doors to keep her in the house.

Mum enjoyed cooking, it clearly tasted good!

Mum had always been a regular church goer and did much for St. Andrew's Alwalton. In recent years I had helped her with several roles and I had joined the PCC and recently become churchwarden. I was disappointed that the Church of England had to cancel all face-to-face services.

One of the best decisions I made before COVID-19 was to register Mum and I at Wansford Surgery near Peterborough, the support received throughout the dementia journey was nothing less than exceptional.

Mum had moved into a hyper-agitated state in late March and was for example kicking windows, gnashing her teeth and trying to bite me (this image will haunt me just as the one from 1987 when my father Arthur was in the depths of mental illness and trying to paint his false teeth), attempting to get out of the car when it was moving, and whipping the carer and me with curtain ties. I tried various physical approaches to improve the situation such as painting the front windows of the bungalow with whitener that is used on garden greenhouses (to reduce the attraction of external movements such as cars arriving), covering internal mirrors (dementia sufferers are commonly disturbed by their reflection), putting child locks onto the gas controls on the cooker hob, nailing cupboards closed and moving all knives to the garage. However, it became clear that medical intervention was necessary to help with Mum's behaviour and mood. A two-month period then began during which various calming and sleeping drugs were tried. With Alison's help we also managed to get Mum's dementia formally diagnosed via a home visit by a psychiatrist who was part of the mental health crisis team. Mum had previously been adamant she didn't have dementia and wouldn't attend the memory clinic, so it was difficult to get access to various drugs. I could understand that with her 10 years as the chair of the Alzheimer's Society in Peterborough she knew, more than most, what she would be facing and for her own wellbeing she was in denial. Perhaps, much of the aggressive behaviour was because she was fighting the symptoms of the disease and was becoming frustrated with its effects. One of the saddest experiences I had throughout the dementia journey was when she asked me one night "Can't you make me better?". The psychiatrist gave a diagnosis of mixed dementia, in Alzheimer's, vascular and Lewy-body forms. I presume this was a cover-all diagnosis as he didn't have access to scans or other information due to the unique times of the first lockdown. However, it opened up access to risperidone, an antipsychotic drug, which helped to manage Mum's behaviour and mood. I was given the authority to titrate this drug. Mum received a regular daily dose, and the same amount was available as PRN (a Latin term "pro re nata", in essence, "as needed"). The psychiatrist's view was that our house wasn't the best place for Mum but other members of the crisis team, who had had firsthand experience of care homes during the lockdown, disagreed. Another major advantage of the diagnosis is that we were allocated a formal community mental health nurse. His advice and assistance throughout the dementia journey proved to be invaluable. To make things more difficult the care manager insisted that our first carer was replaced. The new carer quickly became scared of Mum and locked herself in her bedroom. Fortunately, I managed to get our first carer back and a separate night live-in carer who, despite her young age, managed Mum extremely well. Our residence felt very congested with two live-in carers, Mum, India the dog and me, but there was no other option to keep Mum where she wanted to be.

Living 24/7 with carers and a dementia sufferer, for whom you have unconditional love, exhibiting aggressive behaviour is the toughest experience I have had in my life. It is difficult for those without this experience to understand and this certainly appeared to be the case for my siblings and most of Mum's friends and relatives. I was commonly getting up four or five times during the night as the night carers found Mum difficult when she became agitated.

As such I was often totally exhausted, and sleep deprived however Mum's relentless needs couldn't be ignored. Perhaps one of the few who grasped the complexity of my situation was Patsy one of Mum's special friends. She continued to visit Mum regularly during the early lockdowns, bringing treats such as ice cream and cakes to the door of our house and communicating through the window which was a tremendous uplift. Her husband John (Frank) was diagnosed with Alzheimer's disease in February 2022 via a video conference call with a consultant at the memory clinic. John is able to live at home with the help of lovely carers and Patsy. I visit them regularly as I know how important face-to-face visits were to Mum. Regrettably, I experienced first-hand how some friends and relatives disappear when times become difficult, and seem to conveniently forget about everything the sufferer has given in earlier life to them or their family. I certainly learnt the meaning of "fair-weather friends"; on the other hand, I shall be eternally grateful to everyone who visited Mum to help in her care during the dementia journey.

Patsy and John (Frank) at Mum's granddaughter Nicola's wedding

It was the 75th anniversary of Victory in Europe on the 8th May and we managed to enjoy a form of tea party. It is important to highlight that just as there were periods of aggression and difficult behaviour, there could also be periods of lucidity and communication was still possible with Mum by speech. I found that vestiges of the pre-illness Mum remained even until very late in the dementia journey. Mum's sleep patterns were also improved by the combination of antidepressants and antihistamine drugs prescribed by the psychiatrist. He also helped by prescribing an orodispersible form of risperidone which acted very quickly when circumstances demanded. Unfortunately, all drugs have side effects and the new drug regime including memantine, which is used to treat moderate to severe confusion, and caused oedema in Mum's ankles and feet, led to considerable weight gain due to causing a ravenous hunger together with strain on her kidneys. As for many sufferers of dementia, Mum's taste changed and she became very fond of anything sweet, particularly cake!

We had one carer who was clearly totally unsuitable for the role. He had been chosen to be a night carer. However, I found he had a problem with his legs and couldn't manage Mum at night, so the care company arranged a replacement immediately. Another characteristic common in dementia sufferers is that they become very attached to an item and, for Mum, it was her handbag. She would persistently empty it and became upset if it wasn't in eyeshot.

David, Jenny and our dog India in the garden at Alwalton

At the end of April, I had called Alison and said Mum was very anxious and she offered to make a garden visit that day, working in a hospital in the first COVID-19 lockdown Alison was nervous not to break the COVID-19 regulations and took some convincing that she was in Alwalton as a carer. David made a garden visit with his wife Jenny in June 2020 as did Mum's grandchildren and families which Mum enjoyed.

We then had the good fortune to be allocated a lady, who became the main carer, as Mum's night carer. She would prove to be an ideal match for Mum and would stay with us until the end of the dementia journey. She had spent much of her youth in Southern Africa so fitted in well with the day carer too. The day carer and I benefitted from doing jigsaws together and Mum enjoyed watching and occasionally helping. Alison replenished our supply of jigsaws and acquired some simple ones for Mum. By this time, the first carer had been with me for more than 12 weeks, perhaps the most difficult period of the dementia journey, and needed rest. Fortunately, a very experienced carer replaced her as the day carer and soon after another became Mum's night carer while Mum's main carer took a break. This was that new night carer's first experience of care work in the UK and found Mum too much to handle at first and almost gave up. With the day carer and my support, I split the night with the night carer, she carried on and developed into an excellent carer. There was little positive news at this stage in terms of COVID-19 and no sign of a vaccine during the early summer of 2020.

By the middle of July, the dream team of the first carer and the main carer was back, and the first carer tried her best to keep Mum engaged. They did cooking together and I remember Mum licking out the bowl how she must have done as a child after Grandma (Con) had been baking. The main carer also needed help during the nights as despite Mum's drugs some behavioural issues remained. We had alterations made to the walk-in shower to make it easier to manage Mum by an excellent plumber who was extremely helpful and skilful. David started spending some weekends with me at this time and he enjoyed talking with the carers, particularly as one had a son who played cricket for Derbyshire. The experienced day carer also had connections with South Africa, and we had very good experiences with all the carers from the rainbow nation. Grandma (Con), Betty's Mum, would have been 109 this year, and I took flowers to her grave throughout Mum's dementia journey. She is buried next to her husband Bill, and I often said a prayer to them both to look after their little girl through her terrible illness.

I had another medical challenge to face in August 2020 as Mum developed intertrigo in the skin folds below her breasts. This infection was most likely to have been caused by Mum's increase in weight. Various creams were tried but only strong antibiotics resolved the problem. Alison had thought we should apply for NHS Continuing Health Care (NHS-CHC) funding to help with Mum's care costs. How little we knew about the paperwork involved and how this was totally skewed against dementia sufferers. We had a very difficult interview with what we perceived to be an uninterested NHS staff member and of course were declined. We appealed and had a second interview, but again the outcome was negative. However, we did manage to get Mum's support from Cambridgeshire County Council uplifted to the level of nursing care which did help to a small extent towards the care costs, so the efforts were not completely wasted.

India our lovely White German Shepherd cross, who Mum adored, had a urinary infection at the beginning of September 2020 and I had to adopt the new COVID-19 protocol at the vets. We waited in the car park and were telephoned when she could see the vet who then collected India and took her into the surgery. As for Mum, antibiotics resolved the problem.

A new night carer spent a period with us. Both carers then changed, and we had a relatively settled period including taking Mum by car to Alison's address at Ashwell. The main carer returned to replace the current night carer at the end of the month. The subsidence repairs did not include the floor in the entrance of Forge End, so I arranged for a flooring company to put down a new parquet floor in the dining room and entrance area. It was the same company that had replaced the parquet floor in the living room, and they had done an excellent job. However, they rushed this more recent work and within a week the new floor was lifting. This was a great disappointment as it had been upsetting to Mum to have the work done. I decided to manage the problems with this new floor and consider having it properly repaired later. This was just another problem I didn't need.

Thursday 8th October 2020 was the last day that 747 aircraft were flown by British Airways which was the end of an era as these had been the workhorses of the air for many years and Mum and I had flown on them several times. Mum's mobility was becoming a problem, so I asked the occupational therapist for assistance and wall handles were suggested together with a raised doorstep. It was good to receive visits from Mum's friend from swimming and Mum's contact from the Peterborough Alzheimer's Society, with masks of course! Mum had kept herself really fit throughout her retirement through walking our dogs, swimming and regular Tai Chi.

Throughout the dementia journey I ensured Mum received flu vaccinations and, immediately they became available, COVID-19 vaccinations. One of the earlier night carers returned to be with Mum for the last time as she was moving to live with her new partner in Wales.

**Mum with Alison on her 87ᵗʰ birthday, she is sitting on a commode with wheels
with electric hoist and reclining chair in the background**

Mum's mixed dementia had already stolen her ability to write and much of her old personality, but its next target was her ability to walk. I had to rush to (Auntie) Mary's to borrow a wheelchair as suddenly she could no longer walk from her reclining chair in the living room to her bedroom. Some of the occupational therapists were not very helpful and provided equipment that was unsuitable for Mum. On the other hand, one was excellent and quickly grasped the situation. She provided everything that was needed including a bed-head hoist and a mobile hoist for the rest of the house. It was good equipment and regularly serviced. I had to master the operation of the hoists very quickly as little one-to-one training was offered due to restrictions caused by COVID-19. Moreover, this was a fundamental change in Mum's care needs as hoisting always required two people when a carer from the care company was involved so I became much more tied to our home even cutting India's walks short. I learnt to hoist Mum on my own if she needed the toilet during the carer's two-hour break in the afternoon. Another problem was that we couldn't get Mum into the walk-in shower as it had been built with a step at the entrance. I sketched the type of ramp that we needed, and Alison searched the internet. She found a company in the US which seemed to have exactly what we required, and they put us on to the UK supplier. The ramp arrived on a pallet and its construction was like building with children's play bricks. It cost £1000 but paid for itself many times over during the next two-and-a-half years. Mum had a shower every day until the day before her death, it involved transferring her from her reclining chair in the living room to a plastic commode with wheels, pushing her to the shower room, performing the shower which could be challenging as spraying water onto a dementia sufferer can cause anxiety, drying and dressing her on the commode in her bedroom, and then returning her to the living room. The process always needed two people and could take as much as two hours.

I quickly learnt that continuity of carers is a major issue during the dementia journey. This was reinforced at the beginning of November as the first carer suddenly heard that her mother had been found to have a lump in her breast. After being Mum's day carer for eight months and helping through some exceedingly difficult times, the first carer returned to South Africa. We were unsure however whether it was right for her to return as Mum's carer if she came back to the UK. Mum wore her MBE on Remembrance Day, and it was announced that Mr Biden had won the election in America. A new team of carers was put in place as both the day and the main carer who was performing the night shifts needed a break. There was positive news from the Oxford vaccine trial as it was found to have good efficacy and we started to believe that COVID-19 would be beaten, and some form of normal life would resume with services for dementia sufferers reopening. I helped Mum to write her multitude of Christmas cards, she was always able to forge new friendships throughout the world and commonly received more than 200 cards. The second lockdown ended, and people started to be more adventurous leading up to Christmas, but they were soon disappointed with a third lockdown starting immediately after the holiday period on 6th January 2021. However, Mum received her first Pfizer COVID-19 vaccination just before Christmas which was extremely encouraging as she was particularly vulnerable to the virus being 87 and a dementia sufferer.

Jade, Mum's hairdresser had visited during COVID-19

Mum had a visit from a social worker who proved to be very supportive, and from her hairdresser Jade who was a real gem and always kept Mum's hair neat. We also had visits each week from Sadie and Debbie the cleaners who had known Mum for more than 20 years, which considerably lifted my and India's spirits.

One of the carers returned to their home just before Christmas and Alison, the night carer and I enjoyed Christmas 2020 with Mum. A common challenge for me was that every new carer took a time to become familiar with Mum and the duties. The pressure at least doubled during such periods, and I learnt to dread changeovers. An additional new carer arrived who stayed briefly until another returned. After this time David committed to come up alternate weekends for the remainder of the dementia journey, and Alison in her organised way, thereafter, kept a spreadsheet for the weekend rotas. All face-to-face visits were of inestimable value to maintain my resolve. I found that most electronic and telephone communications had little value and, in fact, could be upsetting for Mum and me.

The third lockdown began on the 6th of January 2021 and Mum received her second Pfizer vaccination on 10th January 2021 at Peterborough City Hospital. I had to lift Mum between the car and her wheelchair due to her lack of mobility which became difficult for my back. At this time a neighbour who had moved into a care home caught COVID-19 and became very ill and died. This made me even more sure that the decision to support Mum in her desire to remain in her house was right. Apparently, 13 people died in the same outbreak at the care home. In fact, January 2021 was the deadliest month of COVID-19 so far as on average more than 1000 people died of it every day through the month in the UK and maybe many of these were in care homes. Despite the medications Mum's behaviour remained very variable and nights continued to be difficult with me having broken sleep. I had had almost a year of sleep deprivation and it was unimaginably hard to keep going. Knowing that dementia is a terminal condition is always at the back of your mind. I also heard that a cousin had just been diagnosed with vascular dementia after his personality changed and he lost his way when driving. Due to experienced nurses being assigned to care duties I lost the support of the initial community mental health nurse for a few months but, fortunately, he did return as the replacement was much less experienced.

In February 2021, for the first time, we had conflict between the day and night live-in carers. It reached such a peak that one wouldn't speak to the other. You could cut the atmosphere in the house with a knife, and I had to call in the care manager to resolve the issue. It became clear an impasse had been reached and at least one of the carers would have to leave otherwise Mum's wellbeing would suffer. In fact, Alison and I were asked to make the decision as to who should remain, and we chose the day carer. The night carer left the same day, but it was very emotional and stressful. It was sad to say but it had become easier to manage Mum now that she was completely immobile and had just started to sleep better through the night. We therefore decided to try to cope with just a day carer and I would oversee issues during the night. This decision was partly driven by cost as I had been paying around £10,000/month to have two live-in carers.

Luckily, this new model worked for the remainder of the dementia journey and thereafter we were generally supported by excellent live-in day carers.

A major advantage of having just one live-in carer in our abode was that it seemed to be less congested which was good for everyone. The amount of washing that must be done whilst caring increases exponentially over that in normal times, hence I had to buy a new washer and separate dryer to manage the situation as it was impossible to tolerate periods of waiting for a repair technician when an old machine failed. It was the beginning of Lent later in February and we liked the pancakes cooked by one of the carers. We all enjoyed Mum's 87th birthday on the 21st of February 2021. This was her first birthday during the time of COVID-19, but she enjoyed a lovely birthday tea and received many flowers and presents. Our care agency, in common with others, was struggling with the recruitment of carers. Many of their carers came from international sources and travel had become more difficult due to COVID-19. Hence this generated another stressor for me as it was difficult to be sure who would be Mum's forthcoming carers, and there were also occasions when we were waiting for a changeover of carer and the new carer didn't show. Luckily, when this happened the current carer generally delayed their break and covered until a replacement was found, although sometimes I was left on my own to cope.

A replacement carer arrived at the beginning of March. We also had an elevator fitted to Mum's bed; fortunately, this allowed us to avoid having a hospital bed throughout the dementia journey. To help during the night I acquired a sensor to monitor Mum including a camera which could be viewed in my bedroom at all times of the day or night, it had a standard video camera and an infrared one. We used home delivery extensively for food and became a weekly customer of a major supermarket. The first carer had produced an extensive list of all the possible shopping items we would need, and the current carer just ticked what we needed, and I submitted the order via the webpage. Another online provider was also extremely useful for everything else. I wrote in my diary that "Mum was spiky/sad/bossy on Friday 19th March", a clear indication of the variability of mood caused by dementia. The replacement carer was good, but she had complications in her private life, and I believe she gave up live-in caring after this first experience of the lifestyle. As I was living so closely with the carers it was impossible not to become very much involved with their problems too, and the replacement carer needed support in what was going on in her private life. With the regular hoisting of Mum, it was important to have toileting slings which made it possible to access her clothes while she was elevated. I had to buy these as the ones provided by the occupational therapist were unsuitable. It was good that the main carer then returned. The Duke of Edinburgh died two months shy of his 100th birthday on the 9th of April 2021 and his funeral followed on 17th April. Mum was able to watch the funeral which was held at Windsor Castle on the television. It was a beautiful day and the pageantry remarkable. At this time the current lockdown ended and non-essential shops, hairdressers, and some sports facilities opened. We then learnt that the turnover in carers also happened with care managers when the current one announced she was leaving the care company to manage a hostel.

Another new carer arrived, and the main carer returned to her abode. This new carer was only with us briefly and then one of the previous carers returned. A fresh care manager was appointed. I had received considerable support from the staff in the Village (Alwalton) Post Office since the beginning of the lockdowns, in fact the owner said she had become my extra sister. Hence, I was extremely sad to discover that her husband had been diagnosed with terminal cancer. There had been so much bad news over the last year. Mum's granddaughter Nicola and her daughter Elinor visited in May as did Mum's grandson Christopher and his wife Philly together with Mum's great grandchildren Annie and Jesse. With Alison and David's help I tried to maintain the garden and Mum seemed to be stimulated by the new hanging baskets we put up for the summer. She said they were "very nice". Fortunately, the occupational therapist had given us a ramp for the back door which allowed me to push Mum outside.

Mum had always suffered from wax in her ears, so it became a regular event to apply drops and to have a professional come to the house to remove the wax. It was necessary to hold Mum's head still, so it was upsetting to her. Another variant of COVID-19 was announced after emerging in the Indian subcontinent named the delta virus. This news reinforced the need to keep vulnerable people such as Mum protected. Strict discipline in washing hands and wearing masks with visitors was necessary. Mum also lost some crowns in one side of her mouth, but the dentist didn't want to take any action. I don't know whether it was because dementia changes the way in which pain is perceived, but I was always amazed how Mum tolerated the remains of the crowns in her mouth for the rest of the dementia journey and, for the most part, continued to eat very well. Her main dentist retired during COVID-19, as many did, and the replacement simply didn't have the experience to manage a patient with severe dementia. We were referred to the community NHS dentist and attended some appointments. This dentist used the trick of brushing Mum's teeth with a conventional toothbrush to get her to open her mouth and hold it open so that she could observe Mum's teeth, apparently this is done with children.

The vacancy for an incumbent at St. Andrew's Alwalton was filled and it was most pleasing that the new vicar chose to visit Mum every month. The vicar had a lovely way with Mum and the hand waving as a gesture of peace a particular joy to watch. One of the churchwardens and his wife who had taken over from Mum as the secretary of the Parochial Church Council also visited our home as did the other churchwarden. A curate arrived in the village too at the end of June and she was very supportive. The main carer had returned earlier in June but her three-weeks were quickly over, and another new carer arrived. Mum took a while to settle with her particularly at night, so I again spent considerable time with Mum overnight. I often slept on the floor next to her bed for reassurance. The Post Office in Alwalton got a new owner. Sadly, this would mean the end of the tearoom in the village as the owner shifted the focus of the business, but he did extend its hours of opening which has been valuable.

The next target of Mum's dementia robber was to make her incontinent.

We had to go through an assessment with the incontinence nurse and, thereafter, Mum was provided with two pairs of disposable knickers per day from the NHS. Alison sourced a further two pairs a day from a different supplier which were delivered to our door. We had to be much more careful to monitor for urinary tract infections. Our neighbour Tony celebrated his 90th birthday and I have since helped him with his garden. Having good neighbours makes life so much easier and Tony has been the best. COVID-19 cases were continuing to rise in Europe, and it was interesting that the Dutch Prime Minister apologised for ending their most recent lockdown too soon. The main carer was hoping to visit her parents who lived in the Netherlands at Christmas, so this was a worry for her. Despite her immobility Mum did have restless legs in bed and therefore I invented a safe barrier with a chair and bungee clips to ensure she didn't fall out of the bed. The current carer was good, but Mum found the smell of nicotine an issue, so we resolved to have solely nonsmoking carers in future. Earlier in the year I had had a three-day break at Ashwell with Simon and then in June Dorothy and Paul invited me to spend three-days with them at their residence in Chesterton. I felt very comfortable with them, and they were generous in every way, and I was close enough to home should there have been a problem. I managed to enjoy some of the matches in Euro 2020 and latest films on their television such as the new James Bond movie "No Time to Die". Alison was happy to replace me briefly when the main carer was with us as she found working with her straightforward but avoided handovers and less experienced carers.

The awareness of a dementia sufferer can vary tremendously, and the 4th of August 2021 was a day to remember. Mum clearly recognised Alison and said she loved her. I think this was also clear evidence of the quality of care Mum was receiving and further confirmation of the benefit of Mum remaining in her home around her family. Perhaps the best decision I made throughout the dementia journey was to buy a wheelchair accessible vehicle to allow Mum to leave the house more frequently and to visit friends and attend appointments. I had a bad experience with one company but was then contacted by a friend who was at that time the manager of a franchise in Peterborough. Mum had really enjoyed the cars he had sold us before her illness. He had taken in a red Ford Tourneo Connect as a part-exchange following the death of its previous owner, it was top of the range and had covered only 5,000 miles. We took delivery on the 20th of August, and it transformed our lives. We called it the "fun bus".

The "fun bus"

Almost every weekend for the next 18 months we would take Mum for a drive in the area and commonly end up at the Mulberry Café at Elton for coffee and cake. The durations of the journeys were constrained by Mum's incontinence, so we didn't venture too far. The vehicle had a ramp and a modern system to secure the wheelchair which only took a matter of minutes to operate. I was so lucky to have the resources to make this happen and so grateful to Mary, Patsy and Brenda who welcomed Mum into their homes despite her being in a wheelchair. Dorothy and Paul also invited Mum to family events at their house, which she clearly enjoyed. We did everything to make her life as pleasurable as possible. The appeal for NHS CHC support triggered another complication that Social Services wished to put in place what is called a Community Deprivation of Liberty (DoL). A DoL is commonly sought for dementia sufferers in care homes and a Community DoL was needed primarily because Mum was receiving drugs for calming. It was a considerable worry as what would happen if this wasn't granted by the Court of Protection? Could she be forced to move out of her house? We had several visits from social workers but despite filling in forms this, thankfully, never happened.

I was asked to do several pieces of work over the dementia journey by universities and the Engineering and Physical Sciences Research Council. This was possible when there wasn't tight time constraints and meetings were held remotely. Video conferencing tools were invaluable, and it was good to keep to some extent technically alert. David and Jenny kindly came up to Alwalton to cover the period while I had a particularly long meeting. In September Steve, Les's friend from Longthorpe, spent a couple of days cutting down trees and bushes in our garden. A friend from church and the village also visited Mum. Another from the village was particularly helpful too in ferrying carers to vaccination appointments. A further change in the care manager happened at the beginning of October. The main carer and I managed to take Mum to see her cousin Gill and husband Don in St. Ives near Huntingdon. We had several such visits but regrettably at the time of writing in September 2023, after a long battle, Don has just died from stomach cancer. Dorothy and Paul had been on a trip around the UK on a cruise ship which visited a very restricted number of locations due to COVID-19. They boarded the ship in Southampton and health regulations were very tight.

As our surgery operates both in King's Cliffe and Wansford, we took Mum to a drive-in location in King's Cliffe in the fun bus to get her flu jab. The care company had arranged a new carer to replace the main carer, but she hadn't been vaccinated for COVID-19 so at the last minute another new carer was found however she turned out to be very experienced and fitted in very well with Mum. I took Mum and the new carer to key attractions around Peterborough including Burghley and Helpston, and to the site of Mum's old school which had been rebuilt as the Welland Academy. The Christmas stamps were published on 2nd November, so it was time to write the Christmas newsletter to go in with Mum's Christmas cards again, I involved Mum in addressing and writing her cards as much as possible.

A good friend of mine who was a Professor at Loughborough University died unexpectedly from a heart problem on 5th November 2021. He was in his mid-60s and had cared for his wife for several years after taking early retirement. He had become the Head of the Electronic, Electrical and Systems Engineering Department but suffered from a poor outcome in the Research Excellence Framework (REF). I received a batch of lovely presents from a recent PhD graduate of mine from Newcastle University. Such Iraqi students are bonded to gain their PhDs and if unsuccessful forfeit considerable financial sums which would impact their whole families.

Hence, he and all the other Iraqi students I helped at Newcastle were very grateful and learned very much about my remarkable mother. Mum received countless boxes of dates and home cooked treats from them.

The main carer returned and spent three weeks with Mum before another carer was found. We were planning for carers over the Christmas and New Year period and wanted to avoid the problems of last year. This year Alison wanted to try to have a family Christmas without a carer. The main carer was back on 26th November and as it turned out it was the last time one of the carers would leave Forge End. She had committed to returning to care for Mum early in January 2022 when the main carer was away but, as it transpired, didn't fulfil her promise. At the beginning of Advent, I put up some Christmas decorations including Mum's favourite Snowman Advent Calendar. This calendar has little pockets and each was filled with treats for India and every morning she would be given the food. This was a practice that we had adopted every year and Mum enjoyed. Unfortunately, due to the latest Omicron variant of COVID-19 I was unable to attend the funeral of my colleague from Loughborough. We had a visitation from a rat in the garden during early December, an unwelcome guest, and I needed to arrange for pest control to visit. This was just another example of an extra task which added to my load.

The usual train of Christmas cards started to arrive for Mum together with messages from across the globe including one from Janice in Australia who had previously lived for a few years with her family in Forge End. Three cousins of Mums visited, as they had come to Peterborough to meet their remaining friends and relatives in the city. One gave an update on her husband who had recently been diagnosed with dementia before the age of 70. The main carer decided very kindly to put off her trip to her parents from 17th to 22nd December as no other carer was available to cover this short period. Although the Netherlands was already in lockdown due to the latest variant of Covid the UK government appeared to be dithering due to data. A real treat for Mum before Christmas was to drive her in the evening around the local villages to see the Christmas lights. Snowmen, penguins, and reindeer were seen, and we chose Castor and Elton as the best locations for lights. Mum certainly appeared to enjoy the trip out. The vicar visited just before Christmas and gave Mum communion and a festive wave of peace! An artificial silver tree was purchased as it was impossible to have a large real tree in the living room as we had done for many years. Mum had, however, always loved such a silver tree when David, Alison and I were children. Alison decorated this on Christmas Eve selecting toy-themed ornaments from Mum's not insignificant collection.

I was busy with church duties on Christmas Day and Alison cooked a lovely Christmas lunch and Mum tucked in. Boxing Day was a most splendid day at Brenda's, and we managed to remain at her house for most of the afternoon. A new carer arrived on 27th December and was very experienced and India benefited from extra walks with her.

She wasn't at all happy that there wasn't sufficient PPE (Personal Protective Equipment) in the house. Mum's grandson Christopher and family visited, and Alison returned to Ashwell before the New Year. New Year's Eve was relatively quiet, and we went to bed well before the arrival of 2022. I wondered what the New Year would bring.

The regular pattern of days continued into 2022 with getting Mum up at 8.30 am, giving medications and breakfast, walking India, showering and dressing, having lunch around 1 pm, carer taking a two-hour break in the afternoon, tea at the dining room table around 6 pm, evening watching television and switching to Classic FM whilst preparing for bed. Although the days had exhausting repetitiveness the time disappeared. Classical music proved to be extremely therapeutic for Mum's mood. We enjoyed coffee and cakes again at the Mulberry Café in Elton. The staff at the Mulberry café were always very understanding and ensured we had a suitable table. A new watch was ordered for Mum as her current one had failed, and her watch was the one piece of jewellery she wore until the end of her life. On 12th January the main carer returned and I took the other carer to the railway station to return to the Midlands with a copy of Mum's book Mr Mayor. JC (Jono Chambers) cabs often figured on changeover days! I had enjoyed the period with the carer from the Midlands, she had a good sense of humour and called me the nutty professor!

Cake was always popular at the Mulberry Café, toffee roulade today

We had watched the latest snooker competition, which was won by Neil Robertson from Australia; we found snooker something that Mum was happy to watch. Perhaps it reminded her of the many times we spent watching snooker in the care home with Uncle Jess. England had capitulated in the cricket test series in Australia, down 4-0, so we felt it was time for the captain to go. The vicar came again to give Mum communion, but Mum found the conventional wafer more difficult, and she (the vicar) suggested we try proper bread. Maybe this was an omen that eating was to become more difficult for Mum. St. Andrew's agreed to introduce the Alzheimer's Society as one of its supported charities and efforts were made to become a more dementia friendly church, such as improving lighting and improving the signage for toilets. The signs were acquired by one of the churchwardens who very sadly had developed a terminal lung condition, and this was one of the last tasks he performed as churchwarden.

At the beginning of February, I received a letter from the care company to say that the care costs were increasing by an amount much higher than inflation. I contacted the care manager to complain but it appeared this was a company-wide non-negotiable decision. I did have worries about how long my monies would last as I was on my own in paying for the care costs and I would soon need to start to use my retirement lump sum. Such worries must be shared by thousands of families across the UK. Sunday 6th February 2022 was 70 years since the accession to the crown by Queen Elizabeth II. A new carer replaced the main carer and I was training her in the role, despite there being a care plan much advice and guidance was always needed. I'm sure the continuity of Mum's care would have suffered at such times had I not been living in the house 24/7. This carer stayed with us until 16th February when the main carer returned in time for Mum's 88th birthday on 21st February.

Some eight months after my previous break, Alison covered, and I was able to take three days of rest at Dorothy and Paul's house after Mum's birthday during which Russia invaded Ukraine. The world appeared to be as confused as Mum, with an extremely dangerous aggression which would soon impact inflation and food supplies, together with major environmental issues including a series of variants of COVID-19, which was continuing to cause 1000s of deaths worldwide. I enjoyed my break, but it was quickly over. Our cleaners repeatedly said that I should be having much more frequent breaks, on a three-monthly basis, this didn't happen. It was John's (Frank's) 88th birthday on the 3rd of March. The main carer was ready for her break, so I dealt with the transfer to another carer. She was new to Mum but very experienced. David then informed me he had caught a cold while visiting Nicola and family in Cambridge, so I was on my own with the carer the next weekend.

Mum was becoming sleepier and on one occasion when we visited Auntie Mary she wouldn't even wake up for cake! I was very much affected by a picture in the media at the time of a man mourning his mother after being killed by shrapnel in a Russian attack in Ukraine. How strange it was that in a matter of years since Mum had enjoyed a unique journey on the Trans-Siberian express that Russia would become an enemy. I celebrated my 62nd birthday on 10th March and it was Mothering Sunday on 27th March. I put flowers on Grandma Con's grave before the weekend and Mum received cards and presents. As there was no one else I accepted to replace the churchwarden who was unwell, and the vicar had asked me to verge at a funeral. I had much to learn in the role of churchwarden as the previous churchwarden with his wife had done considerable work to maintain the church over many years; I feel I'm still serving my apprenticeship! One of the churchgoers kindly agreed to service the fun bus. The main carer had returned by the beginning of April.

Titrating the dosage of risperidone became more difficult with Mum's sleepiness and it was clear that the robber dementia was lurking, this time after Mum's ability to speak (aphasia). This was the time when the Prime Minister and Chancellor received fines from the Metropolitan Police due to COVID-19 parties – uniquely unsettling political times. I wondered at that time if life was better for the early Boyden families when news took days to travel out to parts of East Anglia rather than having a deluge of immediate information on your electronic device. I arranged for the church to be decorated with flowers for Easter Sunday on 17th April and gave Easter Eggs to Alison and the carer. I had my regular weekly two-hour visit to Dorothy and Paul's house on Tuesday. These days had been termed "Terrific Tuesdays" for India by the main carer as she always received many treats and darted into Dorothy's house when she opened the door. I read an excellent monograph about a son caring for his mother through the dementia journey called "Dementia and Mum: Who Really Cares?" by Michael Fassio, certainly as a GP from our surgery put it, it's a real trigger for "burnout" to support someone through dementia. It is only love that drives you on.

One of the carers returned for Mum as the main carer was looking forward to a good break. The care manager was changing again as the current one had decided to leave the care company, change was a constant. We had had troubles with the old boiler in Forge End over the winter, so I decided to get our energy supplier to replace it. This was a good decision as the level of Mum's care needs was escalating. David was very much enjoying interacting with the current carer as it gave him opportunity to practise one of his foreign languages. I visited the previous churchwarden at his address on 16th May and he gave me written instructions of work still needed in the churchyard which he didn't have opportunity to complete. This was to be the last time I would see him alive. On the 23rd of June I heard that David Forbes the husband of Mum's penfriend June in Australia had died, he was born in January 1934 just before Mum, which reminded me of the fantastic trips Mum had enjoyed with June and David. By this time Mum needed special toothpaste with very high fluoride content that was only available by prescription. I had several trips between the dentist and the pharmacy to agree the instructions on the prescription, again extra work which shouldn't have been necessary. Mum had gone through a stage of eating only with her fingers as she couldn't hold cutlery due to the deterioration in her brain's motor control but now needed someone to feed her.

On 4th June the Platinum Party at the Palace was held which was a music celebration for the 70th anniversary of the accession of Queen Elizabeth II. Mum really seemed to enjoy watching this event and particularly the video clip with Paddington Bear.

Switches between carers continued, and we enjoyed a relatively settled period of support. Mum had started to attend the coffee mornings now being held at St. Andrew's in her wheelchair, and they quickly became a highlight of the month. Although Mum's speech was very limited it was clear she recognised the inside of the church and many of her friends. The major challenge of summer 2022 was the heat. There were periods of approaching 40C previously unknown in the UK and a week of daily temperature consistently reaching at least 30C. Keeping Mum cool and hydrated became a major issue but we managed by extensive use of fans and blinds covering windows. The main carer was scrupulous in ensuring Mum drank enough.

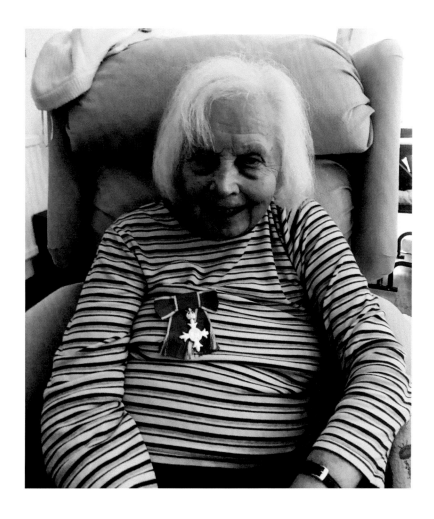

Mum wearing her MBE medal

The churchyard had become very overgrown particularly due to lack of maintenance during the lockdowns. Therefore, I arranged for a company to clear the area and lay new grass seed – this is being completed this week in September 2023. The new and final care manager we would need was appointed. She was very careful to ensure all procedures were followed and was visiting to observe the main carer give Mum ear drops.

David, my brother, was incredibly helpful over the next few months with an administrative issue that I had following a contract of employment with Harbin Engineering University (HEU) in China. Dorothy and Paul hosted a barbeque for (Auntie) Mary as Sarah, her daughter, was visiting with her family from Australia. We took Mum in her wheelchair and she enjoyed the event, drinking a glass of something bubbly! The lockdown in Melbourne Australia had been lifted by July 2022 and Janice, Mum's earlier neighbour, was immediately on a plane to the UK. She so wanted to see Mum and spent two weeks with her during the summer. Janice was extremely kind and, as a trained therapist, massaged Mum and stuffed the little toy dogs we gave Mum to hold with lavender and rosemary to help her relax and avoid claw hands. These fragrant toy dogs were to join Mum for eternity the following year. Janice was one of the very few people who appeared to recognise the demands on me of being Mum's primary carer as her daily visits were long and she helped me by engaging in her care. She also invited me for meals out during her visit.

It was the churchwarden's funeral on Monday 4th July, and it was a pleasure to see the model ships he had made related to his service in the Royal Navy. They had been constructed with the same precision as he had run the maintenance of the church. After more than two years since the beginning of the first COVID-19 lockdown it was time for my fourth three-day break. I stayed with Dorothy and Paul again rather than travelling to Sweden to receive a prize at a conference for work I had done with the team at HEU. It was a good decision as air travel at that time had been incredibly congested due to problems at airports. I was, moreover, too exhausted to make that trip and instead was taken to Tolethorpe, near Stamford, by Dorothy and Paul to see the play the Spider's Web written by Agatha Christie on a beautiful summer's evening. Politically, major events were happening in Downing Street as Boris Johnson finally resigned as leader of the Conservative Party and would soon leave office. The current carer left for a break and a new carer arrived. She was only with us briefly and I was soon back at the railway station collecting the main carer. At times, it was like the foyer of a railway station in the kitchen at home with incoming and outgoing bags piled high. We had enjoyed Wimbledon which was played for the second time after COVID-19 had begun. On the weekends that David visited, Mum would enjoy a meal from a nearby fish and chip shop. We were always shocked by the size of the servings, only one portion of chips was necessary for all of us, and we reminded Mum of when she used to say, "I can smell chippies!", as a child. Mum seemed to enjoy them, and India finished off any remainders. The main carer was planning a six-week trip to South Africa to see friends from her childhood.

Hence, I was concerned that plans were made for the carers to cover the main carer's absence. One of Mum's cousins Ann (Preston) visited with her daughter Jenny at the end of July. She had created a bucket list of things to do as she had been recently diagnosed with a terminal cancer. One of these was to visit Mum (as she had served as one of Mum's bridesmaids). It was to prove a good decision as Ann was to die soon after Mum in 2023. A new carer arrived on 1st August in her car which leaked oil on our entrance drive. It's funny how these trivial types of events remain in your mind.

Constipation had become more of a problem for Mum, possibly due to the hot weather, so senna became a necessary medication. Afternoon ice lollies developed into a daily necessity and Mum's favourite was a Solero, particularly the red berries flavour. After having put lasting power of attorney documents in place for Mum before she became ill, I became something of an expert in helping others to put these in place. I was pleased to do it as the cost charged by solicitors is significant. Mum enjoyed her monthly visit from the vicar, and I again put flowers on Grandma's grave to celebrate what would have been her 111th birthday. The main carer returned for two weeks before her trip to South Africa.

At the time I read a very insightful article related to dementia in the Times, a quote from which read "Dementia is such a horrific thing, utterly horrific. You never know how much is going on in that brain, and for how long someone, is, say, aware of the fact that 'No, I don't know what my name is anymore' – There are parts of the brain that still respond to music". We certainly benefitted from continued regular listening of Classic FM as a method to maintain calmness. The main carer began her long six-week break and another new carer arrived and settled in well. The entire country was in shock, however, on Thursday 8th September 2022 as it was announced that Queen Elizabeth II had died at Balmoral Castle in Scotland at the age of 96. Over the next week there was much media coverage related to the queen who had been our longest serving monarch, Mum appeared to be aware of what was happening. Alison, Simon and friends from Ashwell waited in a 12-hour queue to file past the coffin of Queen Elizabeth II at the lying-in-state in the Palace of Westminster in London. Mum watched all the queen's funeral on 19th September wearing her MBE. It was a very solemn time which clearly impacted everyone, but the accession of King Charles III happened smoothly, and I reminded Mum that he had presented her with her MBE for services to education in Cambridgeshire and Peterborough.

I was pleased that the quinquennial visit to St. Andrew's by the architect went well and he found the church to be generally in excellent repair. It was time for Mum to have her flu jab again at King's Cliffe and this was administered while she was sitting in the fun bus. Liz Truss had become Prime Minister, but she seemed impatient to make changes and caused turmoil in the financial markets.

She resigned from the role only 44 days later.

Rishi Sunak became the third Prime Minister in the year and he remains today, in September 2023. Difficult months ensued for Mum's good friend Patsy as she hurt her spine while caring for her husband John (Frank). Carers had to be found to support John as Patsy was in hospital for a period. Fortunately, Patsy did return home to be with John, but strong painkillers remain necessary to manage the pain. I was particularly pleased when she was able to drive again and regain some independence. 24/7 carers have remained in her house with the concomitant challenges.

I collected the produce from the Harvest service and took it to Thorpe Hall Hospice as Mum had done for years. The carer had done exceptionally well and covered for the whole period while the main carer was away. She flew back to her residence from Luton Airport. She was ready to leave as she was very tired after six weeks. The main carer was only back for three weeks and then, as it turned out, the last new carer would arrive from the Czech Republic where I had been part of the organising team of the very successful International Conference on Acoustics, Speech and Signal Processing in 2011 and Mum had attended.

Dorothy and Paul had invited me to join them at a leisure hotel near to Harrogate at the end of October 2022. I was particularly pleased to do this as (Auntie) Mary and (Uncle) Eric also attended. This was to be my last respite break during the dementia journey, lasting four days. I had had only 16 days over considerably more than three years. They took me to a tearoom which was a lovely experience and I bought Mum an egg custard tart which Dorothy took to her as I returned to Peterborough later.

Blood tests suggested problems with Mum's kidneys and level of potassium. This was monitored over a few days and some adjustments were made to her medications. Mum appeared quite frail when we took her for the tests at the surgery, perhaps the hot summer had taken its toll. The GP wanted to put a ReSPECT (Recommended Summary Plan for Emergency Care and Treatment) form in place. This was done and it was a clear sign that the dementia journey was nearing its end. The new carer quickly fitted in after the main carer's departure on the 7th of November and her experience was obvious. I again did the Christmas cards and wrote Mum's newsletter. David missed another weekend due to a head cold just before the current carer returned to her abode. The familiar switching of carers, with trips to the railway station in Peterborough, happened on the 28th of November and the main carer was back until Christmas. Mum's three cousins did their Christmas visit again on 2nd December and Christmas decorations went up. I put lights up all around the front of the bungalow to make it appear festive. The FIFA World Cup was held in Qatar at the end of 2022, and it was strange to be watching the matches during Advent. As it turned out this was a good distraction from the demands of caring. Christmas cards started to arrive in the post and there were some lovely messages. Mum's grandson Christopher and family visited for a day. It was good to see Mum's colleague from the Alzheimer's Society again.

The main carer and I did the evening trip around the Christmas lights in the villages for a second year, but Mum didn't seem so attentive. The main carer then left for her Christmas break and Alison wanted to attend her friend's father's funeral in Derbyshire, so I loaned her my Mazda 6. I was on my own looking after Mum, but Dorothy very kindly came over to help during the day. Alison's friend Karen who had spent much time at Alwalton in her teenage years and family also visited before Christmas.

Mum developed an abscess on her gum just before Christmas and we had to get antibiotics from the community dentist. Again, with hindsight, I think this was a sign her body was weakening, and she proceeded to develop small blisters on her leg which worryingly could have developed into ulcers. Mum's appetite wasn't so good for the Christmas meal, but Alison did her best to give her a tasty experience in the form of soup which by now featured daily in Mum's diet. Brenda and Simon came over to see Mum on Boxing Day. Mum's granddaughter and family then visited for a day before the New Year. The main carer returned, and we took Mum to Brenda's for the early part of New Year's

Eve. I'd put coal and silver out at our house as custom demands. We watched the New Year's Day concert from Vienna, but we hadn't stayed up to see the New Year in as it was too late for Mum. Sad news came on 5th January 2023 as we heard that the husband of the previous owner of the Alwalton Post Office had died. The care manager visited to update the care plan. The carer from the Czech Republic returned on 16th January 2023. She saw a marked deterioration in Mum, and this continued for the next three weeks. The funeral of the husband of the previous owner of the Post Office was held on Monday 6th February on the same day as the current carer returned to her country via Stansted Airport and the main carer replaced her. Mum did manage to reach her 89th birthday on Tuesday 21st February and we took her to her favourite place for coffee and cake, the Mulberry Café in Elton. Brenda attended too and Mum received many flowers. The carer from the Czech Republic returned for the last time on 27th February and when I was returning from taking the main carer to the station a motorcycle hit the rear of my car. This was certainly inopportune timing but fortunately no one was hurt, and all vehicles were quickly repaired by the corresponding insurance companies, I wasn't at fault.

The last appearance of the dementia robber was to steal Mum's ability to swallow. She started to have difficulties early in March and I managed to arrange a visit from the SALT (Speech and Language Therapy) team who gave some guidance about thickening Mum's drinks. My 63rd birthday was on the 10th of March, and it will always be a fond memory that Mum was still with us. David and I took her to see Brenda on Saturday 11th March, but she had no desire to eat the special ice cream that Brenda served. The carer from the Czech Republic left on the 17th of March and gave a clue that she thought Mum had little time remaining. The main carer was back for the last time. I had worked with around 20 different carers, I always tried to forge good relationships with all of them; even though they were employees living in our home, things wouldn't have worked out if I hadn't adopted a give-and-take approach. I didn't worry about unintended damage to our house which was inevitable with moving Mum on wheelchairs and alike, it could be repaired later.

Mothering Sunday arrived and we had the pleasure to give Mum cards. I fetched some puddings from a supermarket at Oundle to see if I could encourage her to eat. The last thing she ate was an egg custard. As a child, Mum always enjoyed the steamed egg custard her father Bill left her on his plate. The GP visited on Monday 20th March and said Mum wouldn't last until Easter which was on the 9th of April, and he prescribed anticipatory medicines which I collected from the surgery. Mum wasn't drinking at all by that stage and therefore I knew there was little time left. I rang Alison at work on Wednesday 22nd March and she decided to come up immediately. Nicola, Alex and three of Mum's great grandchildren visited. Over the next few days, we had visits from district nurses who administered drugs to minimise any discomfort as Mum was clearly dehydrating. David, Alison, the main carer and I sat around Mum's bed on the evening of Friday 24th March and played music that reminded her of the service of Compline (Night Prayer) she used to attend at Whiteland's College whilst in training as a teacher. Mum managed through the night with Alison's company although her breathing was getting weaker and lasted until after Karen had driven up from Emsworth and Brenda and Simon had come over from Marholm. I kept saying to Mum "hold on" and held her hand tightly. At 10.19 on Saturday 25th March 2023, Lady Day, the Annunciation of the Virgin Mary, our beloved mother died when we were talking about good holiday memories. Plenty of tears were shed but she got her wish to die at home with those who loved her around her. The dementia robber couldn't inflict anymore pain and Christopher, Mum's grandson, said prayers around her body as she was now with her Lord and Saviour. Her body would be laid to rest in the Perkins plot extension of the churchyard of St. Andrew's on Friday 21st April 2023 after being returned to her home for four days and conveyed to the church by the horses of The Fens, two shires…

The final journey on a dray pulled by the shires

Appendix

The following are Betty's notes about some members of the Boyden and Garfield Families.

Perhaps these were early drafts for her (Betty's) life story and are included verbatim as they contain social history from her memories.

Noah's Siblings

Lazarus and Family

Lazarus' life is not well documented. He may have spent many years as a single labourer travelling from village to village but at the age of 50, in 1841, he was working as a carpenter and living in Wereham with his wife Susana, who was 14 years younger than him, and his children Mary Ann aged 14, Elizabeth aged 7 and James aged 4. Ten years later the family were still in Wereham, Elizabeth was 17, Jane aged 11 and Albert, aged 9 had been born, but Mary Ann and James were not registered. James had possibly died but Mary Ann had married, and her husband seems to have been Robert Last who was born in Stoke Ferry and by 1861 their children were Emma born in 1843, Edward born in 1846, John Henry born in 1857 and Philip born in 1860. By 1861 both Elizabeth and Jane had also married. Elizabeth had married Robert Barker of Denver, and they were living in West Dereham. Their children were William aged five, Jane two and Eliza three months. Jane seems to have found domestic employment in London and had married James Carter, a porter who had been born in Bath. They were living near Tottenham Court Road and had two sons Frederick who was three and Henry who was three months. In succeeding censuses, there is no record of Lazarus, Susanna or Albert, so they had possibly all died.

Robert

Robert was married at least twice and died in 1842 in Wimbotsham.

James and Family

James and his family had a chequered life. He was most probably born in Pickenham and married Sarah who came from Prickwillow, in 1818. They followed the family pattern of moving from place to place and were probably in Chatteris in 1821, then went to Downham Market before returning to Chatteris, where they were recorded in the censuses of 1841, 1851 and 1871. James was a brick maker and he and Sarah had four children.

Mary was born soon after 1818, most likely in Wimbotsham where, in 1835, she was married to Philip Bridge, John was born in 1821, Susan in 1825 and Harriett in 1826. In 1841 the family was listed as James 40, Sarah 40, John 20, Susan 15 and Robert Bridge 4. Robert was James and Sarah's

---

grandson, the child of Philip and Mary. Philip was presumably dead because Mary appears to have been working as a female servant for Thomas Ringer at Ponder's Farm in Rougham. Harriett is also unlisted and was most probably working away from home as she married James Priest in 1846 and their first son Thomson was born in 1847, Elizabeth arrived in 1850 and Sarah in probably 1850. In 1851 James' family included his wife Sarah, Susan his daughter and her daughter Mary Ann, who was born in Chatteris, but baptised at St. Andrew's Whittlesea in 1850, her father being Henry Carter from Eldernell. Robert Bridge, the grandson was still with them and there were two lodgers in the house. Susan married the neighbour, George Larkin/g who was 10 years her junior in 1857. George was a brewer's drayman and was born in Biggleswade. They had two children Sarah (born 1856) and Fanny (born 1861). Sarah, James' wife appears to have died by the census of 1871 when James was recorded as being a pauper in Downham Union where he died in 1875 and was buried in Chatteris.

In 1881 Mary Ann was in Doddington and living alone but by 1891 she had married Thomas Goodburn (in 1883) and had a son James who was seven. John followed in his father's footsteps and became a brick maker in Chatteris and married Emma Crowden from Gedney Hill, indicating that there may have been a connection with the Lincolnshire Boydens. John died at 37 years of age in 1858 and was buried at Chatteris. This resulted in Emma having to support the family which consisted of James, born in 1845, Harriett who arrived in 1848, Mary Ann in 1850 and Sarah Jane in 1853. Emma took on the work of a laundress, but James appears to have been forced to take advantage of the scheme where paupers were encouraged to go to work in northern factories with their journey financed and their work found by poor law authorities to reduce 'cash pay outs', because in 1881 he was living in Yorkshire at Attercliffe cum Darnall and was labouring in an iron works. He was married by this time and had a son, John, born in 1875 and a daughter Betsy born in 1880. His wife was Emma, who came from Leeds. James was dead by 1891, probably his health deteriorated in the iron foundry and Emma was working as a housekeeper in Leeds while her children were with her parents. Harriett and Mary Ann both married when they were young which must have been a relief to Emma. Harriett married Frederick Angood in 1866 when she was 20 and he 21 while Mary Ann was only 19 when she married William Ibbott who was 20. Frederick and Harriett produced a large family, Emma in 1869, George in 1870, Eliza in 1873, Elizabeth in 1874, Caroline in 1876, Kate, date not known and Louisa in 1878. George became a successful builder bricklayer who employed workers. He married Mary Ann Buck from Doddington, and their son Percival George was a 2nd Lt in the Royal Flying Corps in World War I and was killed in 1917. His name is on the Chatteris war memorial. Harriett at age 20 married James Priest in 1846, a bricklayer and the following year they had a son Thompson. He was followed in 1849 by Elizabeth and Sarah Jane in 1851. James Priest was recorded as both a brick layer and a beer housekeeper.

William 1800

William whose birth was recorded in 1800 in Wimbotsham married Mary Bowles from March. In concert with his brothers his work was linked to the land. In 1831 he was a groom to 'T. Fryer Esquire', obviously a gentleman of some substance. Twenty years later he was recorded as a gardener, and he was still doing this work in 1881 when he was living in Doncaster with his daughter and son-in-law and had reached the age of 80 years. Mary Ann, his daughter, and her husband Robert Midge had been born in Downham and March respectively and must have moved north to find work under the same scheme as James. However, Robert Midge seems to have done well as he had become a gas engineer, living in a house provided by his work and able to afford a servant.

William 1825

William's first child was born in March in 1825 and was one of the most interesting of the Boydens. He became a Wesleyan Methodist minister and had an extensive family and lived in towns across the country. His wife, Frances, came from Litcham in Norfolk and was the mother of Martha, Frederick, Thomas, Alfred, Mary, Arthur, and Alice. The family lived in Chatteris, Outwell, Litcham, Wellingborough, Preston Lancs, Ripley Derbyshire, Bristol, Clee-with-Weelsby near Grantham and finally after his retirement and the death of Francis in Western-Super-Mare where Martha was his housekeeper.

William 1819

William, Benjamin's brother, was born in Denver and was married in Chatteris, in 1842, although he was still working as an agricultural labourer in Denver in 1841. His wife, Martha Salmon/Sammons was from Haddenham, and it is likely she was working near Chatteris. William and Martha returned to Denver and remained in the village, where their two daughters, Mary Elizabeth and Hannah Marie, were born. William appears to have gained status over the years and by 1881 he had become a coal merchant and featured in White's Gazetteer and Directory of 1883 as a coal dealer. Yet, in 1878, when Hannah Maria married James Scarborough William, he was designated labourer, but that could have been the churchwarden who filled in the marriage certificate not wanting to recognize he had done well. James was a shoemaker, born in March and the couple lived next door to her parents.

It is uncertain whether William Watson's sister Mary Ann died at the young age of 27. His brother John Watson (born 1849) married Sarah Ann who may have been born in Wistow in 1853. It is likely that Sarah Ann lived with her grandfather in Whittlesey before her marriage. John Watson and Sarah Ann had a large family of eight children, John, William, George, Issac, Selina, James, Frederick, David, and Sarah Ann. Two children died David William in 1874 and Harriett in 1881 both at about a year old.

John was designated a brickmaker, which means, no doubt that he worked in a brickyard and his family spent some years in Wistow where John continued with his same work. The family returned to Whittlesey and John and Sarah are buried in Whittlesea cemetery. Of their children, Isaac married Mary Jane, possibly Roberts, of Coates and their daughter Gladys was born in 1914. James also lived in Coates and served in World War 1 and died in St. Bartholomew's. Elizabeth, the sister who was born in Bardney married Henry Redhead in Whittlesey in 1872 and produced eight children, Mary Ann in 1870, George in 1878, Susan in 1881, Sarah 1882, Harriett 1887, Arthur 1889, Ellen 1891, and Annie 1893.

In early 1922 Bill married Minnie Louisa Peacock and his sister Mary Elsie, with Emma as her bridesmaid, married John (Jack) Peacock, but was not related to Minnie. John was born in Buckworth but lived much of his young life in Alconbury Weston. Elsie and Jack went to live at Wistow and had a long-married life of more than 50 years, during which they produced six children Dorothy (Dot) James (Jim), John (Johnny), Sylvia, Freddie, known as Nip, and Pansy (real name Audrey Pearl).

Emma

Eliza's death followed in 1932 and Emma took over the running of the house, looking after her father and Albert who remained unmarried. At the beginning of the Second World War John, Emma and Albert were given notice to quit the tied house and although they appealed against the eviction, they left on Lady Day 25th March 1940/41. Alternative housing was not available because of the Second World War, and they were very distressed when the appeal was dismissed. There was no option but for John to go to live at Wistow with his daughter, Elsie and for Albert and Emma to move in with Bill and Con. Their house was already full and became overcrowded. There was no bed for Albert, and he slept at the home of Grannie Lant, who had, by this time, given up the tenancy of the Plough Inn, and moved with her daughter Phyl, to Peterborough Road about 200 yards from Bill and Con. By this time Albert worked at Perkins Diesel where he met Elsie, whom he married in 1942 and they lived in Walton. In later years John spent time at Farcet, but died at Wistow in 1951. Emma Jane did not marry, but had a son named Donald William, always known as Billy. Bill acted very much as a father figure to Billy. After the war Emma took a flat at 16 Henry Street. I stayed with her on a number of occasions, and I remember a number of things in the flat. She had some hunting pictures where the legs of the horses were in unnatural positions, but most of all I loved her ornament of, I think, a shepherdess. It was so delicate that I wished many times I could have it. One day I was there alone, Emma must have been at work, and I emptied the tea pot down the sink. One of the other residents pointed out that such an action was not a good idea and showed me how to get rid of the leaves by filling a milk bottle with water and washing them down the plug. I think of that episode if I ever tip tea leaves down a sink. I cannot remember if Billy went in the forces, but he certainly became an Eastern Counties bus driver at the end of the Second World War and was often on the route between Farcet and Dogsthorpe, and on Saturdays I was allowed to travel on the bus with him and Jean, who was the conductress. They later married and their two children were Michael and Linda.

Billy and Jean moved around during their married life and Emma died in the early 1960s and is buried in Eastfield Cemetery. Jean later became warden of Stevenson Court, a sheltered housing complex in Peterborough and Billy was the Mayor's chauffeur for some years, a post he filled admirably. After retirement they moved to Gedney Hill where they celebrated their golden wedding before Billy died in the 1990s and Jean later in 2008.

Fred remained true to the land and became a farm manager at Ponders Bridge. He married Ida and they had two sons Barry and Bryan. The farm was an interesting place to visit, but I was always afraid of the geese which ran towards visitors with necks outstretched in a very menacing way. Uncle Fred had two German shepherd dogs and I always wanted a similar dog. Instead, I got Star! The first one was June, loveable and obedient while Major, the second, was more difficult and aggressive, obviously an ancestor of Star. The journey to Ponder's Bridge was by bus and we alighted, and caught the return bus, near the pub next to the bridge. Ponder's Bridge was at a difficult angle and not easy for double-decker buses to manoeuvre. In recent years the road has been changed and now runs some distance from the water and is much easier to negotiate. After retiring Fred and Ida moved to Peterborough Road Farcet to live next to Barry and Mavis. Fred died while driving, he had a heart attack and ran into a garden wall near the turning to Whittlesea.

Albert married Elsie and produced John. Elsie came from Walton, but she and Albert purchased a house in Stanground after the Second World War. They lived there until Elsie moved to nearby Nelson Court, a sheltered housing development, some time after Albert's death, which came after years of ill health. Albert worked at Perkins Diesel, first at Queen's Street and then at Eastfield, after he left Farcet Fen.

The Garfield family

Albert and Eliza

Elsie, Win, Bert and Molly

Elsie was pregnant with their daughter Winnie when she married Tom (Thomas) Turner, a railway guard. Winnie was later joined by a sister and brother, Gillian and Michael. Winnie married Harry.

Winifred was unmarried when her daughter Peggy was born.

The father was a taxi driver, named Arthur who obviously had no intention of marrying Winifred because his wife gave birth to a baby at the time Peggy was born.

Elsie and Winifred were very close as sisters and Winnie and Peggy were brought up together. Winifred married Ezra late in life. Herbert (Bert) worked for the Ladder Company and was a 'lad about town'. At about the age of 18/19 his girlfriend, Kath Hassel, became pregnant, but he was not allowed to marry her. After the birth of the baby who was named Roger, Bert paid regular maintenance of 7/6 each week. Leslie, his brother was sent to buy the postal order and take it to Kath. Bert eventually married Cis Langton, who had a daughter Joan Smith nee Langton at the register office and together they had Danny. Just before his death, Kath contacted Bert. Molly married Jack Powley and had a daughter Ann. They lived in Willesden Ave in Walton and I remember visiting there a great deal. They then moved to Alderman's Drive to an Edwardian House and an old Auntie Molly came to live with them. She had lived in South Wales and was Betty Hart's sister. Betty was probably pregnant when she fell down the stairs and died in 1910. Molly was about three years old, and the death of her mother affected her a great deal. She found it difficult to accept a new 'mother' and probably Florence was not always able to give the same amount of affection to Molly as she should, and Molly had a sense of rejection.

Con etc

Albert and Florence went on to produce six more children after they married early in 1913. They were Florence Muriel in 1913, Kenny in 1915 who died at six months, Leslie Albert Charles arrived in 1916, Betty in 1918, Margaret in 1919, and Kathleen Ethel, the baby in 1922. Con recounted that when Kenny died he had a white coffin but when she lifted the decorative material she found it was made of an orange box and she was only four years old. Florence Muriel was the last of the family to marry. She met Joe Douglas while working at Hotpoint. He was from Southern Ireland and Bill converted to Roman Catholicism before they were married. Their three daughters were Mary, Sally and Joan. Leslie was the apple of his parent's eyes but he was audacious and consistently in mischief. His marriage was to Joan Cooper and their one son was Roger. Betty was the only child who received secondary education. Albert paid for her to attend Fletton Secondary School. Her attendance was unfortunately cut short as Albert was ill and in hospital and his finances seriously reduced. Betty wanted to be a nurse but did not achieve her ambition and worked in a sweet shop and then in the cash office of the International Stores, a grocery shop. Eventually, she achieved her ambition which was to own her own business. She met Jesse through Albert stopping his railway engine near the Cock Inn, a country pub in The Fens near Whittlesea and married him in March 1940. I was the child bridesmaid. They had one daughter, Barbara. Margaret worked for many years in the cash office of Huntings, the butchers. She married John Bates and Judy and Alan were their children. Kathleen Ethel, the youngest of the family served in the WRAC during the Second World War as a driver. She was engaged to an RAF pilot who was killed flying to Malta when the island was blockaded. Jimmy's photograph was displayed in 96 for many years. She subsequently married Charles Coppen who was in the army. Their children were Sue and Jane (Jane died in 2005). Kathleen had a variety of jobs.

Before joining the army, she worked in the office of an estate agent and after her marriage she and Charles became local shop owners before she trained as a care manager and oversaw a number of residential homes. She began her local political career just before her retirement from care work and became the Mayor of the City in 1993. She was extremely proud of the fact that she came from humble Woodston beginnings and became the first citizen of Peterborough.

Certainly, Albert established a friendship with Auntie Sally and Betty which Con continued until their deaths Whether Albert met Florence at Ipswich or if Florence moved to Peterborough for work is not clear, but Bill's brother Jesse and his wife, Phyl, later bought the house which was Con, Bill and my home after we moved from Queen's Walk. I visited them occasionally so retain a vague impression of what it was like. There were no children of the marriage. Jesse was a lorry driver and eventually purchased his own vehicle, but once he no longer felt he should be on the road he became the caretaker of Brewster Avenue School. He was still employed when he had a heart attack and died.

Emma Gertrude Neaverson

Emma Gertrude was the third of seven children, but the eldest daughter of John and Sarah Garfield. She was born in Bread Street and was always know as Gertie. She became a dressmaker and married Herbert Neaverson in 1898. He was born in Peakirk and was one of 12 (maybe 13). His father, William, was born in Whittlesey and moved to Peakirk when he married Harriett, who was 16 years his junior and born in Newborough. Neaverson was an uncommon name in the 19th century and most of the family were living in Northamptonshire. There were limited numbers in Yorkshire and Lincolnshire and a minute number in Cambridgeshire, and in the 20th century it did not occur regularly. William was a publican, but by 1881, he had combined this with farming and had 72 acres of land and employed two men and two boys. Herbert became a businessman and part of Peterborough 'society'. Neaverson's Café was in Long Causeway, and was combined with a shop which sold bread, cakes and confectionery. There were also two sweets shops, one situated in Cowgate, the other at the corner of Oundle Road. Herbert also began a drinks company known as So Bright and was probably associated with Macintosh's of Halifax as director of that confectionary company. Gertrude, it seems, was very proud of this association. Certainly, Herbert did well enough for the couple to have a large house, called Airedale, which they probably had built, in Dogsthorpe Road. Florence once took me to visit but we did not get farther than the kitchen! Con described Gertrude as a 'snob' and said that she acted as if she was a society lady doing good to the poor. She took food to Sarah, her mother and directed Eliza, as if she was a servant rather than her sister, about the way Sarah should be served. Gertrude would, however, have considered she married well and had to maintain her position in the city. Certainly, Herbert and Gertrude employed many relatives, including her father John who looked after the boilers at the café when he retired from the railway, although it is possible that Gertrude did not consider herself as better than her relatives but merely wanted to support her family.

As an old lady Auntie Gertie wore black, was austere and sat in the café, maintaining her control of the business.

John and Sarah Garfield's Children

William (known as Will)

Albert Henry, my grandfather

Emma Gertrude see above

Ethel R. married Alfred Rowlett and lived in Palmerston Road. They had five children. Cyril was a chef at Neaverson's, Phyllis looked after Neaverson's sweet shop on the corner of Oundle Road. (Phyllis married a railwayman and lived in Jubilee Street but later moved to March). Vernon (Vernie) became a window cleaner, Herbert, who was burned as a baby when coal fell out of the fire while he was lying on the hearthrug, and Alec.

Ruth Elizabeth (known as Lizzie) married Edgar Allen and had one child (Bet and Con took this child out in her pram). Later the family moved to Yorkshire.

Nellie married Herbert Christian who perhaps served in the RAF before he also worked at Neaverson's. They lived in Huntly Grove and probably Newark. They had a daughter Muriel and twin boys. Muriel was killed by a bus when she was 12/13 years old while on her way to school and one of the twins died. The survivor was Jack Christian.

Herbert married May and lived in Midland Road. He worked at Baker Perkins where he fell off a ladder and died in the old infirmary. May worked in Neaverson's sweetshop (Near Armstrong's).

The thatched cottage was demolished just after the Second World War and both houses were tied to John's employment as an agricultural worker.

Appendix   The lines of Betty's grandparents

Maternal

3xGreat Grandfather: Robert Garfield, b 1794

Wife Mary

Children *William, b 1818*, John, b 1825, Ruth, b 1830, Joseph, b 1832,

Edward, b 1835, James, b 1837, Robert, b 1840

2xGreat Grandfather: William Garfield, b 1818

Wife Ann

Children Mary Ann, b 1846, *John G., b 1849*, Sarah, b 1850,

James, b 1854, Thomas, b 1856, Joseph, b 1858, Sophy, b 1859,

Henry, b 1861, Ruth, b 1864

Great Grandfather: John G. Garfield, b 1849

Wife Sarah

Children John W., b 1873, *Albert Henry, b 1875*, Emma G., b 1877,

Ethel R., b 1880, Nellie, b 1881, Ruth E., b 1883, Herbert E., b 1888

Grandfather: Albert H. Garfield, b 1875

Wife 1st Betty, 2nd Florence

Children by Betty, Elsie, b 1900, Herbert, b 1904, Winifred, b 1903,

Molly, b 1907; Children by Florence, *Constance, b 1911 (mother)*,

Florence, b 1913, Leslie, b 1916, Kenneth, b 1917, Betty, b 1918,

Margaret, b 1919, Kathleen, b 1922

Paternal

7xGreat Grandfather: Robert Boyden, b 1630

Wife Anne

Children Prudence, b 1659, Ann, b 1660, Mary, b 1661,

Katherine, b 1666, Alice, b 1668, Robert, b 1670, Lucy, b 1672,

John, b 1677

6xGreat Grandfather: John Boyden, b 1677

Wife Susannah

Children Prudence, b 1708, Jon, b 1710, John, b 1712,

Hannah, b 1716, *Robert, b 1718*, Samuel, b 1720

5xGreat Grandfather: Robert Boyden, b 1718

Wife Sarah

Children Mary, b 1743, *John, b 1750*

4xGreat Grandfather: John Boyden, b 1750

Wife Mary

Children Sarah, b 1786, *Noah, b 1787*, Lazarus, b 1789,

Robert, b 1791, James, b 1796, William, b 1800

3xGreat Grandfather: Noah Boyden, b 1787

Wife Maria

Children Sarah, b 1814, Martha, b 1816, *Benjamin, b 1818*,

William, b 1819, Sarah, b 1828, Sarah, b 1833, John, b 1835

2xGreat Grandfather: Benjamin Boyden, b 1818

Wife Mary Ann (Watson)

Children *William Watson, b 1844*, Mary Ann Watson, b 1846,

John Watson, b 1849, Elizabeth Watson, b 1852,

Harriett Watson, b 1860

Great Grandfather: William Boyden, b 1844

Wife Elizabeth

Children Thomas Watson, b 1864, William Watson, b 1866,

John Watson, b 1868, Mary Ann Watson, b 1870,

Emma Jane Watson, b 1873, Elias Watson, b 1878

Grandfather: John Watson Boyden, b 1868

Wife Eliza

Children *Willie (father), b 1897*, Emma, b 1899, Mary Elsie, b 1901,

Fred, b 1905, Albert Ernest, b 1906, Jesse, b 1910

List of Photographs

Index

A

B

G

H

O

P

T

U

X

Y

Z

WHITECHAPEL
IN
50
BUILDINGS

LOUIS BERK &
RACHEL KOLSKY

AMBERLEY

Gwynne House, Turner Street.

First published 2016

Amberley Publishing, The Hill, Stroud
Gloucestershire GL5 4EP

www.amberley-books.com

British Library Cataloguing in Publication Data.
A catalogue record for this book is available from the British Library.

ISBN 978 1 4456 6190 2 (print)
ISBN 978 1 4456 6191 9 (ebook)

Origination by Amberley Publishing.
Printed in Great Britain.

Contents

Enjoy! Rachel, 10/17

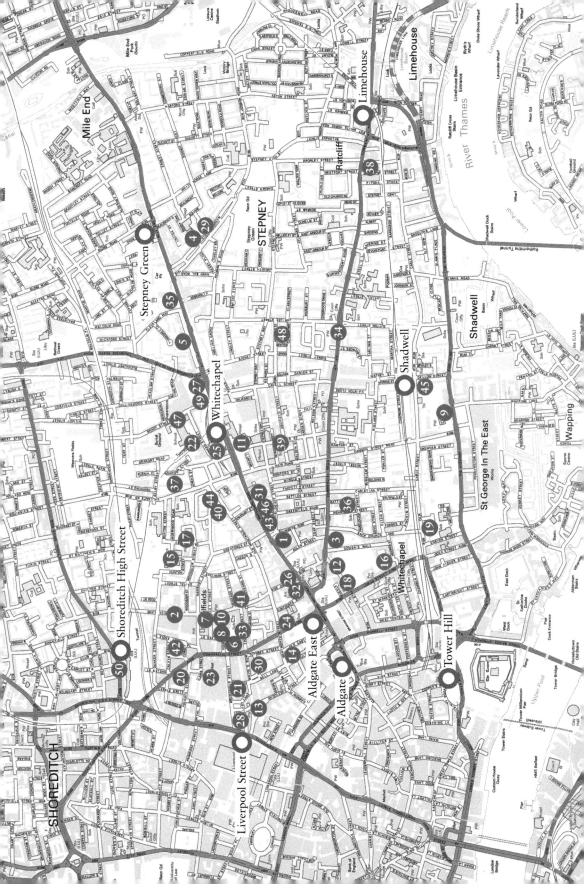

Key

How to use this book

The buildings are listed in chronological order by date of construction, which indicate original building dates and any subsequent significant rebuilding. Where an entry is a listed building, this indicates it is designated a nationally important and protected building, graded by Historic England (historicengland.org.uk). The map enables you to find the buildings within the book as the key uses the same numbers as the text. Information regarding transport and websites was correct at time of writing. Transport for London (tfl.gov.uk) is an excellent resource for planning journeys, and before visiting any of the buildings it is advisable to check their websites for opening hours and access.

A Note from the Authors

In the mid-1990s, working as a researcher in the City of London, I began exploring the area to the east and became enthralled, not only by the intriguing buildings but, in particular, the human stories behind them. I discovered stories of social workers and philanthropists, of industry and commerce, and was captivated by the personalities I 'met' en route. The buildings standing today are a testament to their endeavours.

At the same time, Louis was focusing on the aesthetics of the area, preparing a photographic portfolio of his route to work in Whitechapel. I was treading the same path, but from a social history angle. We met serendipitously at Brady Street Cemetery, Louis fascinated by this tranquil refuge of trees and wildlife and myself researching the development of London's Jewish community. This book grew from our joint passion and enthusiasm for buildings that, in many cases, had been left forlorn or their origins forgotten as they were transformed for new uses. Our challenge was to select just fifty buildings that represent both Whitechapel's intriguing past and present, but also the Whitechapel we love and cherish. Dating from 1695 to the present day, the architectural styles vary from a seventeenth-century home for the aged and elegant eighteenth-century houses to nineteenth-century social housing and twentieth-century art deco. Contemporary steel and glass bring us up to date. In addition, woven into the stories are the different immigrant communities Whitechapel has welcomed over the centuries – Huguenots, Irish, Germans, Jews and Bengalis. I never tire of revisiting Whitechapel and hope our choice of buildings will inspire you to visit this fascinating area of London. Enjoy!

Rachel Kolsky

The renowned British photographer, Don McCullin, once said of Whitechapel 'this district is the most visually fascinating in the whole of London, in fact in the whole of England.' I feel exactly the same way. Even after more than a dozen years photographing in and around the area, there are days I feel I have barely scratched the surface. To me, the key attraction of Whitechapel is the enormous amount of social history contained within its streets and buildings. You can barely walk a single street without finding a gem that links to the impact of immigration, philanthropy and the world. I am not drawn to photographing people. Our lives are but shadows (to echo the sundial of the former Huguenot chapel in Fournier Street) but the buildings have a permanence belying the often powerfully changing circumstances of the people associated with them. It was opportune that, in Rachel, I discovered someone whose passion and interest for the backstreets of this fragile hinterland (increasingly fragile as the City pushes eastwards) matched mine. The combination of her energy and extensive knowledge of Whitechapel, with my attempts to capture the buildings in photographs, brought this book to fruition. We recognise that 'our' fifty buildings may not be 'yours' but this book is a starting point and hopefully it will stimulate you to explore this fascinating area and discover many more of its wonderful and interesting buildings.

Louis Berk

Introduction to Whitechapel

Whitechapel today is easily found on London maps. At the edge of the City of London lies Aldgate, gateway to the East End. Extending east it becomes Whitechapel High Street, then Whitechapel Road and finally it disappears into Mile End Road.

During the fourteenth century, St Mary Matfelon's church, was built. Having been whitewashed in its early life, the parish became known as Whitechapel. The church itself was destroyed during the Second World War and the grounds are now Altab Ali Park.

Whitechapel High Street and Whitechapel Road is a wide and impressive boulevard, following the line of the Roman road to Colchester (now the A11). For centuries, the road linked small settlements and common land. The name Whitechapel Waste survives today as a memory of the common or 'waste' grazing land here prior to the dramatic urbanisation of the eighteenth and nineteenth centuries.

Our collection of historic and interesting buildings is located on this thoroughfare and its tributaries that branch off, reflecting London's rapid eastward development.

Much is made by historians of the 'exclusion' of the East End from the neighbouring settlement of the City of London. This is geographically true, but nevertheless Whitechapel is inextricably linked, through its economic, industrial and social history, to the commerce and banking of the City and beyond. More interestingly, for the times we live in, the

Guardian angel, Whitechapel Waste.

buildings in this book document the important contribution made to the growth of the UK by successive waves of immigrants who brought with them trades and skills that fuelled the enormous economic growth.

Manufacturing in Whitechapel goes back to medieval times and it became an important location for malodorous and polluting industries, including tanning, smelting, dyeing, brewing, brick making and lime-kilning. Acts of Parliament later prevented them being established in the City and beyond. This, and the arrival of London's docks, further concentrated industry in the east. Such industry is now extinct, with the one exception of the Whitechapel Bell Foundry (*see* entry No. 1) existing here since 1570.

Proximity to the River Thames meant that Whitechapel was one of the first areas of England to see an influx of economic migrants and refugees. After the Flemish in the 1100, the French Huguenots arrived fleeing persecution in the late seventeenth century. They lived in new graceful residences, adding attic workshops for their silk looms (*see* entry No. 8 Fournier Street). The authorities endeavoured to impose the supremacy of the state religion by a wave of church-building, which included Christ Church (*see* entry No. 6) and St George in the East (*see* entry No. 9).

German immigrants brought the art of sugar refining to Britain and, like succeeding immigrants, also established their own places of worship (*see* entry No. 12 German Lutheran Church). In the nineteenth century, a wave of Irish immigrants arrived (*see* entry No. 15 St Anne's Church) working on canal and railway construction and of Jewish immigration from Eastern Europe came a profusion of synagogues (*see* entry Nos 13. Sandys Row, 34. Congregation of Jacob, and 43. Fieldgate Street Great Synagogue).

More often than not, the name Whitechapel evokes an image of squalor, depravation and serious crime. It is true that, by the mid-nineteenth century, Whitechapel epitomised the

Ships, Mile End Road (*see* entry No. 5 Trinity Green).

worst aspects of the social impact of the Industrial Revolution. Housing, built as modern and aspirational, became slum accommodation for those lucky enough to afford rent. Others lived from night to night in dosshouses and many more lived on the streets (and even in churchyards, such as Itchy Park next to Christ Church). Life was brutal and, in many cases, short. Charles Dickens, who gave readings at the Hanbury Hall (*see* entry No. 7), was one of the many intellectuals who brought to the middle and upper classes the uncomfortable truth about the enormous divide in wealth, health and happiness in Victorian society.

Improving the conditions of the residents of the East End was not necessarily a new idea; the Trinity Green almshouses (*see* entry No. 5) had been established in 1695 when Whitechapel offered green spaces and fresh air. Other retirement homes followed.

Similarly, the Royal London Hospital (*see* entry No. 11) moved to Whitechapel, just one of five voluntary hospitals established to cater to the needs of those who needed medical help but could not afford it.

The middle of the nineteenth century was still almost 100 years away from the founding of the modern welfare state but, in its absence, many social reformers, spurred on by a combination of religious belief, social conscience and political persuasion, began efforts to improve the lives of the residents of the area.

The mark made by these philanthropists can still be seen today in the shape of the various housing projects that survive (*see* entry Nos 17. Victoria and Albert Cottages, 20. The Cloisters, 21. Providence Row, and 29. Stepney Green Court). The interwar years saw increased social housing provision by local authorities, for example Hughes Mansions (*see* entry No. 37). Following the devastation of the Blitz, slum clearance programmes and new housing estates brought tower blocks to the area (*see* entry No. 44 Pauline House).

In addition to improving housing conditions, the nineteenth-century reformers were also keen to improve the minds and knowledge of the inhabitants of Whitechapel. This included libraries and art galleries (*see* entry Nos 25. Working Lads' Institute, 26. Whitechapel Library, 28. Bishopsgate Institute, and 32. Whitechapel Art Gallery), youth clubs (*see* entry Nos 36 Oxford and St George's Club, and 40. Brady Centre) and settlements, such as Toynbee Hall (*see* entry No. 24), where students from Oxbridge were encouraged to engage with the working classes and improve their skills. Clement Atlee, the Prime Minister most associated with the establishment of the welfare state, spent time at Toynbee Hall in his student days, supporting its programmes for the working poor.

Of course, any place in the world is not just the sum of its places of worship, work and accommodation. Whitechapel has always been a place of entertainment and social interaction. Today, the Bengali market on Whitechapel Waste is as vibrant as it has been for centuries. You can still find evidence of the music halls (*see* entry No. 19 Wilton's) and later, cinemas (*see* entry Nos 38. Troxy, and 41. Mayfair Cinema) would have provided escape from the drudgery of everyday life for local residents. An occupation that exasperated many social reformers was the fondness for drinking oneself away from a desperate life (*see* entry No. 27 The Blind Beggar).

In post-war Whitechapel, despite standards of living rising as the established industries and the docks rapidly rebuilt themselves, residents strived to move out. Many chose the new housing estates in Essex or went northwards to established suburbs. In addition, a new wave of immigrants arrived from Bengal into the Brick Lane area, replacing the large Jewish population who had migrated to Hackney and north-west London. The Bengali population that now dominates a large part of Whitechapel learnt the garment trade in the sweatshops of Brick Lane.

However, in the 1970s, Whitechapel entered a period in which housing and social cohesion went into a downward spiral. It was only when the 1980s brought economic growth to the City and 1991 brought the departure of Spitalfields Market (*see* entry No. 23) that the area began a significant regeneration. The Bengali population is still a vibrant demographic, but the proximity to the docklands and the City has brought a new young community to the area.

This is largely thanks to improved transport infrastructure. The Overground brought a new entrance to Whitechapel at Shoreditch High Street (*see* entry No. 50) and Whitechapel station, also on the Overground, will see Crossrail arrive in 2018.

Whatever the future holds for Whitechapel, its buildings will continue to tell its fascinating and important story. May they remain for future generations to discover and enjoy.

Blue glass and blue bags: Idea Store, Whitechapel Road

The 50 Buildings

Industry came early to East London with brick making, lime-kilning and brewing all well established by the 1600s. Mostly noisy, smelly or both, their sites east of the City ensured there was no negative impact on the City residents.

A small unassuming door on a house dating from 1670 on the corner of Whitechapel Road and Plumbers Row is the entrance to the Whitechapel Bell Foundry. Established by Robert Mot in 1570 during the reign of Elizabeth I and believed to be the oldest manufacturing company in England, it has been on this site since 1738. With over 100 churches in the City by the mid-1500s, there was a constant need for bells. This bell foundry is the only one of several foundries in this area to survive to the present day. It has been managed since 1904 by the Hughes family.

In a maze of cramped staircases, corridors and workshops, the Whitechapel Bell Foundry still makes bells according to traditional methods. It boasts two vast furnaces, one of which can handle up to 6 tons of molten bronze. There are sandpits for cooling the moulds, carpentry shops for assembling the wooden wheels to which the bells are attached, and other departments for making small but essential items like clappers and leather handles, and for tuning and polishing the final product.

Church bells, cathedral bells and handbells are all manufactured here. Ironically, disasters befalling the City and East End have ensured business continues. Following the Great Fire of London of 1666, fifty-one of the eighty-seven churches destroyed were rebuilt. Substantial church rebuilding and renovation also took place after the Blitz, including the German church of St Boniface, just around the corner. Bells were in great demand.

In 1752, the iconic Liberty Bell in Philadelphia was cast here, as was the 13.5-ton bell for Westminster's Big Ben, whose huge mould hangs above the foundry's entrance. It was cast in 1856, being recast in 1858 after a crack appeared. Today, Whitechapel bells chime over parish churches across the UK, peal over Californian vineyards and call schoolchildren in from play.

The foundry might be over 500 years old and still using imperial measures rather than metric, but it is now embracing modern technology, using computers to calculate and test pitch and more recently introducing online purchasing.

Address: Nos 32–34 Whitechapel Road, London, E1 1DY
Built: 1738
Listed status: Grade II
Public access: On tours
Tube: Aldgate East
Website: whitechapelbellfoundry.co.uk

Above: Whitechapel Bell Foundry.

Below: Plumbers Row.

Bells cooling in their moulds.

2. The Old Truman Brewery: The Sign of the Black Eagle

Originally established in 1669 as the Black Eagle Brewery, Truman's Brewery was once the second-largest brewery in England and the largest in London, employing over 1,000 people.

Straddling Brick Lane, the bridge, with its large black eagle, still remains, as does the hanging sign at No. 91. The tall brick chimney with 'Truman' outlined in white tiles still soars above the skyline, its triangular pediment topped by another black eagle. However, no beer is brewed on the site today.

It was Joseph Truman who acquired the brewery in 1694 and Benjamin Truman who then developed the business. The big break came in 1737 when the Prince of Wales (son of George II) was celebrating the birth of his daughter with a bonfire and beer outside Carlton House. The guests didn't like the brew provided by the royal beer master, and Truman's saved the day with their strong porter beer.

Over the centuries, Truman's became a vast enterprise. It acquired a second brewery in Burton-on-Trent in 1873 to produce pale ale. At the height of its popularity, almost 300 publicans were licensed to sell Truman's famous brews. Production of porter ceased in 1930 but mild ale and stout continued to be made in Brick Lane until 1988.

Benjamin Truman was knighted by George III as a reward for loyalty and generous war loans. Along with the Truman family, Sampson Hanbury and Thomas Fowell Buxton played key roles in the development of the brewery and both have streets in the area named after them. Buxton is also commemorated by a plaque alongside the hanging sign.

Most of the Truman's buildings standing today date from the 1800s and include the Directors' House, the Brewmaster's House and the Vat House. The Vat House is the most ornate with a clock and cupola, complete with bell. The stables, with the pediment, were built in 1837 and once housed over 100 horses. They were converted to a boiler house in 1929 and the chimney was added.

The cooperage was rebuilt in 1924/27 and the modern extension along Hanbury Street was built in the early 1970s. Black Eagle Street was renamed Dray Walk and the original loading bays for transporting the beer have been transformed into a row of shops, including the famous Rough Trade Records.

Following the closure of the brewery, the site has been transformed into a hub of creativity and recreation, with architectural changes such as the glass façade linking the Director's House to the Brewhouse.

Over the last twenty years, this large complex of 6 acres has been regenerated and now houses the vibrant Sunday Upmarket, food stalls, art galleries, offices, bars and a tenpin bowling alley.

In 2010, Truman's liquid heritage returned to East London when an artisan brewery was established using the original recipe and trading under the Truman name. Its Eyrie Brewery, built in 2013 in Hackney Wick, retains another eagle-related link to the past.

Address: No. 91 Brick Lane, London, E1 6QR
Built: 1800s various, 1924–27, 1970s, 2000s
Public access: To public areas
Listed status: Brewmaster's House and Vat House – Grade II; Director's House – Grade II*
Tube/Overground: Aldgate East, Liverpool Street, Shoreditch High Street
Website: trumanbrewery.com

Truman Brewery, Brick Lane.

Above: Proof House.

Below: Henry Rudd plaque (*see* entry No. 5 Trinity Green).

3. Proof House

There are 110 City of London livery companies, each responsible for ensuring quality, education and philanthropy linked to their respective industries. The weavers have the earliest charter dating from 1155 and the art scholars have the most recent in 2014. Many companies remain linked to their original industry while some have diversified to reflect changing trends such as fan makers, now linked to the air-conditioning industry, and horners, now linked to plastics. Currently, thirty-nine of the companies have halls in London. Just one is in the London Borough of Tower Hamlets, that of the Worshipful Company of Gunmakers. Its small, unassuming yellow-brick building has few distinguishing marks and it is easily missed by the traffic hurtling by on the busy Commercial Road.

Granted its royal charter in 1637 to promote and regulate gun making, it has continued this work uninterrupted to the present day. All guns sold in the UK must be tested to confirm soundness of barrel and action. Originally sited alongside the Aldgate, in 1675 the Proof House relocated to a less-populated area just outside the City, following an explosion that damaged the City wall.

During the seventeenth and eighteenth centuries, the gun trade expanded, with many companies moving to Birmingham, where, by 1767, there were thirty-five gun and pistol makers plus several other allied specialist trades. An 1813 Act of Parliament created a second Proof House in Birmingham and proof work remains split between the two.

The current London Proof House dates from 1757 and the Livery Hall alongside from 1872. The Receiving Room, where guns are delivered, and the Proof Master's House to the left of the building were both built in 1826. The latter was originally the proof master's residence but is now used as offices. Substantial alterations were made in 1952 and in 1994. In the 1920s, the Livery Hall was sold but was repurchased in 2007.

It is here that the London gun mark 'GP', beneath a crown, is placed on guns suitable for firing and those, following deactivation, safe for collectors. It is a remarkable achievement that for over 300 years guns for private and military use have been inspected, proved and marked here.

Address: Nos 48 and 50 Commercial Road, London, E1 1LP
Built: 1757, 1826, 1872
Listed status: Grade II
Public access: None
Tube: Aldgate East

4. No. 37 Stepney Green: The Oldest House on the Green

Stepney Green Gardens is a series of four interlocking small patches of lawn and path, saved from redevelopment in 1872. On the eastern side is No. 37, a large house set behind ornate wrought-iron railings. The entrance is framed within a scallop-shell-shaped porch.

The house was built for Dormer Sheppherd, a slave owner and merchant. In 1714, Mary Gayer, the widow of the East India Company's governor of Bombay, Sir John Gayer, moved in and it is her initials, 'MG', that are incorporated into the gates. Such houses are a reminder of when this area was East London's 'Millionaire's Row'; their wealth derived from mercantile trade nearby on the River Thames.

Later residents included a chairman of the East India Company, a French Huguenot brewer and Nicholas Charrington, a member of the brewing family. Charrington's Anchor Brewery was nearby on Mile End Road where an original manager's office building remains, while the Anchor Retail Park is on the brewery site.

In 1875, No. 37 became a retirement home for the Jewish community, which for decades dominated this small leafy enclave with an Orthodox synagogue (now the Rosalind Green Hall), Stepney Jewish School, the London Jewish Hospital (this site is now 1990s housing) and Rothschild dwellings (*see* entry No. 29 Stepney Green Court).

In 1907 when the care home relocated to Clapham, No. 37 became a Craft School and then, between 1916 and 1998, the house was used by the local authority. Spitalfields Historic Housing Trust then took ownership, passing it back to residential use. It was fully restored by the new owner and remains in private hands.

Eagle-eyed visitors might recognise the house as it has often been used as a location for film and television, including *The Suspicions of Mr Whicher*.

Address: No. 37 Stepney Green, London, E1 3JX
Built: 1694
Listed status: Grade II*
Public access: None
Tube: Stepney Green

5. Trinity Green

With green space, fresh air and easy access from the City, Whitechapel in the 1600s was the perfect location for almshouses. These retirement homes were sponsored by livery companies and generous merchant families for retired members, their widows or those who fell on hard times. By 1750, travelling east from Aldgate to Bow, there were almshouses funded by the drapers, skinners, mercers and wealthy individuals such as Francis Bancroft. Trinity Hospital (since renamed Trinity Green), established by Trinity House for 'decayed masters and commanders of ships and the widows of such', has survived on its original site since 1695. Funded by Captain Henry Rudd, it was designed by Sir William Ogbourne.

Two magnificent ships, replicas of the original models, guard the entrance gates (*see* image, page 8) and the maritime rope motif on the ironwork links to the work of Trinity House, an organisation founded in 1514 by Henry VIII, whose responsibility is the upkeep of lighthouses and safety of sea vessels sailing around the British Isles.

Two rows of seven houses face each other across a green lawn and their raised ground-floor entrances each lead to a square living and kitchen area, with the bedroom and bathroom located below. Eight dwellings were lost in 1943 during the Blitz, hence the numbering going from 1 to 12 and recommencing with 20. The chapel at the northern end is two storeys high, with the rope motif on the handrail and the word for G-d written in Hebrew characters.

In 1954, the LCC took over responsibility, which later passed to Stepney. Following restoration, neglect set in and it was not until the re-gentrification of Whitechapel that the properties were recognised as the perfect location for City and docklands workers. Several have since been renovated and sold as owner-occupier dwellings.

Number 37 Stepney Green.

Trinity Green almshouses.

This peaceful spot is, at the time of writing, under threat from plans for a twenty-eight-storey tower block just 100 yards away, blighting the human scale of the almshouses. But Trinity Green is a survivor. When threatened with demolition in 1895, public outcry prevented closure. The by-product of that campaign, led by C. R. Ashbee (*see* entry No. 24 Toynbee Hall), was the Survey of London, still produced today as an important record of London's buildings past and present.

Address: Trinity Green, Mile End Road, London, E1 4TS
Built: 1695
Listed status: Grade I
Public access: None
Tube: Stepney Green, Whitechapel

6. Christ Church, Spitalfields

Christ Church Spitalfields is one of six London churches designed by Nicholas Hawksmoor (another is St George in the East – *see* entry No. 9). Constructed between 1714 and 1729, Christ Church's spire still dominates the Commercial Street skyline.

In an area increasingly populated by Huguenot Protestant chapels during the eighteenth century, the bold architecture of this Anglican church stood out, particularly its impressive Portland stone baroque features and Tuscan portico.

However, Christ Church later entered London's collective memory as an ominous presence, witnessing the increasing poverty and misery of the nineteenth century including the Whitechapel murders of 1888. The churchyard was known as Itchy Park, one of several

Christ Church, Spitalfields.

in the capital where the homeless and alcoholics spent their daylight hours. In *People of the Abyss* (1905), Jack London described the scene as one 'he never wanted to see again'. Later twentieth-century authors Iain Sinclair and Peter Ackroyd developed a theory of psychogeography that merged history with folklore, instilling this church with a sense of overpowering malevolence.

The vaulted crypt was used as a bomb shelter during the Blitz but, in 1957 due to extensive damage, the church had to be closed and the congregation moved to the church hall (*see* entry No. 7 Hanbury Hall). Meanwhile, restoration began and from 1965 the crypt was used as a refuge for the homeless.

The eventual reopening of the church in 1987 was, in part, due to the actions of a campaign group, the Friends of Christ Church, formed in 1976. Since then, a remarkable renaissance has taken place. Renovations brought light and majesty to the interior, returning several original features. A more recent project has transformed the crypt into an inviting and spacious area, including a chapel for quiet contemplation and a café. A subtle ramp allows visitors to enter without interrupting the tranquility of the worship area.

A by-product of the Friends' campaign is the biannual Spitalfields Festival for music and the spoken word, which uses Christ Church as one of its venues. From being a sleeping giant, the church is once again connected to its local community.

Address: Commercial Street, London, E1 6LY
Built: 1714–29; 1979–2004; 2015
Listed status: Grade I
Public access: Yes
Tube: Aldgate East, Liverpool Street
Website: ccspits.org

7. Hanbury Hall

For nearly 300 years this small brick building, tucked within Hanbury Street, has witnessed the changing face of Spitalfields.

Built in 1719 as a French Huguenot chapel, it became La Patente Church in 1740. The Royal Arms, previously granted by James II, is still visible in the hall. Later it was used by preachers including John Wesley, the father of Methodism. A newly completed complex of luxury apartments built above Hanbury Hall has been named Wesley Court in his memory.

From 1787, it was a German Lutheran church (*see* entry No. 12 St George's Lutheran Church) and a Baptist chapel. Following enlargement in 1864, it was acquired by Christ Church (*see* entry No. 6 Christ Church, Spitalfields), becoming its church hall and used for public events. Charles Dickens famously visited to recite his own works, and in 1888 it was the venue for meetings gathering support for the girls who were on strike from the Bryant & May match factory in Bow. Between 1957 and 1987 while Christ Church was being restored, services were held here. As local demographics changed, it became the Kobi Nazrul Centre for the Bengali community (now a few doors along in Hanbury Street) and later, the Hanbury Project.

Remodelled between 2014 and 2015, the hall provides a café and a galleried hall for community and arts usage funded by the seven apartments above.

Above left: Hanbury Hall. *Above right*: Christ Church in Fournier Street.

Below: Tiles by Paul Bommer.

In 2015, a series of twelve blue and white Delft-style tiles by Paul Bommer were unveiled on the exterior, evocatively illustrating local Huguenot associations including La Nueve Eglise (*see* entry No. 10 Brick Lane Jamme Masjid), silk and horticulture.

Address: No. 22b Hanbury Street, London, E1 6QR
Built: 1719, 1864, 2015
Listed status: Grade II
Public access: To the hall
Tube: Liverpool Street

5. Fournier Street: A Street with a Church at Both Ends

Between 1718 and 1728, three Spitalfields streets – Fournier, Wilkes and Princelet – were laid out by the developers Charles Woods and Simon Michell, forming an exquisite example of early Georgian residential architecture. The consistent appearance of these streets allows them to be considered as one building.

Fournier Street perhaps boasts the grandest houses, all thirty-four of them, in two elegant rows, including the vicarage for Christ Church (*see* entry No. 6) at the northern end. Originally built with much detailing of brickwork, door canopies and ironwork, the first occupants, the Huguenots, added attics so that the silk weavers working at their looms would have more light.

Following the Huguenots, came the Irish. Then, from the mid- to late nineteenth century, the properties became homes and workshops for Jewish migrants from Russia and Poland, who worked mostly in the garment trade and later also with fruit and fur. The backyards were filled with outbuildings for storage and additional workrooms. Still surviving today is a courtyard, visible through a doorway marked 'S Schwarz'.

After the Second World War, the fur trade predominated above ground and bananas traded at Spitalfields Market (*see* entry No. 23) were still ripened in the semi-basements. However, by 1970, almost all of the Jewish businesses had closed.

The growing Bengali community followed in the footsteps of the departed Huguenots and Jews, working in the clothing industry and worshipping in Fournier Street's former synagogue, now a mosque (*see* entry No. 10 Brick Lane Jamme Masjid). At the same time, the street experienced an influx of artists and designers who recognised the importance of this surviving domestic architecture and created studio space in the outbuildings formerly used for storage. Thus, a creative quarter gradually developed and, when the fruit and vegetable business relocated in 1991, the houses became more attractive, offering affordable and spacious family homes in a wonderful location. Since then, the properties have been extensively renovated, becoming some of the most desirable in London.

Address: Fournier, Princelet and Wilkes Street, London, E1
Built: 1718/1728 (then followed by change of use and subsequent renovations)
Listed status: Several buildings are listed. See historicengland.org.uk/listing for details
Tube: Liverpool Street

Fournier Street looking towards Christ Church.

St George in the East.

9. St George in the East

Shadwell, alongside the Thames on the southern border of Whitechapel, was London's sailor town and designated an area for one of London's fifty new parishes under the 1711 New Churches Act. Nicholas Hawksmoor, a pupil of Christopher Wren, was chosen to build St George in the East, one of his three East London commissions in addition to Christ Church (*see* entry No. 6) and St Anne's Limehouse.

The church, a vast Portland stone baroque edifice was built between 1714 and 1726. The large clock tower dominates the skyline, complemented by two smaller identical 'pepper pot' towers to the east.

Wealthy merchants travelled to services here and Sundays saw rows of coaches awaiting their masters at the end of worship. Henry Raine, a local brewer and founder of Raine's School in 1719, has a large family tomb in the churchyard.

By 1805. the London Docks at Wapping had opened south of The Highway and a large rope walk was established, hence Cable Street to the north. The churchyard was extended and the gardens made public in 1886. By then, views of the church were obscured on the south by housing and to the east and north by the mortuary of 1880, the Town Hall of 1861, a London Board School and a public library, both of 1898.

The Blitz, while bringing destruction to St George's in 1941, also brought opportunities to open up the vista. The southern flank was exposed and a gap appeared to the north following the bombing of the library, now the site of the Cable Street Mural (*see* entry

Below left: The font inside St George in the East. *Below right*: A church within a church.

No. 45). The distinctive Hawksmoor towers survived but the interior was almost totally destroyed. After lying in ruins for over fifteen years, an ingenious solution retained the baroque exterior with a new smaller sanctuary built within. The church was rededicated in 1963. Approaching from the drive, the view through the portico and new plate-glass windows – hence, across the courtyard towards the altar is quite spectacular.

Address: No. 14 Cannon Street Road, London, E1 0BH
Built: 1714,1726, 1960,1963
Listed status: Grade I
Public access: Yes
Tube: Shadwell, Tower Hill
Website: stgeorgeintheeast.org

10. Brick Lane Jamme Masjid

If there is one building in Whitechapel that encapsulates the essence of its history and continuous welcome to new communities who make it their home, it would be the Jamme Masjid Brick Lane mosque. This building has been a place of worship for French Huguenot Protestants, Orthodox members of the Jewish community and currently Muslims.

The sundial atop the Fournier Street frontage states '1743' and, beneath, the inscription reads '*Umbra Sumus*' ('We Are Shadows'). Built as one of several Huguenot chapels in Spitalfields during the late seventeenth and eighteenth centuries, it was called the Neuve Eglise (New French Church). Next door, a three-storey brick house, also built in 1743, originally served as its vestry and school and is now part of the mosque complex. After the French moved on, it became a Wesleyan chapel in 1809, linked to the London Society for Promoting Christianity Amongst the Jews and, in 1819, became a Methodist chapel.

By the end of the nineteenth century, Brick Lane was the backbone of the Jewish East End. A group of ultra-Orthodox Jews linked to the Machzike Hadath ('Strengtheners of the Faith') community formed in 1891, began using the building for worship in 1898. In the attic and building next door they ran a Talmud Torah, a study school, which, at its peak, had over 500 students. There were services at all times of the day and it was known as the Spitalfields Great Synagogue. The synagogue continued to thrive but, by the mid-twentieth century, the number of local Orthodox Jews had declined and the synagogue was busy during the working week only.

While the Jewish businesses had all but disappeared by the mid-1970s, the Muslim community was increasing and in 1975 the building transferred ownership, opening as a mosque in 1976. Refurbishment in 1986 removed the remaining internal galleries and the interior was remodelled. There is capacity for 3,000 worshippers and recently a small basement prayer hall has been added for women. In 2009, the community funded renovation of the ablution area and erected a sculpture on Brick Lane in the form of a tubular steel structure. It resembles a minaret and is decorated with a geometric floral design. Topped with a crescent moon, it is illuminated at night with subtle changing colours providing a beacon of light to the neighbourhood.

The minaret has also brought symmetry to Fournier Street as the steeple of Christ Church, dominating the south end, is now counterbalanced at the north end.

Above: Brick Lane Jamme Masjid.

Below: 'We are shadows'.

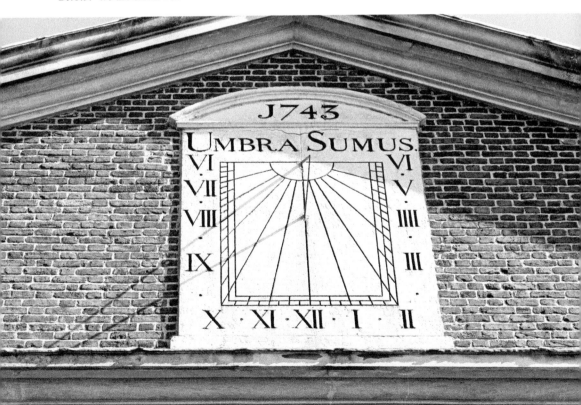

The mosque is surrounded by reminders of the past and present of this ever-evolving area of Spitalfields. Next door is the Bangladesh Welfare Association, established in the 1950s as the Pakistani Welfare Association. In 2016, a budget hotel opened opposite the mosque on Brick Lane, filling a Second World War bombsite, empty since the Russian Vapour Baths were destroyed. Known as Schewzik's after the owner, the metal sign was retrieved from a skip and is now on display in London's Jewish Museum. Nearby, doorways are outdoor art galleries, with examples of the very best of London's street art. Restaurants are no longer exclusively Bengali curry houses but French bistros, Argentine steakhouses and Italian pizzerias.

Address: No. 59 Brick Lane, London, E1 6QL
Built: 1743, 1897, 1986, 2009
Listed status: Grade II*
Public access: Open for services and by arrangement
Tube: Aldgate East
Website: bricklanejammemasjid.co.uk

11. Royal London Hospital

The Royal London Hospital (known affectionately as 'The London'), the UK's leading trauma and emergency care centre, began its life in 1740 as the London Infirmary, a charity providing medical care for the sick poor.

Right from the start, the hospital had to expand and adapt to the changing needs of the population it served. Originally at Moorfields, it soon moved to Prescot Street just east of the City, and subsequently, in 1753, to larger premises in Whitechapel, then still countryside, where it was joined in 1785 by the London Hospital Medical College.

From the early 1800s, the nearby docks and local industry propelled a rapid growth in Whitechapel's population and the hospital adapted accordingly. Responding to a growing Jewish population, kosher food was provided at the hospital from 1837. Later, Jewish benefactors funded designated wards.

By 1876, over 30,000 patients were being treated annually and the hospital started to attract interest from royalty and wealthy patrons, particularly Princess (later Queen) Alexandra. The Alexandra Wing opened in 1864 and, with her support, the UK's first Finsen Lamp was installed here in 1899. Elected president in 1904, Alexandra is commemorated with a statue outside the Luckes Entrance (named after Eva Luckes, matron from 1880 to 1919).

Lord Knutsford, chairman from 1896 to 1931, raised millions of pounds to rebuild the hospital, including the construction of a new outpatients department in 1903 and dental school in 1911. The London hospital joined the National Health Service in 1948 and, in 1990, commemorating its 250th anniversary, Elizabeth II bestowed it the title 'Royal'.

By the turn of the millennium, the Royal London Hospital had become a sprawling estate extending from Cavell to New Streets. A rebuild was the only option and the twenty-first century has seen dramatic change. Between 2007 and 2016, a vast shiny blue complex, built on the site of thirteen previous buildings, appeared above the skyline. The statistics are staggering. Incorporating two seventeen-storey towers and a ten-storey tower, the 727-bed hospital houses Europe's largest renal service, London's second-largest pediatric

Above: Royal London Hospital – the new hospital behind the original building

Below: Royal Hospital London in 2008, before redevelopment.

service and serves a daytime population of 10,000. It is also home to London's Helicopter Emergency Medical Service, established here in 1991.

At the time of writing, some of the original buildings are still visible, derelict and forlorn, but custodian to so many memories. It was here that Joseph Merrick lived, being rescued in 1886 from a life as the 'Elephant Man' by surgeon Frederick Treves. It was here also that the brave nurse Edith Cavell trained, her life commemorated by a blue plaque. The bell, previously hanging in the entrance of the hospital, was cast at the Whitechapel Bell Foundry (*see* entry No. 1) in 1757. It was rung to alert medical staff of an emergency.

The eighteenth-century buildings fronting Whitechapel Road now await their future role, having been purchased in 2015 by the London Borough of Tower Hamlets for conversion into a new town hall.

Address: Whitechapel Road, London, E1 1BB
Built: 1753, various 1800s, 2007–16
Listed status: Grade II
Public access: Yes
Tube: Whitechapel

12 St George's Lutheran Church

Consecrated in 1763, St George's Lutheran Church is the oldest surviving German church in England. With economic migration from Germany plus the establishment of the Hanoverian monarchy in 1714, London saw membership of German Lutheran churches rise to around 4,000 between 1700 and 1750.

Many Germans settled in Whitechapel, where sugar refining was their dominant business ,together with butcher and baking businesses.

In 1762, the lease of this site was funded by Dietrich Beckmann, a wealthy sugar refiner and, in 1859, W. H. Goschen, a German banker, purchased the site next door for a German infant school.

The frontage expanded the east of church in 1877 to enlarge the school and a new organ was installed in 1884. By 1855, most of the congregants were employed in the sugar industry, but by the late 1880s sugar establishments had decreased from thirty to just three and there was much poverty. However, overall between 1851 and 1911, German population continued to rise from 16,082 to 27,290 and East London remained their preferred area. With just 130 people at each service, St George's became London's most active German church. A fire in 1912 destroyed much of the building and the Second World War brought internment of Germans and destruction of their property by local residents. Georg Matzold, pastor here from 1891, remained loyal to his congregation and continued services, but in 1917 the school closed and shortly after Revd Matzold was expelled from England. He returned in 1920 to a much-reduced congregation and died in 1930.

Dr Julius Rieger, from Berlin, followed him. Rieger was anti-Nazi and the church organised rescue work for those escaping Nazi Europe.

The bell tower, demolished in 1934, left an unembellished exterior that belies the elegant and detailed interior. A gallery surrounds three sides of the nave and original gated wooden pews survive. Red and blue stained-glass windows look rather contemporary but date from

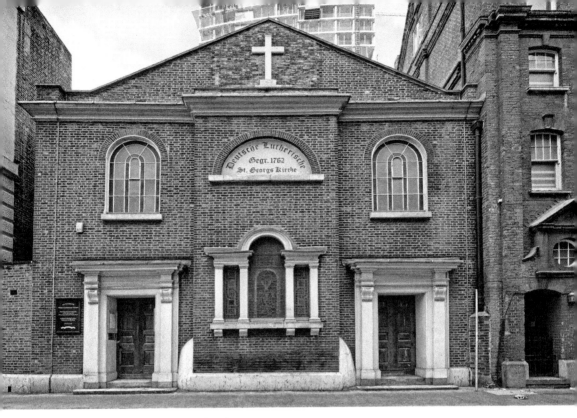

Above: St George's Lutheran Church.

Below: Interior of St George's Lutheran Church.

1812 and above two wooden commandment boards, in German, there is a magnificent royal coat of arms for George III. Following an attempted burglary in 1995, the valuable library, dating back to the eighteenth century and including the personal collection of the first pastor, Gustav Waschel, transferred to the British Library.

By 1995, the congregation numbered barely twenty and services ceased. Currently administered by the Historic Chapels Trust, there was extensive restoration in 2004 and the chapel is now regularly open for organ recitals and events. The school was converted to apartments in 1998.

Address: No. 55 Alie Street, London, E1 8EB
Built: 1763
Listed status: Grade II*
Public access: By arrangement or for events
Tube: Aldgate East
Website: stgeorgesgermanchurch.org.uk

13. Sandys Row Synagogue

When visiting Sandys Row, the oldest Ashkenazi synagogue in London and the last remaining in Spitalfields, the blue and white Delft pottery mezuzah case on the right door post as you enter gives a hint to the origin of this particular Jewish community.

In 1854, fifty Dutch Ashkenazi Jewish economic migrants founded a community, 'The Society for Loving-Kindness and Truth'. By 1867, it had grown to 500 members and acquired the leasehold of a chapel, having outgrown rented premises in Mansell Street.

Sandys Row Synagogue. *Inset*: Delft pottery mezuzah.

Interior, Sandys Row Synagogue.

The chapel, built in 1766 as the French Huguenot chapel L'Eglise d'Artillerie, had subsequently been used by local Baptists since 1786.

This site was particularly suitable for this Orthodox Jewish congregation, having been built with a balcony, which was required for the ladies of the community, and an east–west axis. N. S. Joseph remodelled the exterior on Sandys Row, enclosing the original chapel entrance to make the external steps the current internal staircase. This was later faced with marble. A new three-storey building provided a vestry, kitchens and accommodation.

The chief rabbi, Nathan Adler, opposed its establishment and refused to acknowledge it, so, in 1870, it was consecrated by the rabbi of the nearby Sephardi Bevis Marks synagogue. In 1887, Sandys Row was the largest of the founding congregations of the Federation of Minor Synagogues. Seeking religious independence, it left the federation in 1899, becoming an Associate of the United Synagogue in 1922. In 1949, it returned to independent status and has remained so ever since.

The warm orange and white interior is evocative of the small East End communities. Currently, in 2016, there are around 200 members, many being descendants of previous congregants. Midweek afternoon services attract up to fifty worshippers, mostly from nearby offices and a renaissance has gathered momentum with a variety of communal, cultural and social events. In late 2010, the synagogue embarked on the largest building programme in its history, with a new roof and interior renovation throughout; stories recounted in the 2014 oral history project, 'Our Hidden Histories', are now online.

Address: No. 4a Sandys Row, London, E1 7HW
Built: 1766, remodelled 1869/70
Listed status: Grade II
Public access: Open for services and by arrangement
Tube: Aldgate East, Liverpool Street
Website: sandysrow.org.uk

14. Wash House: 'More Hot Water in No. 6!'

All that survives of the Old Castle Street wash house is the façade. Built in 1846 on what was then Goulston Square, its exterior is adorned with just 'Wash Houses' in relief above the roofline and '1846' below.

Most homes in Whitechapel were still without indoor toilets or bathrooms by the mid-nineteenth century. It was the 'Committee for Promoting the Establishment of Baths and Wash-Houses for the Labouring Classes' and the 1846 Bath and Wash Houses Act that led to many public facilities for bathing and laundry being built, and sometimes swimming baths too.

The Old Castle Street wash house was one of the first to be opened in London. Others followed in Whitechapel and neighbouring districts: Bow Baths on Roman Road in 1892;

Old Castle Street wash house.

Stepney Baths.

Cheshire Street off Brick Lane in 1898; and Mile End Municipal Baths in 1931, the latter indicating the continued need for such facilities well into the twentieth century.

At the wash houses, individual cubicles for bathing provided privacy for those used to overcrowded homes. The occupant could control the temperature of the water by simply calling out for 'more cold' or 'more hot' as required. Soap and towels were also available. The communal laundry area included mangles, dryers and irons.

By 1943, estimates indicate that 90 per cent of homes in Stepney did not have baths but most post-war residential building included toilets and bathrooms. This led to the closure and demolition of many wash houses. The Old Castle Street wash house survived but was finally demolished in 1989 with just the façade retained.

In 1998, Heritage Lottery Funds enabled Guildhall University to purchase the site and build a new home for the Fawcett Library, incorporating the original frontage. Renamed the Women's Library, it remained until 2013 when it relocated to the London School of Economics. The wash house, at time of writing, is being remodelled to accommodate the Frederick Parker furniture collection.

The Mile End Municipal Baths are nearby at No. 159 Mile End Road (Tube: Stepney Green). This sleek, white-tiled bath complex was considered the elite of the bathhouses when opened in 1931 by Miriam Moses, Mayor of Stepney. Closed in 1983 and remodelled in 1995, it is now the Globe Centre for AIDS and HIV patients.

Address: No. 25 Old Castle Street, London, E1 7NT
Built: 1846, 1999–2000
Public access: None (at the time of writing)
Tube: Aldgate East

15. St Anne's Roman Catholic Church

Between the departure of the French Huguenots and the arrival of Russian and Polish refugees, the early nineteenth century saw many Irish people settling in and around Brick Lane as labourers and textile workers. Venturing east of Brick Lane, St Anne's Church is a reminder of this Roman Catholic community.

In 1829, land was acquired for a Catholic school on Spicer Street, now part of Buxton Street, resulting in two classrooms for local boys and girls. From 1848, Mass was celebrated and St Anne's Chapel opened. The Marists, founded in 1817 as the Marist Brothers of the Schools, took over this mission church and from 1853 continued to teach boys in the school, with the girls moving to new premises nearby in Underwood Street (now Road). From 1857 a convent and school were built, designed by Gilbert Blount, an eminent Victorian architect. These exist today at St Anne's and St Patrick's Roman Catholic primary schools.

A chapel was opened in 1850, also on Spicer Street. As the Irish congregation grew, the Marists were invited to take over the services and they purchased a site on the corner of Underwood Street and Deal Street for a church and presbytery.

Building began in 1855 in an early Gothic style and continued until 1894, when the church was completed. It was consecrated in 1905. Today, the church is also used by the Brazilian Chaplaincy.

Address: Underwood Road, London, E1 5AW
Built: 1855/1894
Listed status: Grade II
Public access: Open at service times
Tube/Overground: Whitechapel, Shoreditch High Street

St Anne's Roman Catholic Church.

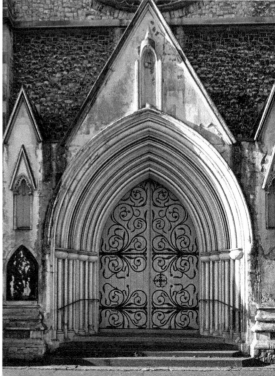

16. The Sugar House (previously the Co-Operative Wholesale Society)

The impressive red-brick building on the corner of Leman and Hooper Streets, complete with an imposing clock tower, was built in 1885–87 for the Co-Operative Wholesale Society (CWS) as its London headquarters, replacing an earlier building badly damaged by fire. Still clearly visible is the name written in full on the recessed brick, the wheat sheaf motif and the motto 'Labor and Wait', written deliberately with American spelling to show support for the anti-slavery campaign.

Founded in 1844, the CWS aimed to offer competitive prices on food and household items by practising collective buying principles. Customers additionally benefitted from stamps or 'the divi' that they could convert into cash savings. By 1900, the CWS was running numerous stores, factories, warehouses and even a shipping line. Leman Street became lined with warehouses for sugar and tea and coffee roasting and the CWS became known as the 'Larder of Leman Street'. From here, with its proximity to the docks, the CWS operated speedy transport links to its national headquarters in Manchester. The London

Door detail, CWS.

CWS Building.
Inset: Co-operation and
Beehive, Prescot Street.

headquarters remained until the late 1960s, when nearby St Katharine and London Docks closed and the need for storage and offices declined.

The beautiful ceilings, inlaid woodwork and fireplaces of the original CWS London headquarters are no longer to be seen as the building was transformed into forty-two luxury apartments and penthouses in 2008–09. However, the clock tower remains. It is said to be a replica of the Palace of Westminster's Big Ben, though a quarter of the size. The maker of the original clock, Thwaites and Read, restored it to working order with a digital mechanism. It no longer chimes, which is obviously an advantage for nearby residents.

Opposite, at No. 1 Prescot Street, is another former block of CWS offices. Built in 1934, this block contrasts with the old buildings around it. It features attractive art deco reliefs of figures shaking hands, representing co-operation, as well as images of a beehive, the motif of the CWS, representing not only diligent labour but also team spirit, a key feature of the bee community. In 1999, it was converted into 150 apartments.

Address: No. 99 Leman Street, London, E1 8GH
Built: 1885–87, 2008
Listed status: Grade II
Public access: None
Tube: Aldgate East, Tower Hill

17. Victoria and Albert Cottages

Walking through the post-Second World War housing estate to the east of Brick Lane, you come across a group of delightful artisan cottage-style homes. Erected in 1858 and 1865, they are named Victoria and Albert Cottages, after the then reigning monarch and consort.

Built by the Metropolitan Association for the Improving of Dwellings of the Industrial Classes (MAIDIC) they housed thirty-two and thirty-six families respectively, included three shops and were intended for those who could not afford the higher rents of the earlier family dwellings blocks alongside, Albert Family Dwellings. Also built by the MAIDIC, the Dwellings were demolished in 1975 and replaced by 1980s housing. While they looked like houses, the cottages were actually two flats leading from the front doors, each with two bedrooms, a living room, scullery and WC. Baths were taken at Cheshire Street public baths.

The cottages attracted criticism at the time for not providing more dwellings on the site as opposed to the adjoining MAIDIC block. Other housing organisations such as Guinness, the Four Per Cent (*see* entry No. 29 Stepney Green Court) and Peabody (*see* entry No. 20, The Cloisters) with dwellings on similar sized sites also housed more people. A close-knit community developed with many Irish and Jewish residents. The properties were refurbished in the 1970s and the gardens remain well maintained. At first glance, nothing seems to have changed at all. However, the Bengali signage for Victoria and Albert Cottages and Tannery House, a nearby warehouse transformed into luxury apartments, indicate the new demographics of the area.

Above: Victoria Cottages.

Below: Victoria Cottages' original doors.

On Woodseer Street, at the junction with Deal Street, several blocks are named after people associated with the neighbourhood, including Vollasky House, built in 1955 and named after Alderman Abraham Vollasky, who was killed at Hughes Mansions in 1945 (*see* entry No. 37)

Address: Deal Street, London, E1 5AJ
Built: 1858 (Victoria), 1865 (Albert)
Listed status: Grade II
Public access: None
Tube: Whitechapel

18. The Dispensary (previously the Eastern Dispensary)

Emerging from Aldgate East tube station for the first time, it is difficult to imagine the rapid changes that are currently transforming the area known as Goodmans Fields. Just a couple of years ago, Second World War bombsites were still being used as car parks and unappealing post-war office blocks lined the main road. Seemingly overnight, high-rise blocks of flats soared into the sky with prices that reflect the proximity of the City.

At the top end of Leman Street on the corner of Alie Street, a gleaming white Italianate building stands out amongst this steel and glass. Built in 1858, it proclaims itself proudly in relief on the parapet as the 'Eastern Dispensary' with 'Supported by Voluntary Contributions' either side of the ornate entrance porch.

Prior to the National Health Service being established in 1948, healthcare provision was not free. Prescriptions, doctors' visits and surgery were all fee-based and those unable to

Eastern Dispensary.

pay relied on charitable foundations, medical missions, benevolent GPs and dispensaries. Public dispensaries provided the medicines free of charge and provident dispensaries were run on a self-help basis via regular subscriptions.

The London Dispensary, later the London Hospital (*see* entry No. 11) was one of the first, followed by The Eastern Dispensary. Founded in 1782 by City doctors in the City, it was originally located on Great Alie Street. Relocating to Leman Street in 1858, it moved into a purpose-built building designed by G. H Simmonds, a local surveyor and secretary to the dispensary. In 1898, it became a branch dispensary to the Metropolitan Provident Medical Association, an organisation formed in 1881 to administer and increase the number of self-supporting dispensaries throughout London.

Remaining as a dispensary until the Second World War, it was leased after the war to various charities before falling into disuse and becoming derelict. To protect it from being sold for redevelopment, it was listed by English Heritage and sold only when the new owner would ensure refurbishment.

In 1997–98 it was restored and reopened as a pub with a mezzanine gallery overlooking the former consulting room. Further refurbishment in 2013–14 has enhanced the period features and the dispensary continues as an award-winning dining establishment.

Address: No. 19a Leman Street, London, E1 8EN
Built: 1858
Listed status: Grade II
Public access: Yes
Tube: Aldgate East
Website: thedispensarylondon.co.uk

19. Wilton's: The Mahogany Mission

One of the oldest and most complete music halls to survive, Wilton's was originally built as the Prince of Denmark pub, later known as the Mahogany Bar because of its wooden counters.

John Wilton opened the music hall at the back of the bar in 1859. The entrance, still used today, was within a row of five terraced houses that Wilton converted. Holding up to 1,500 people, the music hall attracted the famous names of the day, who often performed here late in the evening once they had finished earlier performances in the West End. A vast 'sun burner' chandelier with 300 gas jets lit up the auditorium.

After several name changes and a fire in 1878, Wilton's became a Methodist Mission in 1888, nicknamed the Mahogany Mission. Later it served as a medical centre during the Battle of Cable Street (*see* entry No. 45), then became a tailoring warehouse. In the 1960s, a slum clearance initiative to make way for new housing estates meant that Wilton's was scheduled for demolition. It was saved from this fate by becoming a listed building in 1971.

After a long period of restoration that was completed in 2015, the dusty wreck has been completely transformed thanks to Wilton's Music Hall Trust, who took over the building in 2004 and brought in generous private donations when lottery funding was refused.

Today, Wilton's includes facilities such as dressing rooms and rehearsal spaces while exposed timber and brickwork cleverly retains the ramshackle and distressed atmosphere. The interior has remained a perfect example of a classic music hall with its proscenium

Wilton's Music Hall.

stage, apse and twisted 'barley sugar' pillars supporting the gallery on three sides. Complete with the original mahogany bar, Wilton's is once again alive with theatre, song and dance.

Address: No. 1 Graces Alley, London, E1 8JB
Built: 1859, 2015
Listed status: Grade II*
Public access: Events and tours by arrangement
Tube/Overground: Shadwell
Website: wiltons.org.uk

2c. The Cloisters (previously Peabody Buildings)

This block of flats at the junction of Commercial Street and Folgate Street, built in 1864 was the first Peabody housing estate in London.

The estates are named after George Peabody, a successful American businessman. Arriving in London in 1837, he commemorated his 'silver jubilee' in 1862, endowing a trust of £150,000 to build affordable housing for the industrious classes. By 1890, these funds had created housing for 5,000 people.

This first Peabody block had shops incorporated at ground level. The flats, with affordable rents, varied in size but all used shared toilets, communal baths and laundry facilities. A superintendent lived on the premises. Peabody's architect was Henry Darbishire, who had already designed Columbia Market in Bethnal Green for Angela Burdett Coutts.

The Cloisters, Spitalfields.

Later Peabody estates were constructed according to a similar rapid building system. Many were larger in area, some had separate bath houses and not all included shops. Blocks were never named, merely allocated a letter such as A or B. Many of the estates still stand today. Built in areas of great poverty at the time, the sites are now in expensive inner London neighbourhoods such as Clerkenwell, Covent Garden and Borough. All flats are now self-contained with bathrooms and toilets and most remain rental properties.

Peabody had the honour of having his statue unveiled in his lifetime. You can find him sitting on a large armchair behind the Royal Exchange in the City of London. When he died in 1869, he was honoured with a burial in Westminster Abbey. However, he had requested to be buried in his birthplace, Danvers, Massachusetts. This was duly arranged and the town's name changed to Peabody.

Subsequent philanthropists, such as Edward Guinness, Samuel Lewis, Lord Rothschild (*see* entry No. 29 Stepney Green Court) and Samuel Barnett (*see* entry No. 24 Toynbee Hall) emulated Peabody but their blocks were often considered more aesthetically pleasing.

Today, the Commercial Street building is no longer Peabody accomodation but a private residential block. However, Peabody housing, with over 150 years of experience, remains key to the provision of affordable housing in Whitechapel and in London as a whole, with responsibility for 27,000 homes and 80,000 residents.

Address: The Cloisters, No. 145 Commercial Street, London, E1 6EB
Built: 1864
Public access: None
Tube/Overground: Liverpool Street, Shoreditch High Street

Lilian Knowles House, Crispin Street.

21. Convent of Mercy and the Providence Row Night Refuge and Home

Sandwiched between the newly refurbished Spitalfields Market, and the tall shiny Nido tower block of student accommodation on Bell Lane, stands the imposing façade of Lilian Knowles House. It is named after a 1920s London School of Economics (LSE) economic history professor and since 2006 has been accommodation for LSE students.

The name plaque is very discreet but passers-by might notice the statue of the Virgin Mary above the main entrance and the inscriptions 'Men' and 'Women' above what were entrances on the side and on the main façade respectively.

This was once the Providence Row Night Refuge and Home. In 1858, Father Daniel Gilbert invited four Sisters of Mercy from Wexford in Ireland to establish the Convent of Mercy in Finsbury Square and, in December 1860, they opened a night shelter for the homeless poor in a former stable block off Finsbury Square leading to an alley called Providence Row, hence the name. This was London's first non-sectarian night shelter, with initial accommodation for fourteen women. Demand increased and, with over 14,000 meals having being served by 1862, larger premises were soon required. In 1868, they moved to this purpose-built convent and refuge on Crispin Street, in one of the poorest and most deprived areas of East London. It provided an alternative to the dreaded workhouse where families were split up and the work in lieu of accommodation was arduous and humiliating.

Providence Row included a home for trainee servant girls, a boarders' home for young women and a soup kitchen, while the Sisters ran a school, St Joseph's, next door. By 1939, the charity ran five refuges. Many people who were given shelter, food and education during the post-war years remember the Sisters with great affection. Some were still children, runaways to London or those bombed out of their homes.

Traders at Spitalfields Market (*see* entry No. 23) remember queues for soup and bread at lunchtime remaining well into the 1980s. In 1988, the work of the Sisters was split between Providence Row Charity and Providence Row Housing Association (PRHA) and in 1994 the Dellow Centre was opened on Wentworth Street. This new purpose-built centre houses both the charity's daytime services for homeless people and a hostel managed by PRHA.

Providence Row – Dellow Day, Wentworth Street.

Today the charity assists over 1,000 people each year. Following the relocation, the night refuge and the convent were redeveloped, retaining the façades plus a section of free-standing brick work from Purcell House, seen at the back on Artillery Lane behind the new block of student accommodation.

Memories of the refuge resonate around the world. In 1997, Sister Wright from Australia was visiting London and she asked if the chapel windows with the Mercy Crest could be saved and transferred to Mercedes College in Perth. Finally, in 2012 they were installed.

Address: No. 50 Crispin Street, London, E1 6HQ
Built: 1866, 2013
Public access: None
Tube: Aldgate East, Liverpool Street

22. Trinity Hall (previously Buck's Row Board School)

Buck's Row Board School was one of many schools built in London following the pioneering 1870 Education Act, which established 2,500 school boards to provide elementary education for children between five and thirteen years old. The London School Board (LSB) built its first schools in East London where the need was greatest. The red-brick architecture was always instantly recognisable and tablets in relief would record the year of opening and the name of the school, more often than not, the same as the street.

Built in 1876, this school is a fine square building with brick and stonework details delineating each floor. The large windows are almost full length from floor to ceiling and the flat roof is topped by fine iron-work railings. The school itself does not occupy any additional land than its footprint and the roof formed an open-air area for the pupils, hence the height of the barrier.

Inspection reports show the school improved significantly over its lifetime and, like the more recent Swanlea School (*see* entry No. 47), reached high levels of attainment despite the disadvantaged background of its students.

The school sits on a piece of land created by the construction of the District Line to the south and the East London Line (now Overground) to the east. The construction of these two railways greatly affected the operation of the school and likely contributed to its demise. By 1908, the buildings were already deteriorating and by the 1920s it had closed.

Subsequently used as a factory, it managed to survive the Blitz. However, by the 1980s, when the famed British photographer Don McCullin made Whitechapel a subject of his work, it was derelict and occupied by the homeless.

Now known as Trinity Hall, the building has been entirely refurbished and transformed into private apartments, many with double-height ceilings compared to the original classrooms. Echoing events of almost 120 years previously, the building is now almost entirely hidden from view by the construction of the Crossrail interchange at Whitechapel. The photograph here dates from 2010, just before building works commenced.

The renaming of Buck's Row in 1892 was the result of the association with the notorious events known as the Whitechapel Murders. The first victim, Mary Anne Nichols, was discovered in the early hours of 31 August 1888 at roughly the spot marked by the end of the brick wall in the photograph. However, the school retained its name, the Buck's Row Board School, until it closed.

Address: Durward Street, London, E1 5BA
Built: 1876
Public access: None
Tube: Whitechapel

Left: Buck's Row Board School – Whitechapel 1990. *Right*: Trinity Hall – Whitechapel 2011.

23. Spitalfields Market

Spitalfields Market was established in 1638 for John Balch to sell 'flesh, fowl and roots'. Granted a royal charter by Charles II in 1682 it became one of London's two premier wholesale fruit, vegetable and flower markets, together with Covent Garden in the West End.

Robert Horner, a market porter, acquired the market in the 1870s, rebuilt it and his charming gabled red-brick building, decorated with green paintwork, was completed in 1893. Following sale to the LCC, a low-level extension was added in 1926.

Opposite Spitalfields Market on Brushfield Street, an auction house, the Fruit Exchange, arrived in 1928, joined by the Wool Exchange in 1963. Paper bag vendors, secondary wholesalers and other ancillary services filled the adjoining streets but, by the late twentieth century, the narrow streets proved unsuitable for ever-larger road vehicles. In 1991, the market relocated to Leyton and was renamed New Spitalfields Market.

Once the original market had left, development of the Spitalfields site was the subject of some contention. The City of London planned to open new LIFFE offices there but changed its mind. Archaeological digs further delayed development. Meanwhile, ad-hoc traders started a new market on the site, selling the fruits of their creativity – handmade clothes, jewellery, foodstuffs and stationery. Despite a campaign to save the entire complex, the 1926 extension was demolished. A tall steel and glass office block, designed by Norman Foster, was built for an international law firm. Alongside this, a new glass ceiling allows for all-weather trading. Visitors to this new public space, Bishop's Square, are greeted by 'I Goat', a white painted aluminium goat standing on top of concrete packing cases.

The Horner Buildings, being listed, were never under threat despite the evocatively named campaign, SMUT (Spitalfields Market Under Threat). They have been sympathetically restored with new public gateways. Each is named after an historical association with the area. For example, Montagu because of the nineteenth-century Whitechapel MP; Huguenot because of the French refugees who settled in the area; and Spitfire for the plane market traders sponsored during the Second World War.

Spitalfields Market. *Inset*: Horner Buildings' plaque.

The interior of old Spitalfields Market.

Christ Church Spitalfields once again overlooks a thriving market but now seven days a week. At the time of writing, the fruit and wool exchange has just been demolished to be replaced by a new office block but the front façade has been saved retaining much of the original streetscape.

Address: Brushfield Street, London, E1 6EW
Built: 1883, 2001–05
Listed status: Grade II*
Public access: Yes
Tube: Aldgate East, Liverpool Street
Website: spitalfields.co.uk

24. Toynbee Hall: Britain's First University Settlement

Toynbee Hall was established as a centre of social reform to provide social services and education to the poverty-stricken population of Whitechapel.

The initiative of Samuel and Henrietta Barnett, Toynbee Hall was named after Arnold Toynbee, a noted Oxford historian who died young, a year before it opened in 1884.

Designed by architect Elijah Hoole, his original Arts and Crafts Hall still stands. The tree of life motif by designer C. R. Ashbee can be seen at each of the three entrances and in different styles, from original wooden relief to contemporary signage. Toynbee Studios opened in 2007 and provides theatre and music facilities within original buildings. Blitz damage means that the site of the original Toynbee Hall now features some post-war construction. Two post-war blocks, Profumo and Attlee Houses, are due to be demolished as part of the current redevelopment. A colourful glass community centre has been built as temporary accommodation until June 2017 in advance of new mixed-use spaces opening.

From 1873, Samuel Barnett was vicar at St Jude's Church and he and his wife organised English, art and dressmaking courses in the vicarage. When the classes outgrew this space, they launched the construction of Toynbee Hall.

Toynbee Hall did not just provide opportunities for education but also offered a variety of services to help the poor, including free legal aid, funds for country holidays and a toy library. In addition, Oxford University students lived on-site as social workers. Thus, it became known as a settlement. Attlee House was named after one of these students, Clement Atlee, MP for Limehouse for nearly thirty years and Prime Minister from 1945 to 1951.

The local Jewish community used the Toynbee Hall facilities extensively, including the world's first Jewish Scout troop who donated the small clock tower as a 'thank you'. Also, between 1937 and 2011, the Friends of Yiddish met here every Saturday afternoon. During the Second World War, Toynbee Hall served as a distribution depot for fresh food and unsold clothes, donated by local market traders. A blue plaque commemorates the much-loved Jimmy Mallon, warden at Toynbee Hall between 1919 and 1954. Toynbee Hall was one of many Barnett initiatives in this area. Others include the East End Dwellings Company to build affordable housing for the working poor (1883), Whitechapel Library (1892) (*see* entry No. 26), and in 1902, the Whitechapel Art Gallery (*see* entry No. 32). With Canon Barnett School and Barnett House in a nearby housing estate, the name continues to resonate into the twenty-first century.

Address: No. 28 Commercial Street, London, E1 6LS
Built: 1884, 1970s, 2007
Listed status: Grade II
Public access: Yes
Tube: Aldgate East
Website: toynbeehall.org.uk

25. Working Lads' Institute

Following the London 2012 Olympic Games, there has been a considerable refurbishment programme along the Whitechapel Road. A welcome by-product has been the re-emergence of reliefs on the façades, dating back to the late nineteenth century, many not seen for decades.

Rounded lintels above the shops towards Brady Street have been restored with the short reappearance of names from previous Jewish traders, such as Bressloff the boot maker, while the current shops sell produce for the new Bengali community.

Next to the entrance to Whitechapel tube, newly restored words 'Working Lads' Institute' and 'Lecture Hall' are visible above the doorway and, at first-floor level, 'Gymnasium' and 'Swimming Bath'. This tall majestic red-brick building with white facings, was built in 1885 as purpose-built premises for the Working Lads' Institute, which had been established in 1878 at Mount Place, Whitechapel by City merchant, Henry Hill. This new premises was soon extended in 1886–88, adding a lecture hall and swimming baths.

Above: Toynbee Hall.

Below: Toynbee Hall, new offices on Resolution Plaza. *Inset*: Tree of life motifs.

Left: Working Lads' Institute. *Right*: Lecture Theatre signage.

The institute provided a place of education and refuge, protecting young lads from music halls, pubs and a potential life of crime. Running short of resources, Hill sent a letter to *The Christian* pleading for funds. Revd Thomas Jackson, who had wanted to return to Whitechapel, funded the extension of facilities to homeless and friendless boys, providing beds, clothes and employment in addition to the library and classes.

In 1888, the autopsies for two victims of the Whitechapel Murderer, Mary Ann (Polly) Nichols and Annie Chapman took place at the Institute. Additional signage by 1905 proclaimed Primitive Methodist Mission and Home for Friendless and Orphan Lads. In 1943, the mission relocated to Tulse Hill where it remained until the 1970s.

The building has been converted into apartments and the work of the institute is being continued by the Whitechapel Mission, alongside the Royal London Hospital across the road.

Address: Nos 279/281, Whitechapel Road, London, E1 1BY
Built: 1885, extended 1886/88
Public access: None
Tube: Whitechapel

26. Whitechapel Library: The University of the Ghetto

Opened in 1892, the Whitechapel Library was another initiative of Samuel and Henrietta Barnett. Just around the corner from Toynbee Hall (No. 24), it provided a space for reading and study for the local residents who generally lived in crowded homes. Designed by Potts, Son and Hennings, it was one of several East London libraries funded by Passmore Edwards, hence the name on the front.

Whitechapel Library. *Inset*: Cherubs, Art and Literature.

The Jewish community was the predominant user of Whitechapel Library from the time of its opening until the demise of the Jewish East End in the mid-twentieth century. The reading room became one of East London's liveliest spaces. It was there that schoolchildren did their homework and their Yiddish-speaking parents and grandparents discussed politics. Many of the artists, poets and thinkers who met there became world famous names – Jacob Bronowski, David Bomberg, Mark Gertler and Sir Arnold Wesker.

Another, Isaac Rosenberg, has his memory honoured by a blue plaque. An artist and poet killed in action during the First World War, he is one of fourteen poets from this time commemorated at Westminster Abbey due to his highly regarded *Poems From The Trenches*. His art is found in several collections, including Tate Britain and Ben Uri Gallery.

By the 1930s, Whitechapel library had the largest library collection of Yiddish material in the country. By 2005 when the library closed, Bengali, Gujarati and Somali collections also featured strongly.

The library was replaced by the Whitechapel Idea Store (*see* entry No. 49), and incorporated into the Whitechapel Art Gallery next door (*see* entry No. 32). In 2009, as part of the refurbishment, a weather vane was erected at the top of the library. Made of copper and steel, it depicts its artist Rodney Graham as the sixteenth-century scholar Desiderius Erasmus, riding backwards on a horse, reading a copy of Erasmus's own *The Praise Of Folly*.

A small display inside evokes memories of the past. Writer Bernard Kops, with his poem *Whitechapel Library, Aldgate East*, composed at the time of closure, captures the spirit perfectly. It ends:

> The reference library, where my thoughts were to rage.
> I ate book after book, page after page.
> I scoffed poetry for breakfast and novels for tea.
> And plays for my supper. No more poverty.
> Welcome young poet, in here you are free
> to follow your star to where you should be.
>
> That door of the library was the door into me
>
> And Lorca and Shelley said 'Come to the feast.'
> Whitechapel Library, Aldgate East.

(Courtesy of Bernard Kops.)

Address: Nos 77–82 Whitechapel High Street, London, E1 7QX
Built: 1892
Listed status: Grade II
Public Access: Yes
Tube: Aldgate East
Website: whitechapelgallery.org

27. The Blind Beggar

Positioned on the site of a seventeenth-century inn, where the Whitechapel Road changes name to the Mile End Road, The Blind Beggar public house is a stone's throw from where the toll gate stood before its removal in 1866.

Opened in 1894, this is a typical Victorian pub built in Queen Anne style with red brick, white facings and Dutch gables on the skyline. If the design looks similar to many other pubs, few are linked to such fascinating stories.

The hanging pub sign picture links to the story behind the name. In Bethnal Green, legend has it that Bessy, the daughter of the beggar in the ballad *The Blind Beggar of Bednall Green*, had four suitors but only one was prepared to ask her poor father for permission to marry her. When consent was given, a surprising dowry of £3,000 was provided. He was not a beggar at all but Sir Simon de Montfort's son Henry, who had been blinded in 1265 at the Battle of Evesham. On becoming a borough in 1900, Bethnal Green incorporated the beggar into its coat of arms and a Bessy Street is nearby.

Blind Beggar
public house.

Vallance Road, childhood home of gangsters the Kray twins, Reggie and Ronnie, is not far away. This area of East London was 'their manor'. On 9 March 1966, Ronnie entered the pub and shot dead George Cornell, a member of the rival Richardson gang from South London who, he had been told, was there quietly having a drink. It was this crime that sealed the fate of the Kray twins as they were arrested soon after and, in 1969, jailed for life.

Despite its past criminal associations, the pub is known as family friendly with a large garden, complete with a koi pond and remains a popular eating and drinking venue.

Address: No. 337 Whitechapel Road, London, E1 1BU
Built: 1894
Public access: Yes
Tube: Whitechapel
Website: theblindbeggar.com

28. Bishopsgate Institute: The Battle of the Petticoats

Overshadowed by the vast Broadgate complex and straddling the boundary of the City of London and Tower Hamlets, stands the Bishopsgate Institute, testimony to the educational needs of past and present East End populations.

Designed by architect Charles Harrison Townsend and opened by Lord Rosebery in 1895, the exterior contains both Arts and Crafts and art deco styles with Townsend's trademark pepper-pot towers and rounded arch entrance, similar to his later work on Whitechapel Art Gallery (*see* entry No. 32). The terracotta frontage includes Byzantine and Romanesque design, together with a tree of life motif that incorporates the words 'Bishopsgate Institute'. The ornate gates are replicas of the bronze originals, which had to be relinquished as part of the Second World War effort.

Bishopsgate Institute was funded by charitable work undertaken in the parish of St Botolph's Bishopsgate between 1481 and 1862. The parish had become well-endowed with local but small charities that provided services such as penny loaves for the poor, love feasts for warring businessmen and flannel petticoats for needy women. In 1891, it was decided that the funds could benefit the public more by amalgamating them. Bishopsgate Institute was the result, established 'to promote lectures, exhibitions and otherwise the advancement of literature, science and fine arts' and led by local rector William Rogers.

The institute included a great hall, holding up to 500 people, and reference and lending libraries. The first-floor reading room tables seated up to 250 readers. Separate entrances for men and women ensured strict segregation. As the first public library in the City of London, there was great demand for readers' tickets, with over 4,500 applications on the first day. However, many people were angry that petticoats had been replaced by books! In addition, the institute held lectures and adult education classes, both of which continue to this day.

Expansion of the book collection necessitated an extension, built in 1911. The library, now reference only, has continued to grow and includes a unique collection relating to London history plus special collections and archives relating to protest, campaigning and LGBTQ history.

Substantial renovation in 1994 incorporated an eighteenth-century house on Brushfield Street. Later, in 1997, the library was restored, including Townsend's original colour scheme. Heritage Lottery Fund financed a transformation between 2009 and 2011, including a new

Bishopsgate Institute.

entrance and glass-fronted café. Both on Brushfield Street, they provide direct access to the regenerated Spitalfields Market area.

Address: No. 230 Bishopsgate, London, EC2M 4QH
Built: 1895, 1994, 2009–11
Listed status: Grade II*
Public access: Yes
Tube: Liverpool Street
Website: bishopsgate.org.uk

29. Stepney Green Court

At the eastern end of Stepney Green Gardens, three red-brick housing blocks with white stone decorative reliefs stand as the oldest-surviving examples of housing built under the auspices of the Four Per Cent Industrial Dwellings Society. Founded by the first Lord Rothschild in 1885, the Four Per Cent has been known since 1951 as the Industrial Dwellings Society (IDS).

By the 1870s, the Jewish community was well consolidated, providing support and charity in the form of schools, hospitals, newspapers and lobbying groups. In the 1850s, the first official Jewish Lord Mayor and Jewish MPs were elected. In the early 1880s, a new wave of Jewish immigrants arrived, fleeing persecution in Russia and Poland and putting strain on accommodation in the already crowded area of Whitechapel.

By then, Lord Rothschild had already begun raising funds for affordable housing for the Jewish industrious poor. Named after the 4 per cent return on investment, the first block, built in 1887 near Brick Lane, was named Charlotte de Rothschild Dwellings, honouring his mother. Other Four Per Cent blocks followed quickly, on Brady Street in 1888 and on Wentworth Street in 1892. Designed by N. S. Joseph (*see* entry No. 13 Sandys Row Synagogue), Stepney Green Dwellings were different in that the exterior was more ornate and the apartments were self-contained with toilets, sculleries and constant hot water. By 1901, 4,600 people in London were housed by the Four Per Cent. Building continued, most notably in 1905 outside the East End with Navarino Mansions at Dalston, encouraging earlier Jewish immigrants to migrate northwards, relieving the overcrowded Whitechapel for the new arrivals.

Stepney Green became a microcosm of the Jewish East End. In addition to the Dwellings, there was also an Orthodox synagogue (now the Rosalind Green Hall), the London Jewish Hospital (site now 1990s housing), a Jewish old age home at No. 37 Stepney Green (*see* entry No. 4) and Stepney Jewish School (now studios and flats). Established in 1865 and rebuilt in 1906, the school gate with a curly 'SJS' survives, as does the ornate relief with 1906 in the pediment. One by one, these facilities closed and today only Stepney Green Dwellings retain their original use. Substantial renovation in 1983 closed up the open stairwells, installed lifts, updated the kitchens, carpeted the hallways and gave each flat self-controlled central heating. The original 170 were reduced to 120 but they are still administered by the IDS as Stepney Green Court.

Address: Stepney Green Gardens, London, E1 3LJ
Built: 1896
Public access: None
Tube: Stepney Green
Website: ids.org.uk

Stepney Green Court, looking towards Canary Wharf.

Stepney Green Court.

30. Soup Kitchen for the Jewish Poor

Brune Street is home to one of the most photogenic buildings in Spitalfields – the Soup Kitchen for the Jewish Poor. With a honey-coloured terracotta frontage at ground-floor level, an ornate curly font proclaiming the name and a large tureen of soup above the doorway, this building provided a warm and inviting welcome to those without means to feed themselves.

The charity providing the soup and sustenance was founded in 1854 by wealthy members of the Anglo-Jewish community. First located at Leman Street not far from the docks, it moved to Black Lion Yard off Whitechapel Road and later relocated to Fashion Street (*see* entry No. 33). In 1902, it moved to its first purpose-built site on Butler Street, which was renamed Brune Street in 1937 to commemorate Rose and Walter Brune. They founded the Priory of St Mary Spital in 1197, hence the area being known as Spitalfields.

Designed by Lewis Solomon, the building incorporated milk and meat kitchens, reflecting Jewish dietary laws, a queuing room inside the entrance, a shop and a committee room. Until the 1930s, the main activity was providing soup to be eaten on the premises or taken away in containers for consuming at home, but after the Second World War the premises became more of a food distribution depot. Those in need and known to the charity would be allocated coupons for bread and foodstuffs to be collected at Brune Street. Income to maintain the relief was sourced through appeals to the Jewish community, plus renting out

Soup Kitchen for the Jewish Poor.

the floors above the kitchen as workshops for the tailoring trade and a local girls' youth club. At Passover, special funds were raised to provide matzah for the needy.

In the 1950s, there were still 1,500 regular clients, but by the 1980s the Jewish community had dwindled to such an extent the kitchen was nearly redundant, with only 100 or so elderly people requiring meals.

The building was listed in 1989, vacated in 1991 and the charity's activities merged with those at the Jewish Care day centre in Beaumont Grove, Stepney Green, where there remains today an affordable kosher café. Behind the fascia, the soup kitchen was sympathetically converted by Duncan Thomas in 1997 to mixed-use with apartments and offices.

> Above the doorway are two dates: '5662' and '1902' – one the Hebrew year and the other, the secular. A quick way to convert a Hebrew year is this: remove the 5 and add 1240 to the remaining three digits. It works the other way around too.

Address: Brune Street, London, E1 7NB
Built: 1902, 1997
Listed status: Grade II
Public access: None
Tube: Aldgate East, Liverpool Street

31. Tower House: The Monster Dosshouse

Fieldgate Street is a quiet narrow thoroughfare parallel to Whitechapel Road which, despite a recent and rapid transformation with restaurants, ice-cream parlours and the expansion of the East London Mosque (*see* entry No. 46), remains dominated by the red-brick bulk of Tower House.

Built in 1902, Tower House was once a hostel for itinerant workers. It was funded by a substantial legacy left by Montagu Corry, Lord Rowton, private secretary to Benjamin Disraeli, the famous Victorian Prime Minister. Altogether, six hostels were built, the first in Vauxhall in 1892, followed by King's Cross, 1894, Newington Butts and Hammersmith, both 1897, Tower House in Whitechapel, 1902, and lastly, Arlington House in Camden Town, 1905. Only Arlington and Tower Houses remain.

Most of the Tower House residents were homeless, alcoholics or those the Salvation Army would not admit to their hostel. Equipped with more than 800 beds, the hostel charged a 6*d* entrance fee, later a shilling, which included shelter, a bath and clean clothes. Residents had to abide by several rules, including no cards, no cooking and no admittance before 7 p.m.

Well-known residents include Jack London, a journalist stranded in London in 1902. He lived among the homeless before publishing his experiences as *The People of the Abyss* in which he described Tower House as 'The Monster Doss House'. George Orwell stayed here in 1933 researching his book *Down and Out in Paris and London*. In 1907, London hosted the Fifth Congress of the Russian Social Democratic and Labour Party, and Stalin, Trotsky and Lenin were all in the area. Stalin, then Joseph Djugashvili, spent two weeks here before finding long-term digs nearby in Jubilee Street.

Having lain derelict for decades, Tower House was renovated in the mid-2000s to become a complex of rented upmarket apartments, complete with penthouses and underground parking facilities.

Address: No. 81, Fieldgate Street, London, E1 1GW
Built: 1902, 2005
Public access: None
Tube: Aldgate East, Whitechapel

32. Whitechapel Art Gallery

Built in 1897–98 and opened in 1901, the Whitechapel Art Gallery was designed in art nouveau style by Charles Harrison Townsend, the architect for the Bishopsgate Institute (*see* entry No. 28) where you also see Townsend's distinctive 'pepper pot' towers.

The doorway is off-centre and opens directly onto the street and the semicircular lunette window above brought light into the foyer. Surrounded by a large rounded arch, these elements provided an inviting entrance for the local community and a contrast to the small, dark entrance to the tube station alongside.

The Whitechapel Library (*see* entry No. 26) already stood next door. Following its closure in 2005, it was incorporated into the gallery in 2009, doubling the exhibition space. Aiming to 'bring the finest art in the world to the people of the East End', it was an initiative by Samuel and Henrietta Barnett who, from 1881, held exhibitions with art on loan from

Tower House.

national collections at the schoolhouse on Commercial Street. It was the first space built to offer temporary exhibitions to a mass audience and the first, 'Spring Picture Exhibition' with art by Constable and Hogarth brought 206,000 visitors in six weeks. Such popularity necessitated a purpose-built gallery and Passmore Edwards, having financed the library, once again provided substantial funding.

Sunday afternoon opening catered for the local Jewish community and a group of Jewish artists including David Bomberg and Mark Gertler became known as the Whitechapel Boys.

Other early exhibitions included Chinese Art, Scottish Art and Sporting Pictures and many contemporary modern artists such as Lucien Freud, Andy Warhol and Jackson Pollock saw their first British exhibitions at Whitechapel. In January 1938, Picasso allowed his anti-war painting *Guernica* to be shown in the UK, the first time it was seen outside of Spain. After being exhibited in cities such as Manchester, it arrived at the Whitechapel Gallery in January 1939.

For over 100 years, the façade between the towers remained plain as the original planned mosaic by Walter Crane was considered too big and too costly. In 2012, the empty space was finally filled with an eye-catching sculpture by British artist Rachel Whiteread. Depicting a golden tree of life, the leaves mirror both the emblem of nearby Toynbee Hall (*see* entry No. 24) and the Arts and Crafts decoration on the gallery towers.

Address: Nos 77–82 Whitechapel High Street, London, E1 7QX
Built: 1898–99, 2005m 2009
Listed status: Grade II*
Public access: Yes
Tube: Aldgate East
Website: whitechapelgallery.org

33. Fashion Street: The Moorish Bazaar

By the end of the nineteenth century, London's street markets were well established but those in the East End were among the busiest, noisiest and most cosmopolitan. Brick Lane, Petticoat Lane and Wentworth, Leyden and Cobb Streets created an extensive network in and around Brick Lane. Whitechapel Waste, opposite the London Hospital (*see* entry No. 11), was another vibrant marketplace. When it rained, everyone got wet. When it was cold, everyone shivered. But, the atmosphere was inviting and people came to buy clothes, ribbons, fish, pickles and delicacies. Abraham Davis, a member of a large property developing family who built cinemas and social housing, decided to build an indoor shopping area, so the market traders could be warm and dry. The eastern side of Fashion Street, linking Commercial Street to Brick Lane, was transformed into 244 booths for rent behind an elaborate frontage of Moorish design in red brick. However, the stallholders baulked at paying the rents required and remained in their street markets. Abraham managed to avoid bankruptcy and in 1909 the building, nicknamed 'The Moorish Bazaar', reverted to wholesale trade dominated by Jewish tailoring and fur businesses and later Bengali leather traders. This continued until the early 2000s.

The street has other associations with the Jewish community. It housed the third Soup Kitchen for the Jewish Poor (*see* entry No. 30) and was the childhood home of Israel Zangwill, the writer known as the 'Jewish Dickens'. In his 1892 book, *Children of the Ghetto*, he described the street as 'a dull, narrow, squalid thoroughfare' and wrote

Whitechapel Gallery.

evocatively about the soup kitchen. Decades later, playwright and author Sir Arnold Wesker lived here as a boy. His famous play, *Chicken Soup with Barley*, opens with a scene linked to the Battle of Cable Street (*see* entry No. 45).

The façade was listed by English Heritage in 1973 and restored with substantial rebuilding behind by Buckley Gray Yeoman in 2011. At time of writing new, residents include Glasgow Caledonian University but signs for a leather business and 'Works Office' are vestiges of the past activity.

Address: Nos 10/48 Fashion Street, London, E1 6PX
Built: 1905, 2011
Listed status: Grade II
Public access: None
Tube: Aldgate East

34. Congregation of Jacob

As traffic hurtles down the Commercial Road, almost every building seems to be a wholesale clothing business. However, near the junction of Jubilee Street, you can see a Star of David above the skyline with the words 'Congregation of Jacob' in relief below.

This synagogue for a community, founded in 1903 and now one of just four remaining in the East End, when once there were over sixty-five. Between 1881 and 1914, over

Left: 'The Moorish Bazaar'. Right: Works Office.

100,000 Jewish immigrant arrived in London from eastern Europe and they mostly lived in London. They established a proliferation of chevrot (small congregations based on Friendly Societies), providing facilities for charity and prayer. This community first worshipped in family homes and acquired the current premises in 1921. The building had previously been used as a shoe repairer and was remodelled by Lewis Solomon, a Jewish architect attached to the Federation of Synagogues who also designed the Jewish Soup Kitchen (*see* entry No. 30) and Stoke Newington Synagogue in Dalston.

The building is reminiscent of Eastern European synagogue design and the interior includes folk-art-style painted panels depicting the seven-branched menorah, the Four Species – palm, etrog, willow and myrtle – seven species of Israeli fruit and grain and musical instruments. They were most likely added in the 1950s by artist Philip Steinberg, a synagogue member.

Very few Jewish people now live in this part of the East End but there was a time when this synagogue was one of many in this area. Several have been incorporated into this congregation, including Bikur Cholim (Visitors of Sick), Chevra Yisroel (Society of Israel) and the Stetziver Synagogue. Following renovation in 2009, the community is still active, affiliated to the Federation and providing regular services.

Address: Nos 351–353 Commercial Road, London, E1 2PS
Built: 1921
Public access: Open for services and by arrangement
Tube: Limehouse
Website: congregationofjacob.org

35. Wickhams: The Harrods of the East End

The tower of Wickhams has been a local landmark since the late 1920s. A row of small shops and residences were swept aside for the building of the grandest department store in Whitechapel, to be known as 'The Harrods of the East End'. But it is the dip in the building, where the classical-style stonework wraps itself around a low-level structure before rising again, that everyone finds most intriguing.

This small building at No. 81 Mile End Road had been a jeweller since 1880, run by the Speigelhalters – a German Lutheran family who had been trading in Whitechapel since 1828. In 1850, William Wickham opened a drapery store along the same stretch of road and as his business increased he acquired neighbouring shops resulting in a new store expanding to cover the whole block. Reliefs of '1927' still remain on the corner at Cleveland Way. Spiegelhalters would not sell, resulting in the large store being built around it. This prevented the planned symmetry of a centrally positioned tower. The irony of this David versus Goliath retailing battle is that Wickhams closed in 1969 but Spiegelhalters remained until 1988 before relocating to the West Country, where they still trade in Devon and Cornwall.

Spiegelhalters became a kosher wine and spirits outlet, while Wickhams hosted various different retailers. In the mid-2000s, with local gentrification well established, plans suggested removing Spiegelhalters, by then a roofless shell of a building, and converting Wickhams into retail outlets, a mosque and banqueting suite, demolishing No. 81 and thus obliterating its memory. A vocal local campaign prevented this and the current (at time of writing) redevelopment is including a public right of way through the new frontage but with a first storey incorporating the original fascia of Spiegelhalters.

Address: Nos 68/89 Mile End Road, London, E1 5QN
Built: 1927, ongoing in 2015
Public access: For events
Tube: Stepney Green

Wickhams department store. *Inset*: Date relief.

Left: Bernhard Baron House, memorial stone. *Right*: Berners Road Combined Skills School.

36. Oxford and St George's Club and Settlement

Bernhard Baron House in Henriques Street is a solid red-brick building on the site of Berners Street Board School. Disused by 1929, the school was rebuilt into a youth club and settlement and latterly converted into flats. Baron provided the funding for the first transformation when the street was still Berners Street, the name changing in 1963 to honour the man who ran the club – Sir Basil Henriques.

The density of the Jewish East End necessitated several youth clubs for both boys and girls including the Brady Boys and Girls (*see* entry No. 40), Victoria and the Jewish Lads' and Girls' Brigade. In 1914, supported by West London Synagogue, Henriques established a boys' club in Cannon Street Road. Rose Loewe led a first aid class and he asked that she open a girls' club. They subsequently married in 1917 and opened a joint club in 1919 in Betts Street. Renamed the Oxford and St George's Club after Henriques' university and the local parish, the club incorporated a synagogue linked to Reform Judaism and, despite their wealth, the Henriques' lived within the club building.

The club, now much larger, became known as a settlement and the boys and girls who enjoyed the activities and communal spirit fostered by the Henriques' became the equivalent of a large and close-knit family.

With the demise of the Jewish East End numbers, attending dropped significantly and closure was the only option. Sold in 1973, the club relocated to North London and the synagogue moved to the Brady Centre (*see* entry No. 40), moving again in 1976 to its current site, the Jewish Care Day Centre in Beaumont Grove. Bernhard Baron House reopened in 1980 as apartments.

In 2014, the Troxy (*see* entry No. 38) hosted a centenary club reunion and over 700 past members attended from around the world. A true testimony to the impact of the club and the devotion they had to 'The Gaffer and The Missus', as Sir Basil and Rose were affectionately known. Opposite the settlement was the Berners Street Combined Special School. Built in 1903, reliefs remain as a reminder of the training provided for skills such as cookery and laundry.

Address: No. 71 Henriques Street, London, E1 1LZ
Built: 1929
Public access: None
Tube: Aldgate East, Whitechapel

37. Hughes Mansions

Looking at Hughes Mansions you see two very different styles of architecture. One block fronting Vallance Road was built in 1928 as proclaimed proudly by a plaque at second-floor level. A second block behind dates from the 1950s.

Hughes Mansions was named after Mary Hughes, a local councilor, JP and social worker, who lived across the road. Many of the first residents were Jewish. In the early morning of 27 March 1945, a V2 rocket fell on the flats and 134 people were killed – 120 of them Jewish.

The timing was particularly tragic for the Jewish community as it was the eve of Passover, a festival when families come together and several of the fatalities were only visiting Hughes Mansions. When George VI and Queen Elizabeth visited the East End in May 1945 they visited the devastated area and met survivors. A new block was built after the war.

Mary Hughes is commemorated with a blue plaque at her home, No. 71 Vallance Road, on the corner of Underwood Road. It is a former pub and easily recognisable as such from the double aspect with a corner door. Mary transformed the Earl Grey pub into the Dew Drop Inn, a place for local people to find respite from their overcrowded homes and exhausting manual work. Born into wealth (her father was the author Thomas Hughes), Mary devoted her life to improving working and living conditions, firstly in Berkshire and later in East London, at Bromley by Bow with Muriel and Doris Lester and then in Whitechapel. When Gandhi visited London in 1931, he asked specifically to meet her. She was vegetarian, anti-vivisection, and pro-peace. Local Labour politician George Lansbury said of her: 'Our frail humanity only produces a Mary Hughes once in a century.'

Address: Vallance Road, London, E1 5BJ
Built: 1928, early 1950s
Public access: None
Tube: Whitechapel

Above: Hughes Mansions.
Below: Courtyard, Hughes Mansions.

Dew Drop Inn with blue plaque to Mary Hughes.

38. Troxy: 'Where East is Best'

Built between 1802 and 1806, Commercial Road linked the City with the newly opened West India and East India Docks. Approaching Limehouse on the right-hand side is a vast building with an art deco frontage – the Troxy cinema.

Built on the site of a brewery in 1933, it was designed by George Coles for the Hyams and Gale circuit, run by the brothers Phil, Sid and Mick Hyams who already owned the Trocadero at Elephant & Castle. They would later open the Gaumont State in Kilburn in 1937. Utilising 2.5 million bricks, the side elevations of the Troxy were left plain but the frontage was in faience tiling. It looks the same today with more recent art deco decoration in black and gold.

The interior was very ornate with a black and biscuit marbled floor, sweeping golden onyx staircases and plaster decoration of waterfalls, daisies and sunflowers. With 3,520 seats, it was one of the largest cinemas in the UK at the time. Taken over by Gaumont in 1935, it continued to show films but also hosted live entertainment of the highest calibre. Performers included Vera Lynn and Tommy Steele and the last live performance was by Cliff Richard in 1959. The cinema closed in 1960, remaining empty and unused until 1963.

The London Opera Centre then used it until 1977 as a rehearsal space for the Royal Opera Covent Garden. Mecca Bingo followed and, to protect it from demolition in 1990, the Troxy was listed, remaining a bingo hall until 2006.

Many cinemas closed in the 1960s, including the Hyams's Trocadero, which had the largest Wurlitzer organ in the UK, twice the size of that at the Troxy. When the Trocadero was demolished in 1963, the organ was saved from destruction and in 2004 it was installed at the Troxy.

The Troxy has benefitted from its position at the edge of the revitalised Docklands and a recent refurbishment has brought it back to life as a live entertainment venue with

Troxy Cinema.

banqueting and conference facilities. At last, the publicity quote from the 1930s can be used again - 'Where East is Best!'

Address: No. 490 Commercial Road, London, E1 0HX
Built: 1933, refurbishment 2000s
Public access: For events
Listed status: Grade II
Tube: Limehouse
Website: troxy.co.uk

39. Gwynne House

In a quiet street within the Royal London Hospital estate is one of Whitechapel's most unusual buildings. Surrounded by eighteenth- and nineteenth-century buildings, the modernist Gwynne House appears as though a landlocked ocean liner.

Designed by Hume Victor Kerr in 1934, it consists of twenty-one flats over five storeys, linked by a rounded external staircase on which the name is prominently displayed in a font that is instantly recognisable as art deco. The building has a nautical flavour, with rounded windows in the front doors, reminiscent of portholes in the side of a ship. At ground level, railings separate the building from the street, creating a cottage-style atmosphere; the original white finish of the building survives.

Left: Gwynne House.

Below: Gwynne House.

Owned by the Royal London and eventually the Barts Health NHS Trust, the accommodation was built for trainee doctors and nurses. In 2012, the owners decided to sell the building to private developers, citing that times had changed and medical staff no longer expected or wanted to live in hospital-owned accommodation.

Unusually for an architect, Kerr also had a prolific military career. After lying about his age to fight in the First World War, he went from private to major between 1914 and 1919 and from gunner to colonel between 1939 and 1942.

In between and after the wars, he was prolific as an architect. Also in Turner Street is a factory he designed for M. Levy and in New Road is the imposing Empire House, a warehouse and showroom, sold for redevelopment in 2015. Further north on Middlesex Street, he built Commerce House, which survived until the 1990s when it was demolished. The surviving buildings ensure Hume has definitely left his mark on the area.

Address: Turner Street, E1 2AG
Built: 1934
Public access: None
Tube: Whitechapel

40. Brady Centre

Once a hub of activity for Jewish youth, the Brady Arts Centre is now a local authority venue with education facilities, theatre space, function rooms and workshops for community initiatives. Today the 1930s brick building is decorated with colourful Bengali murals and a contemporary work by Stik, one of London's most famous street artists. However, it is the modest plaques alongside the entrance that tell the story. Designed by Jewish architects Messers Joseph (*see* entry Nos 13 Sandys Row Synagogue and 29. Stepney Green Court), the complex was opened in 1935 by the Duchess of York, wife of the future George VI.

Miriam Moses, mayor of Stepney in 1930, was the driving force behind the establishment of the Brady Centre. It was she who raised the money for the construction of a purpose-built home for the Stepney Girls' Club that she had founded in the 1920s for Jewish girls. After the War, Brady Boys' Club, another Jewish youth movement, shared the premises and, by the 1950s, the centre provided 'cradle to grave' facilities for the Jewish community including a crèche, a settlement with student accommodation and a senior citizens' club. At that time, more than 1,000 people used Brady each week.

During the Second World War, the Brady Centre became a shelter and a refuge and 'Miss Moses', as she was known, lived there. When tragedy struck at Hughes Mansions nearby (*see* entry No. 37), Moses, an ARP warden, was one of the first on the scene assisting rescue efforts.

In 1958, Moses was the subject of *This Is Your Life*, a popular television programme where the subject was reintroduced to people and events linked to their life. Guests included Sir Basil Henriques (*see* entry No. 36 Oxford and St George's Club and Settlement) and stage star, Georgia Brown, an ex-Brady girl.

With the area's rapidly declining Jewish community, the centre was sold in 1976 to Tower Hamlets. Brady continued to operate on just two weekday afternoons and Sundays, later relocating to Edgware, a North-West London suburb with a significant Jewish population.

Address: Nos 192–196 Hanbury Street, London, E1 5HU
Built: 1935
Public access: Yes
Tube: Whitechapel

41. Mayfair Cinema

What remains of the Mayfair cinema nestles at the southern end of Brick Lane in the midst of post-war housing, shops and a few eighteenth-century homes. The original 1930s fascia can still be seen with its black tiling and mint green letters on a cream background, below the roofline, spelling out 'MAYFAIR'.

When cinemas first proliferated in Whitechapel in the late nineteenth century, they were in halls and theatres that were specially converted. Then followed purpose-built cinemas, most notably the Rivoli in 1921. Widespread closures after the Second World War meant that, by 1990, no cinemas remained in the whole of Tower Hamlets. A few cinema buildings, such as the Troxy (*see* entry No. 38) and the Mayfair, survived by changing use to an opera workshop and restaurant respectively. Cinemas returned to the area with the 1999 opening of the Genesis on Mile End Road.

The Mayfair was originally on the site of the Brick Lane Palace Theatre, which was designed by George Coles, the architect of the Troxy. The entrance was on what is now Chicksand Street. It was converted to an independent cinema in 1936, with a new entrance on Brick Lane. It was renamed the Mayfair and the black-tiled façade was added.

Until the late 1950s, the audience was predominantly Jewish, and Yiddish films were frequently shown, including the famous *Yidl with His Fidl* (1937). By 1943, the Mayfair had joined the Odeon chain but it was not renamed until 1950. Later, under the ownership of Rank, it became a fleapit and closed in 1967. However, it soon reopened as the Naz, showing Bollywood films for the growing Bengali community.

In the late 1990s, the Mayfair closed. Following use as a store and indoor car park, the building was demolished with just the fascia saved. The auditorium area became a block of flats, Odeon Court, and the foyer became the Café Naz restaurant which, despite its location, had a largely white clientele. The café was largely destroyed by a nail bomb in 1999 when Brick Lane was one of three London locations targeted by a neo-Nazi terrorist. The café became a popular venue again after rebuilding but has since closed.

At the time of writing, the commercial residents regularly change in advance of planned redevelopment.

Address: Nos 46–48 Brick Lane, London, E1 6RF
Built: 1936, late 1990s
Public access: None
Tube: Aldgate East

Above: Brady Centre.

Below: Foundation plaques, Brady Centre.

'MAYFAIR' signage.

42. Godfrey Phillips

Built in 1935, the Godfrey Phillips factory is a reminder of the once large and prosperous tobacco industry in East London. Officially 'Cambridge House' after the Cambridge Theatre of Varieties that once stood on Commercial Street, it was designed by W. Gilbert Scott and W. H. Scott. The long, cream stone façade still dominates the landscape.

On Jerome Street, a short alleyway within the factory complex, the beautiful gold lettering, Godfrey Phillips Ltd, remains on a black-tiled background as does an industrial chimney behind.

The local Jewish community dominated the tobacco and cigar trade, beginning with the early Dutch Jewish immigrants and later eastern Europeans, who benefitted from the new machinery typically shifting production from cigars to cigarettes and from hand made to machine made products. The most famous was Bernhard Baron who took over Carreras and became a generous benefactor supporting many charities including the Oxford and St George's Settlement (*see* entry No. 36). The company J. Wix & Sons was established in 1901 and began in Buckle Street, Whitechapel and manufactured Kensitas, a brand still around today. Many were smaller concerns such as Zeegen Brothers off Brick Lane in Chicksand Street and Cohen Weenan & Co. in Browns Lane, Spitalfields, both of which had been absorbed into Godfrey Phillips by the 1930s.

Godfrey Phillips was famous for BDV cigarettes, introduced in the early 1900s and likely named after the tobacco from which they were made, Boyd and Dibrell Virginia aka Best Dark Virginia. During the Second World War, the basement shelter here was known as the

Above: Original signage.

Below: Godfrey Phillips factory, now apartments.

BDV. The brand lasted until 1948. This factory also produced rose-tipped Turkish cigarettes, made with real rose petals from roses arriving daily in large boxes directly from the docks.

The company was taken over by Philip Morris in 1968. During the 1990s, the site was converted to a block of apartments and retail outlets.

Address: Nos 112/114, Commercial Street, London, E1 6NF
Built: 1935, 1999
Public access: None
Tube/Overground: Liverpool Street, Shoreditch High Street

43. Fieldgate Street Great Synagogue

The word 'great' seems incongruous when linked to this small, unassuming three-storey building. Over the years, there have been seven synagogues in this narrow street and Fieldgate Street Great Synagogue was the largest of them all – hence the name.

Founded in 1899, amalgamating three existing local synagogues, the memorial stone was laid by Charles Nathaniel Rothschild and the president was Samuel Montagu, both members of the Anglo-Jewish elite of the day. It was badly damaged during the Second World War, so it was rebuilt and reopened in 1959. Post-war, many smaller congregations

Fieldgate Street Great Synagogue.

Left: Fieldgate Street Great Synagogue. *Right*: Fieldgate Synagogue interior.

did not survive and Lubner & Lomzer, Vine Street, Stepney Orthodox, Alie Street, Ezras Chaim, Ain Yacov and Poltava synagogues all closed and merged with Fieldgate Street. Its membership then rose, belying the actual demise of the local Jewish community. While the exterior became somewhat distressed, inside the wood paneling and pews provided a warm welcome to worshippers. Along the ladies' gallery the names on the benefactor boards remained intact complete with their donations.

By the 1990s, the synagogue building was detached and the new dome of the East London Mosque, hovered into view behind. This classic scene captured perfectly the changing demographics and skyline of the area. Care was taken as the mosque expanded to ensure the synagogue was not negatively affected and that light would still illuminate the Star of David on its north-facing window. Regular services ended in 2007. By 2014 it was surrounded on three sides by the mosque, London Muslim Centre and the women's Maryam Centre. The synagogue finally closed in 2015 and was purchased by the mosque. At time of writing, future plans are unknown, but indications are that the interior will be preserved and used for multifaith services and events.

Address: No. 41, Fieldgate Street, London, E1 1JU
Built: Late 1950s
Public access: None
Tube: Aldgate East

44. Pauline House

Pauline House is a typical local authority high-rise block of flats that was built in the post-war period to transform rundown, but community-spirited, neighbourhoods into ones with modern, well-equipped homes. Built between 1960 and 1962, on an area of ground devastated by a bomb during the Second World War, it is nineteen storeys high with seventy-four flats.

Those who moved to such blocks left behind slum dwellings suffering from endemic rising damp, with only cold water for internal plumbing. At Pauline House they found central heating and bathrooms. Not surprisingly, competition for the apartments was fierce. A former resident remembers how her father had threatened the council that he would set fire to his existing home in Old Montague Street unless he was rehoused, saying it seemed 'like moving into a palace!'

Due to its proximity to the docks, the East End suffered particularly badly during the Second World War and its housing stock severely depleted. Records indicate that seventy-two high-explosive bombs fell south of Whitechapel High Street and forty-four to the north, an area that includes Spitalfields. From 1944, the V1 and V2 rockets arrived bringing more fatalities including the tragedy at Hughes Mansions (*see* entry No. 37). Overall, the London Borough of Stepney lost more than 25 per cent of its housing stock.

In the post-war period, major initiatives to replace housing destroyed or damaged beyond repair were launched. Such was the enormity of this task that local authority building continued well into the 1970s and beyond. Flats in the area remain highly sought after due to the excellent location, transport links, and unparalleled views to the City's 'cathedrals of commerce' and over the continually changing landscape of Whitechapel.

Address: Old Montague Street/Hanbury Street, London, E1 5NU
Built: 1960–62
Public access: None
Tube: Whitechapel

City skyline and Pauline House from the top of the former Bucks Row Board School.

Pauline House.

45. Cable Street Mural: 'They shall not pass!'

This mural commemorates the Battle of Cable Street, which took place on 4 October 1936. The battle was sparked by Oswald Mosley and his British Union of Fascists (the 'Blackshirts'), who planned to march through the Jewish East End for a victory parade at Victoria Park. Anglo-Jewish leaders asked Jewish residents to stay away but they turned out in force, together with local Communists and dock workers to prevent the march. The result was a violent confrontation in Cable Street in which an estimated 50,000 to 200,000 protestors took part, with some 6,000 police clearing the way for the Blackshirts.

The mural vividly depicts the barricades and crowds, showing banners proclaiming '*Non Pasaran*' ('They Shall Not Pass'), the call to action for the International Brigade fighting fascism during the Spanish Civil War. It includes splendid detail of marbles being thrown under the police horses' hooves, barricades of mattresses and market stalls and missiles thrown from windows. Caricatures of Hitler and Mosley can be seen on the right-hand side.

Shortly after the 'Battle', the Public Order Act of 1936 banned the wearing of political uniforms in public and any march required official permission.

The mural is mounted on the west wall of St George's Town Hall, which was built in the Italianate style in 1861, originally as the parish vestry hall. Conception of the mural by designer Dave Binnington began in 1976 and it was prepared initially in the basement of the town hall. Final completion was not until 1983. Following vandalism, it was restored in 2011. Also on the wall of the town hall is a plaque commemorating East Enders who fought and died in Spain.

The open space next to the town hall (leading to the churchyard of St George in the East, *see* entry No. 9) used to be the site of a public library but it was destroyed during the Second World War.

As well as the mural, the Battle of Cable Street has also inspired poems, songs and plays and, nearby on the corner of Dock Street, the site of one of the barricades, is a commemorative plaque.

Address: No. 236 Cable Street, Shadwell, London, E1 0BL
Built: 1861 (building); 1976 to 1983 (mural)
Listed status: Grade II
Public access: Yes
Tube/Overground: Shadwell

46. East London Mosque

Sited in a prominent position on Whitechapel Road lies the East London Mosque, one of sixty mosques in Tower Hamlets where 38 per cent of the population is Muslim.

The origins of the mosque date back to 1910 with a fund created by Syed Amir Ali, a member of the Privy Council. Initially, prayer meetings took place in private houses, but by 1938 three houses on Commercial Road were acquired and converted into a place of worship, officially opening in 1941.

The post-war years saw a considerable increase in the local Muslim population and by the 1970s, with the departure of the Jewish community, it became the predominant

St George's Town Hall Cable Street mural.

demographic. In 1975, the mosque was compulsorily purchased and a new site provided in Fieldgate Street backing onto Whitechapel Road. Development took ten years while the present mosque was designed, constructed and completed for opening in 1985. Above the skyline, its three minarets and central onion-shaped dome became a local landmark.

In 1999, the mosque purchased adjacent land and the London Muslim Centre, with multipurpose halls, community facilities and education centre was opened in 2000, providing a new capacity of 7,000 worshippers.

The mosque expanded further in 2013 with the building of the nine-storey Maryam Centre, dedicated to the needs of female worshippers, with a prayer hall, support facilities and a female-only gymnasium.

Almost opposite the mosque, at Nos 183/185 Whitechapel Road, a brightly coloured mosaic entrance leads to an earlier facility established for Bengali women. Now serving all women in Whitechapel, Jagonari, the Women's Educational Resource Centre, was established in 1981 as an offshoot of the Davenant community centre.

One of the few UK mosques permitted to use loudspeakers to call worshippers to prayer, the complex continues to grow. In 2015 the mosque acquired Fieldgate Street Great Synagogue (*see* entry No. 43), where plans are a transformation into a venue for multifaith events and worship.

Address: No. 46 Whitechapel Road, London, E1 1JX
Built: 1985, 2000, 2013
Public access: Open for services and by arrangement
Tube: Aldgate East, Whitechapel
Website: eastlondonmosque.org.uk

East London Mosque.

Left: Crescent moons. *Right*: Jagonari Centre.

47. Swanlea School

Swanlea School is the secondary school closest to the heart of Whitechapel, being located in Brady Street off Whitechapel High Street and behind Whitechapel station. Founded in 1993, it was built upon land made available when, against much public opposition, the Brady Street Buildings, a Four Per Cent block (*see* entry No. 29 Stepney Green Court) were demolished in the 1980s. The site lay unused until the council decided to redevelop it as a secondary school.

The architecture of the school is highly original. At the heart of the building is the mall, a sloping glass canopy running the full length of the school and lined with classrooms. With windows on both sides, it is said that the architect initially envisaged that it would be a public street and that passers-by would be able to observe the teaching. Radiating from this central space are two separate two-storey blocks housing classrooms. There are also two large gymnasia, a restaurant and additional blocks adjoining Durward Street have been added in recent years.

Common to all Inner London schools there is limited external land hence the large enclosed space. There are no playing fields but there is a full-sized all-weather football pitch and a hard full-sized pitch. The green open space to its northern side is the closed Brady Street Jewish Cemetery, which opened in 1761 when Whitechapel was still a relatively rural area.

Swanlea School.

Despite the school's modern appearance, a substantial refurbishment in 2010 was funded under the Building Schools of the Future programme, which upgraded the IT infrastructure to a specification on the par with many of the corporate entities in the City just a mile away.

Address: No. 31, Brady Street, E1 5DJ
Built: 1993
Public access: None
Tube: Whitechapel
Website: swanleaschool.co.uk

48. Elektra House

You can walk by this residential building without even realising it is a home. It is clad with a phenolic resin-based ply, giving it a rusty look to the exterior and no windows are visible. There is a window but it is on the rear side, unseen by passers-by and looks out to the sky above, not to the side. The house, on the site of a former shoe factory, was commissioned by a couple of artists from architect David Adjaye whose work is seen elsewhere in East London.

The house is designed to be one living space at ground level plus a small kitchen to the side and small outside area off the main room. Upstairs there are three bedrooms and a bathroom, but again with no windows. This building represents the cutting edge architecture that is now arriving in Whitechapel and the new residents who are moving into East London.

David Adjaye, Tanzanian with a Ghanian diplomat father, arrived in the UK as a nine-year-old in the mid-1970s, after many different homes and wanted to use the influences of his travels in his career. Moving from fine art to architecture at the Royal College of Art,

Elektra House.

he met students who would become his trademark clients, members of the then emerging YBA (Young British Artists) community. He calls his work 'emotive architecture' using his regular motifs, colourful glass, as with the Idea Stores at Whitechapel (*see* entry No. 49) and Poplar and playful design as at Rivington Place, Shoreditch.

Address: No. 84a Ashfield Street, London, E1 2HV
Built: 2000
Public access: None
Tube: Whitechapel

49. The Idea Store

Opened in 2005, this is the London Borough of Tower Hamlet's (LBTH) flagship public library and learning centre. It is indicative of the changing face of the borough, not only for its contemporary architecture but also for its ability to engage with the ever-changing local demographics.

By the late 1990s, the word 'library' had ceased to resonate with the local community. According to research by LBTH, less than 20 per cent of its residents visited a local library because they were often distant from busy high streets and not easily accessible, and had a fusty old-fashioned image.

Whitechapel Idea Store.

In 1999, LBTH took the drastic decision to close several public libraries, and to rebuild a number, renaming them as Idea Stores. The first, in 2002, was in Bow just off the Roman Road, followed in 2004 in Poplar at Crisp Street. The third was in Whitechapel and opened in 2005 to replace the former Whitechapel Public Library (*see* entry No. 26). All three are in busy shopping areas, with the latter two designed by David Adjaye (*see* entry No. 48 Elektra House). These trailblazers have since been joined by Canary Wharf in 2006 and Watney Street Market, off the Commercial Road, in 2013.

Extensive use of blue and green glass, a trademark feature of Adjaye's work, gives the Whitechapel and Poplar buildings a transparency that is designed to entice people inside. Soaring above the stalls at street level, Whitechapel's Idea Store is a colourful addition to the Whitechapel Market area.

The Idea Stores are funded jointly by LBTH and a variety of local organisations and charities, each Idea Store having a different set of benefactors.

Whitechapel's Idea Store is on a busy thoroughfare with considerable passing trade. It boasts a children's library, café, computer terminals, learning spaces and seminar rooms for a wide range of courses and events. As such, the Idea Store has become an integrated and bustling education and community centre relevant to its neighbourhood. For number crunchers, statistics tell the success story too. Between 2002 and 2013, visitors to Idea Stores and libraries throughout LBTH increased by 240 per cent.

Address: No. 321 Whitechapel Road, London, E1 1BU
Built: 2005
Public access: Yes
Tube: Whitechapel
Website: ideastore.co.uk/idea-store-whitechapel

50. Shoreditch High Street Station: A New Gateway To Whitechapel

Opened in 2010, Shoreditch High Street Overground station is the third station called Shoreditch to serve the northern end of Brick Lane. The largest station on the revived East London Line section of the Overground, known affectionately as the Ginger Line, it is a vast futuristic concrete box built on a track linking to the Kingsland viaduct on the disused North London Railway. Designed by J. S. A. Architects to allow further construction without impact on the rail service, the brick viaduct alongside provides a fascinating insight to the past.

Originally opened as Shoreditch station in 1840 by East Counties Railway, it became a goods yard and renamed Bishopsgate when Liverpool Street station opened on the edge the City as the new passenger terminus. Utilising the 260-metre-long (780 feet) Braithwaite Viaduct, it had eight road entrances, two entrance levels, ten railway tracks and, by 1933, handled 550 wagons a day transferring fresh food produce from rail to truck. Destroyed by fire in 1964, the site remained derelict until demolition began in 2003. Some elements were listed to prevent complete destruction and these include the ornate iron gates, dated 1884, still visible on Shoreditch High Street.

In 1876, further down Brick Lane an earlier Shoreditch Station had opened as part of the East London Railway. By the second half of the twentieth century, this area was rapidly declining. The station opened only at rush hours and within three years, by 2003, traffic had halved to less than 400,000 passengers – just over 1,000 each day. With barely anyone noticing, it closed in 2006 but its site on Pedley Street has become of the foremost enclaves of local contemporary street art.

Today, Sunday mornings bring streams of people pouring out of the new station visiting pop-up businesses in the container Box Park, enjoying sports activities temporarily housed within the brick arches or walking down Sclater Street towards the street markets of Brick Lane and beyond. Passenger traffic per year has increased from 2.6 million in 2012 to 4.8 million in 2015, truly confirming our last entry in this book as not only the new gateway to Whitechapel but unequivocal proof of how Whitechapel has emerged as one of London's top hot spots.

Address: Braithwaite Street, London, E1 6GJ
Built: 2010
Public access: Yes
Overground: Shoreditch High Street

Shoreditch High Street station.

About the Authors

Louis Berk

A photographer and teacher, his work has been published in newspapers and magazines in the UK, US and Italy, as well as in books on subjects as diverse as Banksy and the 'Boris Bus'. In 2008 he published *Walk To Work*, which was the result of a four-year photographic project based in Spitalfields, Shoreditch and Whitechapel. This was followed, in 2010, by *School Work: One Day in the Life of an Outstanding Secondary School*, a unique pictorial investigation into how a modern secondary school operates. In 2012 he published *Ampthill: A Picture Book to Remember Her By*, a personal architectural perspective on the unusual colour-coded tower blocks at Mornington Crescent in London. You can find out more about his books and photographs at his website: louisberk.com.

Rachel Kolsky

Engaging, knowledgeable and well-researched, Rachel Kolsky is a prize-winning London Blue Badge Tourist Guide who is passionate about exploring London's heritage. Her walks and talks (golondontours.com) cover a wide range of themes and areas but always focus on the 'human stories behind the buildings'. Her first book, *Jewish London*, was published in March 2012. When not guiding or writing, she will be found speaking as a guest lecturer on cruise ships or in her local independent cinema, where she is a trustee.

Acknowledgements

The authors would like to thank Amberley for commissioning this book and also acknowledge the following individuals for assistance given and use of materials and images: Anna Kochan for perusing our text, Bernard Kops for generously allowing his poem to be quoted, Stefan Dickers at Bishopsgate Institute, John Bennett, Rob Clack and Adrian Morris regarding Buck's Row Board School, Lorraine Groves and Stephen Pilcher of the Historic Chapels Trust, Paul Westbrook of the IDS, Rose Edmands and Rachel Lichtenstein at Sandys Row Synagogue, Fiona Lawrence and the Clergy at St George in the East, Toby Brown at Spitalfields Market, Brenda Landers at Swanlea School, Kathryn Hughes of the Whitechapel Bell Foundry and John Allen of the Worshipful Company of Gunmakers.

All photographs Copyright LouisBerk.com 2016, except No. 22 Bucks Row School Whitechapel (Copyright Rob Clack, 2016) No. 35 Wickhams and No. 37 Mary Hughes blue plaque (Copyright Rachel Kolsky, 2016).